Dedication

This book is dedicated to
my father
late shri M.L. Goel
and my mother
late smt. Prabha Goel.

Books by author

fganh esa	In English	In Russian
oxZ dqaMfy;ksa ls lVhd Qfyr	Comprehensive Prediction by Divisional Charts	Comprehensive Prediction by Divisional Charts
;ksfxuh n'kk ls Qfyr	Snapshot Prediction using Yogini Dasha	Snapshot Prediction using Yogini Dasha
'kksMk"kksRrjh n'kk ls Qfyr	Predict Through Shodashottary Dasha	
vk;q jgL;	Unravelling Puzzle of longevity	
	Predict Through Shasti Hayani Dasha	
	Locate Disease Astrologically	Locate Disease Astrologically
tSfeuh T;ksfr"k ls Qfyr	Predicting through Jaimini Astrology	Predicting through Jaimini Astrology
uoka'k ls Qfyr	Predict with Navamsha	Predict with Navamsha
lIrka'k ls Qfyr	Predict with Saptamsha	Predict with Saptamsha
n'keka'k ls Qfyr	Predict with Dashamsha	Predict with Dashamsha
	Predict with Trishamsha	
Lkjy T;ksfr"k 1	Saral Jyotish 1	Saral Jyotish 1
Lkjy T;ksfr"k 2	Saral Jyotish 2	Saral Jyotish 2
Lkjy T;ksfr"k 3	Saral Jyotish 3	Saral Jyotish 3
Lkjy T;ksfr"k 4	Saral Jyotish 4	Saral Jyotish 4
Lkjy T;ksfr"k 5	Saral Jyotish 5	
	Saral Jyotish 6	

Yogini Dasha for Accurate Prediction

Author

V. P. GOEL

Published by

Performonks Education and Consulting Services LLP

First edition, 2025

ISBN: 978-81-982134-5-7

Published by
Performonks Education and Consulting Services LLP
44, Tatvam Villas, Sector 48, Sohna Road
Gurgaon, Haryana-122018
Email: rashi@performonks.com

Contents

Preface

Dasha system of Hindu astrology is a unique system for timing of events. Yogini dasha is a prime dasha having universal application.It is not commonly used as the correct method of interpretation is hot known. This is now presented in this book.

The Yogini dasa is generated by Nakshatra. The correct prediction and timing is arrived by erecting progress chart with the sign containing the Nakshatra as lagan. The calculations for birth in in all 27 seven Nakshatra are given.

Interpretation of dasha results is normally a complex processand needs years of experience. A snapshot method has been explained, and the results are seen quickly even by a beginner of astrology.

Ram Navami, 19.04.13
April 2025

V.P. Goel
vpgoel2019@gmail.com
YouTube:saraljyotishbyvpgoel

Chapter 1
Classic

Sage Parashar states that "Now I explain Yogini dasha as enunciated by Lord Mahadeva". Such is the importance of Yogini dasha.

Yogini dasha has universal application and is applicable onall horoscopes.

The total period of one cycle of Yogini is of thirty-six years and there are eight yoginis in one cycle. Compared to Vimshottarydasha having 120 years in one cycle, Yogini is more condensedand gives timing of shorter duration. Small errors in the longitudeof Moon will not make much difference in yogini dasha balance.

Yogini dasha is a planetary dasha and is based on the Nakshtra occupied by Moon in the birth chart.

The yogini dasha comprises of eight yoginis dasha periods.These are Mangla, Pingla, Dhanya, Bhramari, Bhadrika, Ulka, Siddha and Sankata. These dasha periods are lorded by eight planets which are Moon, Sun, Jupiter, Mars, Mercury, Saturn, Venus and Rahu respectively. Ketu is not taken into consideration.Normally while reading Sankata, we can take the Rahu/Ketu axis. The dasha period of each yogini is from one year to eight years. Starting from Mangla with one year and increasing by one year for the next yogini. These yoginis repeat in the samesequence and is now tabulated.

Table 1

S. No.	Name of Yogini	Lord	Dasha\ Period Years
1	Mangla	Moon	One
2	Pingla	Sun	Two
3	Dhanya	Jupiter	Three
4	Bhramari	Mars	Four
5	Bhadrika	Mercury	Five
6	Ulka	Saturn	Six
7	Siddha	Venus	Seven
8	Sankata	Rahu	Eight

The dasha period of benefic planets totals to 16 years and of malefic planets is 20 years. This is the ratio of good and badDasha granted naturally by the creator.

Calculation of Birth Nakshtra

Zodiac is divided in 27 Nakshtra having equal span (excluding Abhijit which do not figure in yogini calculations). Each Nakshtra span is 13° - 20' or 800 minutes. One Nakshtra contributes one yogini dasha. It is, therefore, necessary to knowthe birth Nakshtra occupied by Moon.

Convert the longitude of Moon into minutes (including sign).

Divide this by 800.

The quotient is the number of Nakshtra already coveredby Moon. The remainder is the portion of Nakshtra coveredin the Nakshtra occupied.

Add one to the quotient to get the Nakshtra occupied byMoon.

Example:

Moon is placed in Scorpio 10° – 48' in the birth horoscope. Date of birth is 22 December 1973.

1. The longitude converted into minutes is 13248.
2. After dividing by 800 we get 16.56.
3. Sixteen Nakshtra have passed. Moon has covered 0.56 ofthe seventeenth Nakshtra.
4. Moon is placed in seventeenth Nakshtra i.e. Anuradha.

Yogini Dasha at birth

To get the Yogini Dasha at birth, follow the method given.

1. Work out the number of Nakshtra occupied by Moon at birth. Ashwani Is 1 and Revati is 27.
2. Add 3 in the Nakshtra number.
3. Expunge multiplies of 8 from the sum so arrived till the remainder is 8 or less than 8.
4. The remainder is the number of Yogini Dasha at birth (Table1). The corresponding Yogini is the Yogini Dasha at birth.The first Yogini Dasha Mangla belongs to Ardra Nakshtraand as such three is added to the Nakshtra number.

Example:

We had worked the birth Nakshtra seventeenth i.e. Anuradha.

1. Add 3 to 17 to get 20
2. Expunge multiplies of 8 i.e. 16 and we get remainder as 4.
3. The fourth Yogini Dasha is of Bhramari and is the Dasha at birth.

Dasha balance at birth

Each Yogini Dasha is of one Nakshtra. Therefore, the balance of Yogini Dasha is proportional to the balance of the Nakshtra yet to be covered by Moon at birth in that Nakshtra.

While working to find the Nakshtra at birth, we divided the longitude of Moon (in minutes) by 800. We got the Nakshtra covered by Moon and some fraction. This fraction or the part after decimal is the portion of the Nakshtra covered. Deduct this fraction from 1 to get the portion of Nakshtra yet to be covered.

We have worked out the Yogini Dasha at birth. So, the portion yet to be covered is the proportional part of the Yogini Dasha. Multiply this portion by the full dasha period of Yogini atbirth to get the Dasha balance at birth.

Example:

We had worked the birth Nakshtra is seventeenth i.e. Anuradha.

1. After dividing by 800 we got 16.56. The Nakshtra at birthis seventeenth.
2. The 0.56 parts of 1 seventeenth Nakshtra is already covered.
3. Deduct 0.56 from 1 and we get 0.44 as the balance of Nakshtra of Moon.
4. The Yogini Dasha is of Bhramari at birth. Bhramari full dashais of 4 years. Multiply 0.44 by 4 to get the balance of Bhramari dasha at birth. It works out to 1.76 years or 1 year 9 months 4 days.

A ready table for balance of Yogini Dasha based on Longitude of Moon is given. We can directly work out the balance of Yogini dasa and Nakshtra from the table.

Table 2

Long. Moon	**Dasha Balance**	**Long. Moon**	**Dasha Balance**
Deg. Min.	**Yr. Mo. Day**	**Deg. Min.**	**Yr. Mo. Day**
Aries 00 – 00	Bhramari 04 – 00 – 00	Taurus 00 – 00	Ulka 04 – 06 – 00
00 – 40	03 – 09 – 18	00 – 40	04 – 02 – 12
01 – 20	03 – 07 – 06	01 – 20	03 – 10 – 24
02 – 00	03 – 04 – 24	02 – 00	03 – 07 – 06
02 – 40	03 – 02 – 12	02 – 40	03 – 03 – 18

Long. Moon	Dasha Balance	Long. Moon	Dasha Balance
Deg. Min.	Yr. Mo. Day	Deg. Min.	Yr. Mo. Day
03 – 20	03 – 00 – 00	03 – 20	03 – 00 – 00
04 – 00	02 – 09 – 18	04 – 00	02 – 08 – 12
04 – 40	02 – 07 – 06	04 – 40	02 – 04 – 24
05 – 20	02 – 04 – 24	05 – 20	02 – 01 – 06
06 – 00	02 – 02 – 12	06 – 00	01 – 09 – 18
06 – 40	02 – 00 – 00	06 – 40	01 – 06 – 00
07 – 20	01 – 09 – 18	07 – 20	01 – 02 – 12
08 – 00	01 – 07 – 06	08 – 00	00 – 10 – 24
08 – 40	01 – 04 – 24	08 – 40	00 – 07 – 06
09 – 20	01 – 02 – 12	09 – 20	00 – 03 – 18
10 – 00	01 – 00 – 00	10 – 00	Siddha 07 – 00 – 00
10 – 40	00 – 09 – 18	10 – 40	06 – 07 – 24
11 – 20	00 – 07 – 06	11 – 20	06 – 03 – 18
12 – 00	00 – 04 – 24	12 – 00	05 – 11 – 12
12 – 40	00 – 02 – 12	12 – 40	05 – 07 – 06
13 – 20	Bhadrika 05 – 00 – 00	13 – 20	05 – 03 – 00
14 – 00	04 – 09 – 00	14 – 00	04 – 10 – 24
14 – 40	04 – 06 – 00	14 – 40	04 – 06 – 18
15 – 20	04 – 03 – 00	15 – 20	04 – 02 – 12
16 – 00	04 – 00 – 00	16 – 00	03 – 10 – 06
16 – 40	03 – 09 – 00	16 – 40	03 – 06 – 00
17 – 20	03 – 06 – 00	17 – 20	03 – 01 – 24
18 – 00	03 – 03 – 00	18 – 00	02 – 09 – 18
18 – 40	03 – 00 – 00	18 – 40	02 – 05 – 12
19 – 20	02 – 09 – 00	19 – 20	02 – 01 – 06
20 – 00	02 – 06 – 00	20 – 00	01 – 09 – 00
20 – 40	02 – 03 – 00	20 – 40	01 – 04 – 24
21 – 20	02 – 00 – 00	21 – 20	01 – 01 – 18
22 – 00	01 – 09 – 00	22 – 00	00 – 08 – 12

Long. Moon	Dasha Balance	Long. Moon	Dasha Balance
Deg. Min.	Yr. Mo. Day	Deg. Min.	Yr. Mo. Day
22 – 40	01 – 06 – 00	22 – 40	00 – 04 – 06
23 – 20	01 – 03 – 00	23 – 20	Sankata 08 – 00 – 00
24 – 00	01 – 00 – 00	24 – 00	07 – 07 – 06
24 – 40	00 – 09 – 00	24 – 40	07 – 02 – 12
25 – 20	00 – 06 – 00	25 – 20	06 – 09 – 18
26 – 00	00 – 03 – 00	26 – 00	06 – 04 – 24
26 – 40	Ulka 06 – 00 – 00	26 – 40	06 – 00 – 00
27 – 20	05 – 08 – 12	27 – 20	05 – 07 – 06
28 – 00	05 – 04 – 24	28 – 00	05 – 02 – 12
28 – 40	05 – 01 – 06	28 – 40	04 – 09 – 18
29 – 20	04 – 09 – 18	29 – 20	04 – 04 – 24
Gemini 00 – 00	Sankata 04 – 00 – 00	Cancer 00 – 00	Pingla 00 – 06 – 00
00 – 40	03 – 07 – 06	00 – 40	00 – 04 – 24
01 – 20	03 – 02 – 12	01 – 20	00 – 03 – 18
02 – 00	02 – 09 – 18	02 – 00	00 – 02 – 12
02 – 40	02 – 04 – 24	02 – 40	00 – 01 – 06
03 – 20	02 – 00 – 00	03 – 20	Dhanya 03 – 00 – 00
04 – 00	01 – 07 – 06	04 – 00	02 – 10 – 06
04 – 40	01 – 02 – 12	04 – 40	02 – 08 – 12
05 – 20	00 – 09 – 18	05 – 20	02 – 06 – 18
06 – 00	00 – 04 – 24	06 – 00	02 – 04 – 24
06 – 40	Mangla 01 – 00 – 00	06 – 40	02 – 03 – 00
07 – 20	00 – 11 – 12	07 – 20	02 – 01 – 06
08 – 00	00 – 10 – 24	08 – 00	01 – 11 – 12
08 – 40	00 – 10 – 06	08 – 40	01 – 09 – 18

Long. Moon	Dasha Balance	Long. Moon	Dasha Balance
Deg. Min.	Yr. Mo. Day	Deg. Min.	Yr. Mo. Day
09 – 20	00 – 09 – 18	09 – 20	01 – 07 – 24
10 – 00	00 – 09 – 00	10 – 00	01 – 06 – 00
10 – 40	00 – 08 – 12	10 – 40	01 – 04 – 06
11 – 20	00 – 07 – 24	11 – 20	01 – 02 – 12
12 – 00	00 – 07 – 06	12 – 00	01 – 00 – 18
12 – 40	00 – 06 – 18	12 – 40	00 – 10 – 24
13 – 20	00 – 06 – 00	13 – 20	00 – 09 – 00
14 – 00	00 – 05 – 12	14 – 00	00 – 07 – 06
14 – 40	00 – 04 – 24	14 – 40	00 – 05 – 12
15 – 20	00 – 04 – 06	15 – 20	00 – 03 – 18
16 – 00	00 – 03 – 18	16 – 00	00 – 01 – 24
16 – 40	00 – 03 – 00	16 – 40	Bharamari 04 – 00 – 00
17 – 20	00 – 02 – 12	17 – 20	03 – 09 – 18
18 – 00	00 – 01 – 24	18 – 00	03 – 07 – 06
18 – 40	00 – 01 – 06	18 – 40	03 – 04 – 24
19 – 20	00 – 00 – 18	19 – 20	03 – 02 – 12
20 – 00	Pingla 02 – 00 – 00	20 – 00	03 – 00 – 00
20 – 40	01 – 10 – 24	20 – 40	02 – 09 – 18
21 – 20	01 – 09 – 18	21 – 20	02 – 07 – 06
22 – 00	01 – 08 – 12	22 – 00	02 – 04 – 24
22 – 40	01 – 07 – 06	22 – 40	02 – 02 – 12
23 – 20	01 – 06 – 00	23 – 20	02 – 00 – 00
24 – 00	01 – 04 – 24	24 – 00	01 – 09 – 18
24 – 40	01 – 03 – 18	24 – 40	01 – 07 – 06
25 – 20	01 – 02 – 12	25 – 20	01 – 04 – 24
26 – 00	01 – 01 – 06	26 – 00	01 – 02 – 12
26 – 40	01 – 00 – 00	26 – 40	01 – 00 – 00
27 – 20	00 – 10 – 24	27 – 20	00 – 09 – 18
28 – 00	00 – 09 – 18	28 – 00	00 – 07 – 06

Long. Moon	Dasha Balance	Long. Moon	Dasha Balance
Deg. Min.	Yr. Mo. Day	Deg. Min.	Yr. Mo. Day
28 – 40	00 – 08 – 12	28 – 40	00 – 04 – 24
29 – 20	00 – 07 – 06	29 – 20	00 – 02 – 12
Leo 00 – 00	Bhadrika 05 – 00 – 00	Virgo 00 – 00	Siddha 05 – 03 – 00
00 – 40	04 – 09 – 00	00 – 40	04 – 10 – 24
01 – 20	04 – 06 – 00	01 – 20	04 – 06 – 18
02 – 00	04 – 03 – 00	02 – 00	04 – 02 – 12
02 – 40	04 – 00 – 00	02 – 40	03 – 10 – 06
03 – 20	03 – 09 – 00	03 – 20	03 – 06 – 00
04 – 00	03 – 06 – 00	04 – 00	03 – 01 – 24
04 – 40	03 – 03 – 00	04 – 40	02 – 09 – 18
05 – 20	03 – 00 – 00	05 – 20	02 – 05 – 12
06 – 00	02 – 09 – 00	06 – 00	02 – 01 – 06
06 – 40	02 – 06 – 00	06 – 40	01 – 09 – 00
07 – 20	02 – 03 – 00	07 – 20	01 – 04 – 24
08 – 00	02 – 00 – 00	08 – 00	01 – 01 – 18
08 – 40	01 – 09 – 00	08 – 40	00 – 08 – 12
09 – 20	01 – 06 – 00	09 – 20	00 – 04 – 06
10 – 00	01 – 03 – 00	10 – 00	Sankata 08 – 00 – 00
10 – 40	01 – 00 – 00	10 – 40	07 – 07 – 06
11 – 20	00 – 09 – 00	11 – 20	07 – 02 – 12
12 – 00	00 – 06 – 00	12 – 00	06 – 09 – 18
12 – 40	00 – 03 – 00	12 – 40	06 – 04 – 24
13 – 20	Ulka 06 – 00 – 00	13 – 20	06 – 00 – 00
14 – 00	05 – 08 – 12	14 – 00	05 – 07 – 06
14 – 40	05 – 04 – 24	14 – 40	05 – 02 – 12
15 – 20	05 – 01 – 06	15 – 20	04 – 09 – 18
16 – 00	04 – 09 – 18	16 – 00	04 – 04 – 24

Long. Moon	Dasha Balance	Long. Moon	Dasha Balance
Deg. Min.	Yr. Mo. Day	Deg. Min.	Yr. Mo. Day
16 – 40	04 – 06 – 00	16 – 40	04 – 00 – 00
17 – 20	04 – 02 – 12	17 – 20	03 – 07 – 06
18 – 00	03 – 10 – 24	18 – 00	03 – 02 – 12
18 – 40	03 – 07 – 06	18 – 40	02 – 09 – 18
19 – 20	03 – 03 – 18	19 – 20	02 – 04 – 24
20 – 00	03 – 00 – 00	20 – 00	02 – 00 – 00
20 – 40	02 – 08 – 12	20 – 40	01 – 07 – 06
21 – 20	02 – 04 – 24	21 – 20	01 – 02 – 12
22 – 00	02 – 01 – 06	22 – 00	00 – 09 – 18
22 – 40	01 – 09 – 18	22 – 40	00 – 04 – 24
23 – 20	01 – 06 – 00	23 – 20	Mangla 01 – 00 – 00
24 – 00	01 – 02 – 12	24 – 00	00 – 11 – 12
24 – 40	00 – 10 – 24	24 – 40	00 – 10 – 24
25 – 20	00 – 07 – 06	25 – 20	00 – 10 – 06
26 – 00	00 – 03 – 18	26 – 00	00 – 09 – 18
26 – 40	Siddha 07 – 00 – 00	26 – 40	00 – 09 – 00
27 – 20	06 – 07 – 24	27 – 20	00 – 08 – 12
28 – 00	06 – 03 – 18	28 – 00	00 – 07 – 24
28 – 40	05 – 11 – 12	28 – 40	00 – 07 – 06
29 – 20	05 – 07 – 06	29 – 20	00 – 06 – 18
Libra 00 – 00	Mangla 00 – 06 – 00	Scorpio 00 – 00	Dhanya 00 – 09 – 00
00 – 40	00 – 05 – 12	00 – 40	00 – 07 – 06
01 – 20	00 – 04 – 24	01 – 20	00 – 05 – 12
02 – 00	00 – 04 – 06	02 – 00	00 – 03 – 18
02 – 40	00 – 03 – 18	02 – 40	00 – 01 – 24
03 – 20	00 – 03 – 00	03 – 20	Bharamari 04 – 00 – 00
04 – 00	00 – 02 – 12	04 – 00	03 – 09 – 18

Long. Moon	Dasha Balance	Long. Moon	Dasha Balance
Deg. Min.	Yr. Mo. Day	Deg. Min.	Yr. Mo. Day
04 – 40	00 – 01 – 24	04 – 40	03 – 07 – 06
05 – 20	00 – 01 – 06	05 – 20	03 – 04 – 24
06 – 00	00 – 00 – 18	06 – 00	03 – 02 – 12
06 – 40	Pingla 02 – 00 – 00	06 – 40	03 – 00 – 00
07 – 20	01 – 10 – 24	07 – 20	02 – 09 – 18
08 – 00	01 – 09 – 18	08 – 00	02 – 07 – 06
08 – 40	01 – 08 – 12	08 – 40	02 – 04 – 24
09 – 20	01 – 07 – 06	09 – 20	02 – 02 – 12
10 – 00	01 – 06 – 00	10 – 00	02 – 00 – 00
10 – 40	01 – 04 – 24	10 – 40	01 – 09 – 18
11 – 20	01 – 03 – 18	11 – 20	01 – 07 – 06
12 – 00	01 – 02 – 12	12 – 00	01 – 04 – 24
12 – 40	01 – 01 – 06	12 – 40	01 – 02 – 12
13 – 20	01 – 00 – 00	13 – 20	01 – 00 – 00
14 – 00	00 – 10 – 24	14 – 00	00 – 09 – 18
14 – 40	00 – 09 – 18	14 – 40	00 – 07 – 06
15 – 20	00 – 08 – 12	15 – 20	00 – 04 – 24
16 – 00	00 – 07 – 06	16 – 00	00 – 02 – 12
16 – 40	00 – 06 – 00	16 – 40	Bhadrika 05 – 00 – 00
17 – 20	00 – 04 – 24	17 – 20	04 – 09 – 00
18 – 00	00 – 03 – 18	18 – 00	04 – 06 – 00
18 – 40	00 – 02 – 12	18 – 40	04 – 03 – 00
19 – 20	00 – 01 – 06	19 – 20	04 – 00 – 00
20 – 00	Dhanya 03 – 00 – 00	20 – 00	03 – 09 – 00
20 – 40	02 – 10 – 06	20 – 40	03 – 06 – 00
21 – 20	02 – 08 – 12	21 – 20	03 – 03 – 00
22 – 00	02 – 06 – 18	22 – 00	03 – 00 – 00

Long. Moon	Dasha Balance	Long. Moon	Dasha Balance
Deg. Min.	**Yr. Mo. Day**	**Deg. Min.**	**Yr. Mo. Day**
22 – 40	02 – 04 – 24	22 – 40	02 – 09 – 00
23 – 20	02 – 03 – 00	23 – 20	02 – 06 – 00
24 – 00	02 – 01 – 06	24 – 00	02 – 03 – 00
24 – 40	01 – 11 – 12	24 – 40	02 – 00 – 00
25 – 20	01 – 09 – 18	25 – 20	01 – 09 – 00
26 – 00	01 – 07 – 24	26 – 00	01 – 06 – 00
26 – 40	01 – 06 – 00	26 – 40	01 – 03 – 00
27 – 20	01 – 04 – 06	27 – 20	01 – 00 – 00
28 – 00	01 – 02 – 12	28 – 00	00 – 09 – 00
28 – 40	01 – 00 – 18	28 – 40	00 – 06 – 00
29 – 20	00 – 10 – 24	29 – 20	00 – 03 – 00
Sagittarius 00 – 00	Ulka 06 – 00 – 00	Capricorn 00 – 00	Sankata 06 – 00 – 00
00 – 40	05 – 08 – 12	00 – 40	05 – 07 – 06
01 – 20	05 – 04 – 24	01 – 20	05 – 02 – 12
02 – 00	05 – 01 – 06	02 – 00	04 – 09 – 18
02 – 40	04 – 09 – 18	02 – 40	04 – 04 – 24
03 – 20	04 – 06 – 00	03 – 20	04 – 00 – 00
04 – 00	04 – 02 – 12	04 – 00	03 – 07 – 06
04 – 40	03 – 10 – 24	04 – 40	03 – 02 – 12
05 – 20	03 – 07 – 06	05 – 20	02 – 09 – 18
06 – 00	03 – 03 – 18	06 – 00	02 – 04 – 24
06 – 40	03 – 00 – 00	06 – 40	02 – 00 – 00
07 – 20	02 – 08 – 12	07 – 20	01 – 07 – 06
08 – 00	02 – 04 – 24	08 – 00	01 – 02 – 12
08 – 40	02 – 01 – 06	08 – 40	00 – 09 – 18
09 – 20	01 – 09 – 18	09 – 20	00 – 04 – 24
10 – 00	01 – 06 – 00	10 – 00	Mangla 01 – 00 – 00
10 – 40	01 – 02 – 12	10 – 40	00 – 11 – 12
11 – 20	00 – 10 – 24	11 – 20	00 – 10 – 24

Long. Moon	Dasha Balance	Long. Moon	Dasha Balance
Deg. Min.	Yr. Mo. Day	Deg. Min.	Yr. Mo. Day
12 – 00	00 – 07 – 06	12 – 00	00 – 10 – 06
12 – 40	00 – 03 – 18	12 – 40	00 – 09 – 18
13 – 20	Siddha 07 – 00 – 00	13 – 20	00 – 09 – 00
14 – 00	06 – 07 – 24	14 – 00	00 – 08 – 12
14 – 40	06 – 03 – 18	14 – 40	00 – 07 – 24
15 – 20	05 – 11 – 12	15 – 20	00 – 07 – 06
16 – 00	05 – 07 – 06	16 – 00	00 – 06 – 18
16 – 40	05 – 03 – 00	16 – 40	00 – 06 – 00
17 – 20	04 – 10 – 24	17 – 20	00 – 05 – 12
18 – 00	04 – 06 – 18	18 – 00	00 – 04 – 24
18 – 40	04 – 02 – 12	18 – 40	00 – 04 – 06
19 – 20	03 – 10 – 06	19 – 20	00 – 03 – 18
20 – 00	03 – 06 – 00	20 – 00	00 – 03 – 00
20 – 40	03 – 01 – 24	20 – 40	00 – 02 – 12
21 – 20	02 – 09 – 18	21 – 20	00 – 01 – 24
22 – 00	02 – 05 – 12	22 – 00	00 – 01 – 06
22 – 40	02 – 01 – 06	22 – 40	00 – 00 – 18
23 – 20	01 – 09 – 00	23 – 20	Pingla 02 – 00 – 00
24 – 00	01 – 04 – 24	24 – 00	01 – 10 – 24
24 – 40	01 – 01 – 18	24 – 40	01 – 09 – 18
25 – 20	00 – 08 – 12	25 – 20	01 – 08 – 12
26 – 00	00 – 04 – 06	26 – 00	01 – 07 – 06
26 – 40	Sankata 08 – 00 – 00	26 – 40	01 – 06 – 00
27 – 20	07 – 07 – 06	27 – 20	01 – 04 – 24
28 – 00	07 – 02 – 12	28 – 00	01 – 03 – 18
28 – 40	06 – 09 – 18	28 – 40	01 – 02 – 12
29 – 20	06 – 04 – 24	29 – 20	01 – 01 – 06

Long. Moon	Dasha Balance	Long. Moon	Dasha Balance
Deg. Min.	Yr. Mo. Day	Deg. Min.	Yr. Mo. Day
Aquarius 00 – 00	Pingla 01 – 00 – 00	Pisces 00 – 00	Bhramari 01 – 00 – 00
00 – 40	00 – 10 – 24	00 – 40	00 – 09 – 18
01 – 20	00 – 09 – 18	01 – 20	00 – 07 – 06
02 – 00	00 – 08 – 12	02 – 00	00 – 04 – 24
02 – 40	00 – 07 – 06	02 – 40	00 – 02 – 12
03 – 20	00 – 06 – 00	03 – 20	Bhadrika 05 – 00 – 00
04 – 00	00 – 04 – 24	04 – 00	04 – 09 – 00
04 – 40	00 – 03 – 18	04 – 40	04 – 06 – 00
05 – 20	00 – 02 – 12	05 – 20	04 – 03 – 00
06 – 00	00 – 01 – 06	06 – 00	04 – 00 – 00
06 – 40	Dhanya 03 – 00 – 00	06 – 40	03 – 09 – 00
07 – 20	02 – 10 – 06	07 – 20	03 – 06 – 00
08 – 00	02 – 08 – 12	08 – 00	03 – 03 – 00
08 – 40	02 – 06 – 18	08 – 40	03 – 00 – 00
09 – 20	02 – 04 – 24	09 – 20	02 – 09 – 00
10 – 00	02 – 03 – 00	10 – 00	02 – 06 – 00
10 – 40	02 – 01 – 06	10 – 40	02 – 03 – 00
11 – 20	01 – 11 – 12	11 – 20	02 – 00 – 00
12 – 00	01 – 09 – 18	12 – 00	01 – 09 – 00
12 – 40	01 – 07 – 24	12 – 40	01 – 06 – 00
13 – 20	01 – 06 – 00	13 – 20	01 – 03 – 00
14 – 00	01 – 04 – 06	14 – 00	01 – 00 – 00
14 – 40	01 – 02 – 12	14 – 40	00 – 09 – 00
15 – 20	01 – 00 – 18	15 – 20	00 – 06 – 00
16 – 00	00 – 10 – 24	16 – 00	00 – 03 – 00
16 – 40	00 – 09 – 00	16 – 40	Ulka 06 – 00 – 00
17 – 20	00 – 07 – 06	17 – 20	05 – 08 – 12

Long. Moon	Dasha Balance	Long. Moon	Dasha Balance
Deg. Min.	**Yr. Mo. Day**	**Deg. Min.**	**Yr. Mo. Day**
18 – 00	00 – 05 – 12	18 – 00	05 – 04 – 24
18 – 40	00 – 03 – 18	18 – 40	05 – 01 – 06
19 – 20	00 – 01 – 24	19 – 20	04 – 09 – 18
20 – 00	Bhramari 04 – 00 – 00	20 – 00	04 – 06 – 00
20 – 40	03 – 09 – 18	20 – 40	04 – 02 – 12
21 – 20	03 – 07 – 06	21 – 20	03 – 10 – 24
22 – 00	03 – 04 – 24	22 – 00	03 – 07 – 06
22 – 40	03 – 02 – 12	22 – 40	03 – 03 – 18
23 – 20	03 – 00 – 00	23 – 20	03 – 00 – 00
24 – 00	02 – 09 – 18	24 – 00	02 – 08 – 12
24 – 40	02 – 07 – 06	24 – 40	02 – 04 – 24
25 – 20	02 – 04 – 24	25 – 20	02 – 01 – 06
26 – 00	02 – 02 – 12	26 – 00	01 – 09 – 18
26 – 40	02 – 00 – 00	26 – 40	01 – 06 – 00
27 – 20	01 – 09 – 18	27 – 20	01 – 02 – 12
28 – 00	01 – 07 – 06	28 – 00	00 – 10 – 24
28 – 40	01 – 04 – 24	28 – 40	00 – 07 – 06
29 – 20	01 – 02 – 12	29 – 20	00 – 03 – 18

Table 3 Proportional Parts

Long of Moon Minutes	Mangla M D	Pingla M D	Dhanya M D	Bhra--mari M D	Bhad--rika M D	Ulka M D	Siddha M D	Sankata M D
1	00 – 00	00 – 01	00 – 01	00 – 02	00 – 02	00 – 03	00 – 03	00 – 04
2	00 – 01	00 – 02	00 – 03	00 – 04	00 – 05	00 – 05	00 – 06	00 – 07
3	00 – 01	00 – 03	00 – 04	00 – 05	00 – 07	00 – 08	00 – 09	00 – 11
4	00 – 02	00 – 04	00 – 05	00 – 07	00 – 09	00 – 11	00 – 13	00 – 14
5	00 – 02	00 – 04	00 – 07	00 – 09	00 – 11	00 – 13	00 – 16	00 – 18
6	00 – 03	00 – 05	00 – 08	00 – 11	00 – 13	00 – 16	00 – 19	00 – 22
7	00 – 03	00 – 06	00 – 09	00 – 13	00 – 16	00 – 19	00 – 22	00 – 25
8	00 – 04	00 – 07	00 – 11	00 – 14	00 – 18	00 – 22	00 – 25	00 – 29
9	00 – 04	00 – 08	00 – 12	00 – 16	00 – 20	00 – 24	00 – 28	01 – 02
10	00 – 04	00 – 09	00 – 13	00 – 18	00 – 22	00 – 27	01 – 01	01 – 06

Long of Moon	Mangla	Pingla	Dhanya	Bhra- -mari	Bhad- -rika	Ulka	Siddha	Sankata
Minutes	M D	M D	M D	M D	M D	M D	M D	M D
11	00 – 05	00 – 10	00 – 15	00 – 20	00 – 25	00 – 30	01 – 05	01 – 10
12	00 – 05	00 – 11	00 – 16	00 – 22	00 – 27	01 – 02	01 – 08	01 – 13
13	00 – 06	00 – 12	00 – 18	00 – 23	00 – 29	01 – 05	01 – 11	01 – 17
14	00 – 06	00 – 13	00 – 19	00 – 25	01 – 01	01 – 08	01 – 14	01 – 20
15	00 – 07	00 – 13	00 – 20	00 – 27	01 – 04	01 – 10	01 – 17	01 – 24
16	00 – 07	00 – 14	00 – 22	00 – 29	01 – 06	01 – 13	01 – 20	01 – 28
17	00 – 08	00 – 15	00 – 23	01 – 01	01 – 08	01 – 16	01 – 24	02 – 01
18	00 – 08	00 – 16	00 – 24	01 – 02	01 – 10	01 – 19	01 – 27	02 – 05
19	00 – 09	00 – 17	00 – 26	01 – 04	01 – 13	01 – 21	02 – 00	02 – 08
20	00 – 09	00 – 18	00 – 27	01 – 06	01 – 15	01 – 24	02 – 03	02 – 12

Dasha Sequence of Major Period (Maha Dasha)

We have worked out that the dasha balance at birth is 1 year 9 months 4 days for the example. The date of birth is 22 Dec 1973. The Yogini Dasha follows the sequence as given in the table 1 above. This sequence is repeated after 36 years in thesame order. We will now write the major dasha periods for the example.

Table 4

Yogini Dasa	From	To
Bhramari	22.12.1973	26.9.1975
Bhadrika	26.9.1975	26.9.1980
Ulka	26.9.1980	26.9.1986
Siddha	26.9.1986	26.9.1993
Sankata	26.9.1993	26.9.2001
Mangla	26.9.2001	26.9.2002
Pingla	26.9.2002	26.9.2004
Dhanya	26.9.2004	26.9.2007
Bhramari	26.9.2007	26.9.2011
Bhadrika	26.9.2011	26.9.2016

Sub Periods

Each major period of Yogini Dasha is further divided intoeight parts called sub periods or Antar dasha. The duration ofeach major period is shared by all eight Yoginis in proportion oftheir major period. Each major period Yogini keeps the first subperiod to herself and the others follow in the sequence.

The total of major periods of eight Yoginis in one cycle is36 years. Thus, each major period is shared by the eight Yoginiswhose total periods are 36 years. Each major period is thereforebroken into 36 parts. Each sub period lord takes its period according to its share in 36 years.

We can write it as

$$\text{Sub Period} = \frac{\text{Major Period x Sub Period Year}}{36}$$

To simplify we multiply it by 360.

The result is sub period = Major period x sub periodx 10 days.

The quick rule to find sub period of a Yogini Say A in themajor period of a Yogini Say B is A in years x B in years x 10 days.

For example: we find sub period of Ulka in Siddha. We multiply their Dasha period and again multiply by 10 i.e. 6 x 7 x10 = 420 days.

Sub Period rule states that the major period Yogini keepsthe first sub period to itself. Therefore, to work the sub period atbirth, we must start the sub periods from beginning of birth major period. The start can be known by deducting the full dasha period of Yogini.

Dasha at birth from the ending date ofbirth dasha Yogini. In the example the Yogini Dasha at birth isBhramari which ends on 26 September, 1975. The full dashaperiod of Bhramari is 4 years. Deducting 4 years from ending date we get 26 September, 1971 as the start date of Bhramari.

Sub Period of Bhramari major dasha at birth to get AD at birth

D	M	Y	
26 10	9 5	1971 0	Bhramari 4 x 4 x 10
6 20	3 6	1972 0	Bhramari 4 x 5 x 10
26 0	9 8	1972 0	Ulka 4 x 6 x 10
26 10	5 9	1973	Siddha 4 x 7 x 10

Since date of birth is 22 December 1973 which falls in Siddha Sub period, the sub period at birth is Siddha in Bhramarimajor period.

We now calculate the sub period in Sankata major period.

D	M	Y	
26 10	9 9	1993 1	Sankata 8 x 8 x 10
6 20	7 2	1995 0	Mangla 8 x 1 x 10
26 10	9 5	1995 0	Pingla 8 x 2 x 10
6 0	3 8	1996 0	Dhanya 8 x 3 x 10
6 20	11 10	1996 0	Bhramari 8 x 4 x 10
26 10	9 1	1997 1	Bhramari 8 x 5 x 10
6 0	11 4	1998 1	Ulka 8 x 6 x 10
6 20	3 6	2000 1	Siddha 8 x 7 x 10

The shortest sub period is of 10 days of Mangla / Mangla and the longest sub period is 1 year 9 months 10 days of Sankata/ Sankata.

A ready table for sub period is given.

Table 4.1 – Sub Periods in Yogini Dasa - Mangla

Sub Periods	Sub Period Y-M-D	Total Period Y-M-D
Mangla	00 – 00 – 10	00 – 00 – 10
Pingla	00 – 00 – 20	00 – 01 – 00
Dhanya	00 – 01 – 00	00 – 02 – 00
Bhramari	00 – 01 – 10	00 – 03 – 10
Bhadrika	00 – 01 – 20	00 – 05 – 00
Ulka	00 – 02 – 00	00 – 07 – 00
Siddha	00 – 02 – 10	00 – 09 – 10
Sankata	00 – 02 – 20	01 – 00 – 00

Table 4.2 – Sub Periods in Yogini Dasa - Pingla

Sub Periods	Sub Period Y-M-D	Total Period Y-M-D
Pingla	00 – 01 – 10	00 – 01 – 10
Dhanya	00 – 02 – 00	00 – 03 – 10
Bhramari	00 – 02 – 20	00 – 06 – 00
Bhadrika	00 – 03 – 10	00 – 09 – 10
Ulka	00 – 04 – 00	01 – 01 – 10
Siddha	00 – 04 – 20	01 – 06 – 00
Sankata	00 – 05 – 10	01 – 11 – 10
Mangla	00 – 00 – 20	02 – 00 – 00

Table 4.3 – Sub Periods in Yogini Dasa - Dhanya

Sub Periods	Sub Period Y-M-D	Total Period Y-M-D
Dhanya	00 – 03 – 00	00 – 03 – 00
Bhramari	00 – 04 – 00	00 – 07 – 00
Bhadrika	00 – 05 – 00	01 – 00 – 00
Ulka	00 – 06 – 00	01 – 06 – 00
Siddha	00 – 07 – 00	02 – 01 – 00
Sankata	00 – 08 – 00	02 – 09 – 00
Mangla	00 – 01 – 00	02 – 10 – 00
Pingla	00 – 02 – 00	03 – 00 – 00

Table 4.4 – Sub Periods in Yogini Dasa - Bhramari

Sub Periods	Sub Period Y-M-D	Total Period Y-M-D
Bhramari	00 – 05 – 10	00 – 05 – 10
Bhadrika	00 – 06 – 20	01 – 00 – 00
Ulka	00 – 08 – 00	01 – 08 – 00
Siddha	00 – 09 – 10	02 – 05 – 10
Sankata	00 – 10 – 20	03 – 04 – 00
Mangla	00 – 01 – 10	03 – 05 – 10
Pingla	00 – 20 – 20	03 – 08 – 00
Dhanya	00 – 04 – 00	04 – 00 – 00

Table 4.5 – Sub Periods in Yogini Dasa - Bhadrika

Sub Periods	Sub Period Y-M-D	Total Period Y-M-D
Bhadrika	00 – 08 – 10	00 – 08 – 10
Ulka	00 – 10 – 00	01 – 06 – 10
Siddha	00 – 11 – 20	02 – 06 – 00
Sankata	01 – 01 – 10	03 – 07 – 10
Mangla	00 – 01 – 20	03 – 09 – 00
Pingla	00 – 03 – 10	04 – 00 – 10
Dhanya	00 – 05 – 00	04 – 05 – 10
Bhramari	00 – 06 – 20	05 – 00 – 00

Table 4.6 – Sub Periods in Yogini Dasa - Ulka

Sub Periods	Sub Period Y-M-D	Total Period Y-M-D
Ulka	01 – 00 – 00	01 – 00 – 00
Siddha	01 – 02 – 00	02 – 02 – 00
Sankata	01 – 04 – 00	03 – 06 – 00
Mangla	00 – 02 – 00	03 – 08 – 00
Pingla	00 – 04 – 00	04 – 00 – 00
Dhanya	00 – 06 – 00	04 – 06 – 00
Bhramari	00 – 08 – 00	05 – 02 – 00
Bhadrika	00 – 10 – 00	06 – 00 – 00

Table 4.7 – Sub Periods in Yogini Dasa - Siddha

Sub Periods	Sub Period Y-M-D	Total Period Y-M-D
Siddha	01 – 04 – 10	01 – 04 – 10
Sankata	01 – 06 – 20	02 – 11 – 00
Mangla	00 – 02 – 10	03 – 01 – 10
Pingla	00 – 04 – 20	03 – 06 – 00
Dhanya	00 – 07 – 00	04 – 01 – 00
Bhramari	00 – 09 – 10	04 – 10 – 10
Bhadrika	00 – 11 – 20	05 – 10 – 00
Ulka	01 – 02 – 00	07 – 00 – 00

Table 4.8 – Sub Periods in Yogini Dasa - Sankata

Sub Periods	Sub Period Y-M-D	Total Period Y-M-D
Sankata	01 – 09 – 10	01 – 09 – 10
Mangla	00 – 02 – 20	02 – 00 – 00
Pingla	00 – 05 – 10	02 – 05 – 10
Dhanya	00 – 08 – 00	03 – 01 – 10
Bhramari	00 – 10 – 20	04 – 00 – 00
Bhadrika	01 – 01 – 10	05 – 01 – 10
Ulka	01 – 04 – 00	06 – 05 – 10
Siddha	01 – 06 – 20	08 – 00 – 00

Yogini Dasha Results of Maha dasha

Mansagari have given the interpretation of Dasha Results ofYogini

Maha dasha and antar dasha (Sub periods). These are given here for the benefit of readers. The results given are in line with the names of the Yogini.

Four Yoginis are of benefic planets and four are of maleficplanets. The results given in classic are auspicious or inauspiciousaccording to the Yogini belonging to benefics or malefic.

These are not to be taken literally. We have demonstrated the correct method of analyzing the Yogini Dasha later in this book. It is the total horoscope that matters.

Mangla

During Mangla Dasha, the person will be religious. He will be devoted to gods, religious persons and his Guru. He will have gains of conveyance, riches, fame, and growth of family. Auspicious ceremonies at home, praise from ruler, gain of ornaments, comfort from wife and gain of knowledge.

Pingla

There will be physical and mental sufferings. Troubled by evil association. Suffer from blood disorder, bilious disease, heart problems, and immoral relation with a wicked woman. Sufferingto children and servant. Loss of fame and reputation and have unfulfilled desires.

Dhanya

Gain of wealth and grains, business will increase. There will be all round happiness and good ceremonies in the family.The enemies will be destroyed; Gets honor from the king. Comfort from woman. Holy pilgrimages will be undertaken. Theperson is lucky to have this Dasha of Dhanya.

Bhramari

Aimless wondering in the places like mountains, and denseforests in scorching heat like a deer wanders in illusion. Even the king will sleep on the ground after loss of kingdom.

Bhadrika

There will be harmony in the family. The social status is elevated and the person mixes with eminent people thus improving his career. He develops business skills and benefitsfrom the rulers. He will enjoy the company of beautiful woman.

Ulka

Ulka Dasha gives loss of fame, wealth, cattle's, conveyance,business and clothes. He will face punishment from ruler. He will be troubled by spouse, servants, children etc. He will developdisease of heart, ears, feet, teeth and eyes.

Siddha

All desires will be fulfilled. Gain of wealth, education, fameand prosperity. Authority granted by the ruler (status given byking). Expansion of business. Marriage of children. Gets company of friends and enjoys luxurious from king.

Sankata

The position or the kingdom is lost. Destruction due to firein the house or village. Unworthy desires. Separation from theson and family. Loss of precious metals like gold. weakness ofbody and the fear of death.

Results of sub periods of Yoginis from classics

Mangla Maha Dasa

1. Mangla – This is giver of happiness from friends, sons, spouse and business. The sub period of Mangla in ManglaMaha dasha is giver of auspicious ceremonies.
2. Pingla – It is giver of enmity with friends and relatives. There is anxiety in mind. In this dasha all types of suffering will happen.
3. Dhanya – There will be gains of elephants, cows and wealth. Derives happiness from son, friends and relatives. There are all types of luxuries.

4. Bhramari - There will be rift with wife and friends. Lives in other lands and there is loss of wealth. He will develop friendship with the rulers.
5. Bhadrika – He will enjoy the wealth of all types with sons,wife, friends and relatives in a cordial way. He will have devotion to Gods. This will be a period of making merry.
6. Ulka – Loss of wealth and fame. Children, wife, friends and animals will suffer. He will be in constant fear of punishment from the king.
7. Siddha - He will have happiness from wife, children and wealth. All types of pleasure will be enjoyed. Friends and relatives will gather at his home.
8. Sankata – There will be fear from water, fire, thieves andthe king. He will suffer death like situation.

Pingla Maha Dasa

1. Pingla - He will develop addiction and will suffer from ailments, mental tension and have troublesome travelling.
2. Dhanya – Will have wealth, plenty of food and gain of progeny. The sexual enjoyments will be there. He will acquire landed property and all desires will be fulfilled.
3. Bhramari - He will live in foreign land and suffer loss dueto house, village or city and from relatives. There will be discord in the family.
4. Bhadrika – It will give all round prosperity. He will earn fame, profits from business and gain of son. The residencewill be changed.
5. Ulka – There is opposition from relatives and friends. Danger from king, thieves and trouble from society.
6. Siddha – He will master the mantras. There will be gain of wealth and grains. He will suffer from respiratory problemsand diabetes.
7. Sankata – Loss of wealth. Danger from king and enemies.He will have fear of some serious diseases.

8. Mangla – The person suffers from sorrows and unfounded fears. He gets various diseases and his longevity is affected.

Dhanya Maha Dasa

1. Dhanya - The person gains property, lands, wealth and grains. There is earning from the king. Happiness from wife and children.
2. Bhramari - The travel will be troublesome. Loss of wealth.He gains by change of residence. He will oppose his friends and relatives.
3. Bhadrika – it is an auspicious time. He gets happiness from family and friends. He will gain conveyance and honor fromthe king. There will be acquisition of clothes.
4. Ulka – This is a troublesome period and suffers losses. Hewill experience pain in heart and waist.
5. Siddha – Will get great happiness from children. Many friends will visit his house and he gets many kinds of enjoyments and gets pleasure.
6. Sankata – This is a period of bondage. He will not be having interest in his work like business, policies and the works given by the king.
7. Mangla – All round happiness in the home. He will enjoy the comfort of food, wife, children and precious metals.
8. Pingla – There will be loss of property and wealth of manyways. There will be fear of king and he will have pains andailments in his body. There is no enthusiasm in his work.

Bhramari Maha Dasa

1. Bhramari - It will be a period of frightfulness. There will be trouble from poison. He will be shifted from his place. Hewill be away from friends, relatives and enemies.
2. Bhadrika – He will have association of friends and will travel abroad. Good education and gets honor from King.
3. Ulka - This dasha is giver of fever, pains and troubles fromblood disorder. Sufferings to wife, children. There will be loss of

wealth and other things.

4. Siddha – The desired things will be accomplished. This dasha will give the wealth of wisdom, education and relief from diseases and fears.
5. Sankata – Great death like sufferings and will have sorrow, sickness and attachments leading to disappointment. He faces theft charges in the court of king.
6. Mangla – Auspicious events will happen and there will be comfort and pleasure around. He will get prosperity and happiness by serving the king.
7. Pingla – The person will have disease of rectum, mouth, feet etc. There will be fear of injuries caused by animals like elephant, horses, buffaloes and tigers.
8. Dhanya – Accumulation of wealth, vehicles and pleasurable amenities. He will gain from the king. There will be losseson account of tribals.

Bhadrika Maha Dasa

1. Bhadrika – He will receive honors and there will be gain of horses, cows etc. He will get freedom from wrong habitsand sorrows and will get to know the correct path of life.
2. Ulka – In this dasha, there will be conflict with people, suffers ill wealth and loss of job or home. There will be loss of wealth and have great worries.
3. Siddha – Will have devotion to gods and Brahmins. Thereis happiness from wife, children and relatives. Will have comforts, enjoyments at home, village with celebration.
4. Sankata – Will face many troubles, sorrows, obstacles. There will be troubles in travelling abroad.
5. Mangla – Will be honored and there is increase in land assets, business and the family will expand.
6. Pingla – Have bilious disorders. He will get good advice from elders which will increase his agriculture, property and in many ways.

7. Dhanya – Happiness from wife, children, friends and relatives. There will be auspicious celebrations at home. Have great gains of wealth and food.
8. Bhramari – Diseases of blood, danger from fire. Death like fears. This dasha destroys a person who is the enemy in the village. He will have happiness from relatives.

Ulka Maha Dasa

1. Ulka – Sudden loss of wealth which is caused by enemy. Will have great fear of loss of kingdom.
2. Siddha – This antardasha delivers unfavorable results andthe auspiciousness of Venus is not felt. He will undertakejourney to foreign countries.
3. Sankata – Fear of death, children will suffer. There will beharm to wife, relatives and servants.
4. Mangla – The person will have wrong notions. He gets happiness from wealth, friends, wife and wisdom. He willget rid of disease and wickedness.
5. Pingla – Will be troubled by skin disease like leprosy and disease of head. He will be a wanderer or aimless traveler.
6. Dhanya – No gains and no comforts. Diseases of wind and phlegm will trouble. There will be rift with wife, children and relatives.
7. Bhramari - The mind will be agitated and there is fear or enemies. Many types of Sufferings are faced during this period.
8. Bhadrika – There will be all round prosperity and gain of wealth. Will suffer loss of clothes and ornaments. He willhave happiness from friends and relatives.

Siddha Maha Dasa

1. Siddha – Accomplishes all his undertakings. Gets happiness from relatives. There is increase in comforts of children and friends.
2. Sankata – Faces confinement and loss of wealth throughthe

king. It may be by way of penalty or by theft. He is under fear and made to leave the country.

3. Mangla – Will enjoy sensual pleasures. His own people willgive him happiness and will earn wealth through the king. There will be success all-round.
4. Pingla – Will be given to anger and arrogance. He will havefear of fire and develop rift with his own people. He gets illegal income.
5. Dhanya – The good results of good deeds done in past lifewill be bestowed. His all desires are fulfilled.
6. Bhramari – Due to serious bad habits he has to desert his residence. He will face danger due to the anger from king's family.
7. Bhadrika – Auspicious events at home. He indulges in sensual pleasures. There is increase of comfort, educationand virtues. Success in all undertakings.
8. Ulka – Destruction of wealth and grains. He faces troubles, sorrows and indulges in bad habits. Suffers from diseasesof rectum.

Sankata Maha Dasa

1. Sankata – will have grave danger of death, losses due tothe king. Have to leave the country and destruction of wealth.
2. Mangla – Suffering from many diseases and ill health. Painsto wife. He will be addicted to many evil habits.
3. Pingla – There will be sudden financial loses. Grief from son. Danger from enemies and separation from near relatives.
4. Dhanya – Due to problems of spleen, he will suffer pain in stomach. Great happiness from son. Enjoys fame and popularity among the people of own country.
5. Bhramari - There will be travels in his own and foreign countries. Harm will be caused to his home, village or county. There is fear of loss of kingdom.

6. Bhadrika – The person will acquire knowledge and education. Increase in ornaments, fame and clothes. He will have quarrel with ordinary people.
7. Ulka – The accumulated wealth will be lost. The propertywill be lost and faces death like situations. The animals willsuffer. There will be problems to maternal family.
8. Siddha - The person will be active. There will be birth of children and gets happiness from own progress. The personwill be in elated state of mind.

Chapter 2
Research

The description given in chapter 1 is the classical method of computing Yogini Dasha. This method is also followed for our calculations also. We are following the classics but the interpretation of result is the tested research.

Yogini Dasha repeats every thirty-six years. The events are not repeating every 36 years. Some people say that we shouldconsider the age of the person. We agree but the nature of events should remain same. This is also not so. Suppose a personjoin service at the age of 24 years in a Yogini Dasha. The same Yogini will repeat at 60 years of age and the person retires fromwork. For example, a person gets married at an age of 24 years. Will he marry again at 60?

The Yoginis are generated through the Nakshtra and this is the hidden secret of analyzing the Yogini.

It is the Nakshatra which generates the Yogini.

Thus, we have to understand the Yogini Nakshtra.

The problem came while linking the Yoginis with Nakshtra sequence. There are twenty-seven Nakshtra and twenty-four yoginis in three cycles. Three Yogini dasha originate from four Nakshtra. Other five Yogini originate from three Nakshtra each.

The classics have laid down the sequence or Yogini dashafrom Mangla to Sankata and cannot be altered. The solution came through the analysis of Navamsha of Nakshtra. Thus, three Nakshtra Ashwani, Bharani and Kritika were left before Rohini to maintain the sequence.

This is akin to the frog jumps of Kalachakra dasha or Mandook dasa.

We have taken Nakshtra lords as the Vimshottary lords. The Yogini dasha is microscopic view of Vimshottary. The unfolding of events is seen with a clear view since yogini dashais of 36 years cycle and Vimshottary is 120 years. The dasha periods in Vimshottary are longer as compared to Yogini Dasha.To aid this further, we are having different progress lagna for each dasha according to the Nakshtra generating the dasha. As the lagna changes, the role of the planets also changes.

Method to get progress chart

A step-by-step method of working out the Yogini with Nakshtra and getting progress lagan for a Yogini dasa is given. A condensed table of Nakshtra and Yogini dasa is given which is useful to decide the Nakshtra of a Yogini dasa.

Condensed Table

Nakshtra	Yogini Dasa
Ashwini	Bharamari
Bharani	Bhadrika
Kritika	Ulka
Rohini	Siddha
Mrigshira	Sankata
Ardra	Mangla
Punarvasu	Pingla
Pushya	Dhanya
Ashlesha	Bharamari
Magha	Bhadrika
P. Phalguni	Ulka
U. Phalguni	Siddha
Hasta	Sankata
Chitra	Mangla

Nakshtra	Yogini Dasa
Swati	Pingla
Visakha	Dhanya
Anuradha	Bharamari
Jyeshtha	Bhadrika
Moola	Ulka
P. Ashadha	Siddha
U. Ashadha	Sankata
Shravan	Mangla
Dhanishta	Pingla
Shatbhisaj	Dhanya
P. Bhadrapad	Bharamari
U. Bhadrapad	Bhadrika
Revati	Ulka
Rohini	Siddha

1. Workout the Yogini dasha and the balance at birth.
2. Note down the Nakshtra and the Nakshtra lord of Moon at birth. (Vimshottary lord of Nakshtra).
3. Write the dasha at birth along with Nakshtra of Moon like Bhramari / Anuradha.
4. For next Yogini dasha write the next Nakshtra along with dasha. Continue writing dasha and Nakshtra for the subsequent dasha. Take the sequence from the condensed table given.
5. When you reach Revati, jump to Rohini for next dasha. The Yogini dasha for Revati is Ulka. So, for next dasha of Siddha we jump to Rohini.
6. This way we have a Nakshtra for each Yogini dasha period.Each Yogini dasha will have its generating Nakshtra. Forexample,

we take Mangla dasha period. Mangla dasha repeats three times in 27 Nakshtra. Now each Mangla willhave a different Nakshtra which is ruling a particular Mangla dasha.

7. For a Yogini dasha period, recast the birth chart keeping the sign of Nakshtra as Lagna / Ascendant. This re castedchart is called progress chart and the Lagna or Ascendantis called progress lagna (PL).
8. Planets remain in the signs as occupied by them in birth chart.
9. When a Nakshtra occupy two signs, the progress lagna will change to the next sign according to span of Nakshtrain each sign. The time of change will be in proportion to dasha period and span of Nakshtra in each sign.

   For example, for Mrigshira Nakshtra, the dasha is of Sankataof eight years. Mrigshira falls in Taurus and Gemini. TwoPadas are in Taurus and two Padas are in Gemini. So, thisNakshtra is equally divided in these two signs. The Sankatadasha is of eight years. These eight years will be equally divided in Taurus and Gemini. Thus, the progress lagna willchange to Gemini after four years have passed in Sankata.

   This is applicable to Nakshtra of Sun and Jupiter. For dasha generated by a Nakshtra of Sun, we have one pada in one sign and three Padas in next sign. So, the progress lagna will change after one – fourth dasha period of Yoginigenerated by the Nakshtra.

   Similarly for Nakshtra of Jupiter, there are three Padas infirst sign and one pada in next sign. The progress lagna will change to next sign after three –fourth of the dasha period of the Yogini generated by the Yogini.
10. This way we have different lagans for each dasha. This progress chart now is interpreted for results and timing of events.

We illustrate the method with an example: -

Example Indira Gandhi DOB 19 November 1917 TOB 23.11 POB Allahabad

Birth Chart

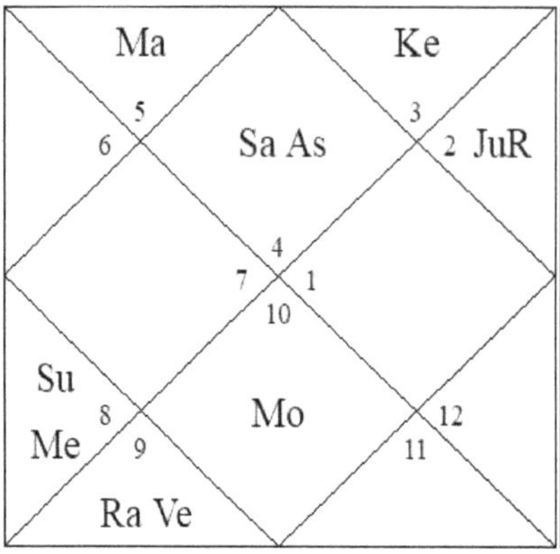

Birth Chart

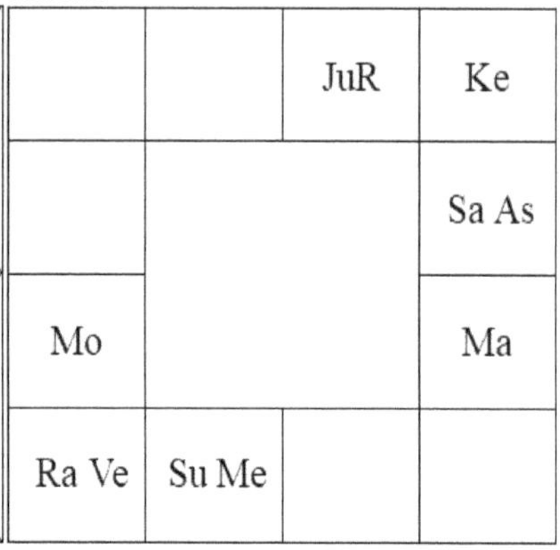

Birth Nakshatra U. Ashadha

Longitude of Moon is 5° – 35' in Capricorn. The Nakshtrais Uttara Ashadha. The balance of Yogini Dasha at Birth is Sankata2 years 7 months and 24 days. The dasha sequence will be –

Yogini	Nakshtra	From	To
Sankata	U. Ashadha	19.11.1917	13.7.1920
Mangla	Shravan	13.7.1920	13.7.1921
Pingla	Dhanishta	13.7.1921	13.7.1923
Dhanya	Shatbhisaj	13.7.1923	13.7.1926
Bhramari	P. Bhadrapad	13.7.1926	13.7.1930
Bhadrika	U. Bhadrapad	13.7.1930	13.7.1935

Yogini	Nakshtra	From	To
Ulka	Revati	13.7.1935	13.7.1941
Siddha	Rohini	13.7.1941	13.7.1948
Sankata	Mrigshira	13.7.1948	13.7.1956
Mangla	Ardra	13.7.1956	13.7.1957
Pingla	Punarvasu	13.7.1957	13.7.1959
Dhanya	Pushya	13.7.1959	13.7.1962
Bhramari	Ashlesha	13.7.1962	13.7.1966
Bhadrika	Magha	13.7.1966	13.7.1971
Ulka	P. Phalguni	13.7.1971	13.7.1977
Siddha	U. Phalguni	13.7.1977	13.7.1984
Sankata	Hasta	13.7.1984	13.7.1992

A full table for Nakshatra, Yogini and the sign of progress lagna is given.

Yogini Dasha	Yr	Lord of Yogini	Nak-shatra	Nakshatra Lord	Sign of PL	Change sign after
Bhramari	4	Mars	Ashwani	Ketu	Aries	X
Bhadrika	5	Mercury	Bharani	Venus	Aries	X
Ulka	6	Saturn	Kritika	Sun	Aries / Taurus	1 Y 6 M
Siddha	7	Venus	Rohini	Moon	Taurus	X
Sankata	8	Rahu	Mrigshira	Mars	Taurus/ Gemini	4 Y 0 M
Mangla	1	Moon	Ardra	Rahu	Gemini	X
Pingla	2	Sun	Punarvasu	Jupiter	Gemini / Cancer	1Y 6 M

Yogini Dasha	Yr	Lord of Yogini	Nak-shatra	Nakshatra Lord	Sign of PL	Change sign after
Dhanya	3	Jupiter	Pushya	Saturn	Cancer	X
Bhramari	4	Mars	Ashlesha	Mercury	Cancer	X
Bhadrika	5	Mercury	Magha	Ketu	Leo	X
Ulka	6	Saturn	P. Phalguni	Venus	Leo	X
Siddha	7	Venus	Phalguni	Sun	Leo / Virgo	1 Y 9 M
Sankata	8	Rahu	Hasta	Moon	Virgo	X
Mangla	1	Moon	Chitra	Mars	Virgo / Libra	0 Y 6 M
Pingla	2	Sun	Swati	Rahu	Libra	X
Dhanya	3	Jupiter	Vishakha	Jupiter	Libra / Scorpio	2 Y 3 M
Bhramari	4	Mars	Anuradha	Saturn	Scorpio	X
Bhadrika	5	Mercury	Jyeshtha	Mercury	Scorpio	X
Ulka	6	Saturn	Moola	Ketu	Sagittarius	X
Siddha	7	Venus	Poorva Ashadha	Venus	Sagittarius	X
Sankata	8	Rahu	Uttara Ashadha	Sun	Sagittarius/ Capricorn	2 Y 0 M
Mangla	1	Moon	Shravan	Moon	Capricorn	X
Pingla	2	Sun	Dhanishta	Mars	Capricorn/ Aquarius	1 Y 0 M
Dhanya	3	Jupiter	Shatbhisaj	Rahu	Aquarius	X
Bhramari	4	Mars	Poorva Bhadrapad	Jupiter	Aquarius/ Pisces	3 Y 0 M
Bhadrika	5	Mercury	Uttara Bhadrapad	Saturn	Pisces	X
Ulka	6	Saturn	Revati	Mercury	Pisces	X
Siddha	7	Venus	Rohini	Moon	Taurus	X

Note: Jump to Rohini after Revati (Ignore Ashwani, Bharani and Kritika)

If birth is in Ashwani or Bharani or Kritika then proceed in normal order.

Examination of Dasha Periods

1. The re casted chart for the running dasha is examined in totality.
2. The Nakshtra lord is important as well as the progress lagna.
3. We must identify the Nakshtra lord in the birth chart andthe new role in the progress chart.
4. Any planet connected to a house in birth chart makes connection with the same house in progress chart assures the events of that house in the duration of dasha period of progress chart.
5. A planet is related to a house in birth chart. Now in progress chart, another planet is related to the same house in progress chart. If these two planets are related then eventsignified by the house materializes. Suppose Mars is seventhlord of birth chart. In progress chart Jupiter is the seventhlord. Mars is aspecting Jupiter; the marriage will take placeduring the currency of progress chart.
6. Work out the significators of an event and note these planets. During a dasha period if the same planets becomethe significator of the event in progress chart, it will takeplace. The significator can be the Nakshtra lord of the dasha.
7. For example, Mars is maraca for Libra lagna. When a dasha generated by Nakshtra of Mars operates, it can give problems.
8. Also, if Mars is influencing another planet, then this planetis also capable of giving results of Mars.
9. The progress chart is examined for the dasha period. Wemust see any Raj Yoga, Dhana Yoga etc. forming in the progress chart. We will experience their effects within thelimits of promises ofbirth chart and during the dasha period.
10. In the progress chart, if we see any serious affection to any

house, it is a danger signal for the significations of that house.

11. The sub period of events will be of the planets related tothe house. They may be lord of the house; the planets placed in the house or aspecting it and associated with lord.
12. The sub period of Nakshtra Lord and the planets relatedto it is also important.
13. Any planet who is related to Nakshtra lord and the lord ofthe house gives the events of that house.
14. Rahu and Ketu acts as their dispositor and the planet associated with them.
15. The events promised by Ketu are given in sub period of Sankata.

We illustrate this with an example.

Example DOB 30 April 1945 TOB 9.27 POB Delhi

Birth Chart

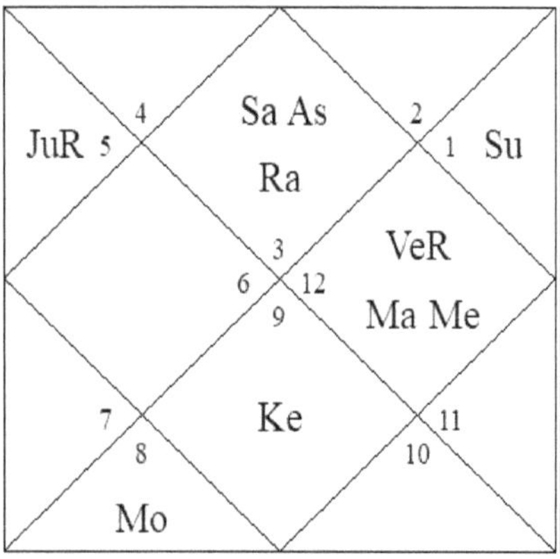

Birth Chart

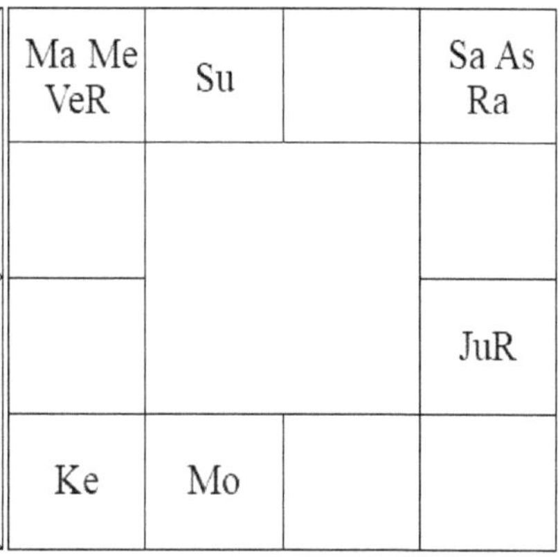

He was born in Bhramari / Anuradha. He was a class oneofficer with ministry of Defence.

The dasha sequence is,

Yogini	Nakshtra	From	To
Bharamari	Anuradha	30.4.1945	15.5.1945
Bhadrika	Jyeshtha	15.5.1945	15.5.1950

Yogini	Nakshtra	From	To
Ulka	Moola	15.5.1950	15.5.1956
Siddha	P. Ashadha	15.5.1956	15.5.1963
Sankata	U. Ashadha	15.5.1963	15.5.1971

Here we illustrate selection in class I service in 1969. The Nakshtra is U. Ashadha and its lord is Sun. The progress lagna moves to Capricorn on 15.5.65 i.e. after two years of Sankata.

The progress chart is,

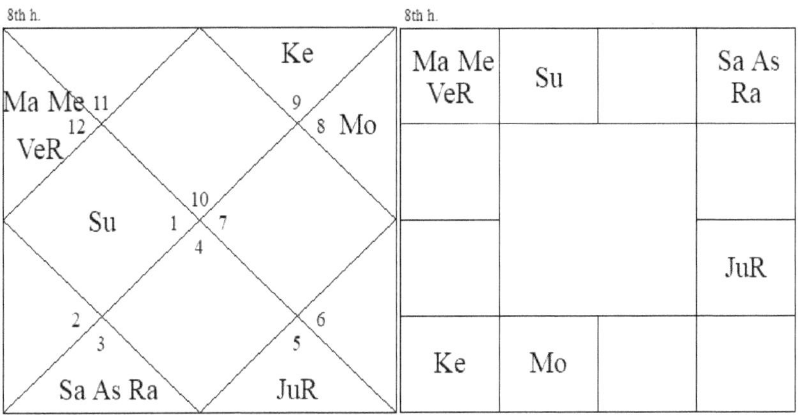

Sun is the Nakshtra Lord. It is influenced by Jupiter. Jupiteris the tenth lord of birth chart. In the progress chart, Sunis aspecting tenth house. The results of tenth are expectedthro' exalted Sun. The sub period was of Siddha. Venus is in tenth houseofbirth Chart and is the tenth lord of progresschart.

If we move further and reach Bhramari of P. Bhadrapad from 15 May 1977 to 15 May 1981. The progress Lagna isPisces from 15 May 1980. The star lord is Jupiter. Jupiter is birth tenth lord and also the progress tenth lord. Jupiter is in sixth from progress lagna. The tenth house is occupied by Ketu and aspected by Saturn. He resigned from class I job. The aspect of Jupiter on Sagittarius gave another job.

Chapter 3
Mangla

Mangla Yogini dasha is of one year duration. As the nameimplies, this is considered auspicious. It is not always so.

Mangla dasha belongs to three Nakshtra. These are Ardra,Chitra, and Shravan. The table below gives the Nakshtra lordetc. for each of Mangla Yogini period.

Nakshtra	Nakshtra Lord	Sign of Nakshtra	Remarks
Ardra	Rahu	Gemini	For entire period Progress Lagna is Gemini
Chitra	Mars	Virgo / Libra	First six months PL is Virgo and forlast six months PLis Libra.
Shravan	Moon	Capricorn	PL is Capricorn.The Nakshtra and dasha lord are same.

We will examine some charts for each of Mangla period.

Mangla / Ardra

Rahu is the Nakshtra lord. Rahu do not have lordship ofany sign. It gives results of the sign lord occupied by it and ofthe planet conjunct with it. Gemini is the progress lagna. Placement of Rahu in Kendra /Trikona from Gemini as well as from birth lagna makes it give good results. Association of Rahuwith lords of trine is also auspicious.

Example Marriage DOB 15 November 1918 TOB 21.49.26 POB Srinagar JK

Birth Chart

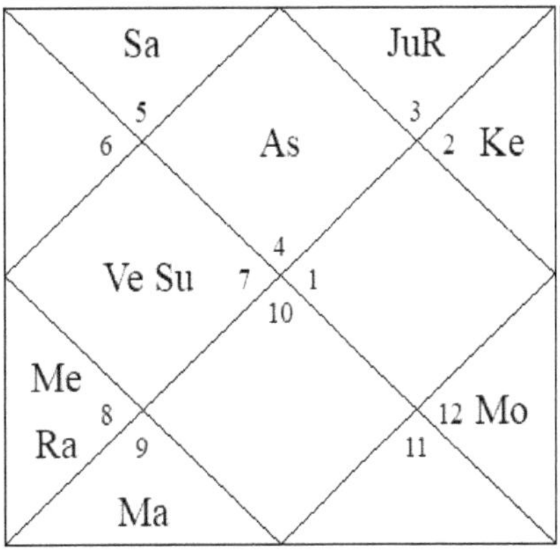

Birth Chart

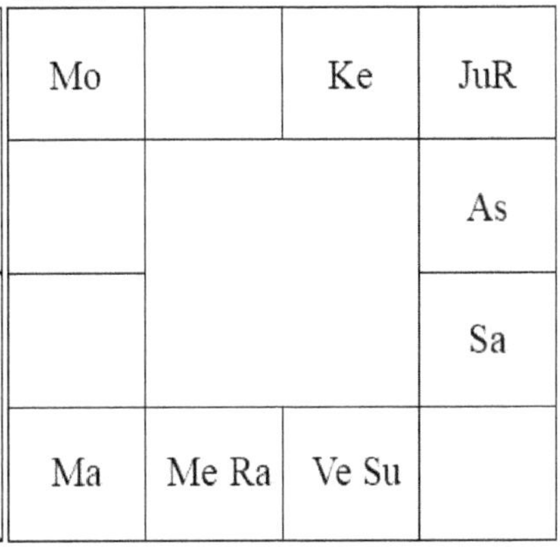

Birth Nakshatra Nakshtra – Revati

First, we will calculate the Yogini dasa along with Nakshtra.

He was born in Ulka of Revati. The dasa sequence is given.

Yogini	Nakshtra	From	To
Ulka	Revati	15. 11. 1918	11. 2. 1922
Siddha	Rohini	1.2. 1922	11.2.1929
Sankata	Mrigashira	11.2.1929	11.2.1937
Mangla	Ardra	11.2.1937	11.2.1938
Pingla	Punarvasu	11.2.1938	11.2.1940
Dhanya	Pushya	11.2.1940	11.2.1943
Bharamari	Ashlesha	11.2.1943	11.2.1947

He was married on 7 May 1937 in the Yogini Dasha period of Mangla / Ardra. The progress chart is casted. (Note - In progress Yogini we go to Rohini after Revati). Ardra Nakshtra falls in Gemini. The progress lagan will be Gemini.

Progress chart for Mangla/ Ardra

12th h.

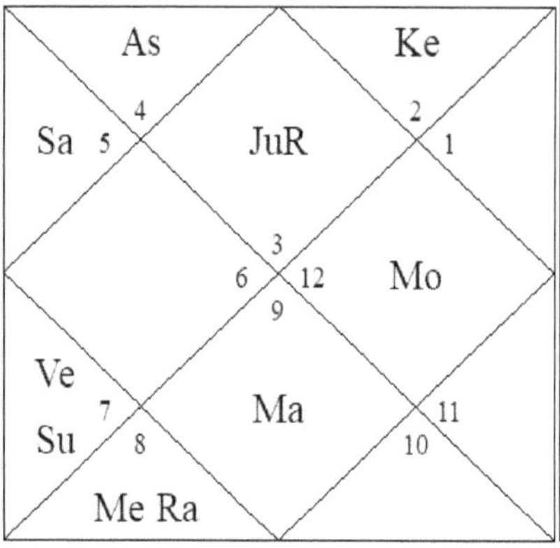

12th h.

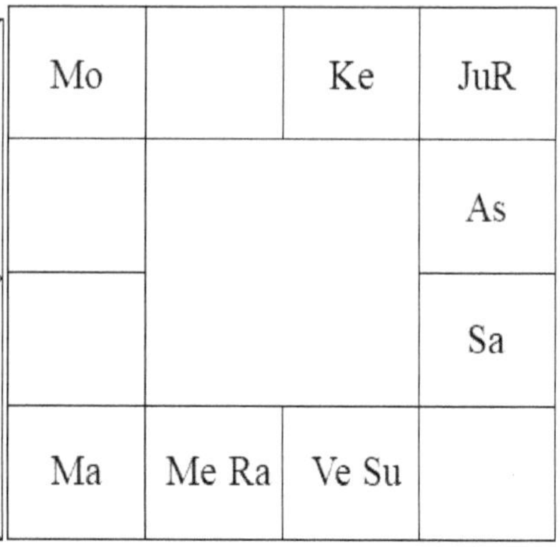

Rahu is in Scorpio and with Mercury. It acts as Mars. From progress Lagna, Mars is placed in seventh house and aspected by seventh lord Jupiter. Marriage took placed in Mangla / Bhramari or Moon / Mars.

Example Jail DOB 23 December 1902 TOB 7.23 POB Baghpat

Birth Chart

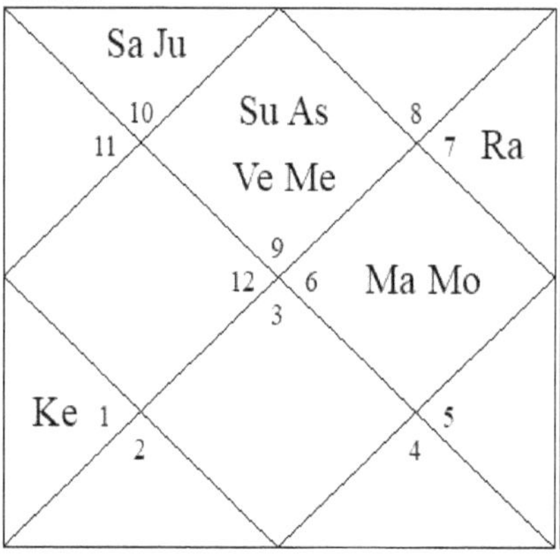

Birth Chart

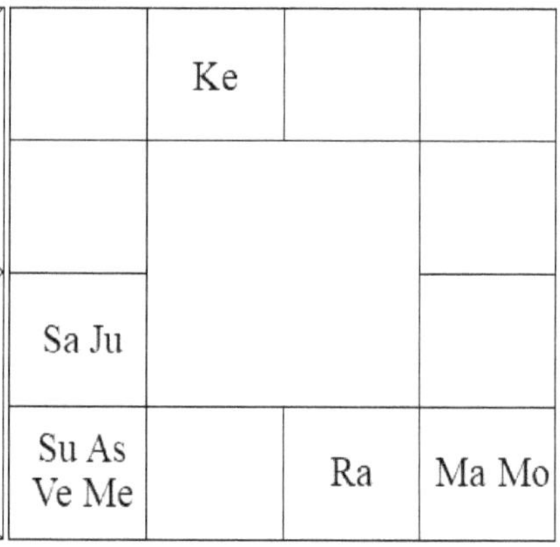

Birth Nakshatra Hasta

He remained in jail during emergency in 1975. The dasa sequence was,

Yogini	Nakshtra	From	To
Sankata	Hasta	23. 12.1902	26.5. 1903
Mangla	Chitra	26.5. 1903	26.5. 1904
Pingla	Swati	26.5. 1904	26.5. 1906
Dhanya	Visakha	26.5. 1906	26.5. 1909
Bharamari	Anuradha	26.5. 1909	26.5. 1913
Bhadrika	Jyeshtha	26.5. 1913	26.5. 1918
Ulka	Moola	26.5. 1918	26.5. 1924
Siddha	P. Ashadha	26.5. 1924	26.5. 1931
Sankata	U. Ashadha	26.5. 1931	26.5. 1939
Mangla	Shravan	26.5. 1939	26.5. 1940
Pingla	Dhanishta	26.5. 1940	26.5. 1942
Dhanya	Shatbhisaj	26.5. 1942	26.5. 1945
Bharamari	P. Bhadrapad	26.5. 1945	26.5. 1949
Bhadrika	U. Bhadrapad	26.5. 1949	26.5. 1954
Ulka	Revati	26.5. 1954	26.5. 1960
Siddha	Rohini	26.5. 1960	26.5. 1967
Sankata	Mrigshira	26.5. 1967	26.5. 1975
Mangla	Ardra	26.5. 1975	26.5. 1976

Progress chart for Mangla/Ardra

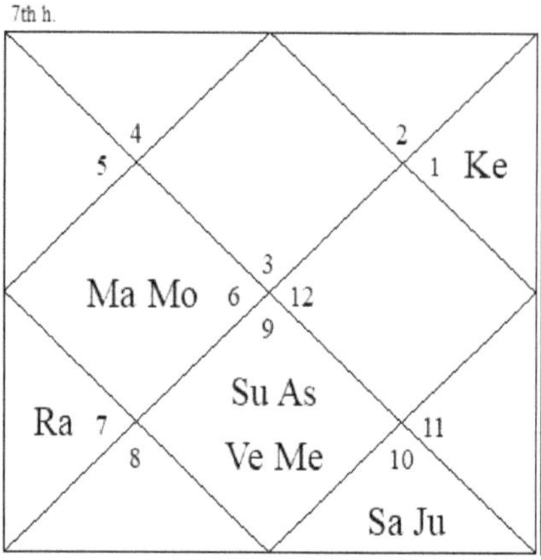

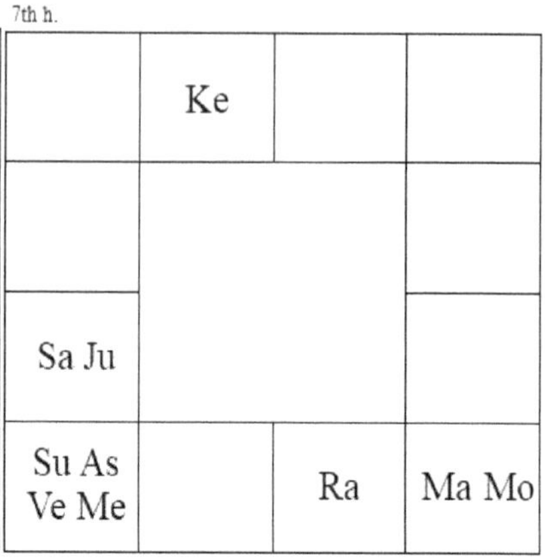

Now Rahu is in Libra and acts as Venus. Rahu is aspected by eighth lord Saturn from eighth house. The relation of eighthlord shows problems.

This Rahu is not aspected by any beneficand as such the malefic effect is prominent. Rahu in a trine aspected by eighth lord conjoined with maraca give problems.

Here Saturn is with Jupiter who is lord of seventh house. Saturnis in Pasha / Nigada Dreshkana. Saturn is maraca of birth chart. The star lord is now afflicted.

Birth lagna lord is in eighth house. Progress lagna lord is with twelfth lord and aspected by Mars. He remained in jail during emergency of 1975.

Example Grace of God DOB 13 May 1956 TOB 0.0 POB Papanasam

Birth Chart

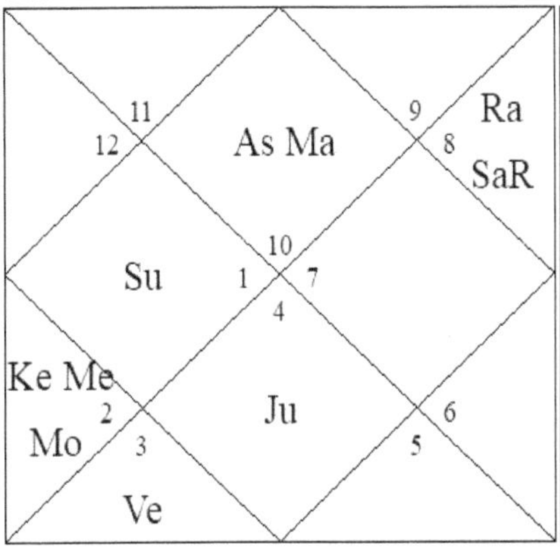

Birth Chart

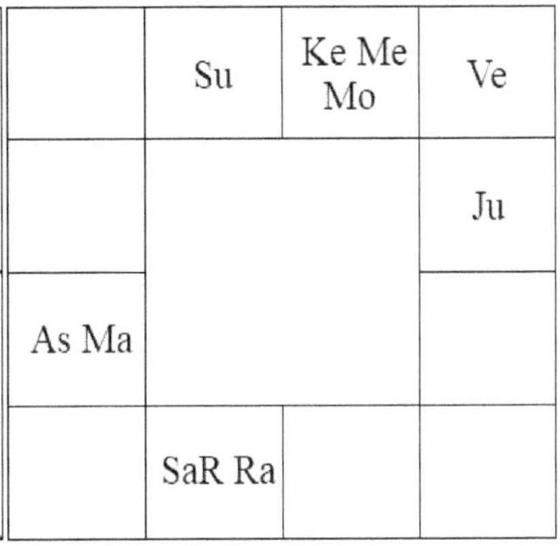

Birth Nakshtra Mrigshira

Basic chart is very strong with three exalted planets in Kendra. Mercury and Venus exchange sign. Moon is exalted. Ketu is with ninth lord and aspected by lagna lord. There is anexchange of lagna lord and eleventh lord

Progress Chart Mangla/ Ardra

6th h.

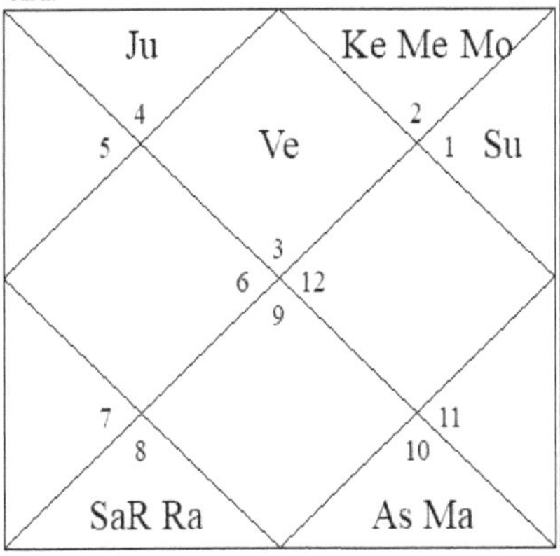

6th h.

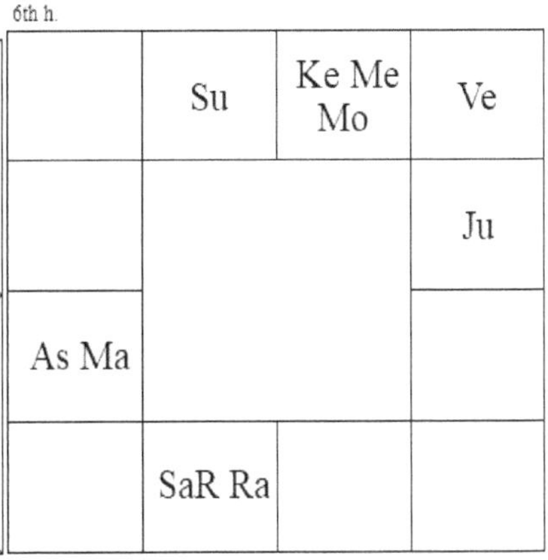

Dasha sequence is,

Yogini	Nakshtra	From	To
Sankata	Mrigshira	13. 5.1956	5.1.1961
Mangla	Ardra	5.1.1961	5.1.1962

Mangla / Ardra operated in 1961 when Sri Sri Ji was fouryears old. In the progress chart Rahu is in sixth house and is placedwith ninth lord Saturn. Sixth house shows efforts and is the house of Sadhna. Rahu is aspected by lagna lord Mercury andexalted Moon and Jupiter. He could recite the entire Bhagwat Gita during this Mangla Period.

Example Job DOB 11 September 1968 TOB 12.45 POB Shahjahanpur UP

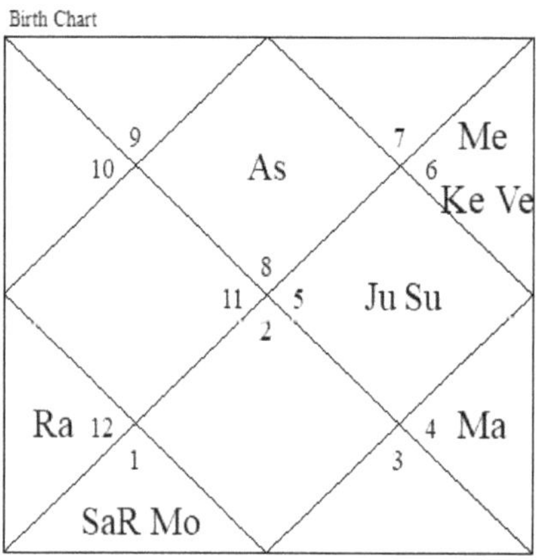

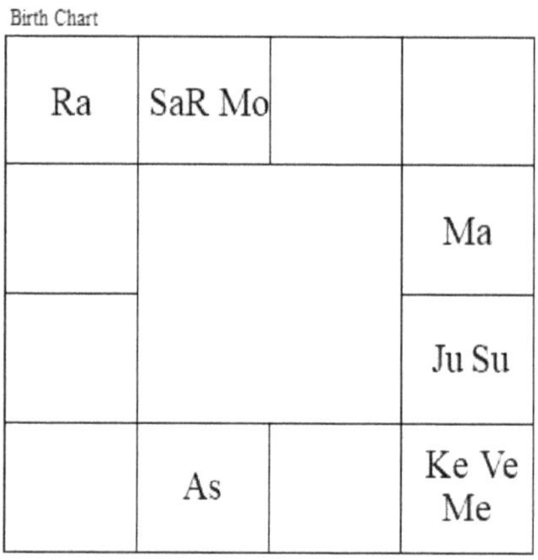

Birth Nakshtra Bharani

Dasa sequence

Yogini	Nakshtra	From	To
Bhadrika	Bharani	11.9.1968	1.8.1972
Ulka	Kritika	1.8.1972	1.8.1978
Siddha	Rohini	1.8.1978	1.8.1985

Sankata	Mrigshira	1.8.1985	1.8.1993
Mangla	Ardra	1.8.1993	1.8.1994

Progress Chart Mangla/ Ardra and Gemini lagan.

8th h.

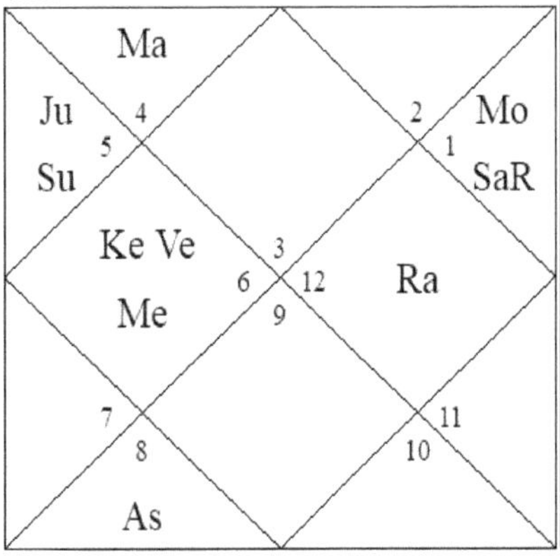

8th h.

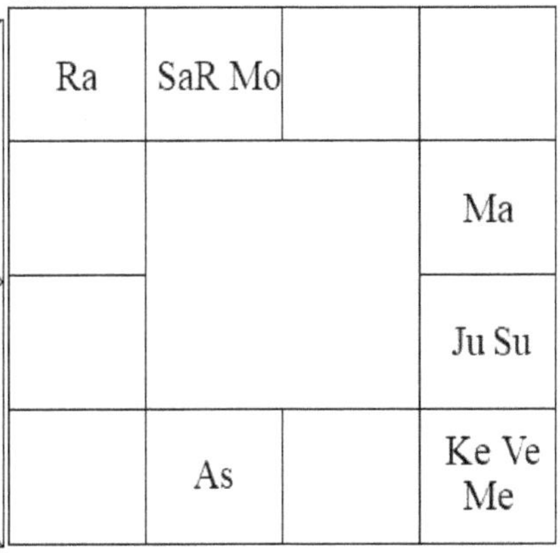

He started his service on 1 September, 1993 in the YoginiDasha of Moon/ Jupiter. Jupiter sub period started on 1. September, 1993.

The Nakshtra lord Rahu is placed in tenth house from progress Lagna. Rahu acts as Jupiter. In the birth chart Jupiteris placed in tenth house with tenth lord. The job was started inMoon / Jupiter.

Example childbirth DOB 30 July 1975 TOB 18.45 POB Delhi

Birth Chart

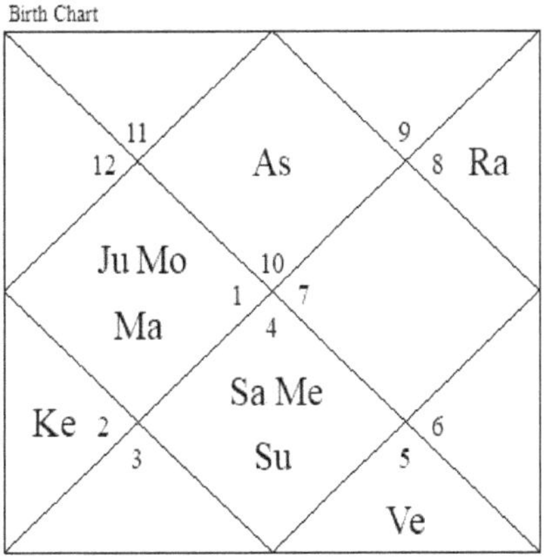

Birth Chart

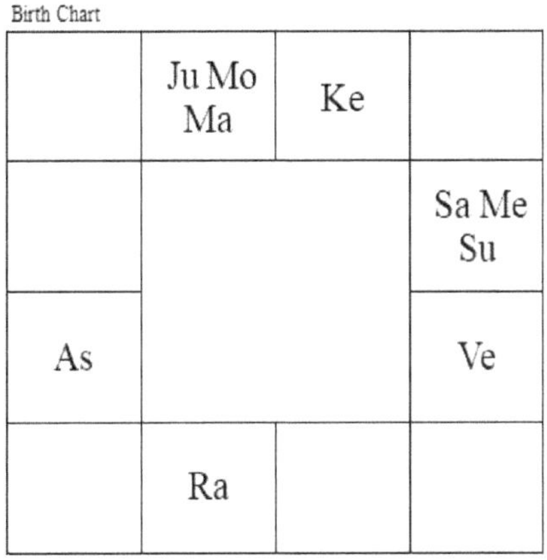

Birth Nakshtra Ashwani

This horoscope is of a lady who is a school teacher. Her husband is an executive working in Dubai. She got a baby girlon 22.5.2004 in Mangla / Pingla.

Dasa sequence

Yogini	Nakshtra	From	To
Bharamari	Ashwani	30.7.1975	1.5.1978
Bhadrika	Bharani	1.5.1978	1.5.1983
Ulka	Kritika	1.5.1983	1.5.1989
Siddha	Rohini	1.5.1989	1.5.1996
Sankata	Mrigshira	1.5.1996	1.5.2004
Mangla	Ardra	1.5.2004	1.5.2005

Progress Chart Mangla/ Ardra and Gemini lagan.

6th h.

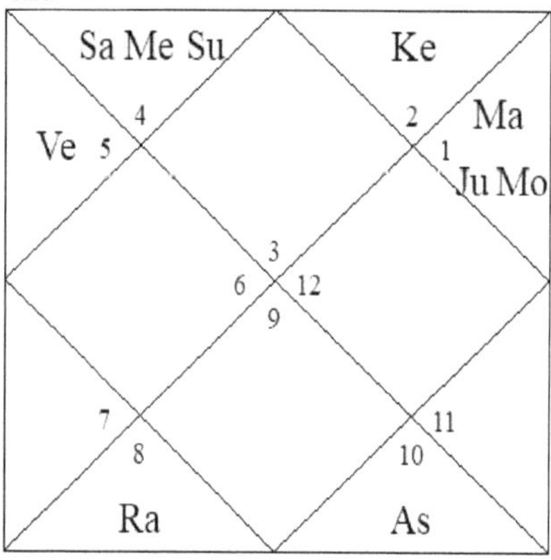

6th h.

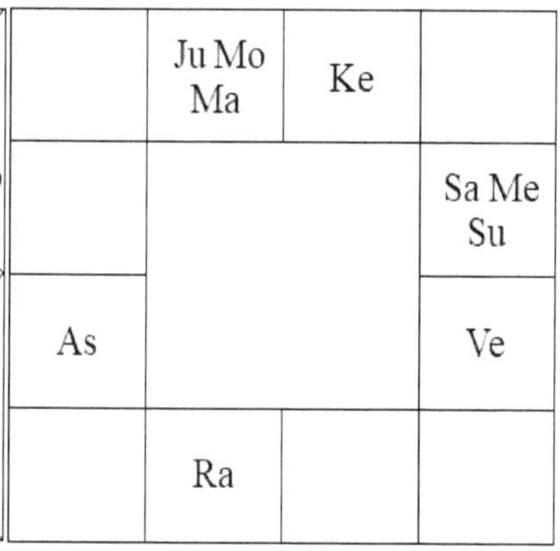

Rahu acts as Mars. Mars is in eleventh house and aspects fifth house and Rahu. The ninth lord Saturn is aspecting Mars and Moon.

Example Party president DOB 19 November 1917 TOB 23.11 POB Allahabad

Birth Chart

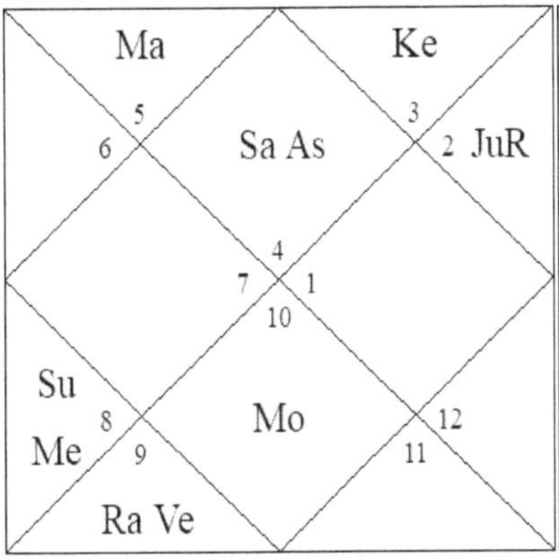

Birth Chart

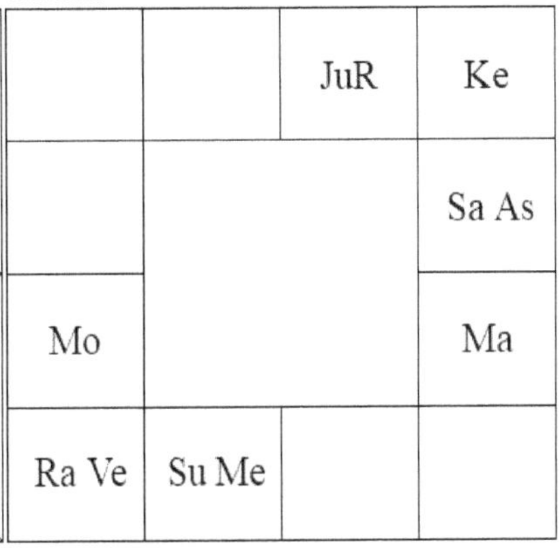

Birth Nakshtra U. Ashadha

She was appointed Congress President in Mangla/ Mangla. This was her big exposure to active political life.

Dasa sequence

Yogini	Nakshtra	From	To
Sankata	U. Ashadha	19.11.1917	13.7.1920
Mangla	Shravan	13.7.1920	13.7.1921
Pingla	Dhanista	13.7.1921	13.7.1922
Dhanya	Shatbhisaj	13.7.1922	13.7.1925
Bharamari	P. Bhadrapad	13.7.1925	13.7.1929
Bhadrika	U. Bhadrapad	13.7.1929	13.7.1934
Ulka	Revati	13.7.1934	13.7.1940
Siddha	Rohini	13.7.1940	13.7.1947
Sankata	Mrigshira	13.7.1947	13.7.1955
Mangla	Ardra	13.7.1955	13.7.1956

Progress Chart Mangla/ Ardra and Gemini lagan.

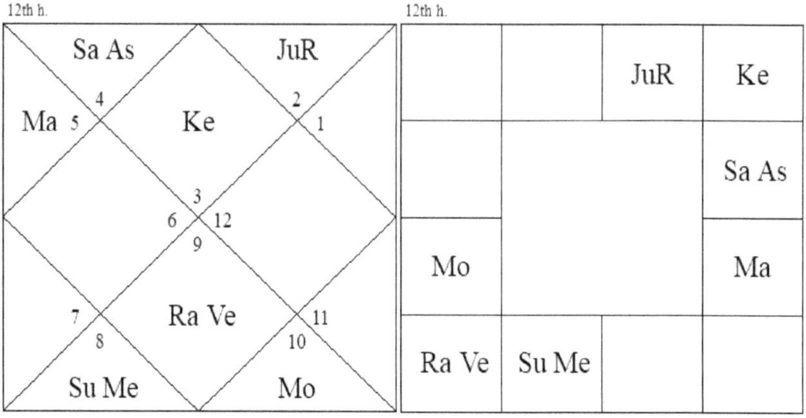

Now Rahu acts as Jupiter and is placed in seventh house. Conjunction of Venus with Rahu is like raj yoga of Kendra and Trikona. Moon is aspected by ninth and tenth lord of progress lagna.

Mangla / Chitra

Mars is the lord of the progress Nakshtra. Chitra Nakshtrafalls in Virgo and Libra. Two pada are in Virgo and two Padas are in Libra. Thus, the dasha period covers two signs. The first six months of Mangla (Chitra) will have Virgo as progress lagnaand for last six months the progress lagna is Libra.

When Virgo is the progress lagna, Mars is the lord of thirdand eighth house indicating suddenness and efforts. Mercury isthe lord of tenth and lagna.

With Libra is the progress lagna, Mars is the seventh andsecond lord. Badly placed Mars can give ill health even death.As Kendra lord when with good association can give position and wealth.

Example Secretary of state DOB 26 October 1947 TOB 20.0 POB Chicago

Birth Chart

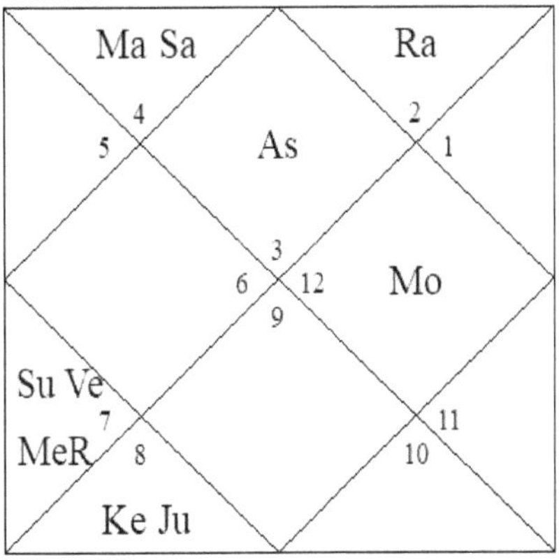

Birth Chart

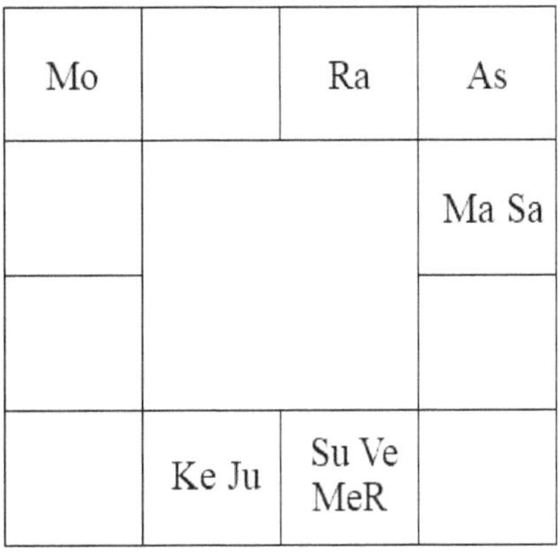

Birth Nakshtra U. Bhadrapad

She was appointed secretary of state on 20 January 2009. The Yogini dasha was Mangla / Bhramari. The progress chart for Mangla / Chitra is given. The Mangla dasha started on 16 Oct 2008 and the progress lagna will be Virgo up 16 April 2009.

Dasha sequence

Yogini	Nakshtra	From	To
Bhadrika	U. Bhadrapad	26.10.1947	17.10.1951
Ulka	Revati	17.10.1951	17.10.1957
Siddha	Rohini	17.10.1957	17.10.1964
Sankata	Mrigshira	17.10.1964	17.10.1972
Mangla	Ardra	17.10.1972	17.10.1973
Punarvasu	Pingla	17.10.1973	17.10.1975
Pushya	Dhanya	17.10.1975	17.10.1978
Ashlesha	Bharamari	17.10.1978	17.10.1982

Yogini	Nakshtra	From	To
Magha	Bhadrika	17.10.1982	17.10.1987
P. Phalguni	Ulka	17.10.1987	17.10.1993
U. Phalguni	Siddha	17.10.1993	17.10.2000
Hasta	Sankata	17.10.2000	17.10.2008
Chitra	Mangla	17.10.2008	17.10.2009

Progress Chart Mangla/ Chitra and Virgo lagan.

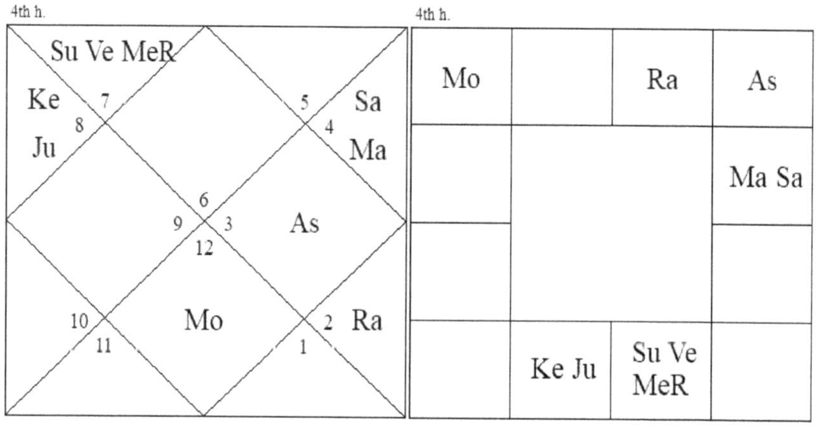

Mars is the lord of eighth and third house and is debilitated.The lords of third and eighth give Yoga Karak results when theyare debilitated. From Virgo the ninth and tenth lord is making excellent Raj Yoga but with Sun. Sun is twelfth lord and she hadto accept the secretary of state instead of Presidency.

Example Promotion DOB 24 December 1942 TOB 0.21.40 POB Gazipur

Birth Chart

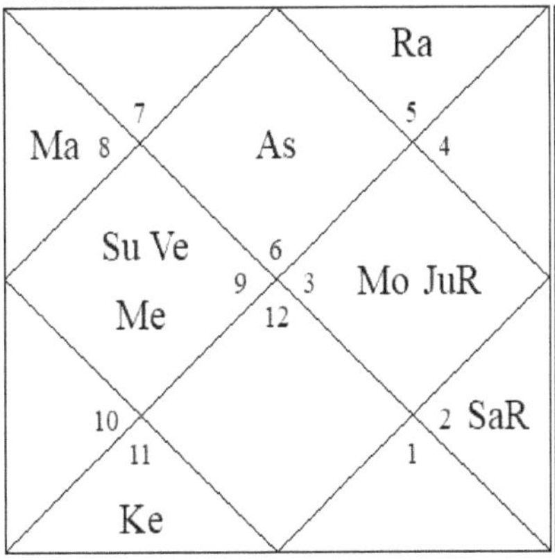

Birth Chart

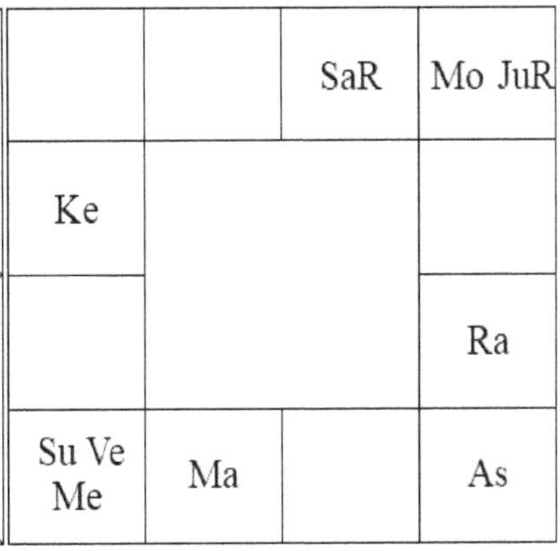

Birth Nakshtra Punarvasu

Dasa sequence

Yogini	Nakshtra	From	To
Punarvasu	Pingla	24.12.1942	5.12.1944
Pushya	Dhanya	5.12.1944	5.12.1947
Ashlesha	Bharamari	5.12.1947	5.12.1951
Magha	Bhadrika	5.12.1951	5.12.1956
P. Phalguni	Ulka	5.12.1956	5.12.1962
U. Phalguni	Siddha	5.12.1962	5.12.1969
Hasta	Sankata	5.12.1969	5.12.1977
Chitra	Mangla	5.12.1977	5.12.1978

He got promotion in Mangla / Bhadrika. The Mangla / Chitra started on 5 Dec. 1977 and Virgo will be the progress lagna till5 June 1978.

Progress Chart Mangla/ Chitra is same as birth chart.

From progress lagna, the lord of tenth Mercury is aspectingtenth house. Venus and Mercury are forming Raj yoga. Mars isin third house in its own sign and aspects tenth house. The promotion came with transfer.

Example GS of Lok Sabha DOB 15 November 1918 TOB 21.49.26 POB Srinagar

Birth Chart

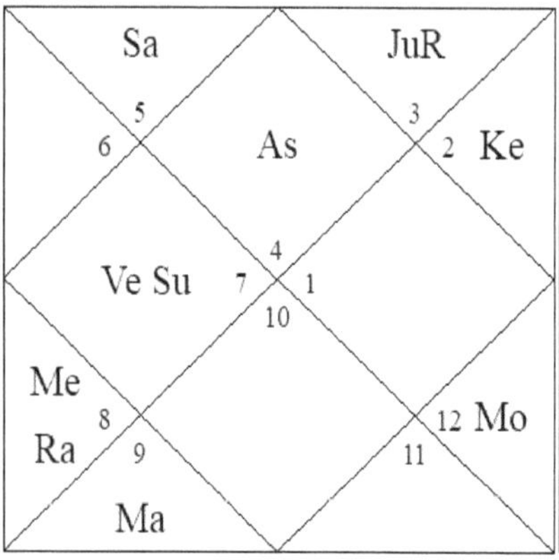

Birth Chart

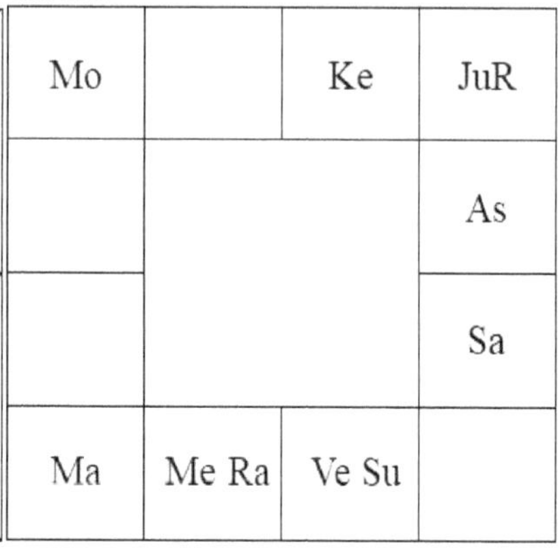

Birth Nakshtra – Revati

Dasa sequence

Yogini	**Nakshtra**	**From**	**To**
Ulka	Revati	15.11.1918	11.2.1922
Siddha	Rohini	11.2.1922	11.2.1929
Sankata	Mrigshira	11.2.1929	11.2.1937
Mangla	Ardra	11.2.1937	11.2.1938
Pingla	Punarvasu	11.2.1938	11.2.1940
Dhanya	Pushya	11.2.1940	11.2.1943
Bharamari	Ashlesha	11.2.1943	11.2.1947
Bhadrika	Magha	11.2.1947	11.2.1952
Ulka	P. Phalguni	11.2.1952	11.2.1958
Siddha	U. Phalguni	11.2.1958	11.2.1965

Yogini	Nakshtra	From	To
Sankata	Hasta	11.2.1965	11.2.1973
Mangla	Chitra	11.2.1973	11.2.1974

The Progress chart for Mangla/ Chitra and Libra lagan.

4th h.

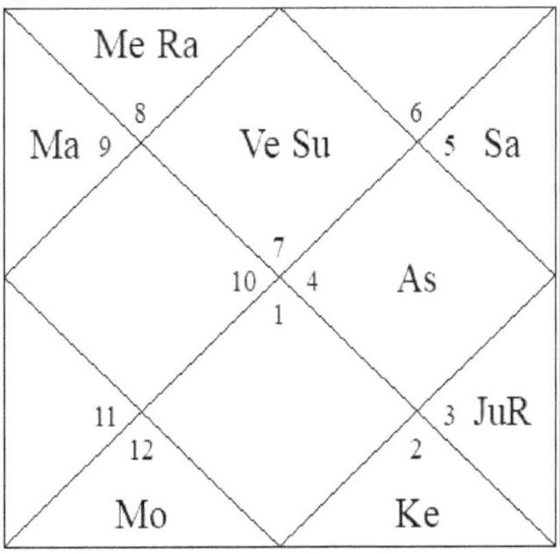

4th h.

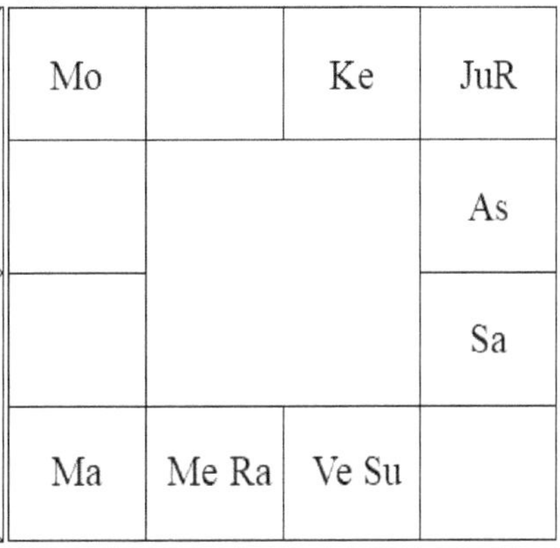

With Virgo progress lagna, the lord of tenth house, Mercury is afflicted by Rahu. With Libra as progress lagna, the tenth house is aspected by Nakshtra lord Mars. (With Virgo also the tenth house is aspected by Mars) Now the lord of tenth houseMoon is also aspected by Mars. The lagna is occupied by its lordVenus. The sub period was Siddha.

Example Lost election DOB 13 October 1925 TOB 9.0 POB Grantham UK

Birth Chart

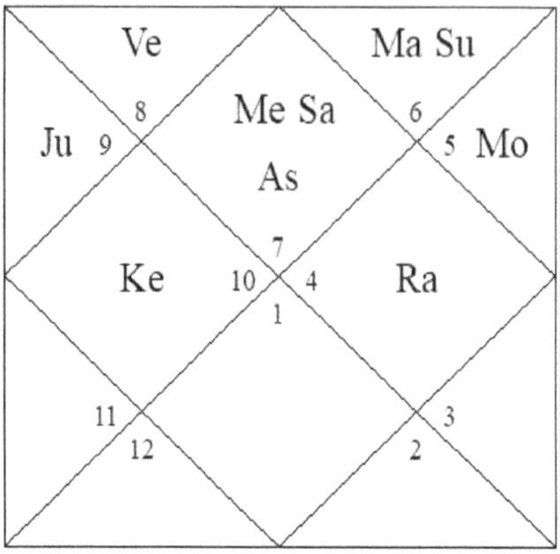

Birth Chart

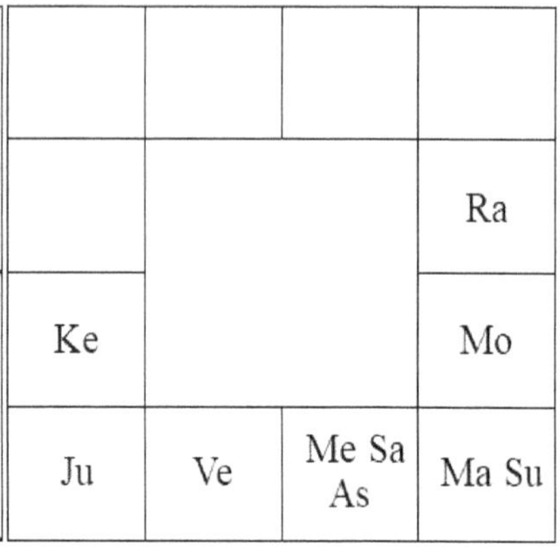

Birth Nakshtra Magha

She was the conservative party candidate for safe labor seat, Dart Ford, and lost elections in 1950. She reduced the margin of labor candidate, Norman Dodds, and emerged as a force in politics. Dasa sequence

Yogini	Nakshtra	From	To
Magha	Bhadrika	13.10.1925	8.8.1928
P. Phalguni	Ulka	8.8.1928	8.8.1934
U. Phalguni	Siddha	8.8.1934	8.8.1941
Hasta	Sankata	8.8.1941	8.8.1949
Chitra	Mangla	8.8.1949	8.8.1950

Progress Chart for Mangla/ Chitra and Virgo lagan

12th h.

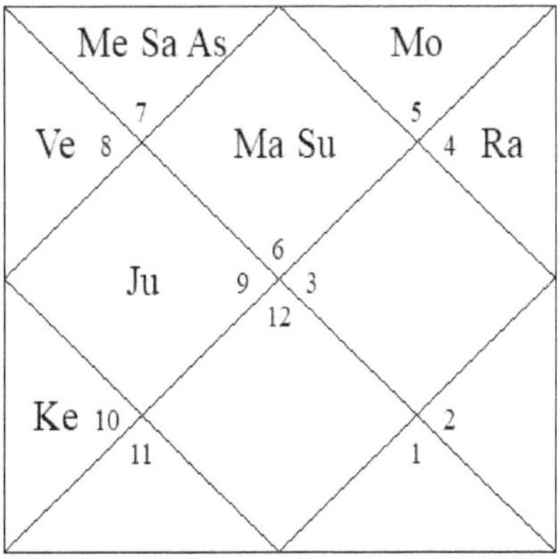

12th h.

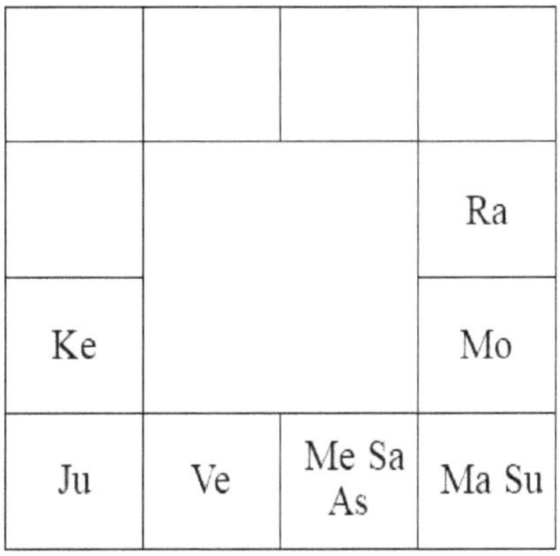

The star lord Mars is not connected with tenth house or tenth lord Mercury. Mars is with twelfth lord Sun. The dasha lord is in twelfth. Next progress lagna is Libra and again Mars isin twelfth. The gain of position is not seen.

Example Death of Father DOB 24 December 1937 TOB 4.27 POB Delhi

Birth Chart

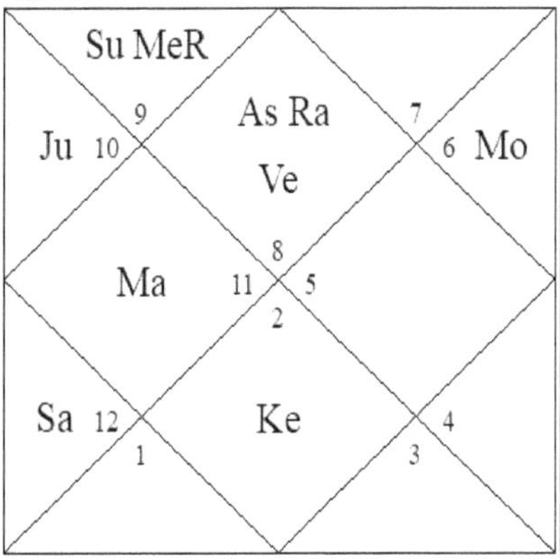

Birth Chart

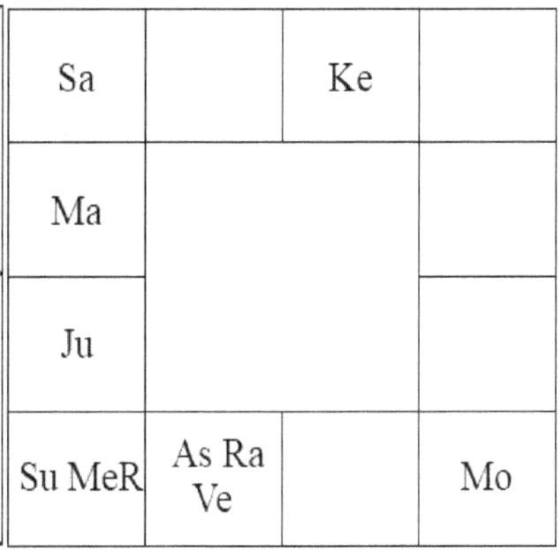

Birth Nakshtra U. Phalguni

His father died on 15 October 1950 in Yogini dasa of Mangla/ Dhanya.

Dasa sequence

Yogini	Nakshtra	From	To
U. Phalguni	Siddha	24.12.1937	25.8.1942
Hasta	Sankata	25.8.1942	25.8.1950
Chitra	Mangla	25.8.1950	25.8.1951

Progress Chart for Mangla/ Chitra and Virgo lagan.

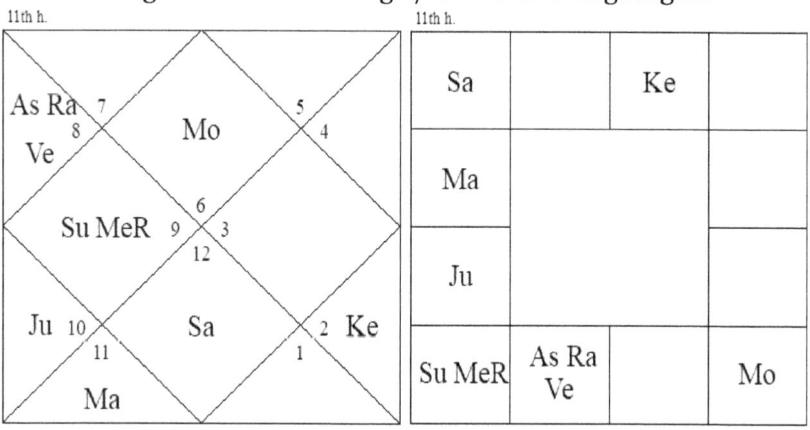

Mangla/ Chitra started on 25 August 1950. The progress lagan will be Virgo for first six months till 25 April 1951.

Ninth house from progress lagna is afflicted by Ketu and is aspected by Saturn and Mars. Eighth lord from Taurus is Jupiter and is aspecting it. The karaka of father is in fourth house whichis eighth from ninth. Sun is with Mercury that is maraca of father i.e. Second lord from ninth house. The dasha Nakshtralord Mars is also aspecting the ninth house. All malefic association is with ninth house. The ninth house is badly afflicted. The AD lord Jupiter is eighth lord for father.

Mangla / Shravan

This is an important Mangla period. The Nakshtra lord isMoon and the dasha lord is also Moon. To top it the seventh lord is also Moon. During this Yogini dasha the relation with outside world or your relations are important. A person experience ups and down in the marriage / business matters. The condition of Moon is important. The events are governed by Moon.

Example Affair DOB 2 July 1974 TOB 9.17.15 POB Deoghar

Birth Chart

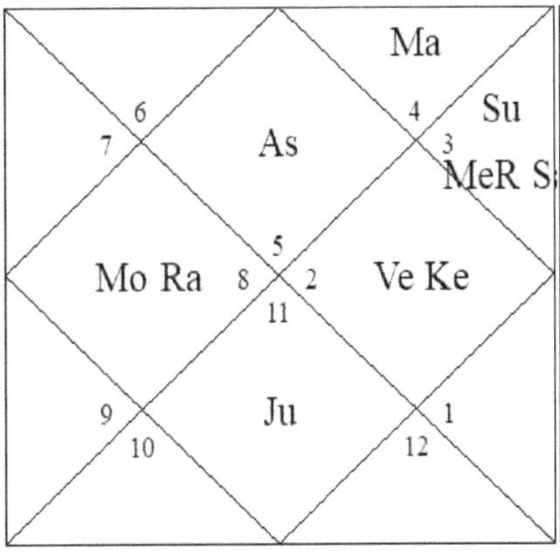

Birth Chart

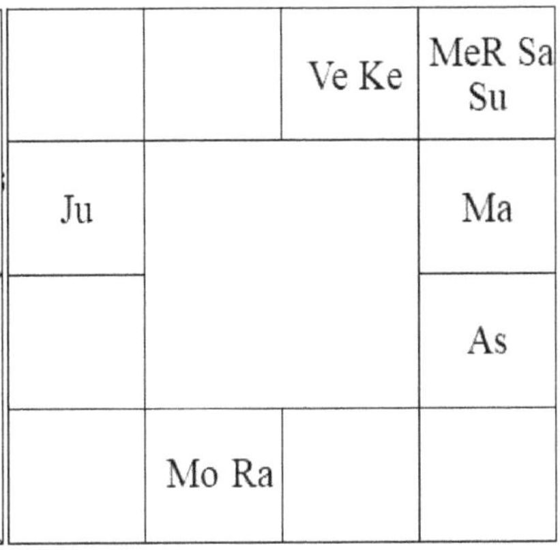

Birth Nakshtra Jyeshtha

Dasa sequence

Yogini	Nakshtra	From	To
Bhadrika	Jyeshtha	2.7.1974	23.3.1978
Ulka	Moola	23.3.1978	23.3.1984
Siddha	P. Ashadha	23.3.1984	23.3.1991
Sankata	U. Ashadha	23.3.1991	23.3.1999
Mangla	Shravan	23.3.1999	23.3.2000
Pingla	Dhanishta	23.3.2000	23.3.2002
Dhanya	Shatbhisaj	23.3.2002	23.3.2005

The Mangla / Shravan operated from 23 March 1999 to 23Mar 2000. The person was running his twenty fifth year of age.This age is the right age for marriage and affairs. The birth Moon will be in Jyeshtha / Moola for this dasha to operate at marriageable age.

Progress chart for Mangla/ Shravan and Capricorn lagan.

6th h.

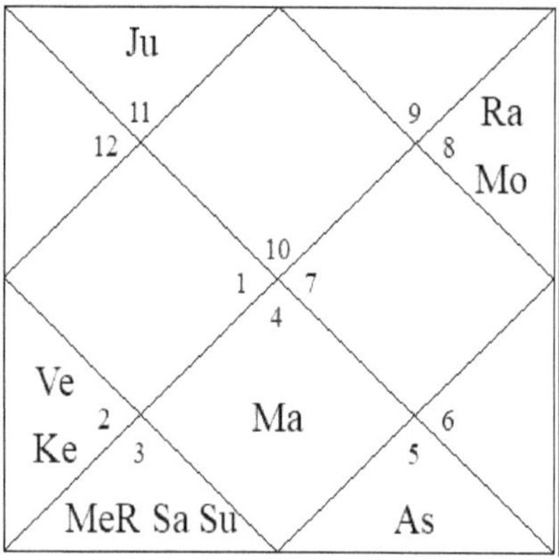

6th h.

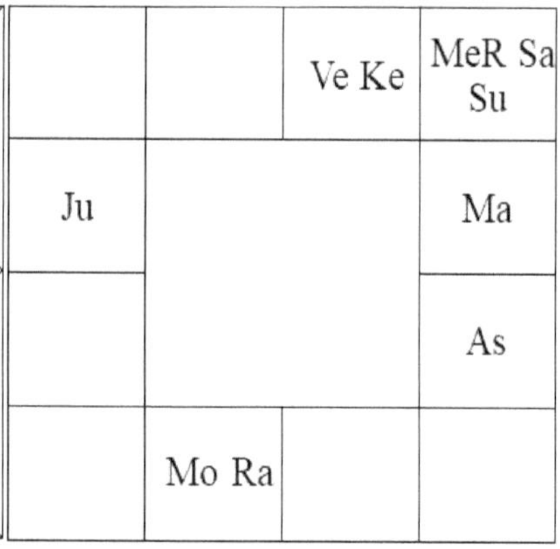

Here Moon is debilitated and afflicted by Rahu / Ketu axis.The fifth and seventh lords are in mutual aspect and both are inRahu / Ketu axis. No benefic is aspecting this combination andas such possibility of marriage is not present. This person hadan intense affair throughout Mangla period which ended with this period. For next period of Pingla, the Nakshtra is Dhanishtaand its lord Mars is in seventh. The marriage happened in Pingla/ Dhanishta.

Example Jail DOB 19 May 1945 TOB 15.0 POB London

Birth Chart

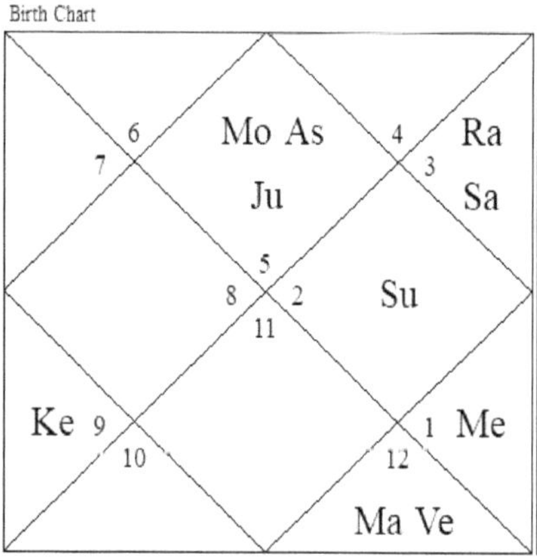

Birth Chart

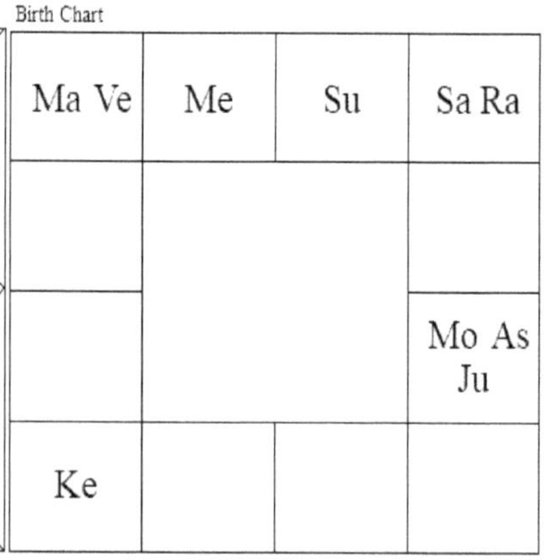

Birth Nakshtra Magha

He was arrested in January 2003 for possessing indecent images of children. He is an English rock guitarist, vocalist, song writer and author. The exposure of massive child porn industry over internet in USA led to his arrest.

Dasa sequence

Yogini	Nakshtra	From	To
Bhadrika	Magha	19.5.1945	13.11.1945
Ulka	P. Phalguni	13.11.1945	13.11.1951
Siddha	U. Phalguni	13.11.1951	13.11.1958
Sankata	Hasta	13.11.1958	13.11.1966
Mangla	Chitra	13.11.1966	13.11.1967
Pingla	Swati	13.11.1967	13.11.1969
Dhanya	Visakha	13.11.1969	13.11.1972
Bharamari	Anuradha	13.11.1972	13.11.1976
Bhadrika	Jyeshtha	13.11.1976	13.11.1981
Ulka	Moola	13.11.1981	13.11.1987
Siddha	P. Ashadha	13.11.1987	13.11.1994
Sankata	U. Ashadha	13.11.1994	13.11.2002
Mangla	Shravan	13.11.2002	13.11.2003

The Mangla/ Shravan period started on 13 November 2002. Mangla/ Bhramari commenced on 12 January 2003.

Progress Chart for Capricorn/ Shravan lagan.

6th h.

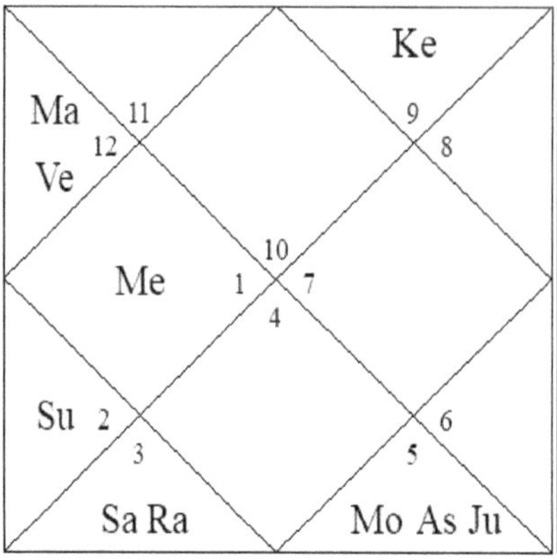

6th h.

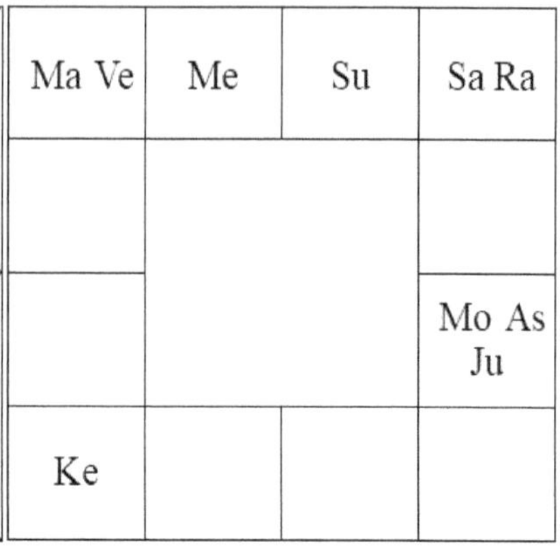

The age of the person is now 57 years. The Moon is in eighth house of the progress chart. It is with Jupiter and aspectedby Saturn. Since Saturn is the progress Lagna lord not much damage was caused. He was jailed on 13 Jan, 2003, a day after Bhramari sub-period started. Mars is in eighth from Moon.

Example Job DOB 2 May 1972 TOB 02.45 POB Nagpur

Birth Chart

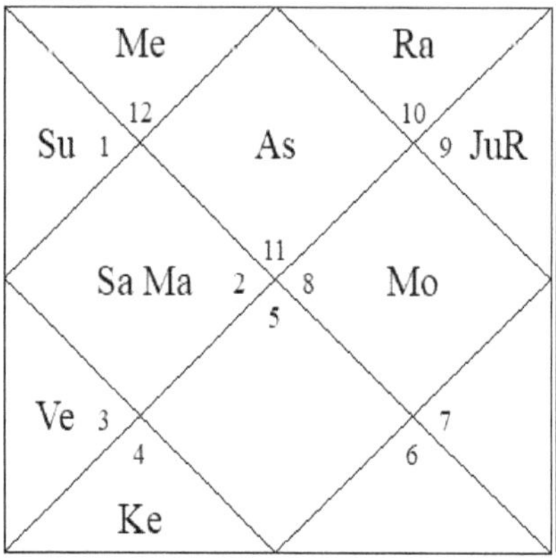

Birth Chart

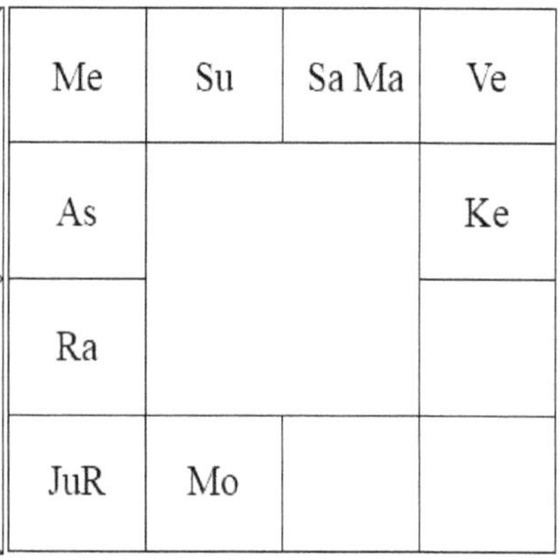

Birth Nakshtra Jyeshtha

Dasa sequence

Yogini	Nakshtra	From	To
Bhadrika	Jyeshtha	2.5.1972	9.4.1974
Ulka	Moola	9.4.1974	9.4.1980
Siddha	P. Ashadha	9.4.1980	9.4.1987
Sankata	U. Ashadha	9.4.1987	9.4.1995
Mangla	Shravan	9.4.1995	9.4.1996

Progress chart for Capricorn/Shravan progress lagan.

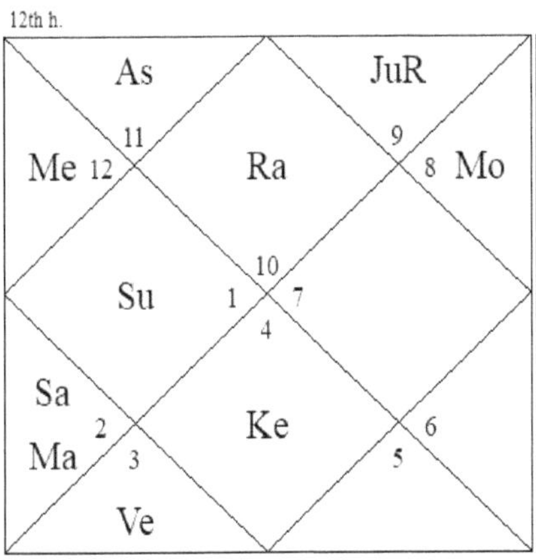

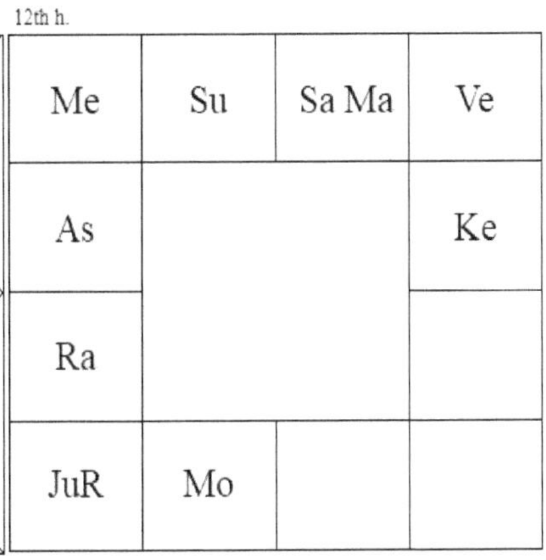

He started his career in Moon / Bhramari. In the above example above, the person was arrested in the same period. Theplacement of Mars / and Moon made the difference. In exampleabove Moon is in eighth house from PL. The birth lagna is also ineighth.

Moon is in eleventh house of progress chart. Moon is aspected by Mars and Saturn. Saturn is lagna lord of birth andprogress chart. He started his job in July 1995 in the Bhramarisub period. Mars is the tenth lord of birth chart and aspect itsown sign Scorpio which is now eleventh house.

Example Promotion DOB 20 November 1949 TOB 2.0 POB Delhi

Birth Chart

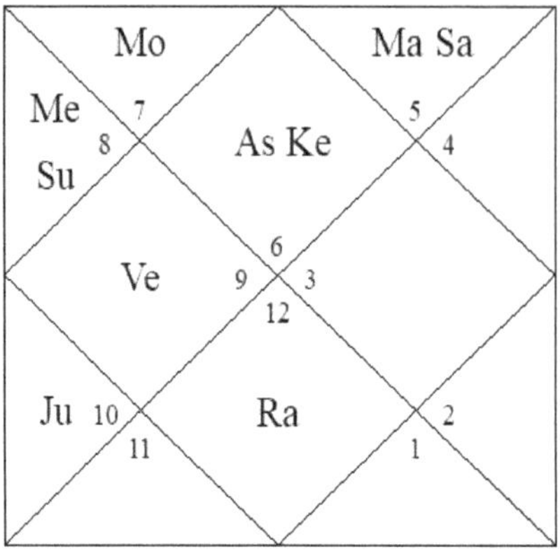

Birth Chart

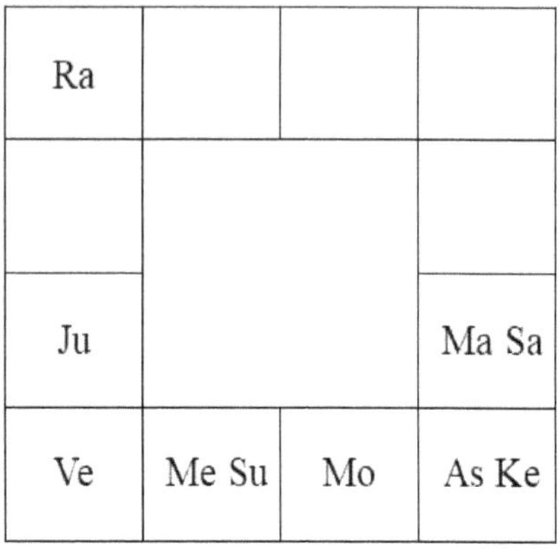

Birth Nakshtra Visakha

He got a good rise in March 1981. The sub period was of Pingla.

Dasa sequence

Yogini	Nakshtra	From	To
Dhanya	Visakha	20.11.1949	3.3.1951
Bharamari	Anuradha	3.3.1951	3.3.1955
Bhadrika	Jyeshtha	3.3.1955	3.3.1960
Ulka	Moola	3.3.1960	3.3.1966
Siddha	P. Ashadha	3.3.1966	3.3.1973
Sankata	U. Ashadha	3.3.1973	3.3.1981
Mangla	Shravan	3.3.1981	3.3.1982

Progress chart for Capricorn /Shravan progress lagan.

5th h.

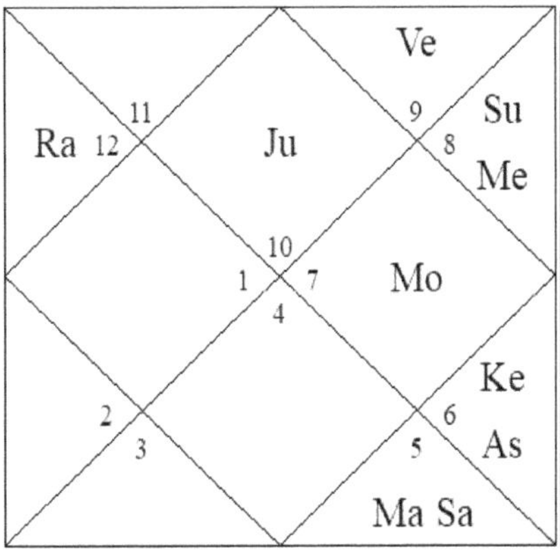

5th h.

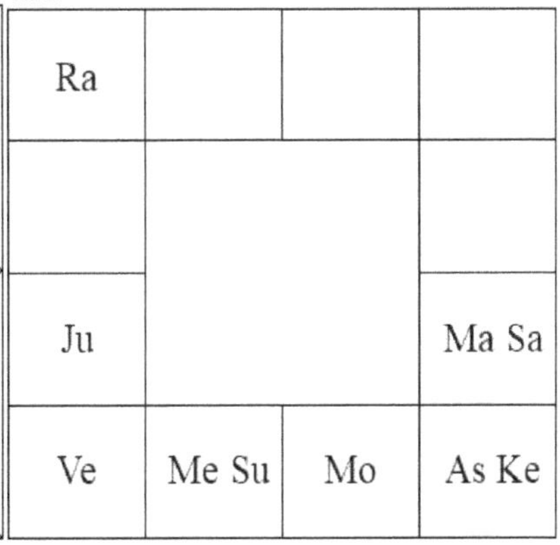

Progress Nakshtra lord, Moon, is in tenth house. Moon is lord of seventh house. he is aspected by progress lagan lord and second lord Saturn. Sun is in eleventh house.

Example Posting abroad DOB 14 August 1975 TOB 03.04 POB Agra

Birth Chart

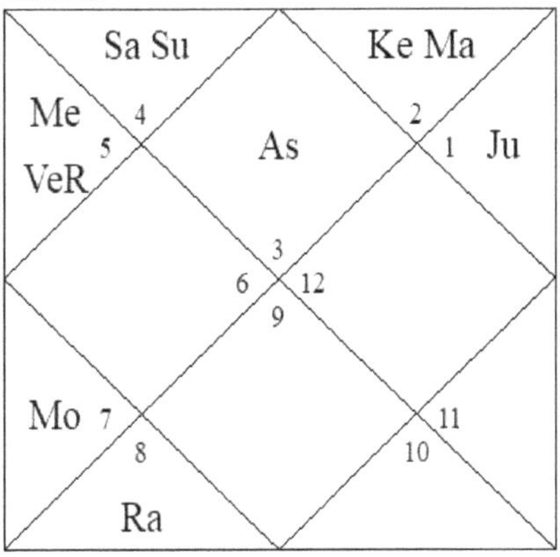

Birth Chart

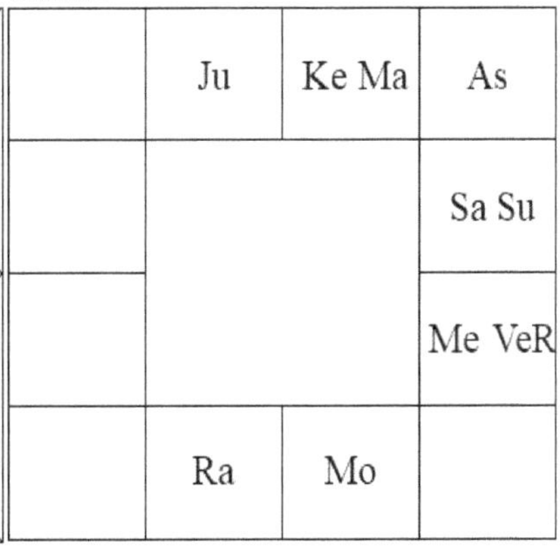

Birth Nakshtra Visakha

This chart belongs to a highly placed executive. The Mangla/ Shravan started on 13 August 2007.

Dasa sequence

Yogini	Nakshtra	From	To
Dhanya	Visakha	14.8.1975	13.8.1977
Bharamari	Anuradha	13.8.1977	13.8.1981
Bhadrika	Jyeshtha	13.8.1981	13.8.1986
Ulka	Moola	13.8.1986	13.8.1992
Siddha	P. Ashadha	13.8.1992	13.8.1999
Sankata	U. Ashadha	13.8.1999	13.8.2007
Mangla	Shravan	13.8.2007	13.8.2008

Progress chart for Capricorn/ Shravan progress lagan.

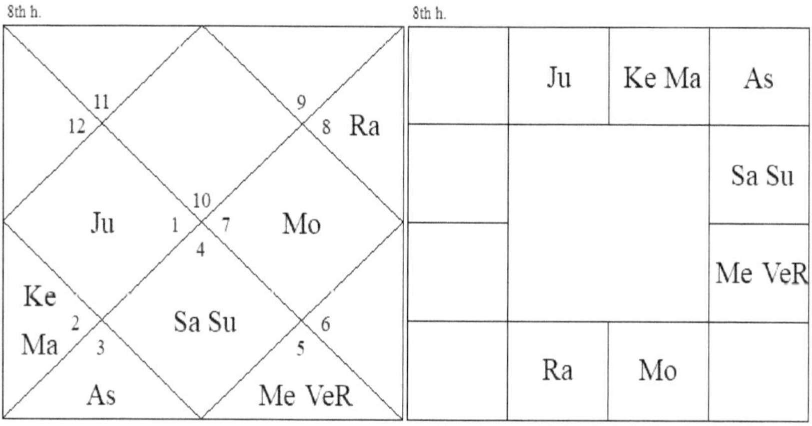

Now Moon is placed in tenth house. He is aspected by birth tenth lord, Jupiter.

She was working with an MNC and was posted abroad. In Mangla/ Mangla, she resigned from that job and returned to India to take a job with another American MNC at a much higher salary and status.

In progress chart, Jupiter is third and twelfth lord. The progress tenth lord is retrograde and is in eighth house. Venus is Yoga Karaka for PL. This progress chart also promise marriage since Jupiter is seventh lord of birth. Marriage did not happen because

Saturn and Sun are in seventh house.

Example Illness of father DOB 24 August 1974 TOB 16.35 POB Mumbai

Birth Chart

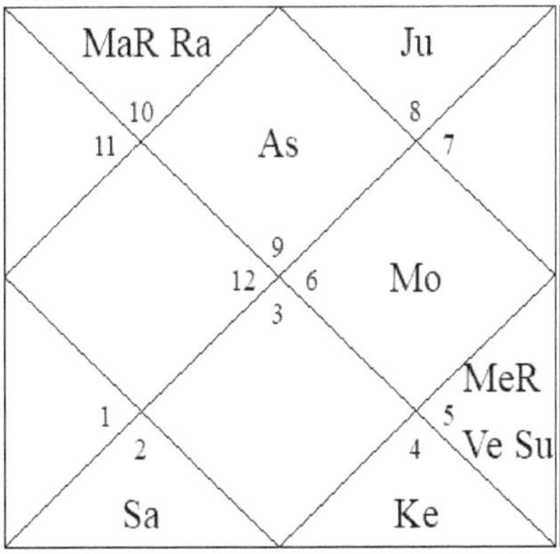

Birth Chart

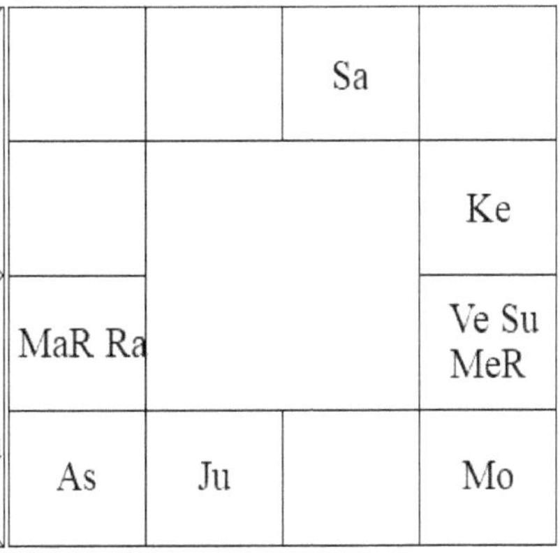

Birth Nakshtra Hasta

Dasa sequence

Yogini	Nakshtra	From	To
Sankata	Hasta	24.8.1974	6.3.1976
Mangla	Chitra	6.3.1976	6.3.1977
Pingla	Swati	6.3.1977	6.3.1979
Dhanya	Visakha	6.3.1979	6.3.1982
Bharamari	Anuradha	6.3.1982	6.3.1986
Bhadrika	Jyeshtha	6.3.1986	6.3.1991
Ulka	Moola	6.3.1991	6.3.1997
Siddha	P. Ashadha	6.3.1997	6.3.2004
Sankata	U. Ashadha	6.3.2004	6.3.2012
Mangla	Shravan	6.3.2012	6.3.2013

Progress chart for Capricorn progress lagan

2nd h.

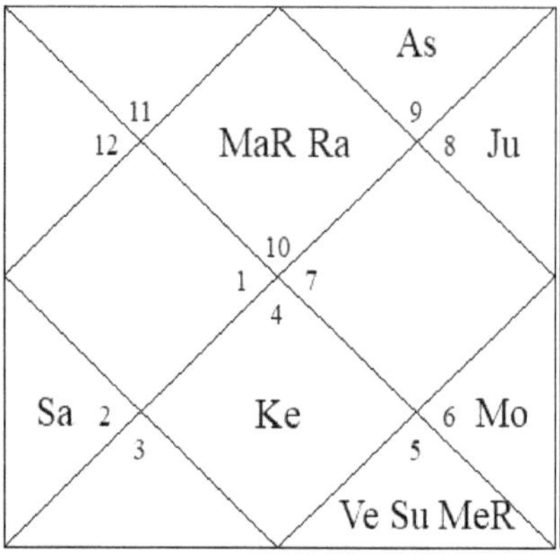

2nd h.

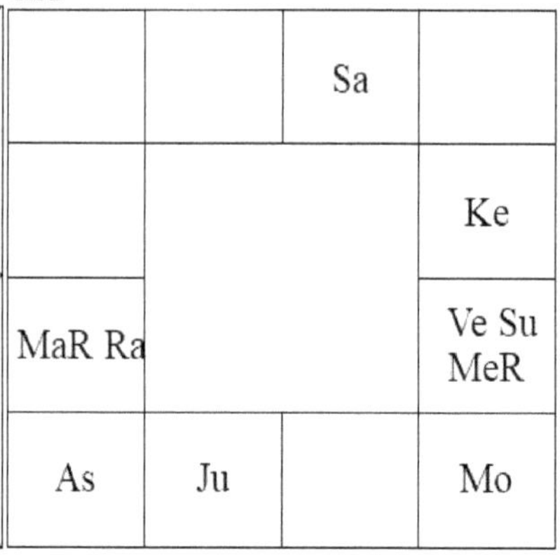

Moon is now in ninth house. The attention is on ninth house.The ninth lord Mercury is in eighth house from PL. It is with Sunwho is the significator of father. It is aspected by afflicted Mars.The sixth lord of birth chart also joins Sun and Mercury in eighth house. Father got seriously ill in Mangla / Pingla.

Chapter 4
Pingla

Pingla dasha is of two years. This can operate in three Nakshtra. This dasha is not considered a benefic in classics. However, the results depend upon the Nakshtra lord.

Punarvasu, Swati and Dhanishta generate this dasha. Tablebelow gives the Nakshtra and lords etc. for Pingla Yogini dasha.

Nakshtra	Nakshtra Lord	Sign of Nakshtra	Remarks
Punarvasu	Jupiter	Gemini / Cancer	For first one yearsix months, the progress lagna is Gemini and last six months it is cancer.
Swati	Rahu	Libra	Libra is the progress Lagna.
Dhanishta	Mars	Capricorn / Aquarius	For first one-year progress lagna is Capricorn and for last one year it is Aquarius.

Pingla / Punarvasu

Punarvasu Nakshtra has three Padas in Gemini and onepada in cancer. In Gemini it is from 20^{0} to 30^{0}. In cancer it is from 0 to 3^{0} – 20'. The Navamsha signs are Aries, Taurus, Gemini and cancer.

Progress lagna is Gemini for first eighteen months of Pingla/ Punarvasu. Jupiter is the lord of seventh and tenth house. Thearea of focus will be related to partner and profession. The position of Jupiter in the birth chart is also important.

For Cancer progress lagna, Jupiter is sixth and ninth lord.

The focus now is on these houses.

Jupiter should normally make relation to the house and house lord for any event related to a house.

Example Marriage DOB 26 October 1947 TOB 20.00 POB Chicago

Birth Chart

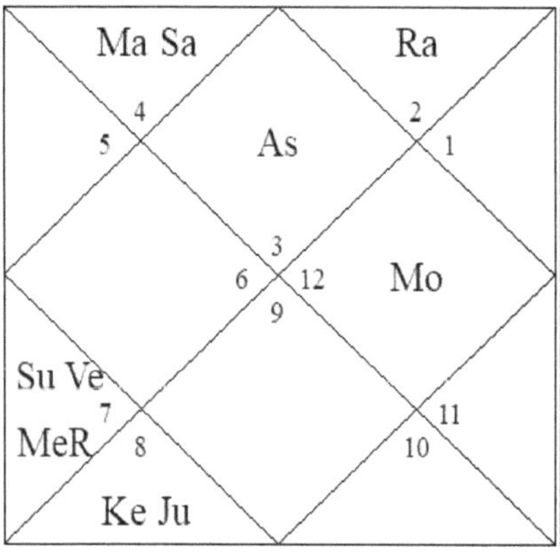

Birth Chart

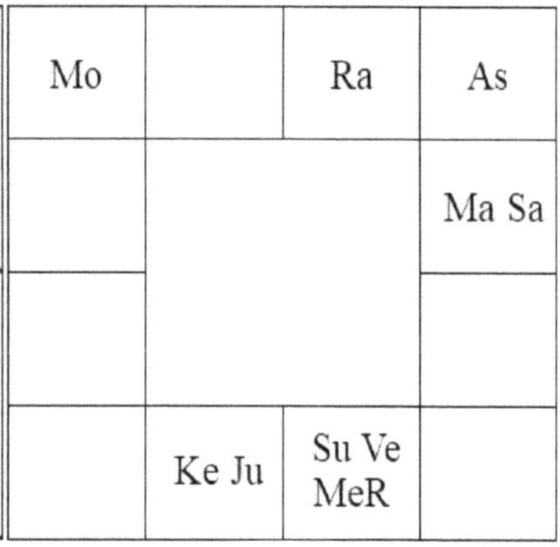

Birth Nakshtra U. Bhadrapad

Dasa sequence

Yogini	Nakshtra	From	To
Bhadrika	U. Bhadrapad	26.10.1947	17.10.1951
Ulka	Revati	17.10.1951	17.10.1957
Siddha	Rohini	17.10.1957	17.10.1964
Sankata	Mrigshira	17.10.1964	17.10.1972
Mangla	Ardra	17.10.1972	17.10.1973
Pingla	Punarvasu	17.10.1973	17.10.1975

She got married on 11 Oct 1975 in the dasha of Pingla / Mangla. The progress lagna is cancer.

Progress chart for Cancer progress lagan

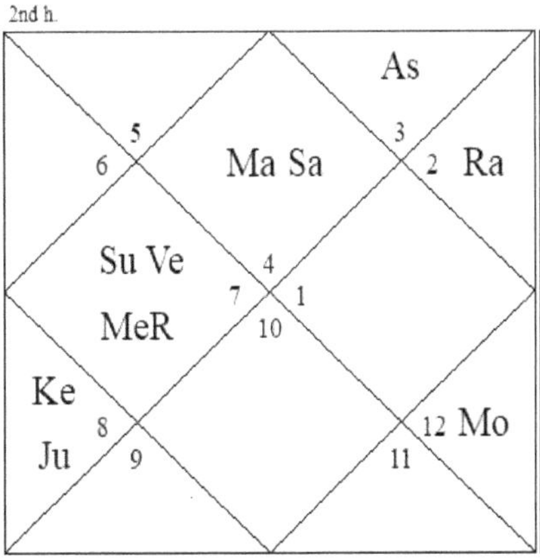

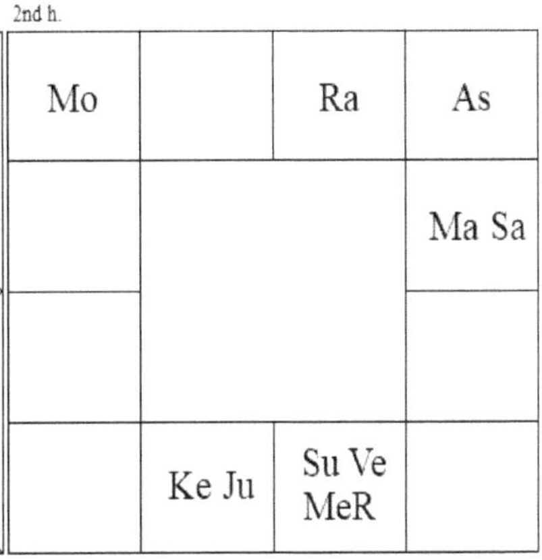

We first examine it from Gemini progress lagna. Jupiter is seventh lord but placed in sixth house. It is not making any relation with seventh house or the lagna. Since Jupiter is seventh lord and is afflicted, it gave relationship but could not convert it in marriage.

With cancer progress lagna, the stage is now set. Jupiteris the seventh lord of birth chart and now aspects lagna lord, lagna and seventh lord of progress chart.

Let us examine this event from the dasha lord Sun in birth chart. Sun isthe third lord and placed in fifth house of affairs. It is not relatedto seventh house / seventh lord in any way in birth chart.

Example Job DOB 15 November 1918 TOB 21.49.26 POB Srinagar

Birth Chart

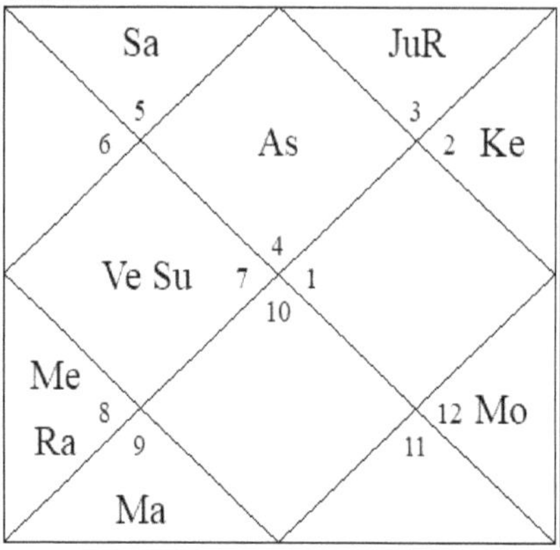

Birth Chart

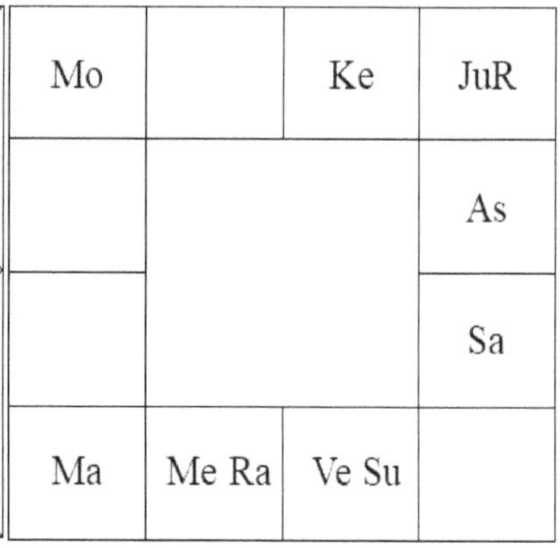

Birth Nakshtra Revati

Dasa sequence

Yogini	Nakshtra	From	To
Ulka	Revati	15.11.1918	11.2.1922
Siddha	Rohini	11.2.1922	11.2.1929
Sankata	Mrigshira	11.2.1929	11.2.1937
Mangla	Ardra	11.2.1937	11.2.1938
Pingla	Punarvasu	11.2.1938	11.2.1940

He started his career as an LDC in Pingla/ Pingla. The progress lagan is Gemini.

Progress chart for Gemini progress lagan.

12th h.

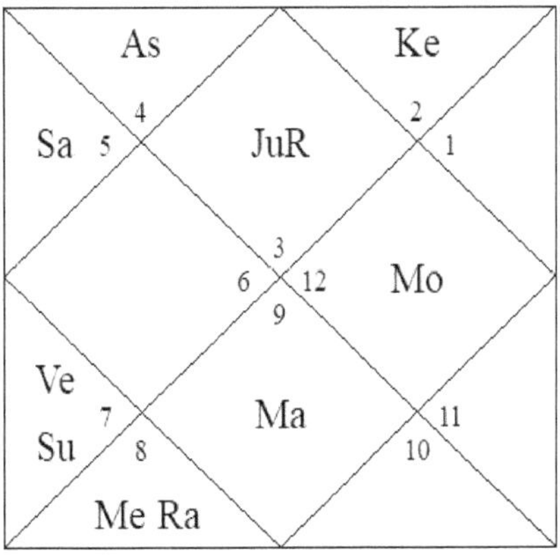

12th h.

Jupiter is now tenth lord and placed in Lagna. Jupiter is aspected by Mars who is now eleventh lord. Mars is the tenth lord of birth chart. Mars is also aspecting the progress tenth house. Mars is the lord of sixth house indicating service. He started his career as an LDC in Pingla/ Pingla. Sun is aspectedby Jupiter.

Example Deputy PM DOB 23 December 1902 TOB 7.23 POB Baghpat

Birth Chart

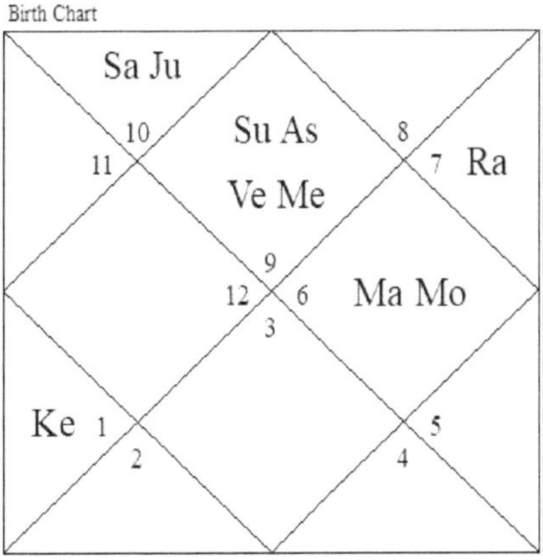

Birth Chart

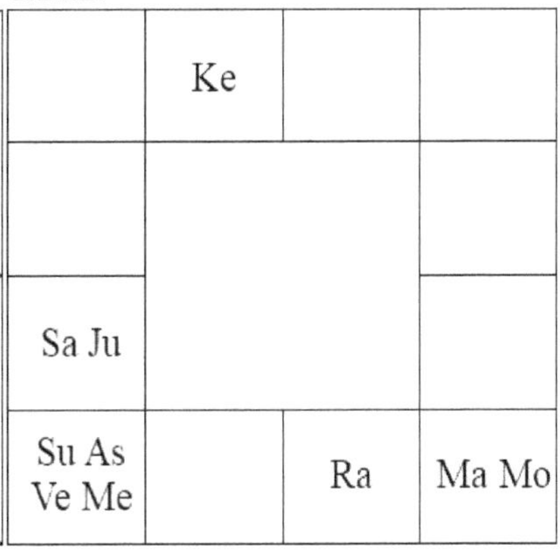

Birth Nakshtra Hasta

Dasa sequence

Yogini	Nakshtra	From	To
Sankata	Hasta	23.12.1902	26.5.1903
Mangla	Chitra	26.5.1903	26.5.1904
Pingla	Swati	26.5.1904	26.5.1906
Dhanya	Visakha	26.5.1906	26.5.1909
Bharamari	Anuradha	26.5.1909	26.5.1913
Bhadrika	Jyeshtha	26.5.1913	26.5.1918
Ulka	Moola	26.5.1918	26.5.1924
Siddha	P. Ashadha	26.5.1924	26.5.1931
Sankata	U. Ashadha	26.5.1931	26.5.1939
Mangla	Shravan	26.5.1939	26.5.1940
Pingla	Dhanishta	26.5.1940	26.5.1942
Dhanya	Shatbhisaj	26.5.1942	26.5.1945
Bharamari	P. Bhadrapad	26.5.1945	26.5.1949
Bhadrika	U. Bhadrapad	26.5.1949	26.5.1954
Ulka	Revati	26.5.1954	26.5.1960
Siddha	Rohini	26.5.1960	26.5.1967
Sankata	Mrigshira	26.5.1967	26.5.1975
Mangla	Ardra	26.5.1975	26.5.1976
Pingla	Punarvasu	26.5.1976	26.5.1978

He became Deputy Prime Minister of India on 24 March1977 and remained DPM till 28.7.79. After that he was Prime Minister till 14 January 1980.

Progress chart for Gemini progress lagan.

7th h.

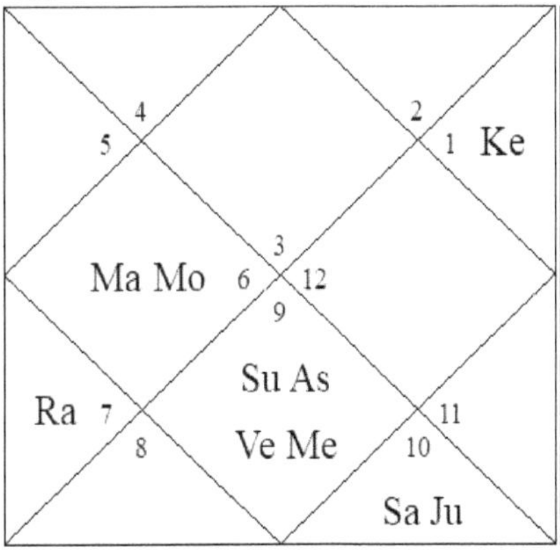

7th h.

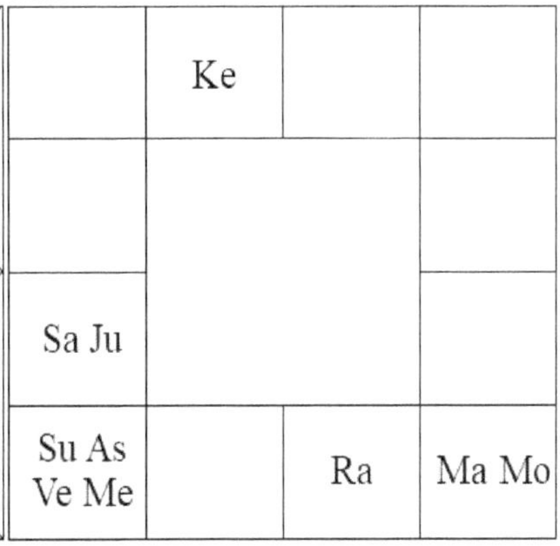

The Pingla dasha started on 25 May, 1976. For first one year six months i.e. till 25 November, 1978 the progress lagnais Gemini. The Nakshtra lord Jupiter is the lord of tenth houseand forms a powerful Raj Yoga with ninth Lord Saturn. This isnot associated or aspected by any planet. The formation of yoga is in the eighth house which is good for politician and helps in political moves.

Example Scriptures DOB 13 May 1956 TOB 0.00 POB Papanasam

Birth Chart

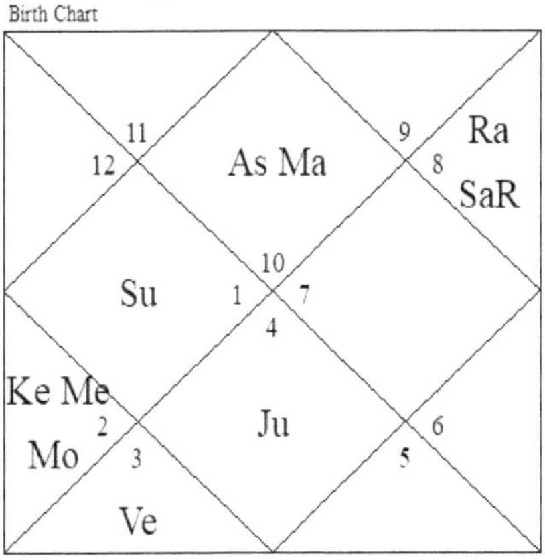

Birth Chart

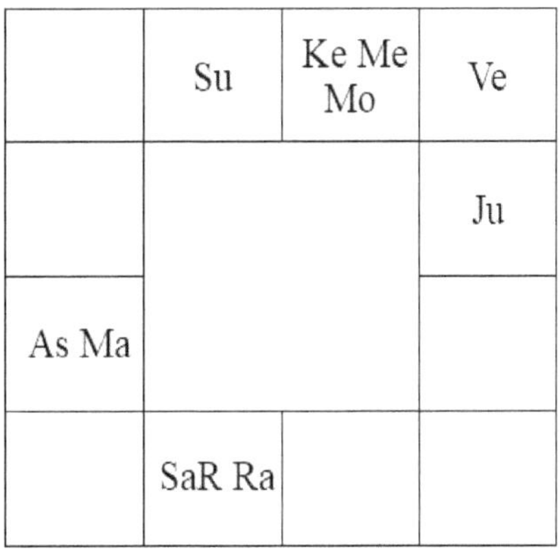

Birth Nakshtra Mrigshira

Dasa sequence

Yogini	Nakshtra	From	To
Sankata	Mrigshira	13.5.1956	5.1.1961
Mangla	Ardra	5.1.1961	5.1.1962
Pingla	Punarvasu	5.1.1962	5.1.1964

Progress chart for Cancer progress lagan.

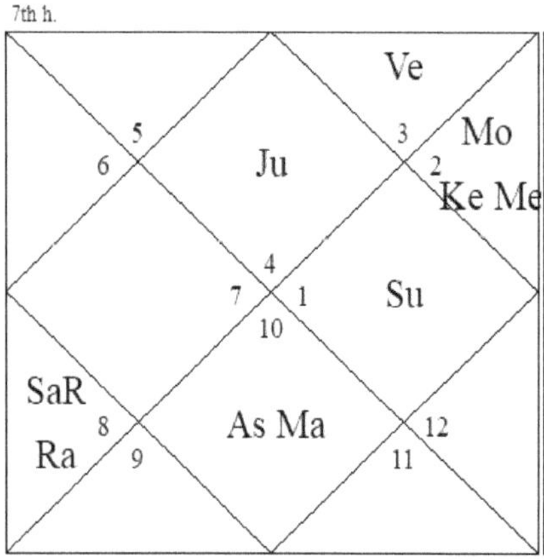

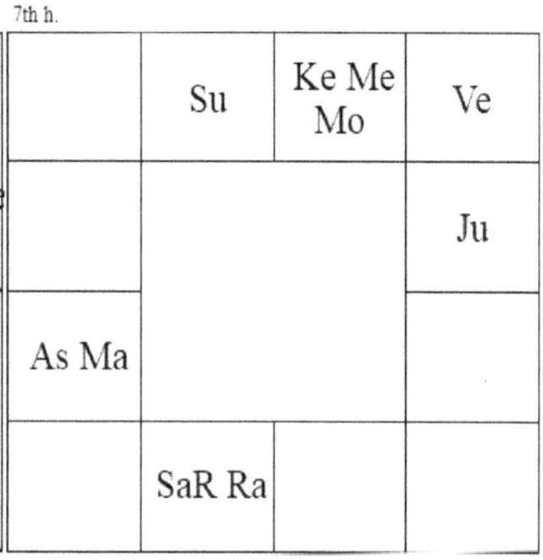

The Nakshtra lord is ninth lord and is exalted in lagna. The ninth and tenth lords are in mutual aspect. The fifth and lagna lords are exalted. A wonderful placement of lords of dharma trikona. He mastered the Rig Veda at the young age starting with this dasha at an age of six years.

Example Marriage DOB 11 September 1968 TOB 12.45 POB Shahjahanpur

Birth Chart

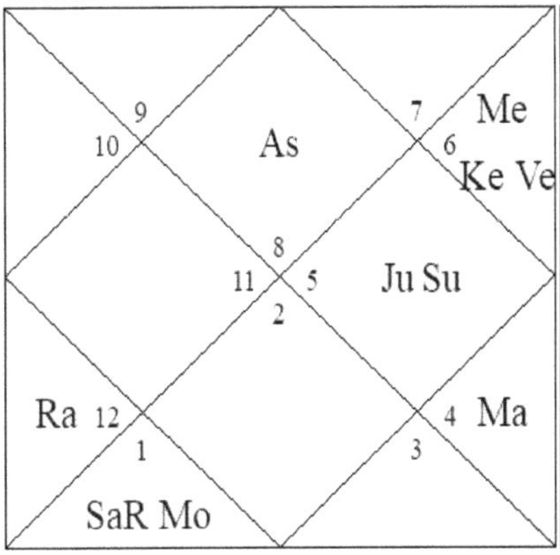

Birth Chart

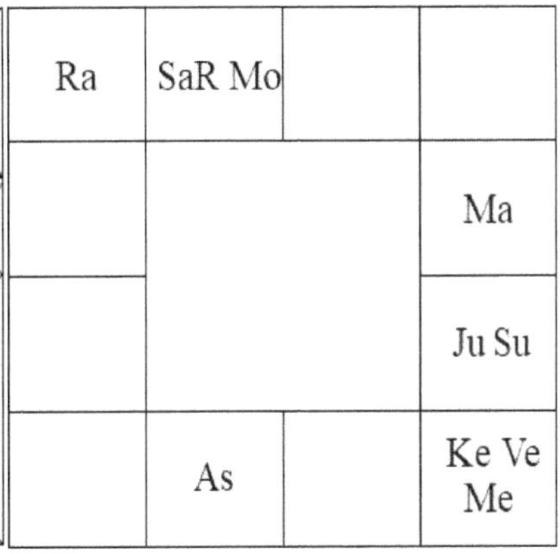

Birth Nakshtra Bharani

She was married on 18 November 1995 in the progress Yogini lagan of Gemini.

Dasa sequence

Yogini	Nakshtra	From	To
Bhadrika	Bharani	11.9.1968	1.8.1972
Ulka	Kritika	1.8.1972	1.8.1978
Siddha	Rohini	1.8.1978	1.8.1985
Sankata	Mrigshira	1.8.1985	1.8.1993
Mangla	Ardra	1.8.1993	1.8.1994
Pingla	Punarvasu	1.8.1994	1.8.1996

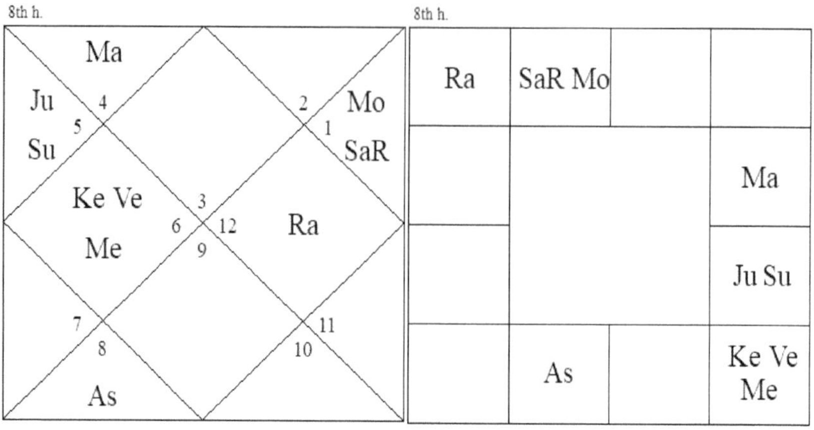

Pingla / Punarvasu started on 1 August 1994. In the progressYogini Dasha, we go to Rohini after Revati.

The Nakshtra lord Jupiter is seventh lord and aspects seventh house. The sub period was of Siddha. It will be interesting to examine Sun for its promise to give marriage during Pingla dasha. Sun is the tenth lord placed in tenth housein the birth chart. It is associated with Jupiter. Jupiter is not the lord of seventh house but fifth and second lord of birth chart. Sun is not related to seventh house or lord. The dasha of Sun is not promising marriage. **The Nakshtra lord is more important than dasa lord.**

Pingla / Swati

The Nakshtra lord is Rahu. The progress lagna is Libra for the entire Pingla dasha. The placement and association of Rahuin the birth chart is important. Rahu gives the result of the signand sign lord occupied by it and the planets it associates.

Example Death of wife DOB 27 November 1907 TOB 05.24.54 POB Allahabad

Birth Chart

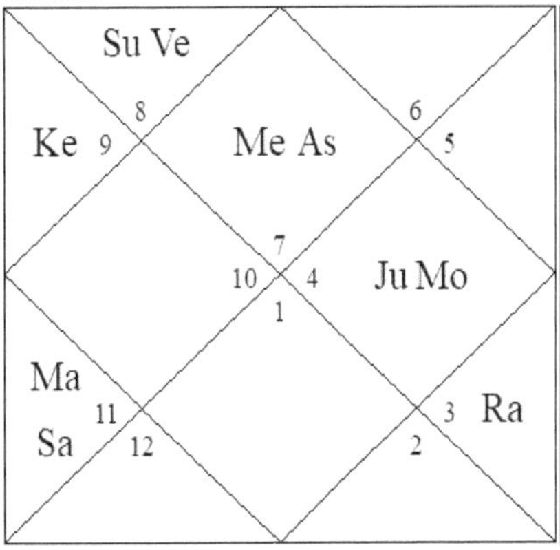

Birth Chart

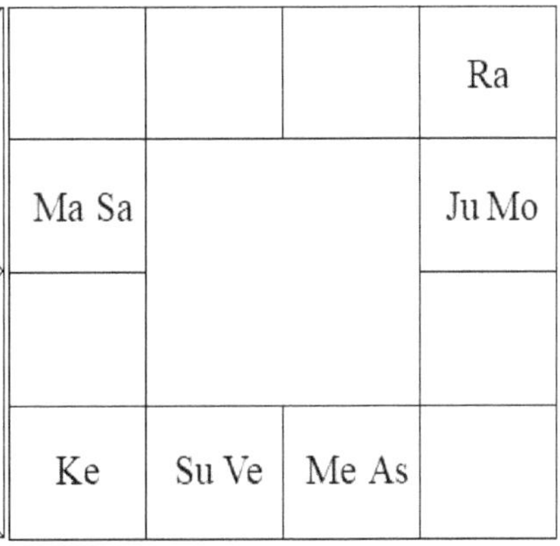

Birth Nakshtra Ashlesha

Dasa sequence

Yogini	Nakshtra	From	To
Bharamari	Ashlesha	27.11.1907	30.6.1908
Bhadrika	Magha	30.6.1908	30.6.1913
Ulka	P. Phalguni	30.6.1913	30.6.1919
Siddha	U. Phalguni	30.6.1919	30.6.1926
Sankata	Hasta	30.6.1926	30.6.1934
Mangla	Chitra	30.6.1934	30.6.1935
Pingla	Swati	30.6.1935	30.6.1937

Progress lagan is same as birth lagan.

The progress and birth lagna are same as Libra. The seventhhouse and seventh lord are afflicted. From seventh house, Venusis the lord of second and seventh and is placed in second house.

Example Marriage DOB 13 October 1925 TOB 9.0 POB Grantham UK

Birth Chart

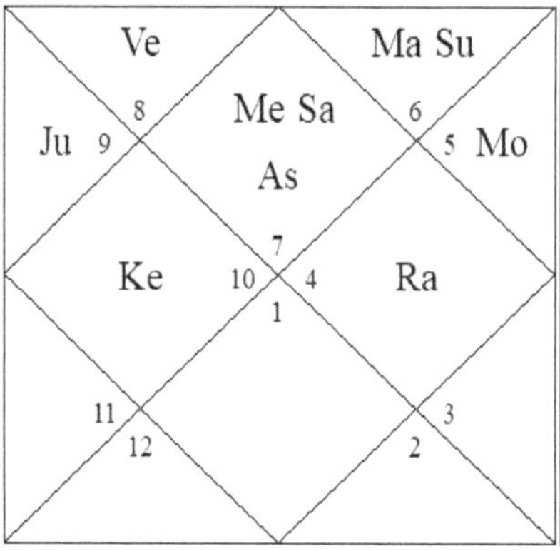

Birth Chart

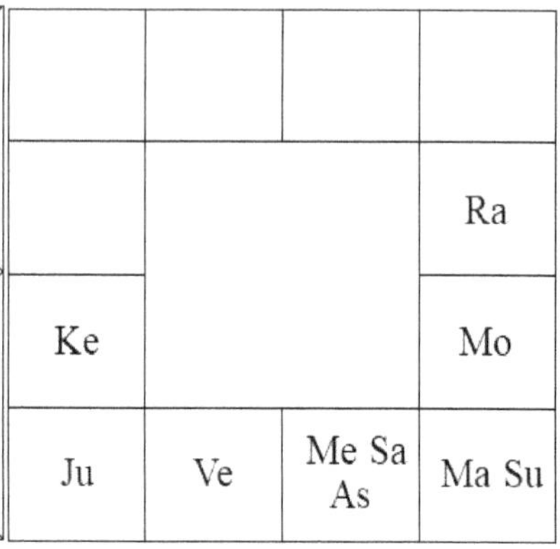

Birth Nakshtra Magha

Dasa sequence

Yogini	Nakshtra	From	To
Bhadrika	Magha	13.10.1925	8.8.1928
Ulka	P. Phalguni	8.8.1928	8.8.1934
Siddha	U. Phalguni	8.8.1934	8.8.1941
Sankata	Hasta	8.8.1941	8.8.1949
Mangla	Chitra	8.8.1949	8.8.1950
Pingla	Swati	8.8.1950	8.8.1952

For person born in Libra lagan, the progress chart for Swati Nakshtra will be same as the birth chart.

She married Sir Denis Thatcher on 13 Dec. 1951. They had met in Feb 1949. Sir Thatcher was ten years senior to her and had married three times before his marriage with Margret.

With Libra progress Lagna, the focus is on Seventh and tenth house. The seventh house is aspected by four planets. Rahu is in tenth house and its dispositor is in eleventh. It was marriage and professional rise.

Mars, Saturn, Mercury and Jupiter are aspecting seventhhouse. The fifth and seventh lord is both influencing the seventhhouse.

Example Job DOB 15 November 1918 TOB 21.49.26 POB Srinagar

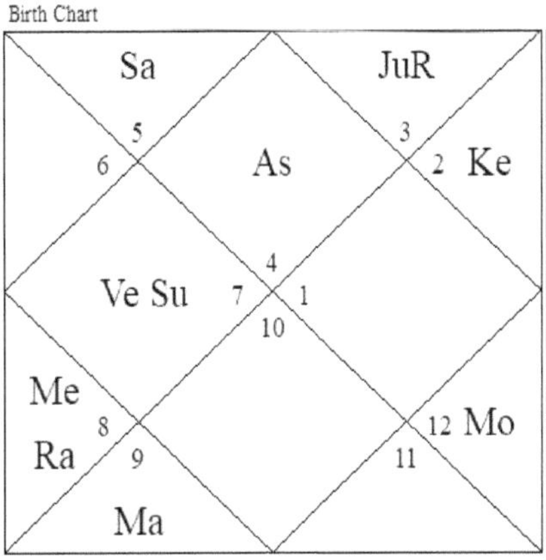

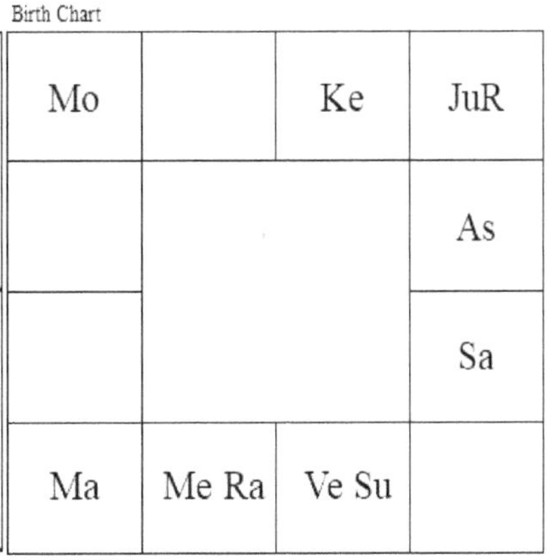

Birth Nakshtra Revati

Dasa sequence

Yogini	Nakshtra	From	To
Ulka	Revati	15.11.1918	11.2.1922
Siddha	Rohini	11.2.1922	11.2.1929
Sankata	Mrigshira	11.2.1929	11.2.1937
Mangla	Ardra	11.2.1937	11.2.1938
Pingla	Punarvasu	11.2.1938	11.2.1940
Dhanya	Pushya	11.2.1940	11.2.1943
Bharamari	Ashlesha	11.2.1943	11.2.1947
Bhadrika	Magha	11.2.1947	11.2.1952
Ulka	P. Phalguni	11.2.1952	11.2.1958
Siddha	U. Phalguni	11.2.1958	11.2.1965
Sankata	Hasta	11.2.1965	11.2.1973

Yogini	Nakshtra	From	To
Mangla	Chitra	11.2.1973	11.2.1974
Pingla	Swati	11.2.1974	11.2.1976

Let us examine Rahu in birth chart. Rahu is in fifth houseand acts as maraca for mother. It is with Mercury, which is twelfth lord of mother and is a maraca for Moon. Mars is lord of tenthhouse also and is Yoga Karaka for Cancer lagna. Thus, Mars aregiver of yoga also. He was promoted to General Secretary. In Pingla/ Punarvasu, he started his job as an LDC.

The progress lagna is Libra which is fourth house of birthchart. The eighth lord from fourth is Sun and is debilitated. The eighth house from fourth house is occupied by Saturn. The fourth lord of progress chart is in eighth from fourth. Mother died in Pingla / Pingla.

Let us see why mother did not expire in Mangla of Ardra Nakshtra. The progress lagna was Gemini. The fourth lord is in sixth house of PL and can give illness only.

Pingla / Dhanishta

Dhanishta Nakshtra occupies Capricorn and Aquarius. First two pada of Dhanishta falls in Capricorn and last two in Aquarius. Therefore, for first half dasha period i.e. one year the progress lagna will be Capricorn and for last one year the progress lagnawill be Aquarius. This change happens in Ulka Sub period.

For both progress lagna, Saturn is the lord of lagna and Venus is the Yoga Karak. Therefore, attention should be given to these planets also.

For Capricorn, Mars is the lord of fourth and eleventh houseand activates these houses. The lordship and placement of Marsin natal chart is important.

For Aquarius, Mars is the lord of third and tenth house. The matters regarding profession, father, travels etc. come intoplay.

Example Serious Accident DOB 30 April 1945 TOB 9.27 POB Delhi

Birth Chart

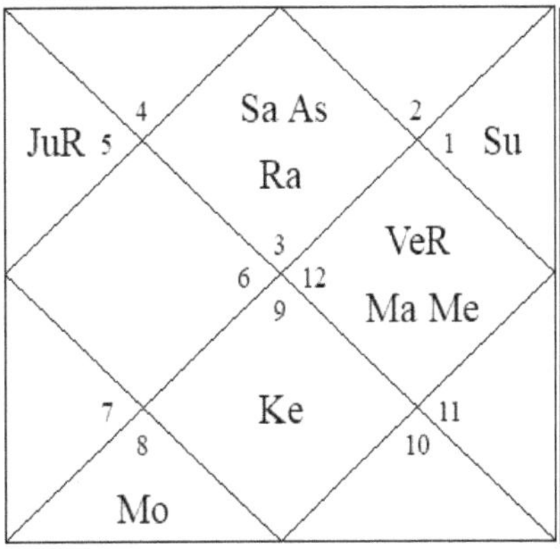

Birth Chart

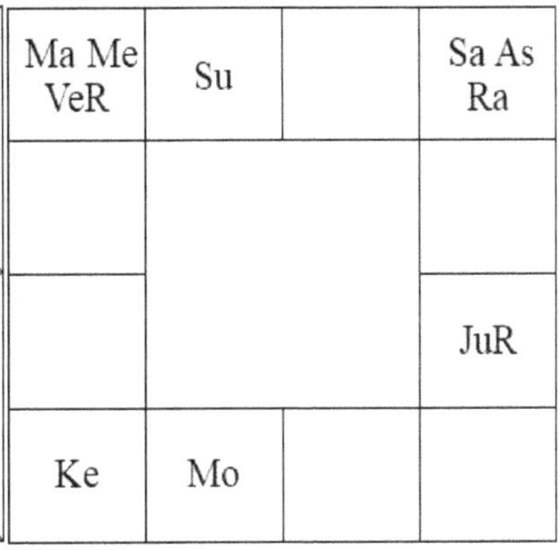

Birth Nakshtra Anuradha

Dasa sequence

Yogini	Nakshtra	From	To
Bharamari	Anuradha	30.4.1945	15.5.1945
Bhadrika	Jyeshtha	15.5.1945	15.5.1950
Ulka	Moola	15.5.1950	15.5.1956
Siddha	P. Ashadha	15.5.1956	15.5.1963
Sankata	U. Ashadha	15.5.1963	15.5.1971
Mangla	Shravan	15.5.1971	15.5.1972
Pingla	Dhanishta	15.5.1972	15.5.1974

A near fatal accident happened in September 1972 when he was driving a Jeep. Four other co passengers were hurt. The dasha was Pingla / Bhramari.

Progress chart for Pingla/ Dhanishta and Capricorn lagan.

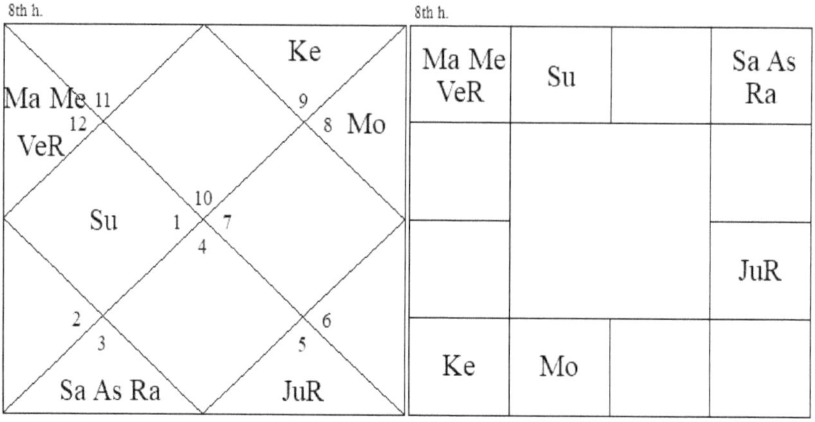

Eighth house is the progress lagna. Mars is the sixth lordof the birth chart.

In thc progress chart Mars is fourth lord and is placed withsixth lord of Progress chart. A very serious accident involving sixth and fourth Lords of Birth and progress chart happened inSept. 1972.

The saving grace came from the conjunction of Mars withfifth and ninth lord and aspect of lagna lord.

He remained hospitalized for six months and recovered when the progress lagna moved to Aquarius.

It will be of interest to see the changes which happened after the progress lagna moved to Aquarius. Daughter was bornon 22 Dec. 1973 in the sub period of Sankata.

Progress chart for Pingla/ Dhanishta and Aquarius lagan.

9th h.

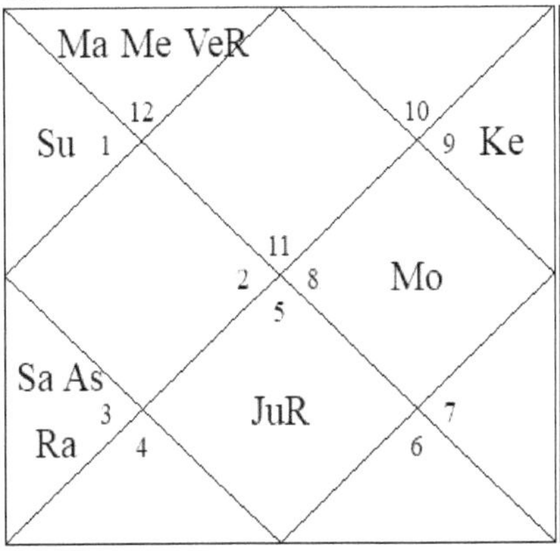

9th h.

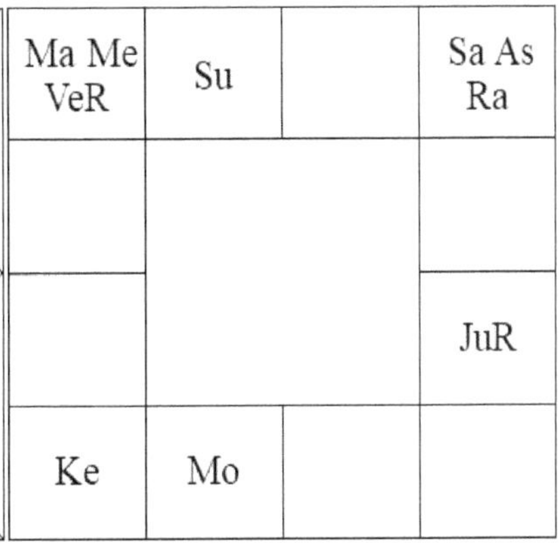

Now also Mars is with fifth, ninth and aspected by LagnaLord. The relation with sixth lord of progress is not there.

Saturn and Rahu are in fifth house. The effect of trine lords is still present. After the birth of daughter, he wastransferred. Mars is third and tenth lord now.

Example Chief Minister DOB 31 March 1912 TOB 5.44 POB Saraikela

Birth Chart

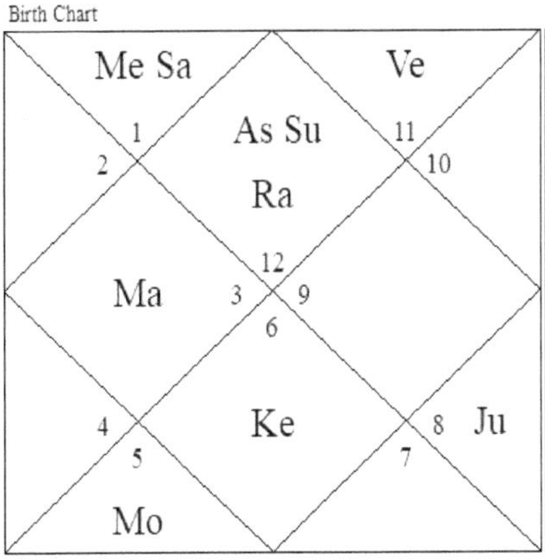

Birth Chart

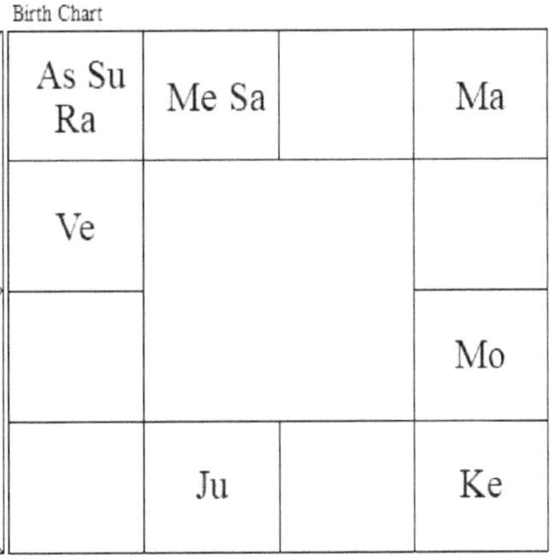

Birth Nakshtra P. Phalguni

Dasa sequence

Yogini	Nakshtra	From	To
Ulka	P. Phalguni	31.3.1912	28.2.1914
Siddha	U. Phalguni	28.2.1914	28.2.1921
Sankata	Hasta	28.2.1921	28.2.1929
Mangla	Chitra	28.2.1929	28.2.1930
Pingla	Swati	28.2.1930	28.2.1932
Dhanya	Visakha	28.2.1932	28.2.1935
Bharamari	Anuradha	28.2.1935	28.2.1939
Bhadrika	Jyeshtha	28.2.1939	28.2.1944
Ulka	Moola	28.2.1944	28.2.1950
Siddha	P. Ashadha	28.2.1950	28.2.1957
Sankata	U. Ashadha	28.2.1957	28.2.1965
Mangla	Shravan	28.2.1965	28.2.1966
Pingla	Dhanishta	28.2.1966	28.2.1968

He became chief minister of Orrisa in Pingla/ Bhadrika in progress lagan Aquarius.

Progress chart with Aquarius lagan.

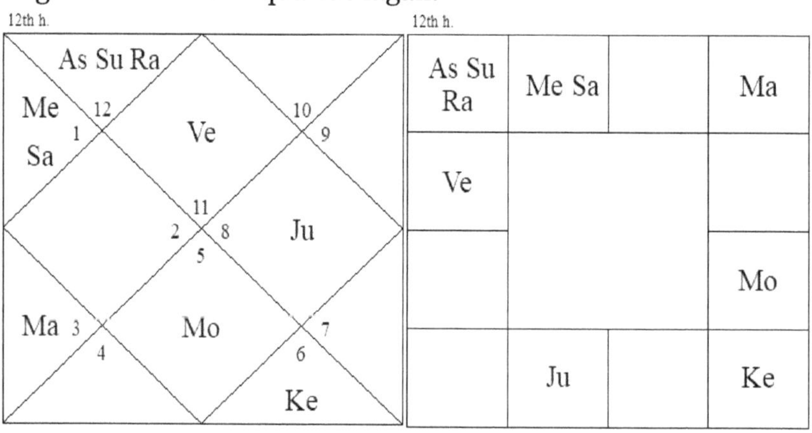

Mars is the tenth lord. Mars is aspected by lagna lord Saturn. There is exchange of fifth and third lord. Birth tenth lord is in tenth house of PC. Yoga Karaka Venus is in lagan.

Example Fame DOB 7 April 1920 TOB 10.13 POB Varanasi

Birth Chart

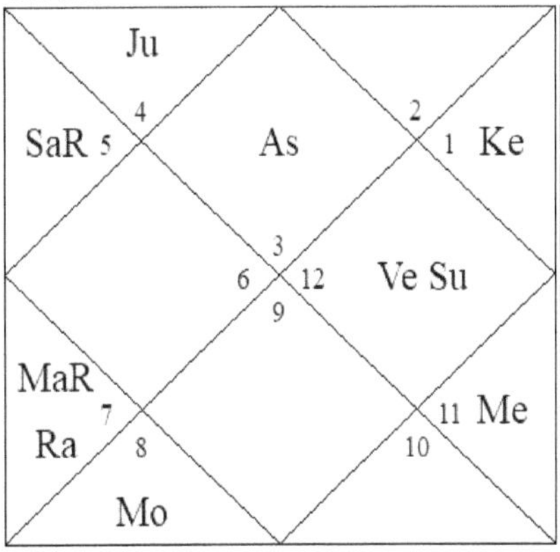

Birth Chart

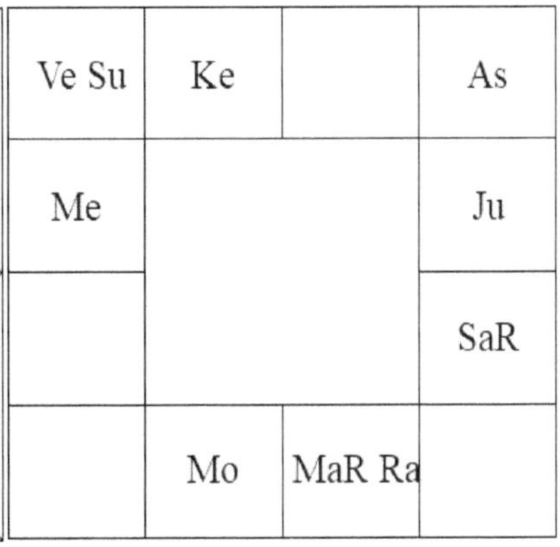

Birth Nakshtra Anuradha

Dasa sequence

Yogini	Nakshtra	From	To
Bharamari	Anuradha	7.4.1920	28.3.1923
Bhadrika	Jyeshtha	28.3.1923	28.3.1928
Ulka	Moola	28.3.1928	28.3.1934
Siddha	P. Ashadha	28.3.1934	28.3.1941
Sankata	U. Ashadha	28.3.1941	28.3.1949
Mangla	Shravan	28.3.1949	28.3.1950
Pingla	Dhanishta	28.3.1950	28.3.1952

Progress chart with Capricorn lagan.

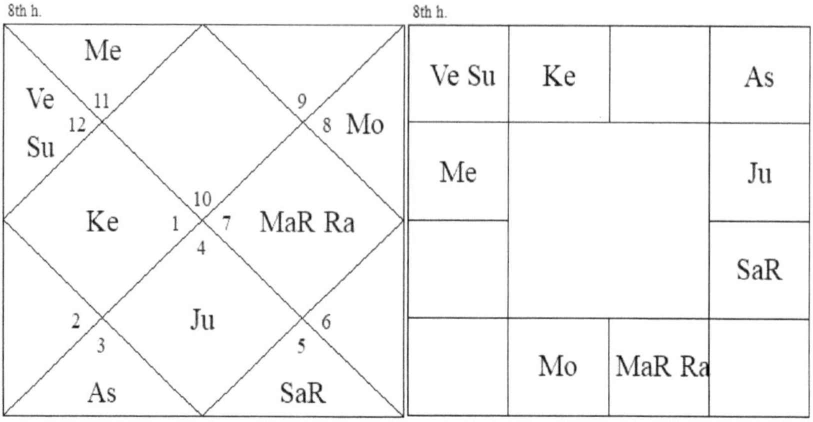

He was music director with All India Radio. He composed music for Satyajit Ray and got international fame.

Nakshtra lord Mars is in tenth house of progress chart and is with Rahu. Lagan lord Saturn is aspecting Mars.

Example Marriage DOB 18 August 1972 TOB 12.13.32 POB Kolkata

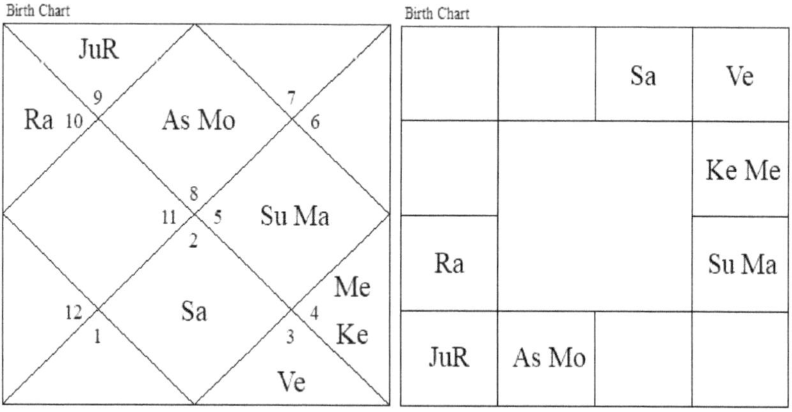

Birth Nakshtra Anuradha

Marriage took place in January 2001. The Pingla dasa started on 2 January 2000 and the progress lagan moved to Aquarius in January 2001.

Dasa sequence

Yogini	Nakshtra	From	To
Bharamari	Anuradha	18.8.1972	2.1.1973
Bhadrika	Jyeshtha	2.1.1973	2.1.1978
Ulka	Moola	2.1.1978	2.1.1984
Siddha	P. Ashadha	2.1.1984	2.1.1991
Sankata	U. Ashadha	2.1.1991	2.1.1999
Mangla	Shravan	2.1.1999	2.1.2000
Pingla	Dhanishta	2.1.2000	2.1.2002

Progress chart with Aquarius lagan.

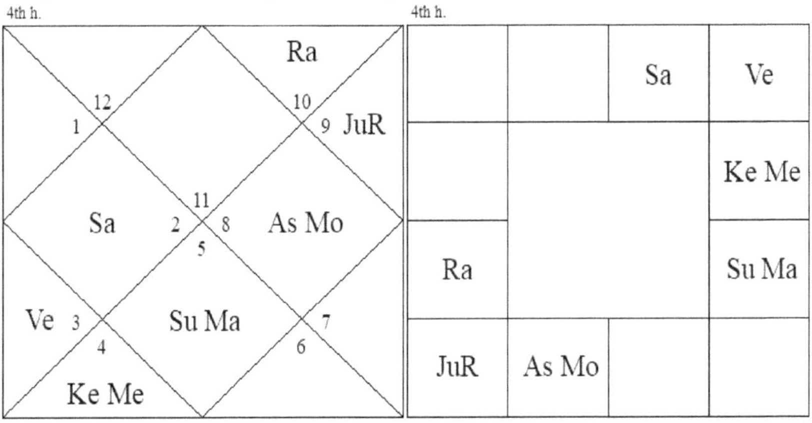

A clear picture emerges. Mars is the birth lagna lord. In the progress chart, it is in seventh house with seventh lord and is aspected by Jupiter. Saturn is the lagna lord and aspects lagna. Saturn is in seventh house of birth chart.

With the traditional approach in the birth chart Sun is in tenth house making no relation with seventh house or seventh lord. Only when we progress Yogini with the Nakshtra, the promise comes out clear and loud

Chapter 5

Dhanya

Dhanya Maha dasha is generated by three Nakshtra. Thelord of Dhanya Yogini is Jupiter and classics have rated Jupiteras the most benefic planets and give mostly auspicious resultsduring this period.

The Nakshtra of Dhanya Dasha are given:

Nakshtra	Lord	Sign of Nakshtra	Remarks
Pushya	Saturn	Cancer	Cancer in progress lagna
Vishakha	Jupiter	Libra / Scorpio	First two years 3 months progress lagna in Libra. Last 9 months progress lagna is Scorpio.
Shatbhisaj	Rahu	Aquarius	Aquarius is the progress Lagna.

Dhanya / Pushya

Pushya Nakshtra is considered auspicious. Both heavy weights and the ninth and tenth lord of Kaal Purush are controlling this period.

It is our experience that this Yogini period **brings major changes which have lifelong effects.**

Example Queen DOB 24 May 1819 TOB 2.26.54 POB London Colney

Birth Chart

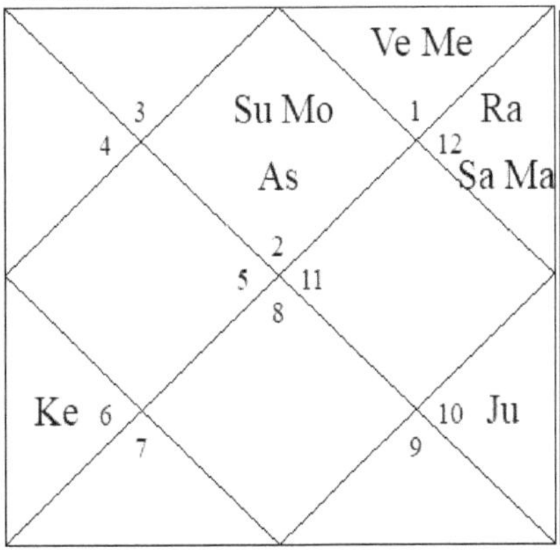

Birth Chart

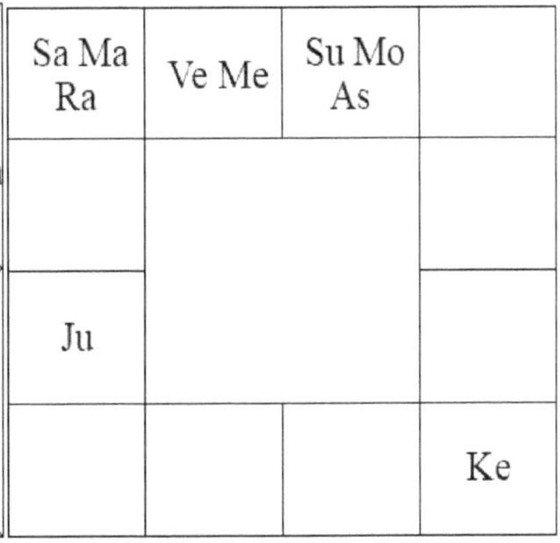

Birth Nakshtra Rohini

She was coronated on 20 June 1836 at the age of 18 years.

Dasa sequence

Yogini	Nakshtra	From	To
Siddha	Rohini	24.5.1819	27.2.1825
Sankata	Mrigshira	27.2.1825	27.2.1833
Mangla	Ardra	27.2.1833	27.2.1834
Pingla	Punarvasu	27.2.1834	27.2.1836
Dhanya	Pushya	27.2.1836	27.2.1839

Progress chart for Dhanya/ Pushya. Progress lagan is Cancer.

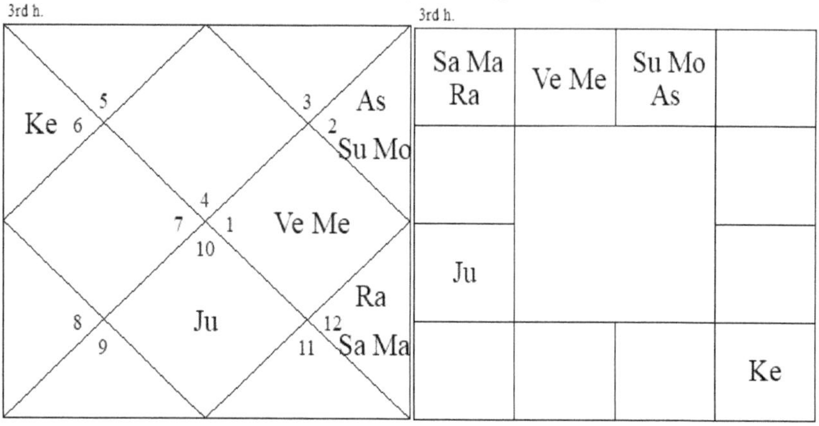

She was coroneted on 20 June 1836 at age of 18 years. She remained queen till her death on 22 Jan 1901.

She was fifth in the line of succession to the throne but theturn of events made her the queen. Dhanya/ Pushya changedthe life.

Saturn is the yoga Karaka ninth lord of birth chart and hasbecome the dasha Nakshtra. Examine the progress chart. Thelagna lord Moon is exalted in eleventh house. Both Lagna andlagna lord are aspected by Jupiter. Jupiter is debilitated ninth lord and shows death of father. Saturn and Jupiter haveexchanged seventh and ninth houses.

The coronation came in Dhanya/ Bhadrika.

Example Change of residence DOB 30 April 1945 TOB 9.27 POB Delhi

Birth Chart

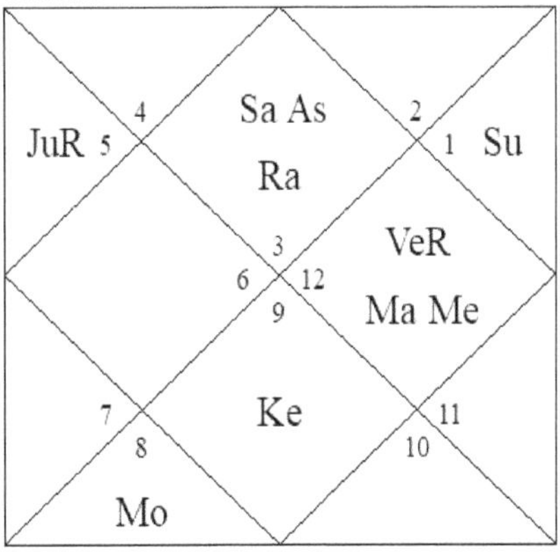

Birth Chart

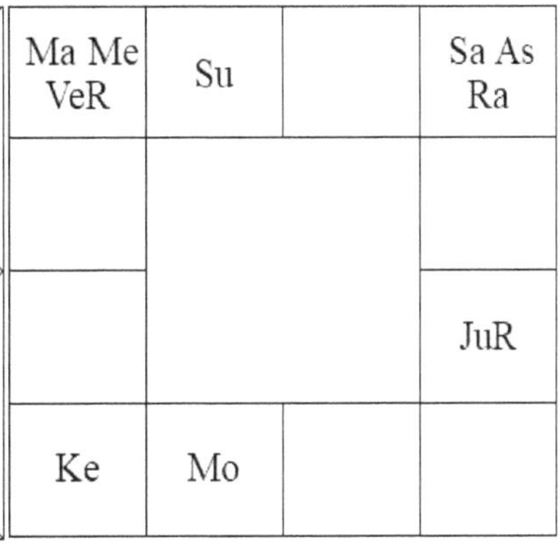

Birth Nakshtra Anuradha

He was born and brought up in Delhi. In May 2012 he shifted to Gurgaon at the age of 67 years to settle there. This will be a permanent shift. This is a major change in life of a person.

Dasa sequence

Yogini	Nakshtra	From	To
Bharamari	Anuradha	30.4.1945	15.5.1945
Bhadrika	Jyeshtha	15.5.1945	15.5.1950
Ulka	Moola	15.5.1950	15.5.1956
Siddha	P. Ashadha	15.5.1956	15.5.1963
Sankata	U. Ashadha	15.5.1963	15.5.1971
Mangla	Shravan	15.5.1971	15.5.1972
Pingla	Dhanishta	15.5.1972	15.5.1974
Dhanya	Shatbhisaj	15.5.1974	15.5.1977
Bharamari	P. Bhadrapad	15.5.1977	15.5.1981
Bhadrika	U. Bhadrapad	15.5.1981	15.5.1986
Ulka	Revati	15.5.1986	15.5.1992

Yogini	Nakshtra	From	To
Siddha	Rohini	15.5.1992	15.5.1999
Sankata	Mrigshira	15.5.1999	15.5.2007
Mangla	Ardra	15.5.2007	15.5.2008
Pingla	Punarvasu	15.5.2008	15.5.2010
Dhanya	Pushya	15.5.2010	15.5.2013

Dhanya/Pushya commenced on 15 May 2010. In May 2012 he shifted out of Delhi to settle in Gurgaon at the age of 67 years and it should be the home for rest of life. This is a majorchange for the person born in Delhi and lived in Delhi throughout.

Progress chart for Dhanya/ Pushya and Cancer lagan.

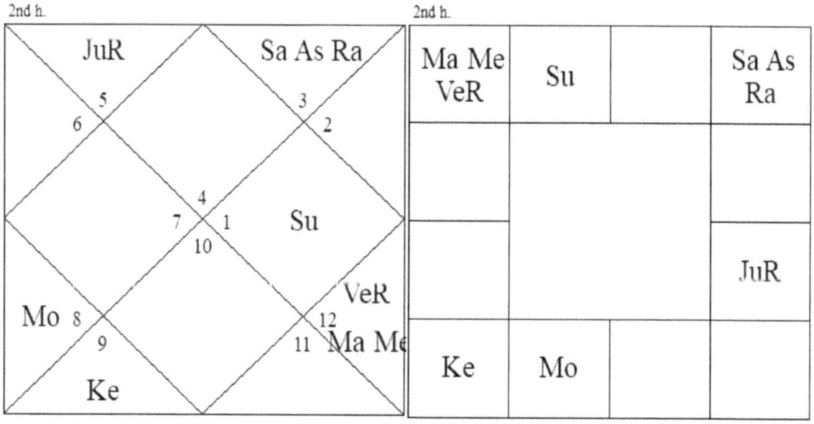

Saturn and the birth lagna are in 12th house. Saturn is with Rahu and aspected by Mars. It is a big disturbance and affliction to Nakshtra lord. Venus is the fourth lord of progresslagna. Both fourth lords of birth chart and progress chart are afflicted. The change came in Dhanya/Siddha. Jupiter and Venusare retrograde but Saturn in not.

Example Marriage at young age DOB 8 December 1884 TOB 8.18.30 POB Chapra Bihar

Birth Chart

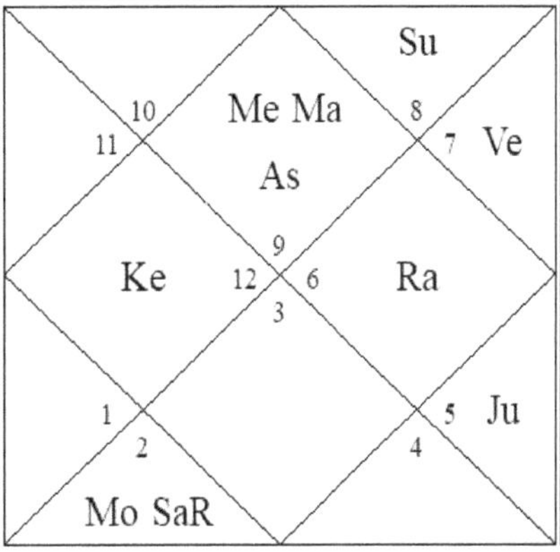

Birth Chart

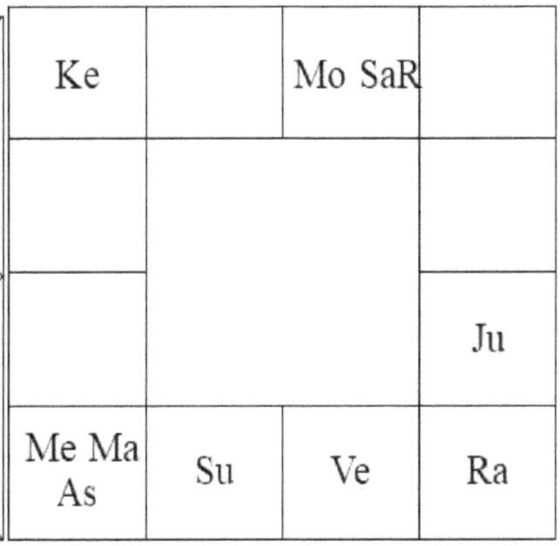

Birth Nakshtra Mrigshira

He was married at an early age of 12 years.

Dasa sequence

Yogini	Nakshtra	From	To
Sankata	Mrigshira	8.12.1884	28.7.1892
Mangla	Ardra	28.7.1892	28.7.1893
Pingla	Punarvasu	28.7.1893	28.7.1895
Dhanya	Pushya	28.7.1895	28.7.1898

Progress chart for Dhanya/ Pushya and Cancer lagan.

8th h.

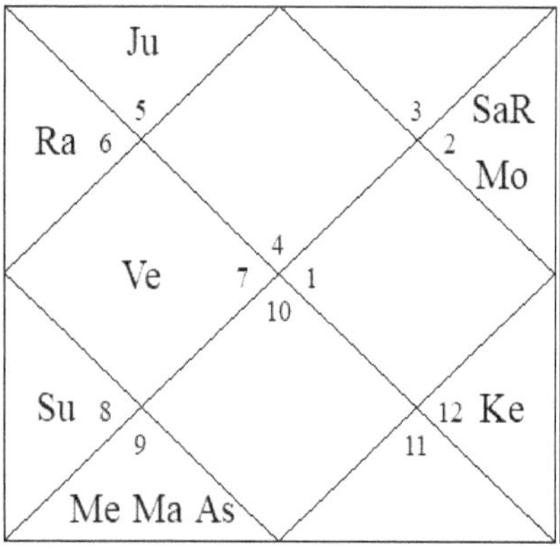

8th h.

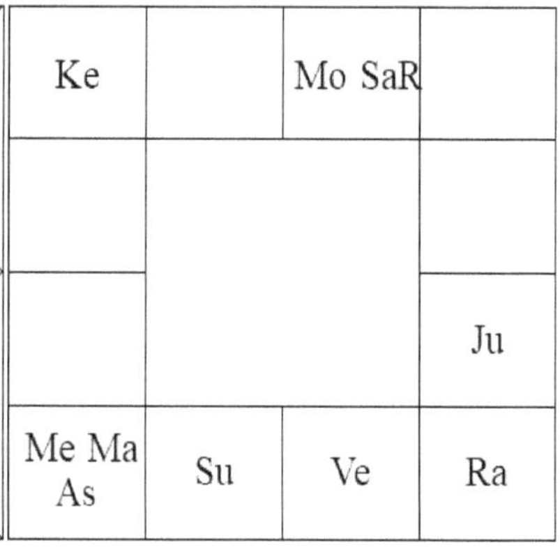

Saturn is the seventh lord of progress chart. It is with Lagnalord of progress chart. Both are placed in eleventh house.

Example Death of husband DOB 19 November 1917 TOB 23.11 POB Allahabad

Birth Chart

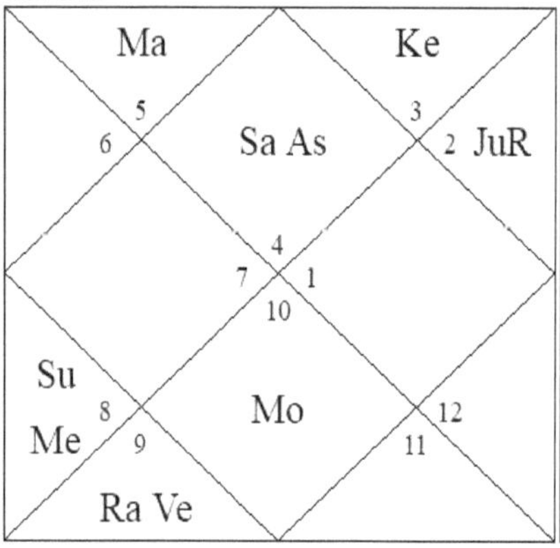

Birth Chart

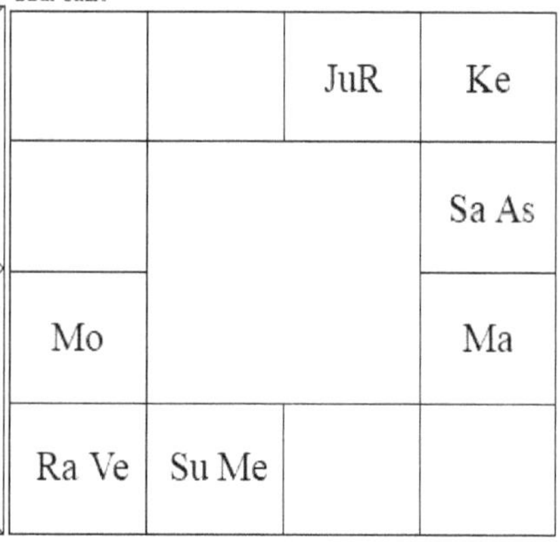

Birth Nakshtra U. Ashadha

Dasa sequence

Yogini	Nakshtra	From	To
Sankata	U. Ashadha	19.11.1917	13.7.1920
Mangla	Shravan	13.7.1920	13.7.1921

Yogini	Nakshtra	From	To
Pingla	Dhanishta	13.7.1921	13.7.1923
Dhanya	Shatbhisaj	13.7.1923	13.7.1926
Bharamari	P. Bhadrapad	13.7.19226	13.7.1930
Bhadrika	U. Bhadrapad	13.7.1930	13.7.1935
Ulka	Revati	13.7.1935	13.7.1941
Siddha	Rohini	13.7.1941	13.7.1948
Sankata	Mrigshira	13.7.1948	13.7.1956
Mangla	Ardra	13.7.1956	13.7.1957
Pingla	Punarvasu	13.7.1957	13.7.1959
Dhanya	Pushya	13.7.1959	13.7.1962

Firoz Gandhi died on 8 September 1960 in the sub period of Ulka. The progress chart for Dhanya / Pushya is same as birth chart.

The Nakshtra Lord Saturn is the seventh and the eighthlord of Birth Chart. In progress chart, we take seventh house asthe house of spouse. The maraca for husband is Saturn and Moon. Both are in natural aspect in one/seven axis.

Example Death DOB 9 November 1931 TOB 12.27.30 POB Jodhpur

Birth Chart

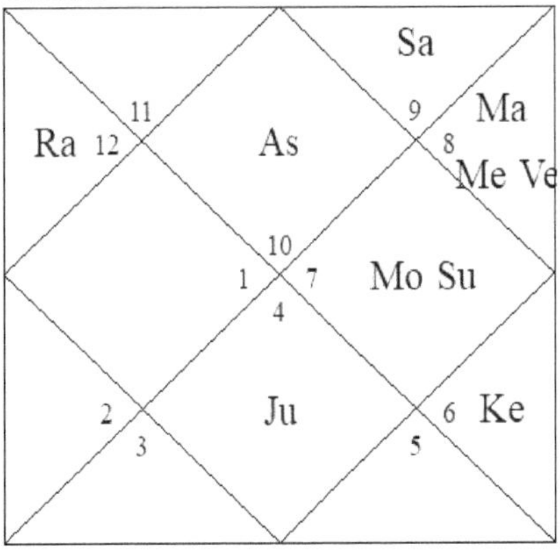

Birth Chart

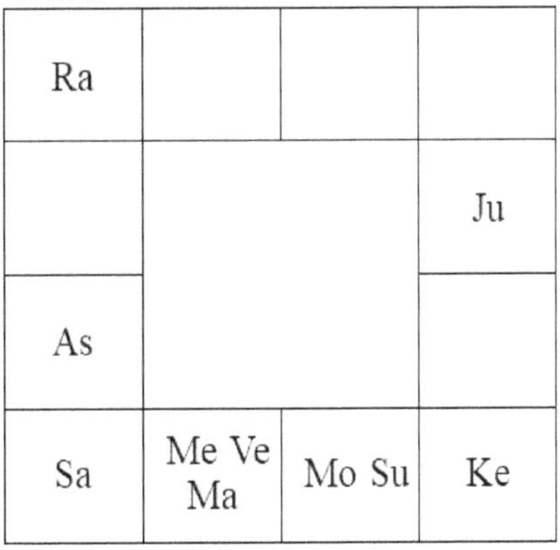

Birth Nakshtra Swati

Dasa sequence

Yogini	Nakshtra	From	To
Pingla	Swati	9.11.1931	18.10.1932
Dhanya	Visakha	18.10.1932	18.10.1935
Bharamari	Anuradha	18.10.1935	18.10.1939
Bhadrika	Jyeshtha	18.10.1939	18.10.1944
Ulka	Moola	18.10.1944	18.10.1950
Siddha	P. Ashadha	18.10.1950	18.10.1957
Sankata	U. Ashadha	18.10.1957	18.10.1965
Mangla	Shravan	18.10.1965	18.10.1966
Pingla	Dhanishta	18.10.1966	18.10.1968
Dhanya	Shatbhisaj	18.10.1968	18.10.1971
Bharamari	P. Bhadrapad	18.10.1971	18.10.1975
Bhadrika	U. Bhadrapad	18.10.1975	18.10.1980
Ulka	Revati	18.10.1980	18.10.1986
Siddha	Rohini	18.10.1986	18.10.1993
Sankata	Mrigshira	18.10.1993	18.10.2001
Mangla	Ardra	18.10.2001	18.10.2002
Pingla	Punarvasu	18.10.2002	18.10.2004
Dhanya	Pushya	18.10.2004	18.10.2007

Laxmi Mal Singhvi was the longest serving high Commissioner to U.K. He expired on 13 Oct 2007 in Dhanya / Pingla.

Progress chart for Dhanya/ Pushya and Cancer lagan.

7th h.

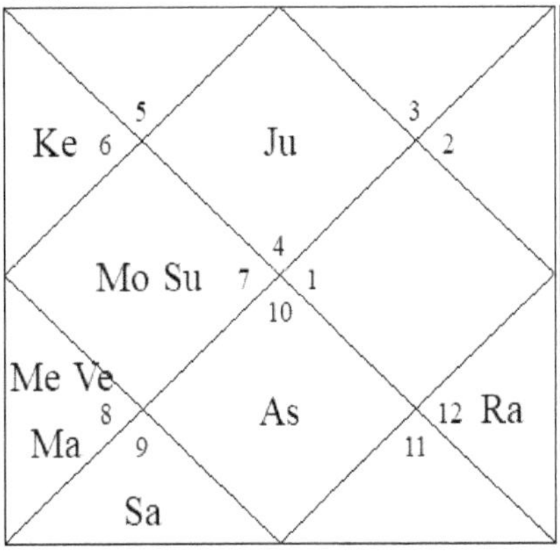

7th h.

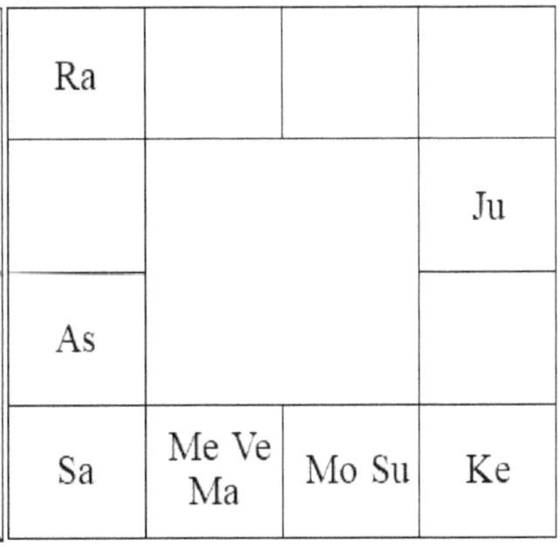

Saturn is the second lord of Birth Chart. In the progress chart Saturn is the seventh and eighth lord. The maracastatus of Saturn is confirmed. For earlier dasha generated by Saturn Nakshtra did not confirm the maraca status of Saturn.

Sun is the eighth lord of birth chart and the second lord of progress chart. The end came in Dhanya / Pingla

Example Promotion DOB 3 October 1960 TOB 12.10.40 POB Delhi

Birth Chart

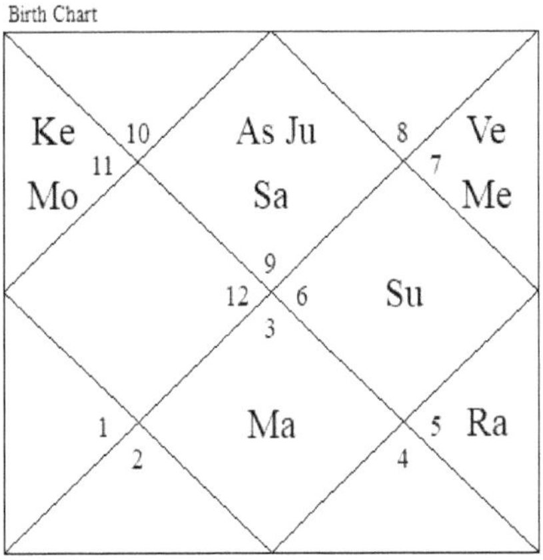

Birth Chart

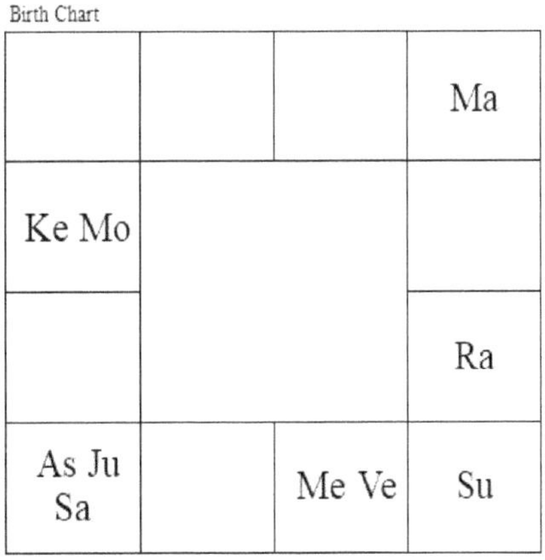

Birth Nakshtra P. Bhadrapad

He got an excellent promotion on 23 January 1992 in dasa of Dhanya/ Dhanya.

Dasa sequence

Yogini	Nakshtra	From	To
Bharamari	P. Bhadrapad	3.10.1960	21.1.1963
Bhadrika	U. Bhadrapad	21.1.1963	21.1.1968
Ulka	Revati	21.1.1968	21.1.1974
Siddha	Rohini	21.1.1974	21.1.1981
Sankata	Mrigshira	21.1.1981	21.1.1989
Mangla	Ardra	21.1.1989	21.1.1990
Pingla	Punarvasu	21.1.1990	21.1.1992
Dhanya	Pushya	21.1.1992	21.1.1995

Progress chart for Dhanya/ Pushya and Cancer lagan.

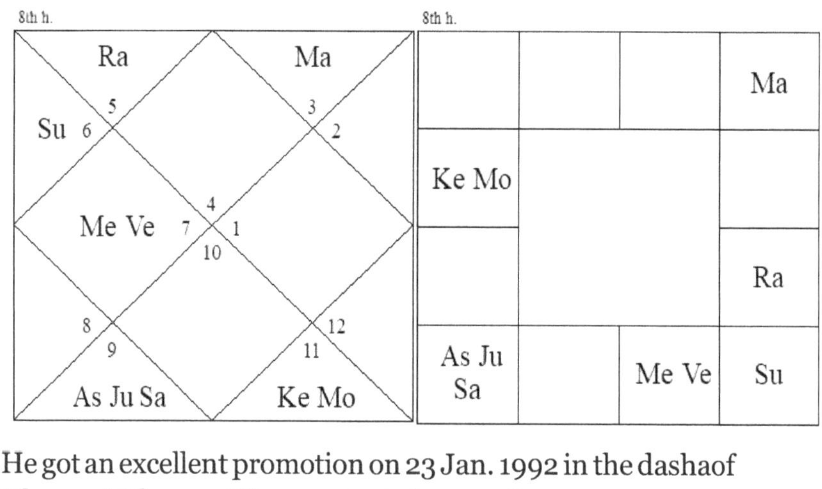

He got an excellent promotion on 23 Jan. 1992 in the dashaof Dhanya/ Dhanya. Dhanya started on 21 Jan. 1992.

Saturn is aspecting tenth house in the birth chart. It is aspected by lord of fifth house Mars.

In the progress chart Saturn is again making relation with progress tenth lord Mars. Jupiter is aspecting the progress tenth lord and tenth house. Jupiter is the dasha lord and is with Nakshtra Lord.

Example Promotion DOB 10 March 1951 TOB 23.30 POB Hoogly WB

Birth Chart

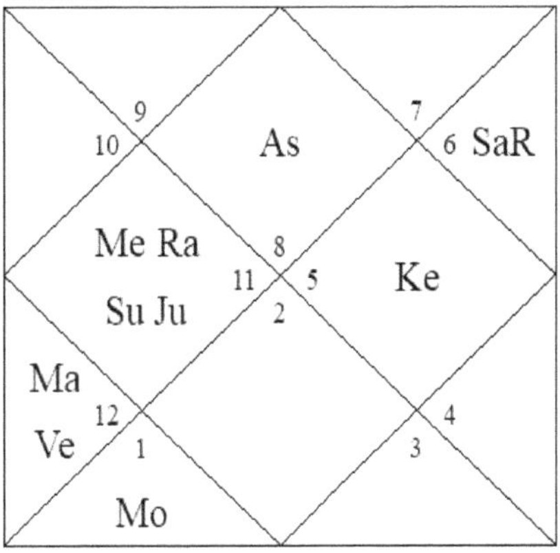

Birth Chart

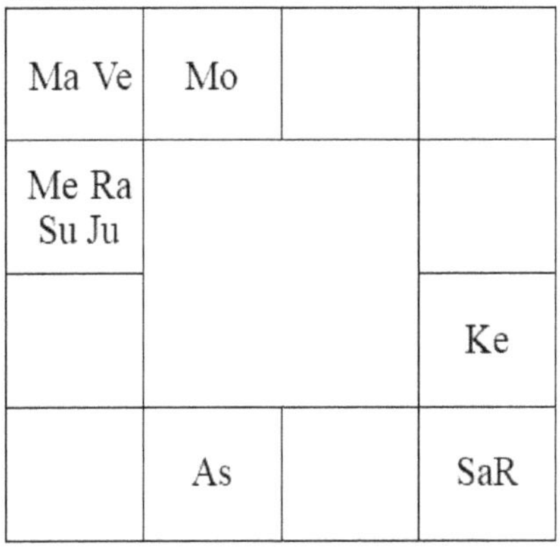

Birth Nakshtra Ashwani

Dasa sequence

Yogini	**Nakshtra**	**From**	**To**
Bharamari	Ashwini	10.3.1951	13.12.1954
Bhadrika	Bharani	13.12.1954	13.12.1959
Ulka	Kritika	13.12.1959	13.12.1965
Siddha	Rohini	13.12.1965	13.12.1972
Sankata	Mrigshira	13.12.1972	13.12.1980
Mangla	Ardra	13.12.1980	13.12.1981
Pingla	Punarvasu	13.12.1981	13.12.1983
Dhanya	Pushya	13.12.1983	13.12.1986

This is another case of a government officer who got promoted on 13 Aug. 1986.

Progress chart for Dhanya/ Pushya and Cancer lagan.

9th h.

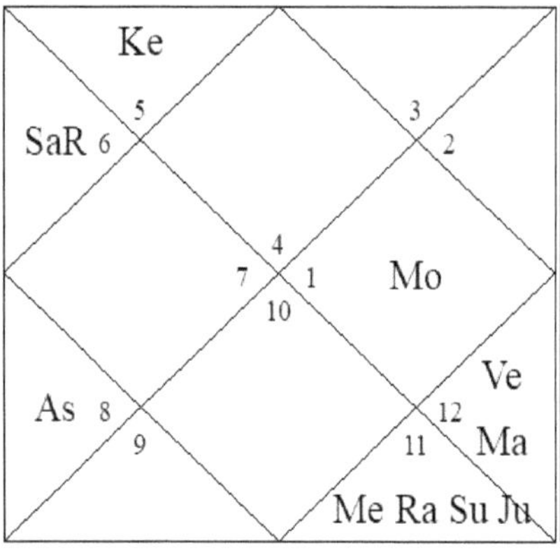

9th h.

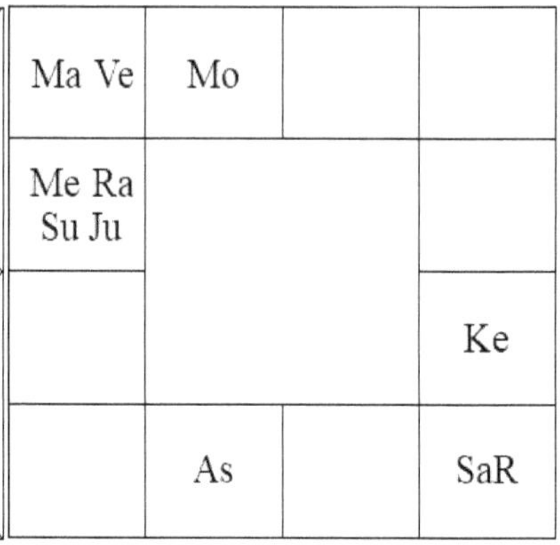

Saturn is aspected by Mars in the birth chart. Mars is thetenth lord in the progress chart.

Rahu act as Saturn and give result of Saturn also. It is conjoined with tenth lord of birth chart.

The promotion came in Sankata sub period.

Example Jailed DOB 19 August 1973 TOB 8.55 POB Delhi

Birth Chart

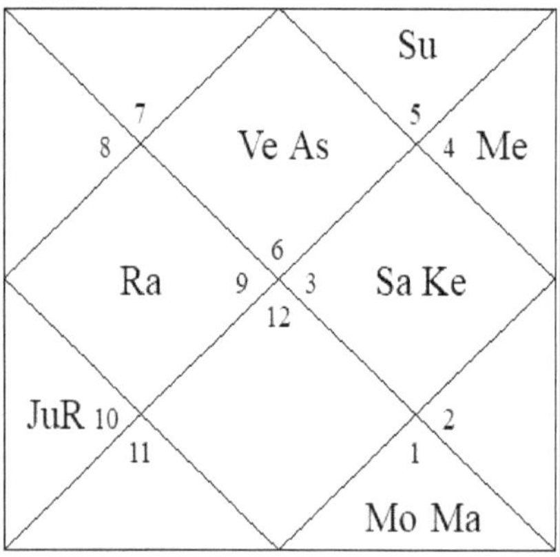

Birth Chart

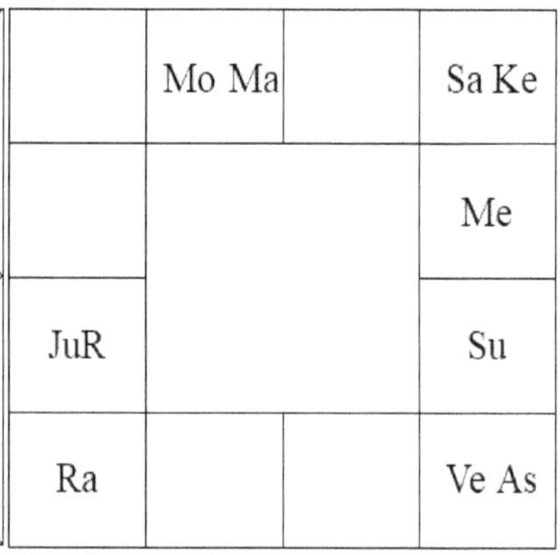

Birth Nakshtra Ashwani

He was with Merchant Navy. In Jan 2006 he was arrested in a

foreign country on the charge of murder and was jailed.

Dasa sequence

Yogini	Nakshtra	From	To
Bharamari	Ashwini	19.8.1973	30.8.1976
Bhadrika	Bharani	30.8.1976	30.8.1981
Ulka	Kritika	30.8.1981	30.8.1987
Siddha	Rohini	30.8.1987	30.8.1994
Sankata	Mrigshira	30.8.1994	30.8.2002
Mangla	Ardra	30.8.2002	30.8.2003
Pingla	Punarvasu	30.8.2003	30.8.2005
Dhanya	Pushya	30.8.2005	30.8.2008

Progress chart for Dhanya/ Pushya and Cancer lagan.

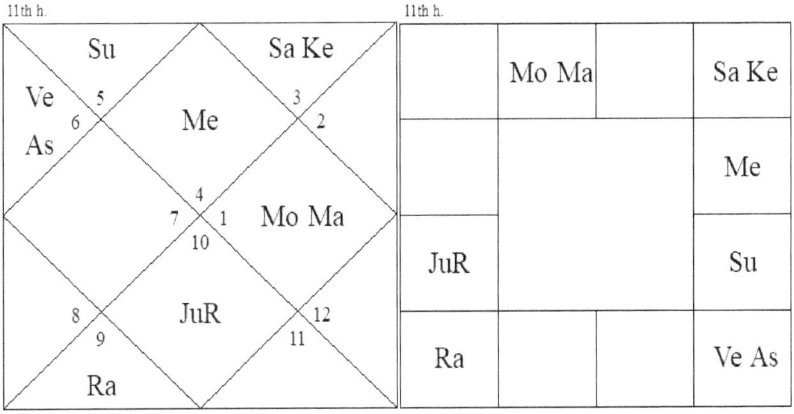

Saturn is fifth and sixth lord of birth chart and is placed intenth house. It is with Ketu.

In the progress chart, Saturn is in twelfth house in Rahu /Ketu axis. Lagna is in Papa Kartari and is a typical bandana yoga. Saturn is not having any benefic relation. Twelfth houseis also the house of confinement. Mars is eighth lord of birth chart and is in tenth house with progress lagan lord.

Example Marriage and child birth DOB 25 September 1969 TOB 14.40 POB Swansea UK

Birth Chart

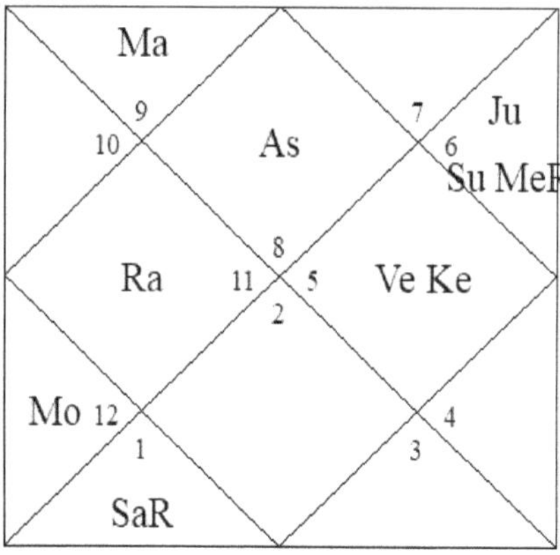

Birth Chart

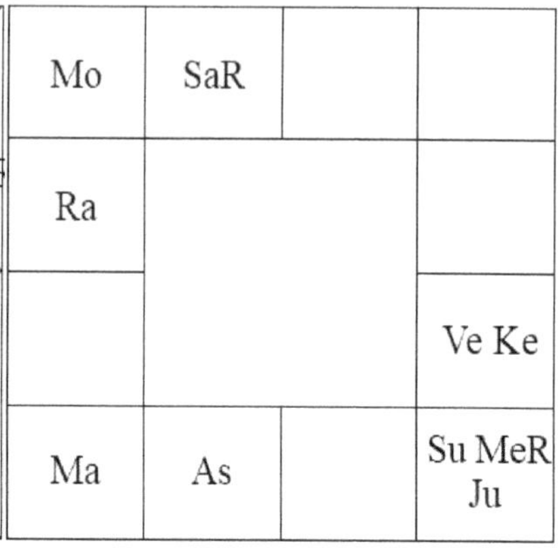

Birth Nakshtra U. Bhadrapad

She is the British Film actor. She married Michael Douglas in 2000. The formal marriage was performed on 18 November 2000. Her first child was born on 8 August 2000 much before her formal marriage. What should now be the date of marriage. Do we take the date of formal marriage or the relationship? The relationship started in the dasha of Dhanya / Siddha.

Dasa sequence

Yogini	Nakshtra	From	To
Bhadrika	U. Bhadrapad	25.9.1969	7.1.1974
Ulka	Revati	7.1.1974	7.1.1980
Siddha	Rohini	7.1.1980	7.1.1987
Sankata	Mrigshira	7.1.1987	7.1.1995
Mangla	Ardra	7.1.1995	7.1.1996
Pingla	Punarvasu	7.1.1996	7.1.1998
Dhanya	Pushya	7.1.1998	7.1.2001

Progress chart for Dhanya/ Pushya and Cancer lagan.

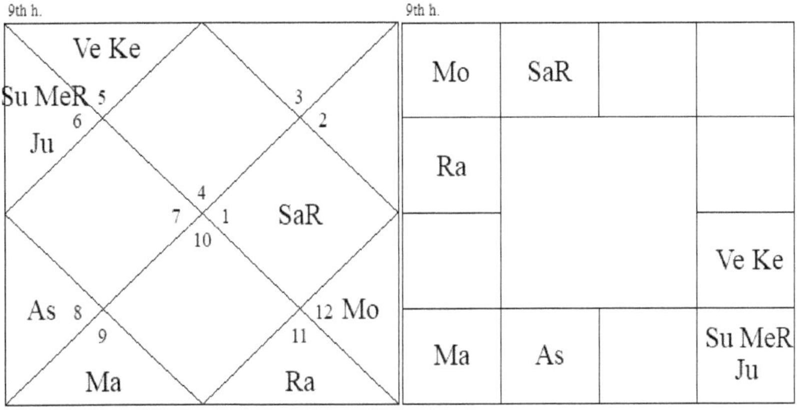

The Nakshtra lord Saturn is in tenth house and aspects progress seventh house. He is also the seventh lord. The sub period of Venus gave the actual marriage since it is birth seventh lord. .

Dhanya Vishakha

Jupiter is the dasha as well as the Nakshtra Lord. The results given by Jupiter are prominent. Vishakha Nakshtra is inLibra and Scorpio sign. First three Pada are in Libra and the last pada is in Scorpio. Dhanya Dasha is of three years and assuch for first two years and three months the progress lagna will be Libra and for last nine months, the progress lagna is Scorpio. The progress Lagna changes to Scorpio in Sankata subperiod.

With Libra progress lagna, Jupiter is lord of third and sixthhouse and is a malefic. It high lights the effect of these housesand is good for competition, service etc.

With Scorpio progress lagna, Jupiter is lord of second andfifth house and the results of Jupiter improve.

Jupiter is the planet for spirituality. In Dhanya / Vishakha, it should turn the person towards spirituality.

Example Twins DOB 13 October 1925 TOB 9.0 POB Grantham UK

Birth Chart

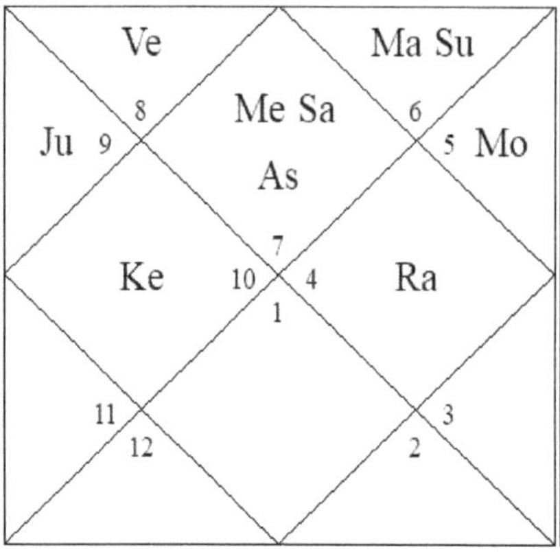

Birth Chart

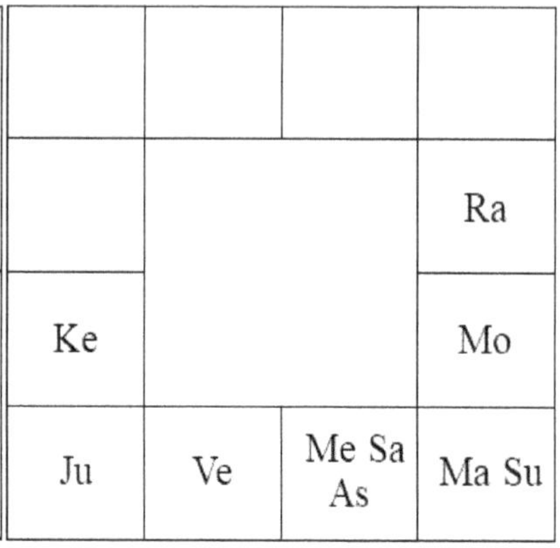

Birth Nakshtra Magha

Twins were born on 15 Aug. 1953. The dasha was Dhanya/ Ulka.

Dasa sequence

Yogini	Nakshtra	From	To
Bhadrika	Magha	13.10.1925	8.8.1923
Ulka	P. Phalguni	8.8.1923	8.8.1923
Siddha	U. Phalguni	8.8.1923	8.8.1923
Sankata	Hasta	8.8.1923	8.8.1923
Mangla	Chitra	8.8.1923	8.8.1923
Pingla	Swati	8.8.1923	8.8.1923
Dhanya	Visakha	8.8.1923	8.8.1923

Progress chart for Dhanya/ Vishakha and Libra lagan is same as birth chart.

Jupiter is placed in third house and aspects ninth house. He is under the aspect of Saturn. Saturn is the fifth lord of birth and progress chart. Twins were born in the sub period of Saturn.

Example Rise DOB 15 November 1918 TOB 21.49.26 POB Srinagar

Birth Chart

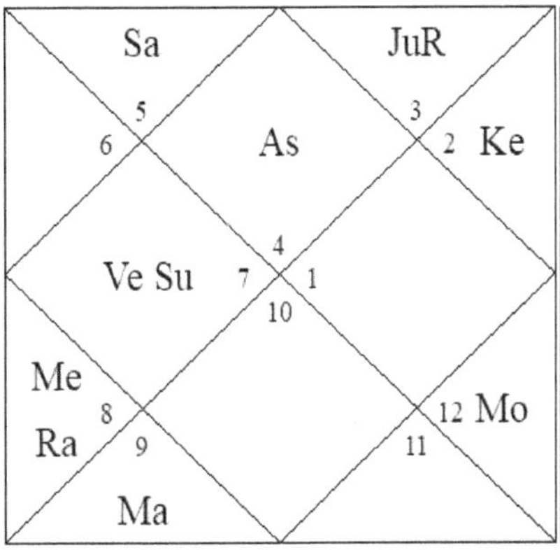

Birth Chart

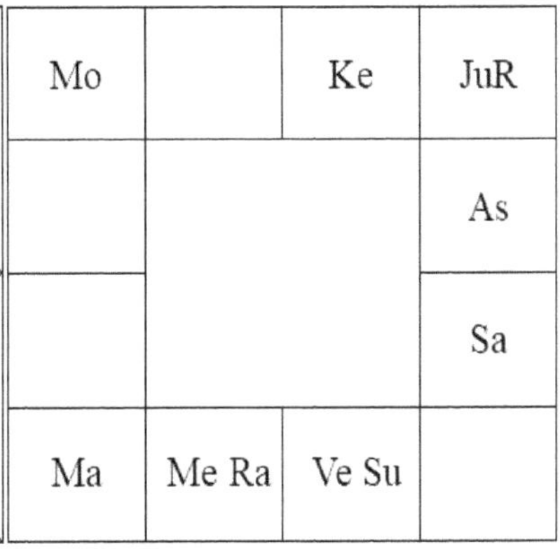

Birth Nakshtra Revati

Dasa sequence

Yogini	Nakshtra	From	To
Ulka	Revati	15.11.1918	11.2.1922
Siddha	Rohini	11.2.1922	11.2.1929
Sankata	Mrigshira	11.2.1929	11.2.1937
Mangla	Ardra	11.2.1937	11.2.1938
Pingla	Punarvasu	11.2.1938	11.2.1940
Dhanya	Pushya	11.2.1940	11.2.1943
Bharamari	Ashlesha	11.2.1943	11.2.1947
Bhadrika	Magha	11.2.1947	11.2.1952
Ulka	P. Phalguni	11.2.1952	11.2.1958
Siddha	U. Phalguni	11.2.1958	11.2.1965
Sankata	Hasta	11.2.1965	11.2.1973
Mangla	Chitra	11.2.1973	11.2.1974
Pingla	Swati	11.2.1974	11.2.1976
Dhanya	Visakha	11.2.1976	11.2.1979

Progress chart for Dhanya/ Vishakha and Libra lagan

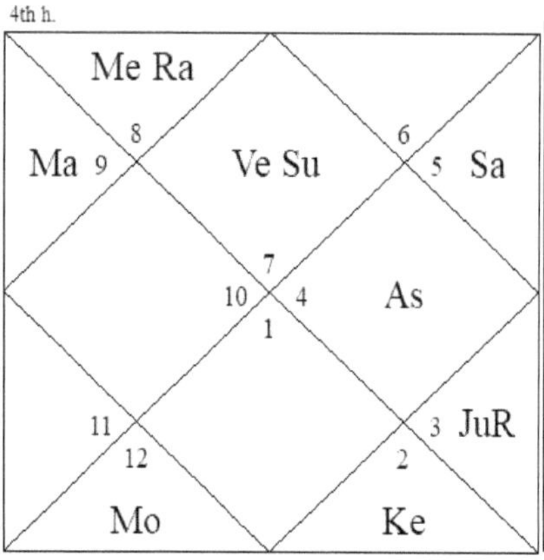

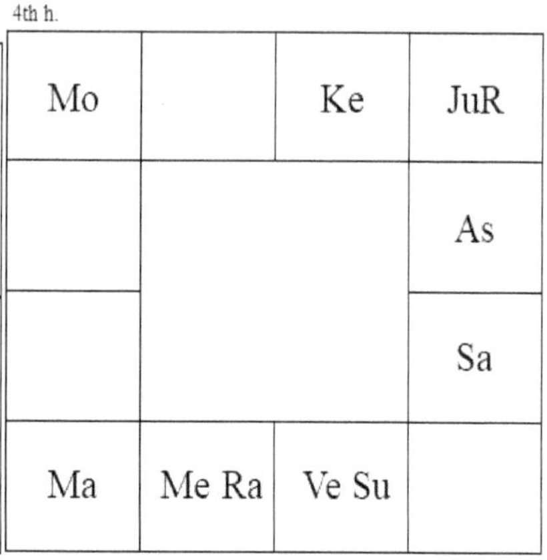

Birth lagna goes to tenth house. Jupiter is in ninth houseaspected by birth tenth lord. The progress tenth lord is also aspected by birth tenth lord. Mars aspected tenth house also.

He was appointed Chief Election Commissioner in Dhanya/ Ulka on 17 June, 1977. The approval came in Dhanya / Bhramari.

Example Death DOB 27 September 1917 TOB 01.38.32 POB Kolkata

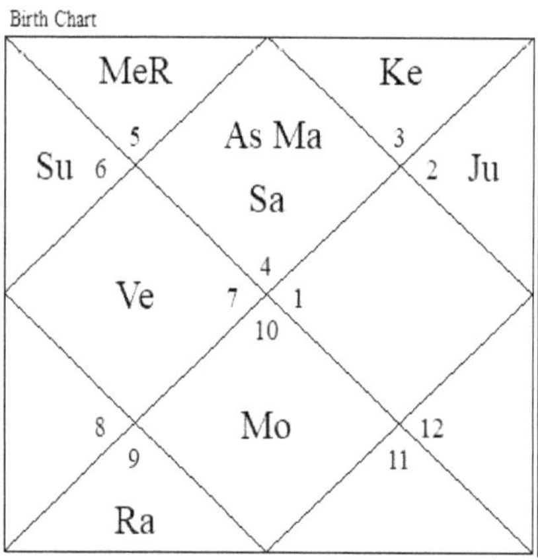

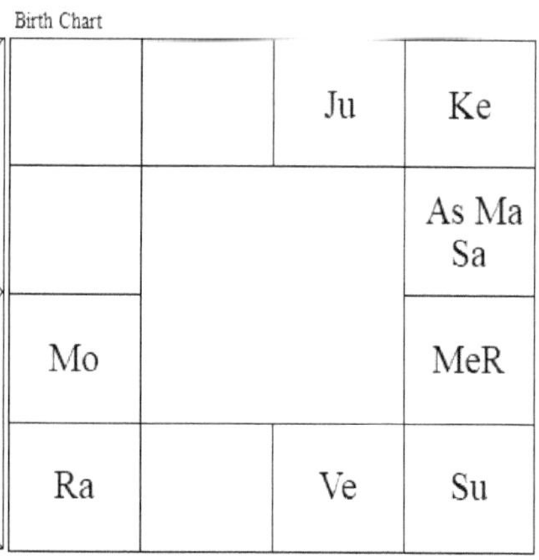

Birth Nakshtra Shravan

She was a great singer and died in October 1993.

Dasa sequence

Yogini	Nakshtra	From	To
Mangla	Shravan	27. 9.1917	9.6.1918
Pingla	Dhanishta	9.6.1918	9.6.1920
Dhanya	Shatbhisaj	9.6.1920	9.6.1923
Bharamari	P. Bhadrapad	9.6.1923	9.6.1927
Bhadrika	U. Bhadrapad	9.6.1927	9.6.1932
Ulka	Revati	9.6.1932	9.6.1938
Siddha	Rohini	9.6.1938	9.6.1945
Sankata	Mrigshira	9.6.1945	9.6.1953
Mangla	Ardra	9.6.1953	9.6.1954
Pingla	Punarvasu	9.6.1954	9.6.1956
Dhanya	Pushya	9.6.1956	9.6.1959
Bharamari	Ashlesha	9.6.1959	9.6.1963
Bhadrika	Magha	9.6.1963	9.6.1968
Ulka	P. Phalguni	9.6.1968	9.6.1974
Siddha	U. Phalguni	9.6.1974	9.6.1981
Sankata	Hasta	9.6.1981	9.6.1989
Mangla	Chitra	9.6.1989	9.6.1990
Pingla	Swati	9.6.1990	9.6.1992
Dhanya	Visakha	9.6.1992	9.6.1995

Progress chart for Dhanya/ Vishakha and Libra lagan

4th h.

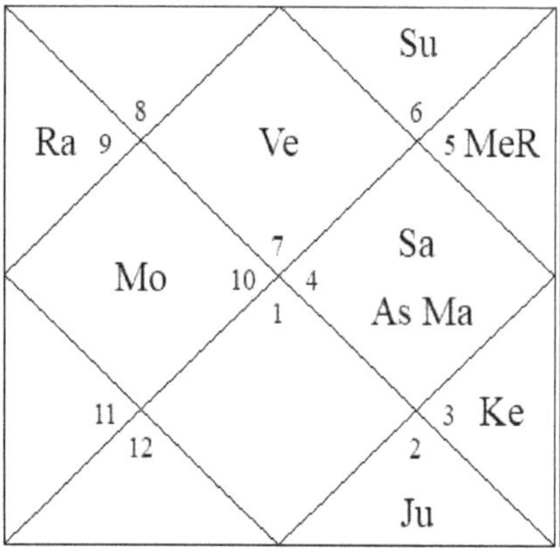

4th h.

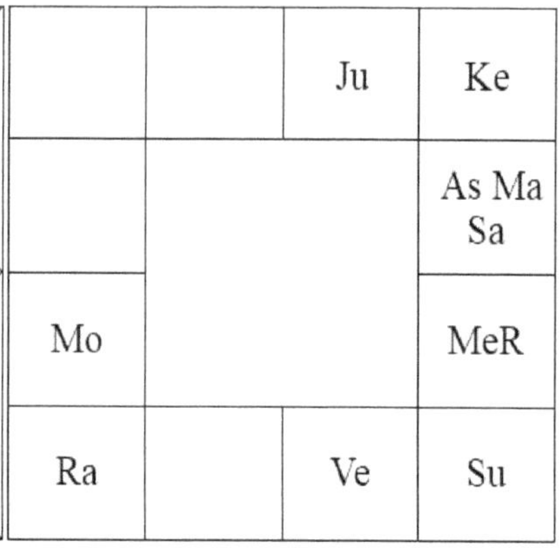

Jupiter is in eighth house of progress lagna. Saturn is themaraca of birth chart and Mars is the maraca of progress chart.Both are placed in tenth house. The end came in Dhanya / Ulka.

Example Job Started DOB 30 July 1957 TOB 14.39 POB Chamoli

Birth Chart

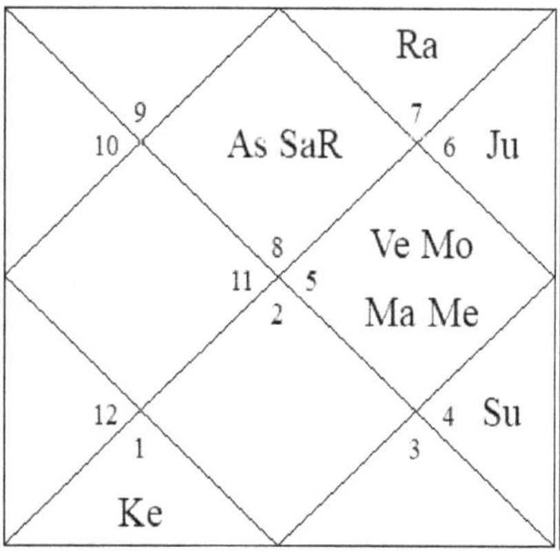

Birth Chart

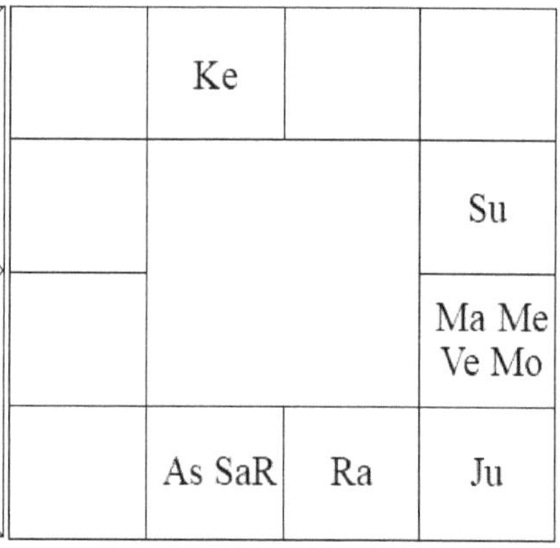

Birth Nakshtra U. Phalguni

He started his job on 28 August 1976 in the sub period of Sankata.

Dasa sequence

Yogini	Nakshtra	From	To
Siddha	U. Phalguni	30.7.1957	13.7.1963
Sankata	Hasta	13.7.1963	13.7.1971
Mangla	Chitra	13.7.1971	13.7.1972
Pingla	Swati	13.7.1972	13.7.1974
Dhanya	Visakha	13.7.1974	13.7.1977

Dhanya started on 13 July 1974. For first two years and three month the progress lagna is Libra. It will change to Scorpioon 13 Oct, 1976.

Progress chart for Dhanya/ Vishakha and Scorpio lagan is same as birth chart.

Jupiter is in eleventh house and aspecting its own sign in fifth house. Birth tenth lord is in progress ninth house. Tenth and ninth lords of progress chart have exchanged places and makes a Raj Yoga. Start of professional career is seen.

Example Marriage DOB 20 August 1944 TOB 8.10.59 POB Mumbai

Birth Chart

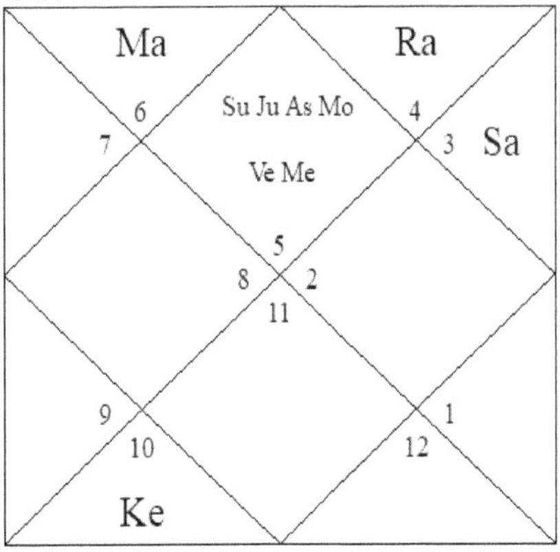

Birth Chart

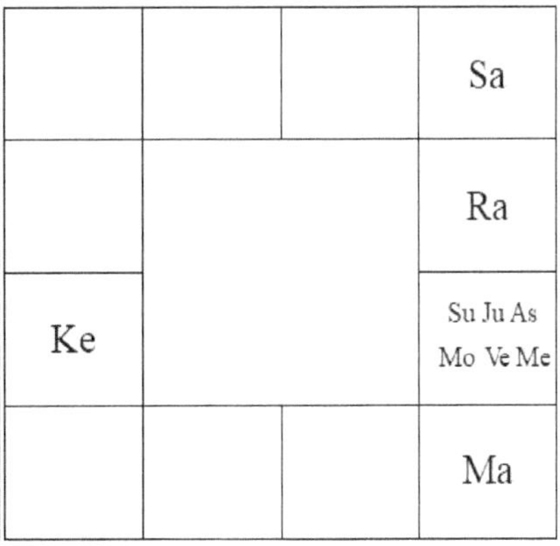

Birth Nakshtra P. Phalguni

He married Antonio Maino in 1968. The progress lagna was Libra.

Dasa sequence

Yogini	Nakshtra	From	To
Ulka	P. Phalguni	20.8.1944	1.12.1948
Siddha	U. Phalguni	1.12.1948	1.12.1955
Sankata	Hasta	1.12.1955	1.12.1963
Mangla	Chitra	1.12.1963	1.12.1964
Pingla	Swati	1.12.1964	1.12.1966
Dhanya	Visakha	1.12.1966	1.12.1969

Progress chart for Dhanya/ Vishakha and Libra lagan

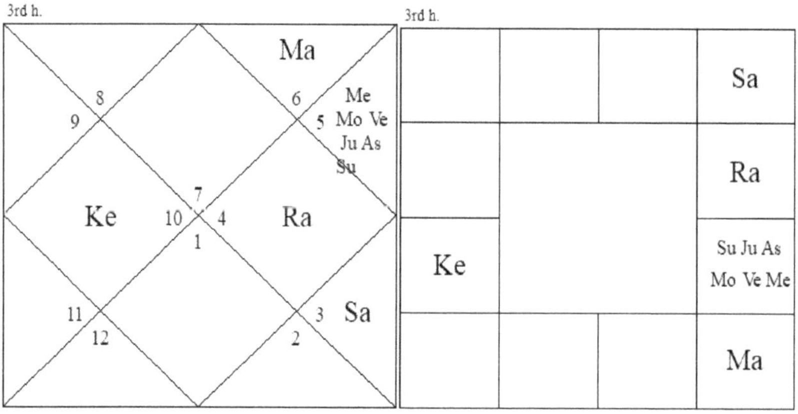

Jupiter is the birth fifth and eighth lord. It is aspected bythe birth seventh lord Saturn. The conjunction of three beneficswith this Jupiter promised love marriage.

Seventh house of progress chart is aspected by progressseventh Lord. In April, 1968 the Sub was of Mars.

The marriage took place in Dhanya / Ulka / Bhramari.

Example Childbirth DOB 21 April 1926 TOB 2.48.40 POB London

Birth Chart

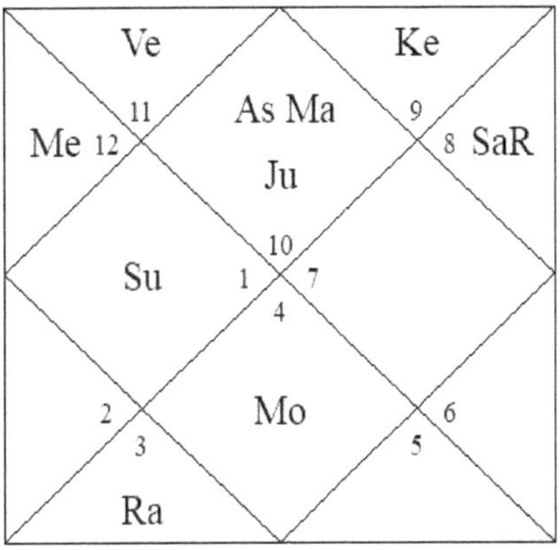

Birth Chart

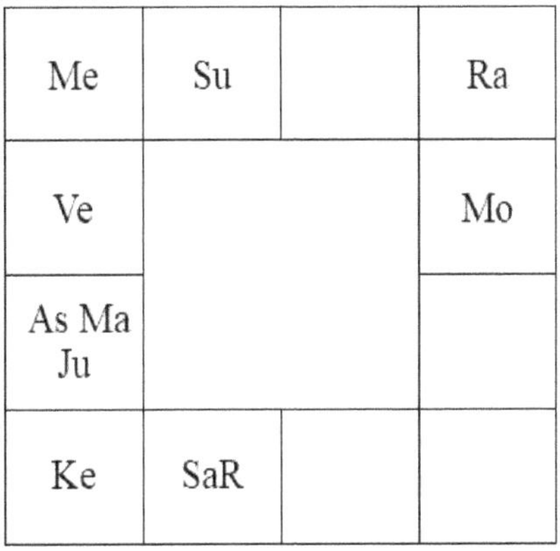

Birth Nakshtra Ashlesha

Dasa sequence

Yogini	Nakshtra	From	To
Bharamari	Ashlesha	21.4.1926	29.6.1929
Bhadrika	Magha	29.6.1929	29.6.1934
Ulka	P. Phalguni	29.6.1934	29.6.1940
Siddha	U. Phalguni	29.6.1940	29.6.1947
Sankata	Hasta	29.6.1947	29.6.1955
Mangla	Chitra	29.6.1955	29.6.1956
Pingla	Swati	29.6.1956	29.6.1958
Dhanya	Visakha	29.6.1958	29.6.1961

Prince Andrew, Duke of York was born on 19 February 1960.

Progress chart for Dhanya/ Vishakha and Libra lagan.

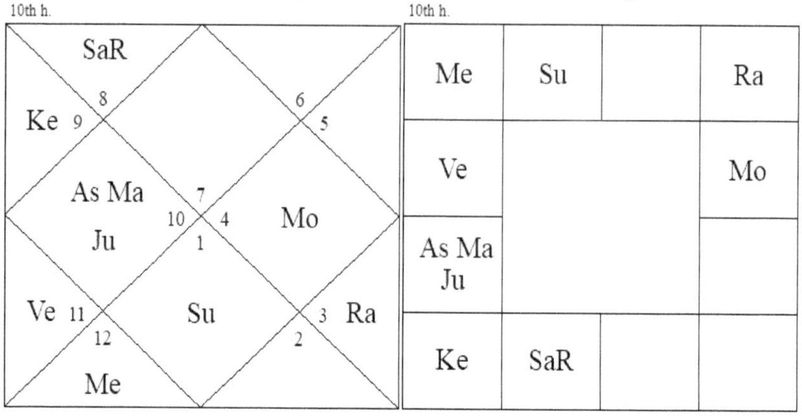

In birth chart Jupiter is in Lagna with exalted Mars and aspected by Moon.

In the progress chart the lord of fifth house of birth chartis in fifth house of progress chart. Jupiter is Karaka of children.The sub period is of Venus.

Dhanya / Shatbhisaj

The progress Lagna is Aquarius. Rahu is the Progress Nakshtra lord. Placement of Rahu is important and also the progresschart with Aquarius lagna.

For Aquarius lagna Venus is Yoga karaka. Jupiter is the lord of second and eleventh house. Its relation with Venus, Saturn or Mercury gives Dhana and Raj yoga in their periods.

Mercury is eighth lord of progress chart also. His relation with lords of trik house lords of birth chart can give problems like accidents etc.

Example Corona DOB 15 August 1947 TOB 0.0 POB Delhi

Birth Chart

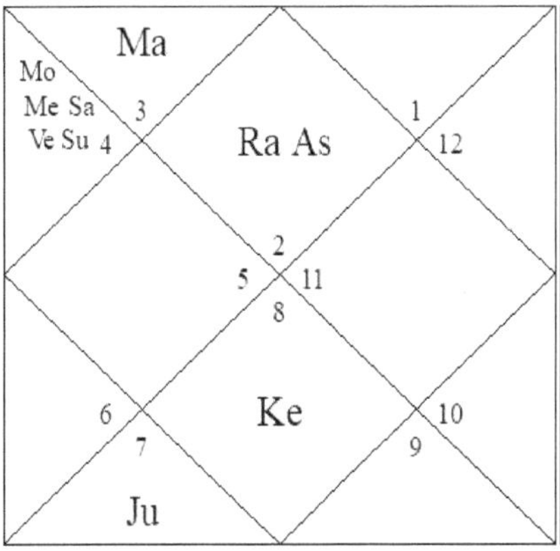

Birth Chart

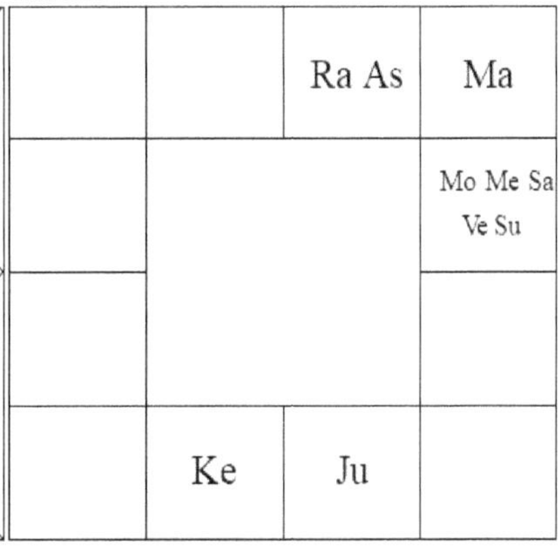

Birth Nakshtra Pushya

Dasa sequence

Yogini	Nakshtra	From	To
Dhanya	Pushya	15.8.1947	22.6.1950
Bharamari	Ashlesha	22.6.1950	22.6.1954
Bhadrika	Magha	22.6.1954	22.6.1959
Ulka	P. Phalguni	22.6.1959	22.6.1965
Siddha	U. Phalguni	22.6.1965	22.6.1972
Sankata	Hasta	22.6.1972	22.6.1980
Mangla	Chitra	22.6.1980	22.6.1981
Pingla	Swati	22.6.1981	22.6.1983
Dhanya	Visakha	22.6.1983	22.6.1986
Bharamari	Anuradha	22.6.1986	22.6.1990
Bhadrika	Jyeshtha	22.6.1990	22.6.1995
Ulka	Moola	22.6.1995	22.6.2001
Siddha	P. Ashadha	22.6.2001	22.6.2008

Yogini	Nakshtra	From	To
Sankata	U. Ashadha	22.6.2008	22.6.2016
Mangla	Shravan	22.6.2016	22.6.2017
Pingla	Dhanishta	22.6.2017	22.6.2019
Dhanya	Shatbhisaj	22.6.2019	22.6.2022

Progress chart for Dhanya/ Shatbhisaj and Aquarius lagan.

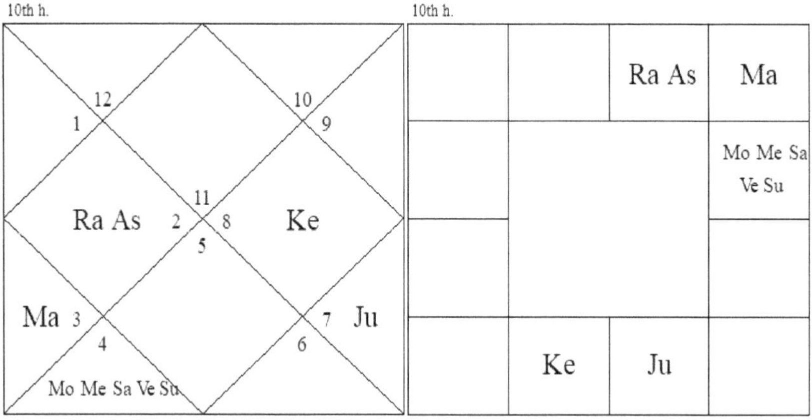

Rahu acts as Saturn and is placed in fourth house in birthchart.

In the progress chart, Rahu is placed in fourth house. Fourth house represent happiness of masses. Fourt lord is in sixth house with sixth lord and lagan lord. Serious accident or illness is indicated. First case of Corona was reported in March 2020 in India. The Corona epidemic ended with Dhanya dasa in June 2022.

India has faced three Dhanya dasa since independence. The first was in 1947 and the country was divided. Lakhs of people were displaced and were murdered. Second came in 1983 and India witnessed murder of Indira Gandhi and killing of thousands of Sikhs and unrest. The third brought Corona epidemic killing lakhs of people. Dhanya is an auspicious dasa in classics.

Example Bharat Ratan DOB 28 September 1929 TOB 22.39.59 POB Indore

Birth Chart

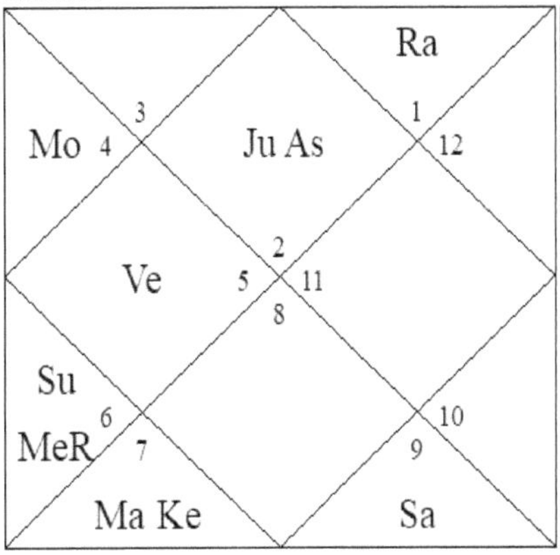

Birth Chart

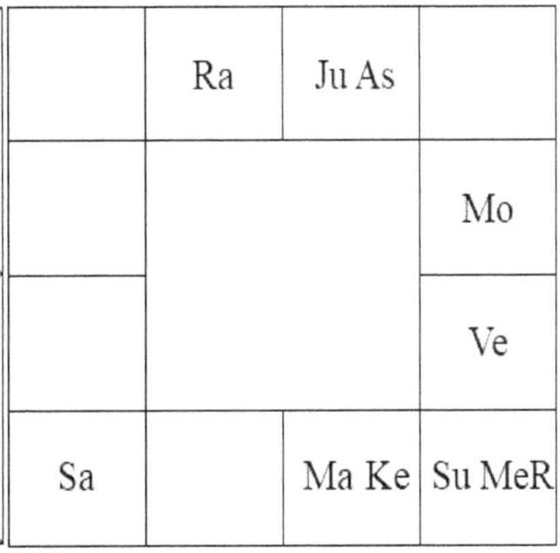

Birth Nakshtra Aslesha

Dasa sequence

Yogini	Nakshtra	From	To
Bharamari	Ashlesha	28.9.1929	14.8.1933
Bhadrika	Magha	14.8.1933	14.8.1938
Ulka	P. Phalguni	14.8.1938	14.8.1944
Siddha	U. Phalguni	14.8.1944	14.8.1951
Sankata	Hasta	14.8.1951	14.8.1959
Mangla	Chitra	14.8.1959	14.8.1960
Pingla	Swati	14.8.1960	14.8.1962
Dhanya	Visakha	14.8.1962	14.8.1965
Bharamari	Anuradha	14.8.1965	14.8.1969
Bhadrika	Jyeshtha	14.8.1969	14.8.1974
Ulka	Moola	14.8.1974	14.8.1980
Siddha	P. Ashadha	14.8.1980	14.8.1987

Yogini	Nakshtra	From	To
Sankata	U. Ashadha	14.8.1987	14.8.1995
Mangla	Shravan	14.8.1995	14.8.1996
Pingla	Dhanishta	14.8.1996	14.8.1998
Dhanya	Shatbhisaj	14.8.1998	14.8.2001

Progress chart for Dhanya/ Shatbhisaj and Aquarius lagan.

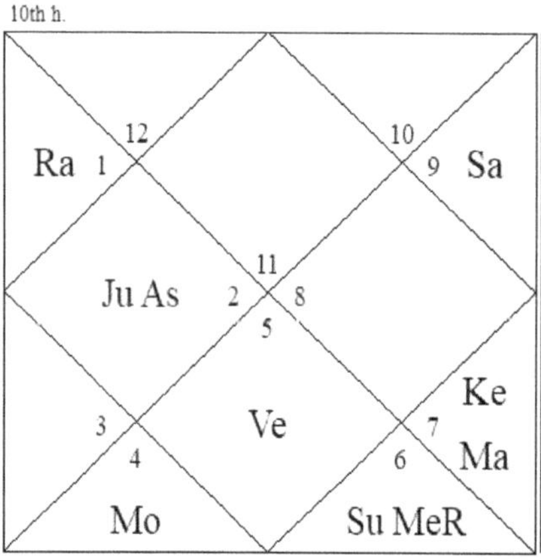

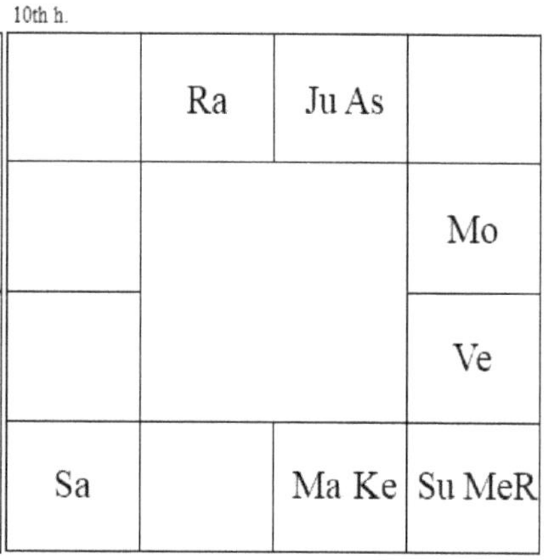

She was conferred the honor of Bharat Ratna in Jan. 2001.The dasha was Dhanya / Sankata. Sankata is the Nakshtra Lord. Tenth house of birth chart rises as Progress lagna. Lagnalord Saturn is aspecting lagna. Saturn is the birth tenth lord.

Mars is tenth lord of progress chart and aspects the Nakshtra lord. Progress lagna is aspected by yoga karaka Venus.

Can we see this event from regular Yogini Dasha? Jupiteris the dasha lord and is the eighth lord of birth chart. He is aspected by afflicted Mars from sixth house. Jupiter is not connected to tenth house.

Example Narrow Escape DOB 27 December 1965 TOB 8.04 POB Anakapalle AP

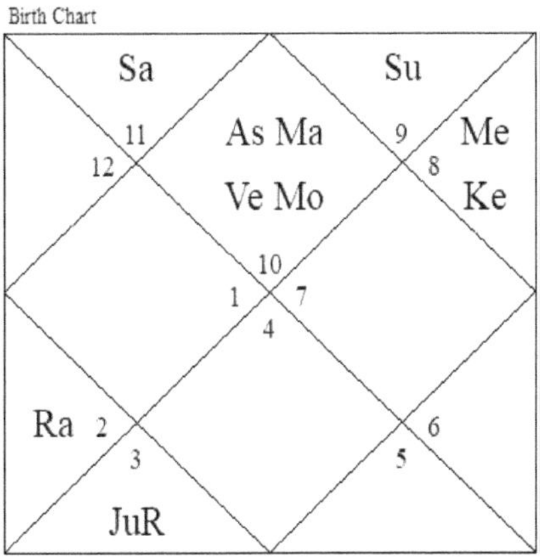

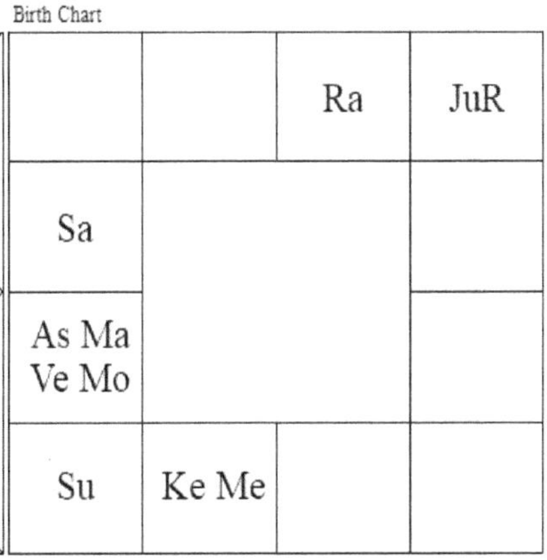

Birth Nakshtra Dhanishta

Dasa sequence

Yogini	Nakshtra	From	To
Pingla	Dhanishta	27.12.1965	26.3.1967
Dhanya	Shatbhisaj	26.3.1967	26.3.1970

Progress chart for Dhanya/ Shatbhisaj and Aquarius lagan.

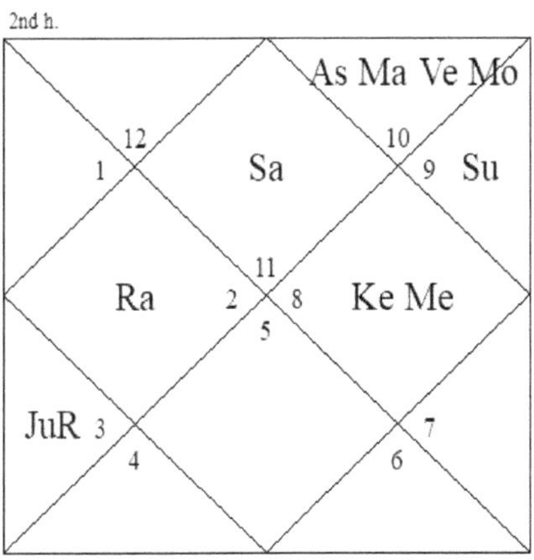

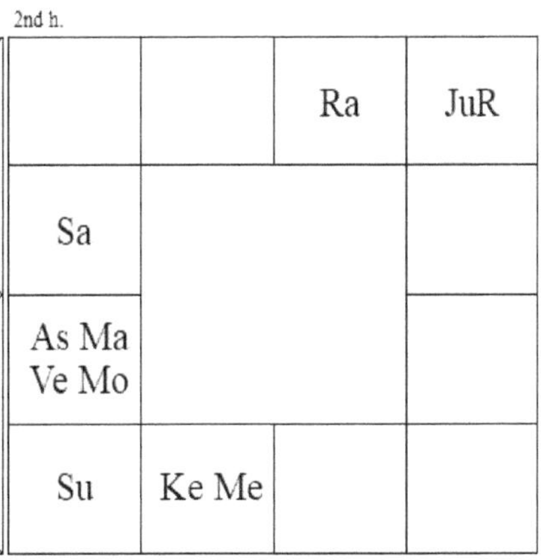

Rahu is aspected by sixth lord of birth chart i.e. Mercury. Mercury is the eighth lord of progress chart.

Thus, the Nakshtra Lord Rahu is connected with sixth lordof Birth Chart and eighth lord of progress chart.

The accident happens in Dhanya / Bhadrika in November1967.

Example Posting Abroad DOB 2 May 1972 TOB 2.45 POB Nagpur

Birth Chart

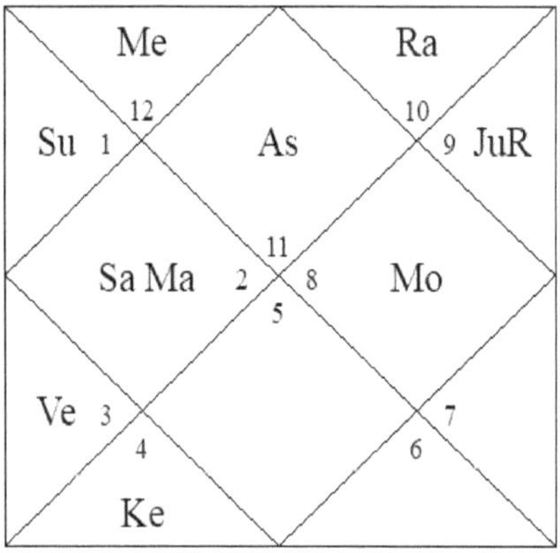

Birth Chart

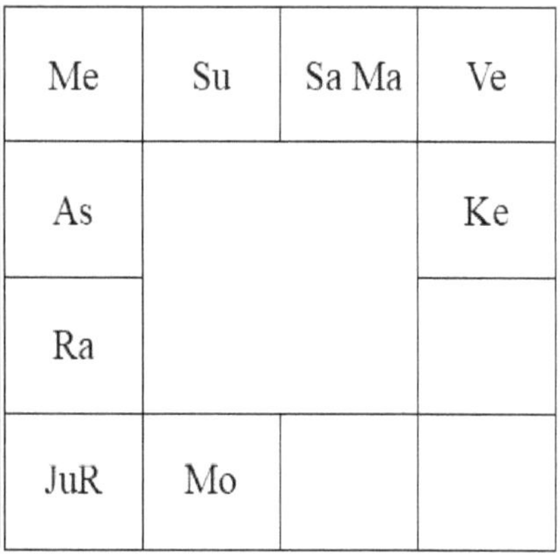

Birth Nakshtra Jyestha

Dasa sequence

Yogini	Nakshtra	From	To
Bhadrika	Jyeshtha	2.5.1972	9.4.1974
Ulka	Moola	9.4.1974	9.4.1980
Siddha	P. Ashadha	9.4.1980	9.4.1987
Sankata	U. Ashadha	9.4.1987	9.4.1995
Mangla	Shravan	9.4.1995	9.4.1996
Pingla	Dhanishta	9.4.1996	9.4.1998
Dhanya	Shatbhisaj	9.4.1998	9.4.2001

He was transferred to Hong Kong immediately after start of Dhanya on 9 April 1998. He joined in May 1998.

Progress chart for Dhanya/ Shatbhisaj and Aquarius lagan is same as birth chart.

The progress chart gives clear indication of change of residence. The Nakshtra lord is in twelfth house. He is in the sign of Saturn who is in fourth house with tenth lord and aspected by sixth lord. The shift is seen.

Example Higher Education DOB 30 April 1945 TOB 9.27 POB Delhi

Birth Chart

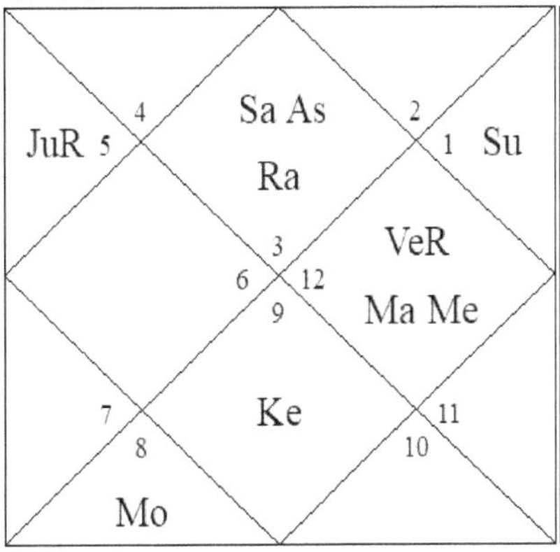

Birth Chart

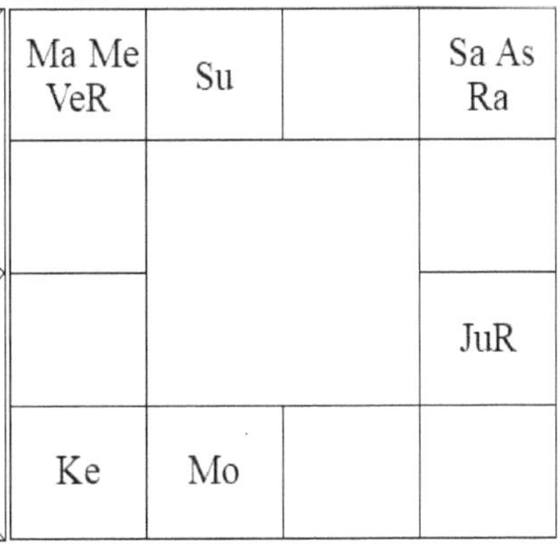

Birth Nakshtra Anuradha

Dasa sequence

Yogini	Nakshtra	From	To
Bharamari	Anuradha	30.4.1945	15.5.1945
Bhadrika	Jyeshtha	15.5.1945	15.5.1950
Ulka	Moola	15.5.1950	15.5.1956
Siddha	P. Ashadha	15.5.1956	15.5.1963
Sankata	U. Ashadha	15.5.1963	15.5.1971
Mangla	Shravan	15.5.1971	15.5.1972
Pingla	Dhanishta	15.5.1972	15.5.1974
Dhanya	Shatbhisaj	15.5.1974	15.5.1977

He was serving with MOD since 1969. He graduated in 1968. The MOD sent him to pursue higher studies to IIT Kharagpur in July 1975. This was a long gap to start education again. He was married and even with the family responsibilities, he completed the studies with distinction.

Progress chart for Dhanya/ Shatbhisaj and Aquarius lagan.

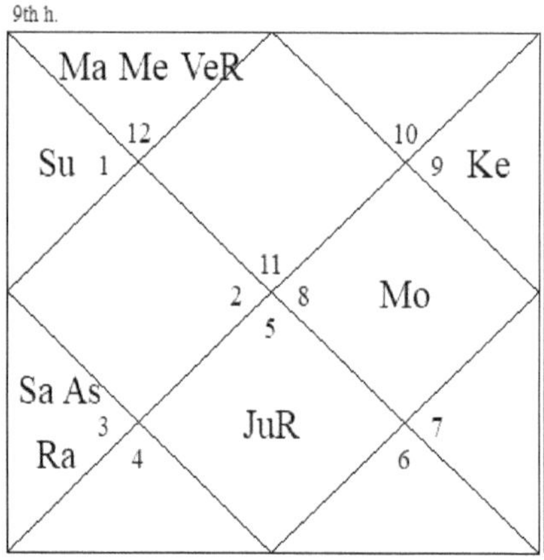

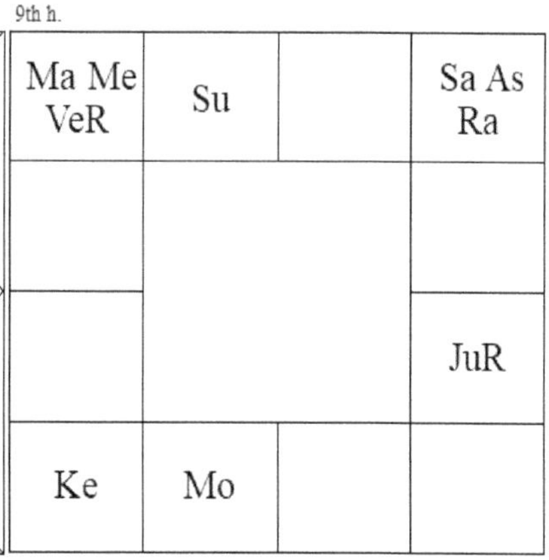

The progress lagna is the ninth house of birth chart. Rahu is now in fifth house with lagna lord and aspected by tenth lord Mars. The dasha period was Dhanya/Ulka. Saturn is infifth house.

As the fifth house is prominent during this dasha, daughterwas born in the same period on 14 Aug1975.

Can the normal interpretation of yogini lead us to this conclusion?

Chapter 6
Bhramari

Bhramari dasha is generated by four Nakshatras i.e. Ashwini Ashlesha, Anuradha and P. Bhadrapad.

Nakshtra	Nakshtra Lord	Sign	Remarks
Ashwini	Ketu	Aries	Progress Lagna is Aries
Ashlesha	Mercury	Cancer	Progress lagna is Cancer
Anuradha	Saturn	Scorpio	Progress Lagna is Scorpio
P. Bhadrapad	Jupiter	Aquarius / Pisces	For first three years progress Lagna is Aquarius.For last one year progress lagna is Pisces.

Bhramari / Ashwini

The dasha can only be operative in the first four years periodof birth. In this system of progress yogini, we jump to Rohiniafter Revati Nakshtra.

During infancy we can only see the health, death or the problems to parents and shift of residence. This is a period generally said to be related to the past karma of mother.

We cannot find many examples for this dasha. Twoexamples are taken from Astro data Bank.

Example Adoption DOB 10 January 1946 TOB 18.17 POB Los Angeles

Birth Chart

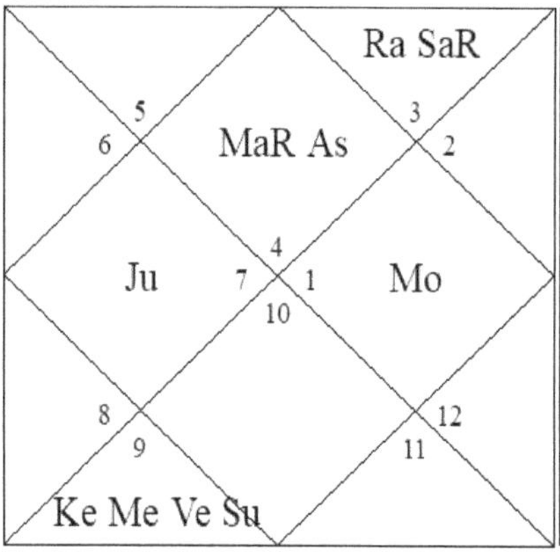

Birth Chart

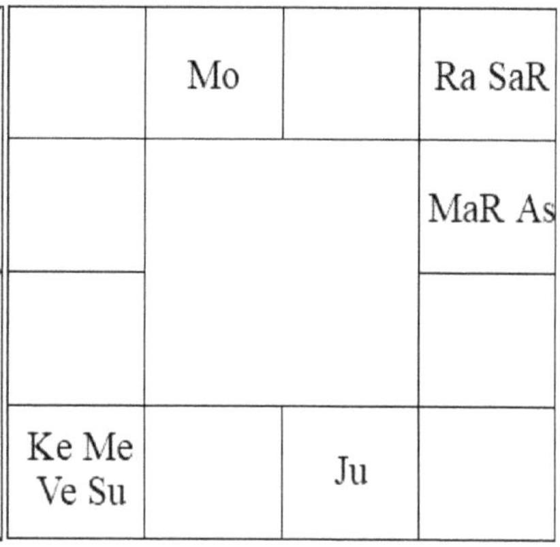

Birth Nakshatra Ashwini

In the birth chart, the ninth house is aspected by retrogradeeighth lord Saturn. The ninth lord is in eighth from ninth and aspected by retrograde debilitated Mars.

Dasa sequence

Dasa at birth is Bhramari/ Ashwini and will last till 4 December 1949.

Progress chart for Bhramari/ Ashwini and Aries lagan.

10th h.

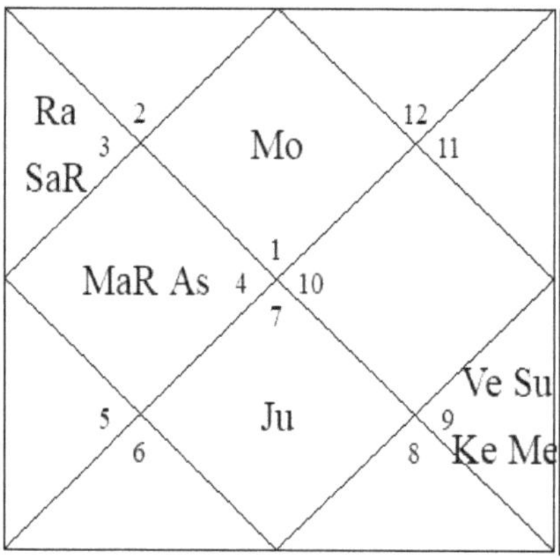

10th h.

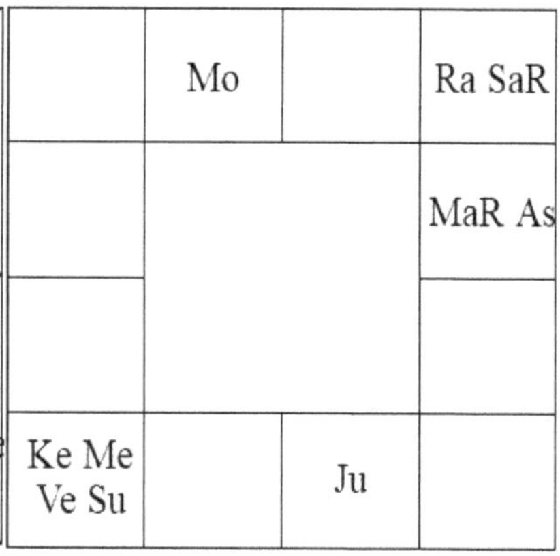

The progress chart gives confirmation to this effect. Ninthhouse is again afflicted in Rahu / Ketu axis and aspected by Saturn. Jupiter is aspected by Mars who is again eighth lord. Mars is now lagna lord also and ensure life to father. He was adopted and moved out of home.

Example Infant Mortality DOB 10 March 1932 TOB 18.25 POB 79W43, 41N38

Birth Chart

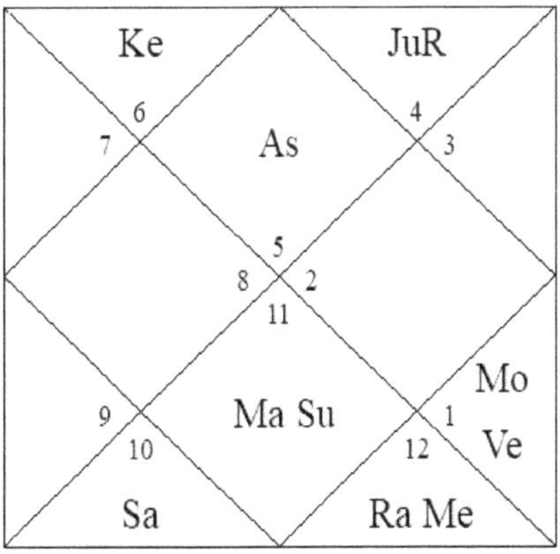

Birth Chart

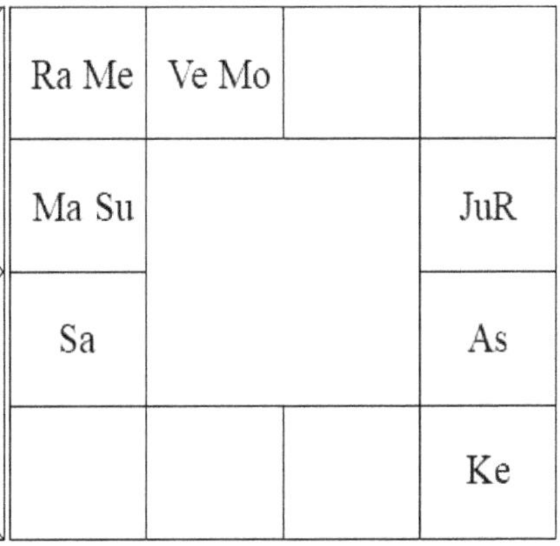

Birth Nakshatra Ashwini

Progress chart for Bhramari/ Ashwini and Aries lagan.

9th h.

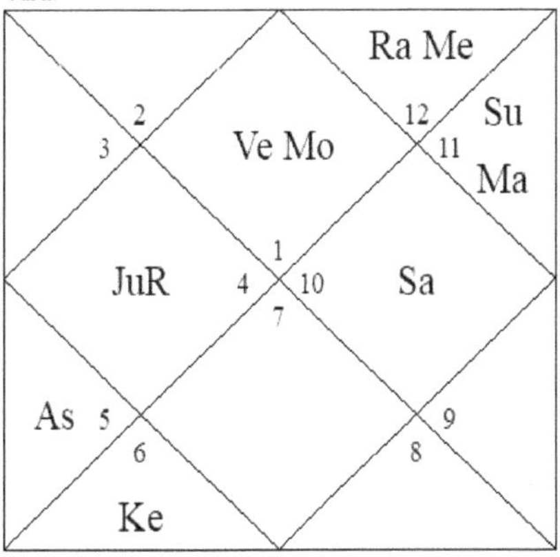

9th h.

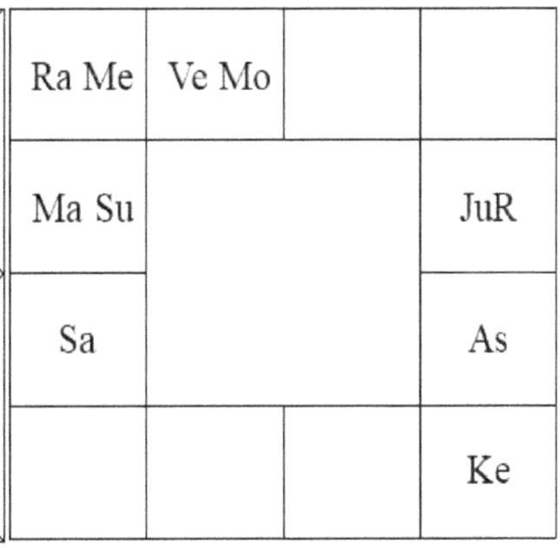

Let us first examine birth chart for longevity. The eight house is with Rahu and aspected by Saturn. The aspect of Jupiteron his own sign should be the saving factor. The dasha at birthwas Ketu. Both maracas are connected with eighth house. Lagnais aspected by its lord and yoga karaka Mars. The lagna is strong.

Dasa sequence

Dasa at birth is Bhramari/ Ashwini and will last till 19 February 1935.

In the progress chart, the eighth house is vacant. Now wesee lagna. Venus is the maraca now and is placed in lagna. TheNakshtra lord Ketu is in sixth house of illness. He developed Pneumonia and died on 17 Jan 1933. The sub period was Rahu.

Since Ketu do not have any dasha period in Yogini, we can take Rahu in its place.

Bhramari / Ashlesha

Mercury is the Nakshtra lord and cancer is the progress lagna. Mars is the yoga karaka for progress chart. Saturn is lordof seventh and eighth house. Generally good results will be experienced during this dasha period.

Example Death of Father DOB 19 November 1917 TOB 23.11 POB Allahabad

Birth Chart

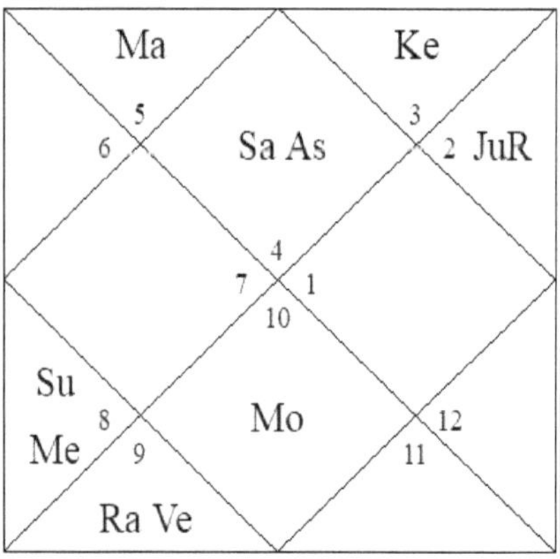

Birth Chart

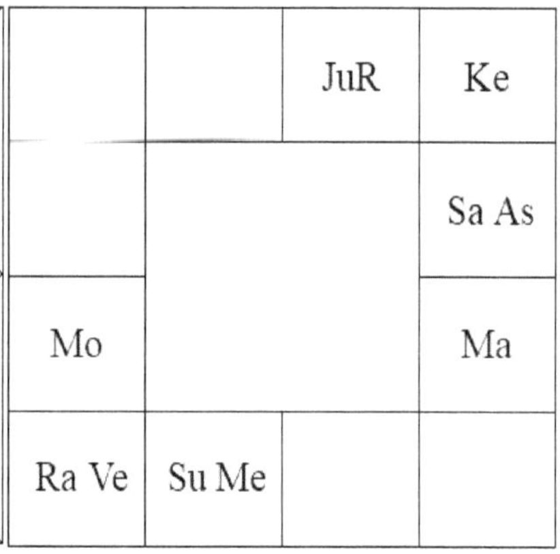

Birth Nakshatra U. Ashadha

Dasa sequence

Yogini	Nakshatra	From	To
Sankata	U. Ashadha	19.11.1917	13.7.1920
Mangla	Shravan	13.7.1920	13.7.1921
Pingla	Dhanishta	13.7.1921	13.7.1923
Dhanya	Shatbhisaj	13.7.1923	13.7.1926
Bharamari	P. Bhadrapad	13.7.1926	13.7.1930
Bhadrika	U. Bhadrapad	13.7.1930	13.7.1935
Ulka	Revati	13.7.1935	13.7.1941
Siddha	Rohini	13.7.1941	13.7.1948
Sankata	Mrigshira	13.7.1948	13.7.1956
Mangla	Ardra	13.7.1956	13.7.1957
Pingla	Punarvasu	13.7.1957	13.7.1959
Dhanya	Pushya	13.7.1959	13.7.1962
Bharamari	Ashlesha	13.7.1962	13.7.1966

Her father expired on 27 May 1964 and she became Prime Minister of India on 24 Jan. 1966. All happened in Bhramari / Ashlesha.

Mercury is Nakshtra lord and is aspected by ninth and tenth lord in birth chart. Ninth lord is retrograde.

Progress chart for Bhramari/ Ashlesha and Cancer lagan is same as birth chart.

For father Mars and Mercury are maracas. Venus is the third and eighth lord. Both dasha and Nakshtra are maracas for father. Venus is afflicted in sixth house. Father died in the subperiod of Venus after illness.

Mercury has to give the result of ninth and tenth also. Therelation of ninth and tenth have forced him to give Yoga karaka results which happened in sub period of Sun who is conjoined with Mercury and is having aspects of Jupiter and Mars. Sun is in exchange with Mars the tenth lord.

She became Prime Minister in Bhramari / Pingla.

Example Prime Minister DOB 17 April 1916 TOB 15.35.30 POB Colombo

Birth Chart

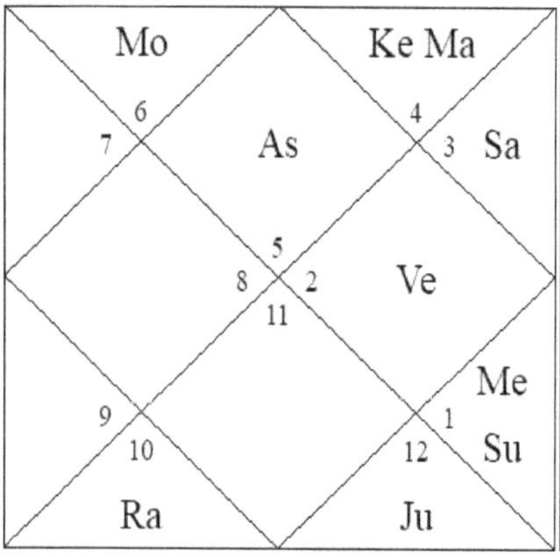

Birth Chart

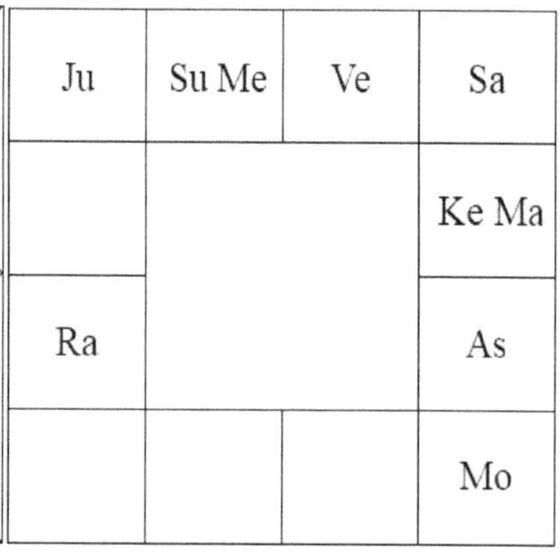

Birth Nakshatra Chitra

She was elected Prime Minister of Colombo for third timeafter a long gap. She took over on14 Nov 1994. The dasha was

Bhramari / Bhadrika.

Dasa sequence

Yogini	Nakshatra	From	To
Mangla	Chitra	17.4.1916	29.3.1917
Pingla	Swati	29.3.1917	29.3.1919
Dhanya	Visakha	29.3.1919	29.3.1922
Bharamari	Anuradha	29.3.1922	29.3.1926
Bhadrika	Jyeshtha	29.3.1926	29.3.1931
Ulka	Moola	29.3.1931	29.3.1937

Yogini	Nakshatra	From	To
Siddha	P. Ashadha	29.3.1937	29.3.1944
Sankata	U. Ashadha	29.3.1944	29.3.1952
Mangla	Shravan	29.3.1952	29.3.1953
Pingla	Dhanishta	29.3.1953	29.3.1955
Dhanya	Shatbhisaj	29.3.1955	29.3.1958
Bharamari	P. Bhadrapad	29.3.1958	29.3.1962
Bhadrika	U. Bhadrapad	29.3.1962	29.3.1967
Ulka	Revati	29.3.1967	29.3.1973
Siddha	Rohini	29.3.1973	29.3.1980
Sankata	Mrigshira	29.3.1980	29.3.1988
Mangla	Ardra	29.3.1988	29.3.1989
Pingla	Punarvasu	29.3.1989	29.3.1991
Dhanya	Pushya	29.3.1991	29.3.1994
Bharamari	Ashlesha	29.3.1994	29.3.1998

Progress chart for Bhramari/ Ashlesha and Cancer lagan.

12th h.

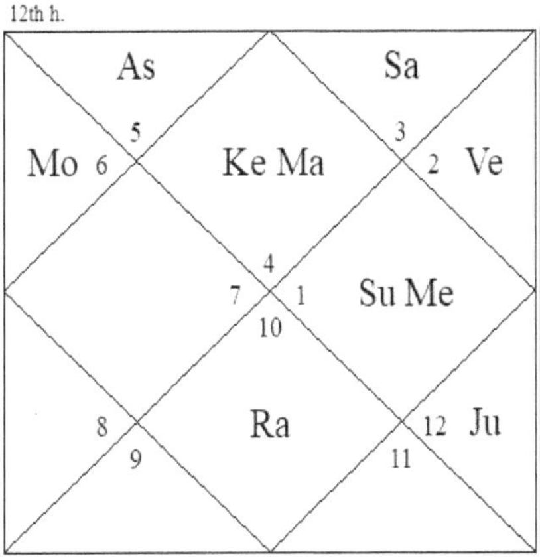

12th h.

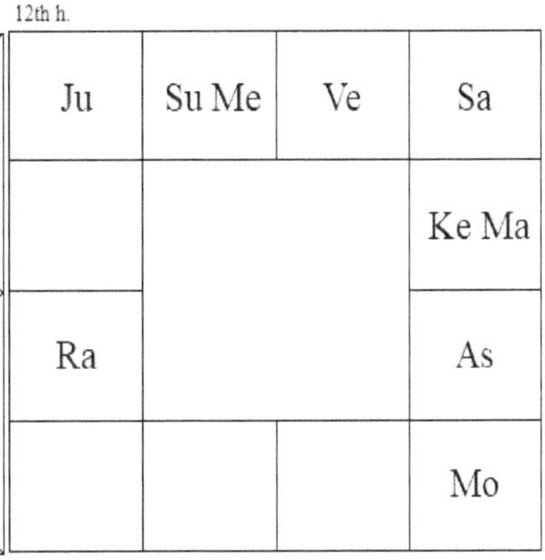

Mercury is in tenth house with exalted Sun. Sun is the lagna lord of birth chart. The tenth lord is in lagna and aspectedby ninth lord

Jupiter.

Regular analysis of Bhramari dasha gives no idea of this elevation. Mars is in twelfth house and afflicted by Ketu. The eighth lord Jupiter aspects Mars which is good for politicians.

Example Brain Cancer DOB 6 December 1965 TOB 9.40 POB Delhi

Birth Chart

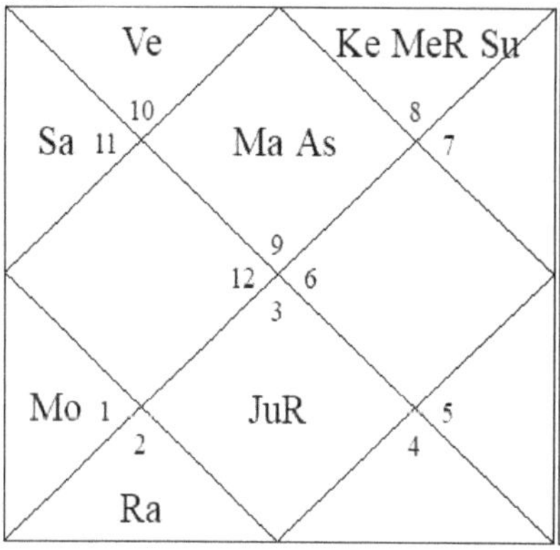

Birth Chart

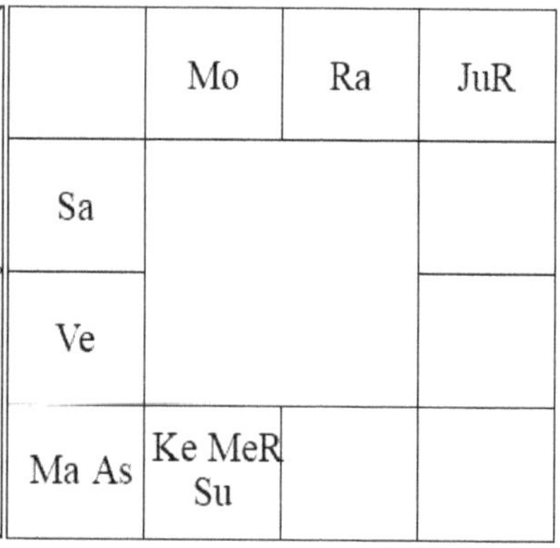

Birth Nakshatra Bharani

Dasa sequence

Yogini	Nakshatra	From	To
Bhadrika	Bharani	6.12.1965	23.4.1969
Ulka	Kritika	23.4.1969	23.4.1975
Siddha	Rohini	23.4.1975	23.4.1982
Sankata	Mrigshira	23.4.1982	23.4.1990
Mangla	Ardra	23.4.1990	23.4.1991
Pingla	Punarvasu	23.4.1991	23.4.1993
Dhanya	Pushya	23.4.1993	23.4.1996
Bharamari	Ashlesha	23.4.1996	23.4.2000

Progress chart for Bhramari/ Ashlesha and Cancer lagan

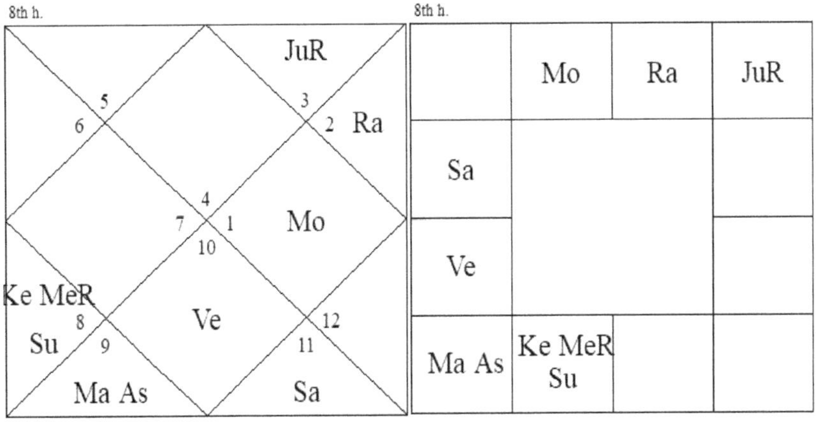

He died on the operation table during the brain surgery.
Dasha was Bhramari / Bhadrika.

A very clear picture of this unfortunate event is seen in progress chart.

Mercury and Saturn are maracas of birth chart. This dashabelongs to Mercury.

In the progress chart Saturn and Sun are the maracas. Mercury is with Ketu. Sun joins it and Saturn aspects it from eighth house. All the maracas are influencing Mercury who is the Nakshtra lord. The end came in Mercury sub period.

Example Hanged to death DOB 28 April 1937 TOB 8.11.45 POB Tikrit

Birth Chart

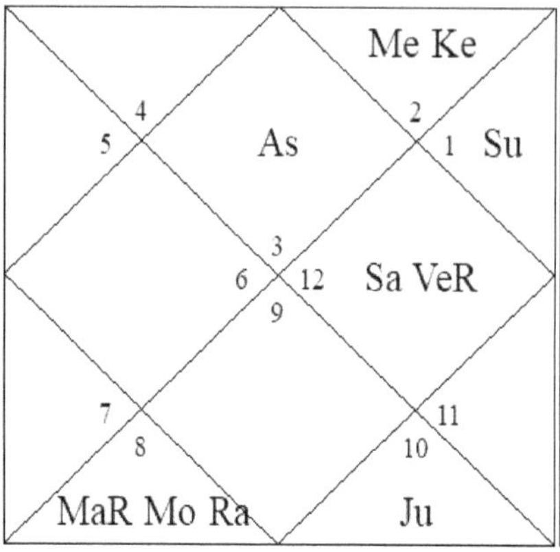

Birth Chart

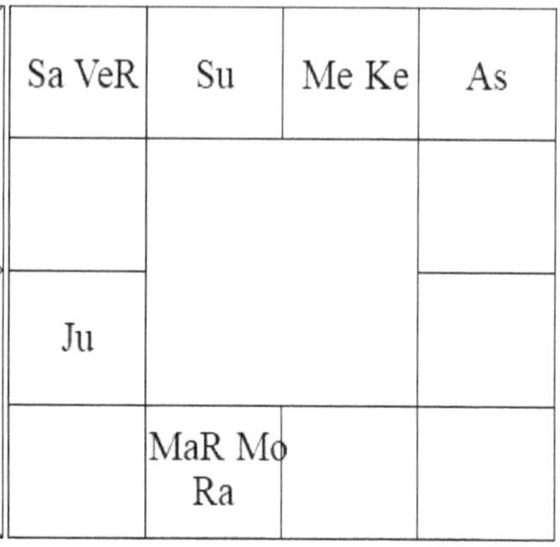

Birth Nakshatra Anuradha

Dasa sequence

Yogini	Nakshatra	From	To
Bharamari	Anuradha	28.4.1937	31.7.1938
Bhadrika	Jyeshtha	31.7.1938	31.7.1943
Ulka	Moola	31.7.1943	31.7.1949
Siddha	P. Ashadha	31.7.1949	31.7.1956
Sankata	U. Ashadha	31.7.1956	31.7.1964
Mangla	Shravan	31.7.1964	31.7.1965
Pingla	Dhanishta	31.7.1965	31.7.1967
Dhanya	Shatbhisaj	31.7.1967	31.7.1970
Bharamari	P. Bhadrapad	31.7.1970	31.7.1974
Bhadrika	U. Bhadrapad	31.7.1974	31.7.1979
Ulka	Revati	31.7.1979	31.7.1985

Yogini	Nakshatra	From	To
Siddha	Rohini	31.7.1985	31.7.1992
Sankata	Mrigshira	31.7.1992	31.7.2000
Mangla	Ardra	31.7.2000	31.7.2001
Pingla	Punarvasu	31.7.2001	31.7.2003
Dhanya	Pushya	31.7.2003	31.7.2006
Bharamari	Ashlesha	31.7.2006	31.7.2010

He was hanged to death on 30 December, 2006 in the dasha of Bhramari / Bhramari.

Progress chart for Bhramari/ Ashlesha and Cancer lagan.

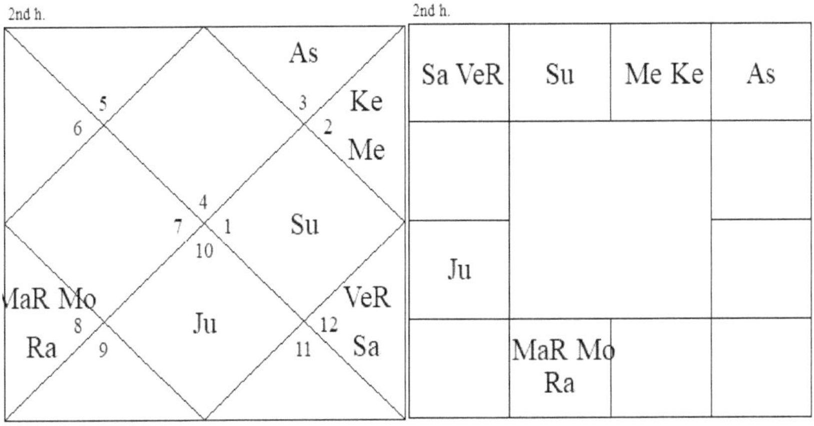

A freighting situation emerges. Moon and Jupiter are maracain the birth chart. In the progress chart Sun and Saturn are maraca. Saturn is more serious planet.

Mercury is the progress, Nakshtra. It is with Ketu and aspected by Mars and Saturn. Jupiter is aspecting lagna. The Nakshtra lord is badly afflicted by the maracas.

Mars is the participating planet with Nakshtra lord. The end came in Mars period.

Bhramari / Anuradha

The progress lagna is Scorpio and the Nakshtra lord is Saturn.

Sun and Moon are the lords of tenth and ninth house of progress chart. Their relation gives good yoga. Also, Saturn andJupiter are fourth and fifth lord.

Mercury is the malefic planet and its relation with a planetcan be harmful to the effects of the planet and more so if Saturnis also related.

Example Empress DOB 24 May 1819 TOB 2.26.54 POB London

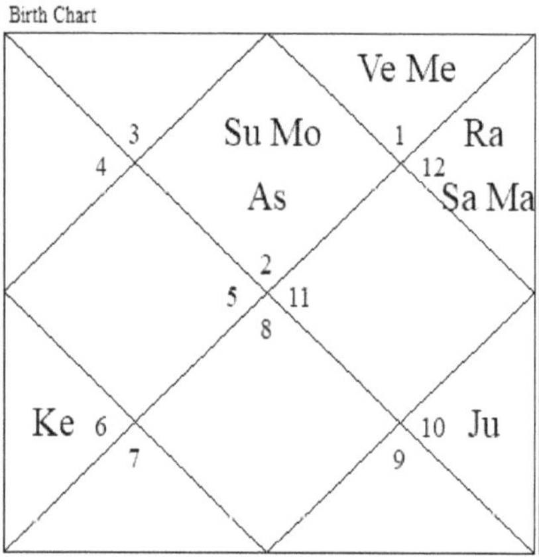

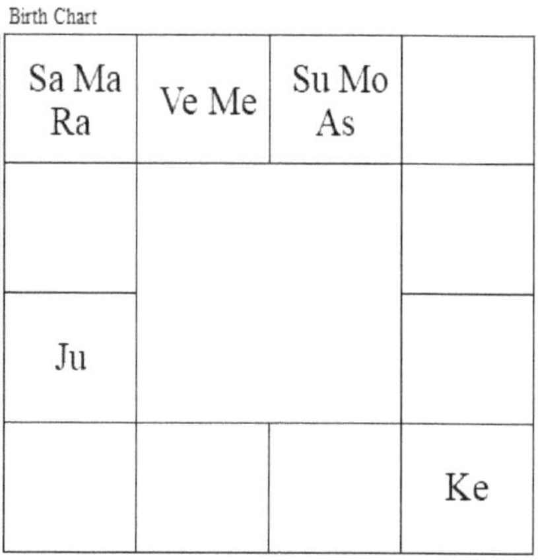

Birth Nakshatra Rohini

Yogini	Nakshatra	From	To
Siddha	Rohini	24.5.1819	27.2.1825
Sankata	Mrigshira	27.2.1825	27.2.1833
Mangla	Ardra	27.2.1833	27.2.1834
Pingla	Punarvasu	27.2.1834	27.2.1836
Dhanya	Pushya	27.2.1836	27.2.1839
Bharamari	Ashlesha	27.2.1839	27.2.1843

Yogini	Nakshatra	From	To
Bhadrika	Magha	27.2.1843	27.2.1848
Ulka	P. Phalguni	27.2.1848	27.2.1854
Siddha	U. Phalguni	27.2.1854	27.2.1861
Sankata	Hasta	27.2.1861	27.2.1869
Mangla	Chitra	27.2.1869	27.2.1870
Pingla	Swati	27.2.1870	27.2.1872
Dhanya	Visakha	27.2.1872	27.2.1875
Bharamari	Anuradha	27.2.1875	27.2.1879

She started using the title of Empress of India from 1 May 1876. It was a feather in her crown.

Progress chart for Bhramari/ Anuradha and Scorpio lagan.

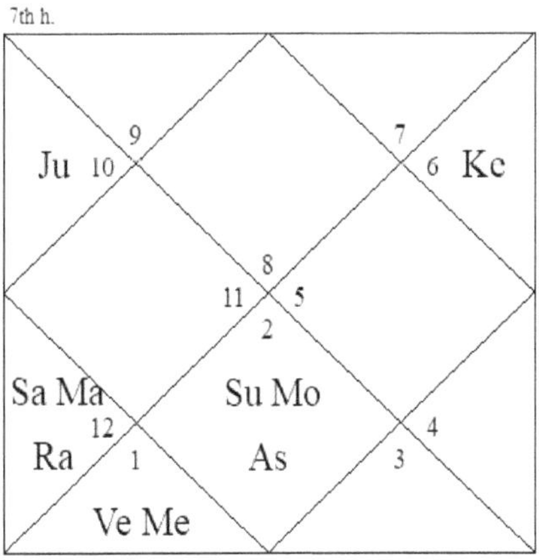

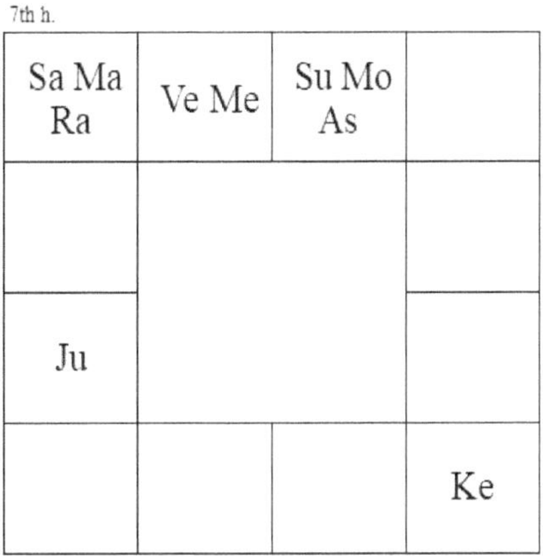

Sun and Moon are in seventh house. The lords of ninthand tenth house are conjoined.

Nakshtra lord Saturn is the ninth and tenth lord of birthchart. Saturn aspects Sun and Moon. It is with Mars.

The Antar Dasha was of Nakshtra lord Saturn. Third andfifth lords are in exchange of sign. It was a calculated move.

Example Death of father DOB 30 August 1927 TOB 7.16 POB Bulandshahar

Birth Chart

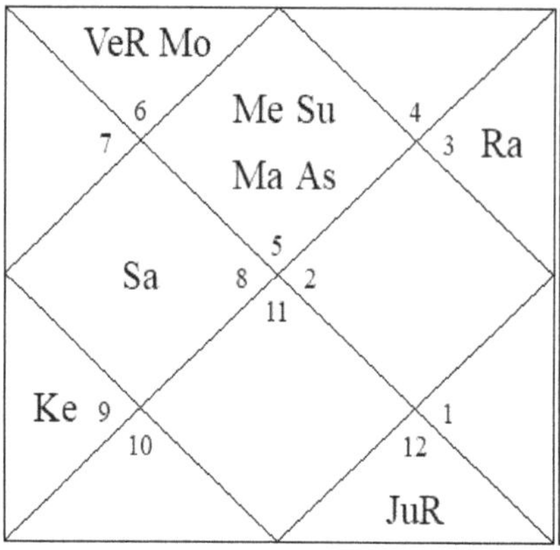

Birth Chart

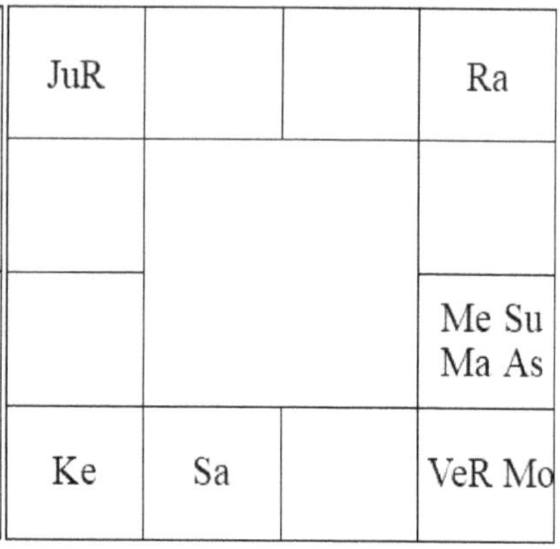

Birth Nakshatra Hasta

Dasa sequence

Yogini	Nakshatra	From	To
Sankata	Hasta	30.8.1927	4.4.1933
Mangla	Chitra	4.4.1933	4.4.1934
Pingla	Swati	4.4.1934	4.4.1936
Dhanya	Visakha	4.4.1936	4.4.1939
Bharamari	Anuradha	4.4.1939	4.4.1943

Progress chart for Bhramari/ Anuradha and Scorpio lagan.

4th h.

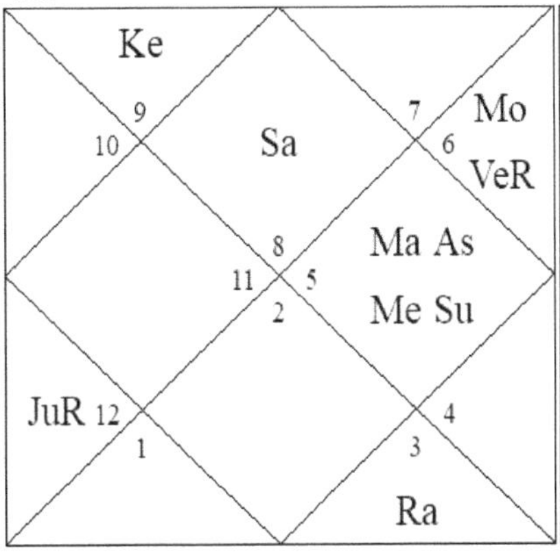

4th h.

JuR			Ra
			Me Su Ma As
Ke	Sa		VeR Mo

His father expired in Bhramari / Bhramari.

Saturn is in the eighth house from ninth house in the birthchart. Venus is the maraca of father in birth chart.

In the progress chart, Saturn, the Nakshtra lord is lord ofseventh and eighth house from ninth house. The birth maraca is with progress ninth lord. Saturn is aspecting Sun, Mars andMercury which are placed in tenth house i.e. maraca house forfather.

Thus, the maracas are influenced by Saturn.

Example Won Election DOB 13 October 1925 TOB 9.0 POB Grantham

Birth Chart

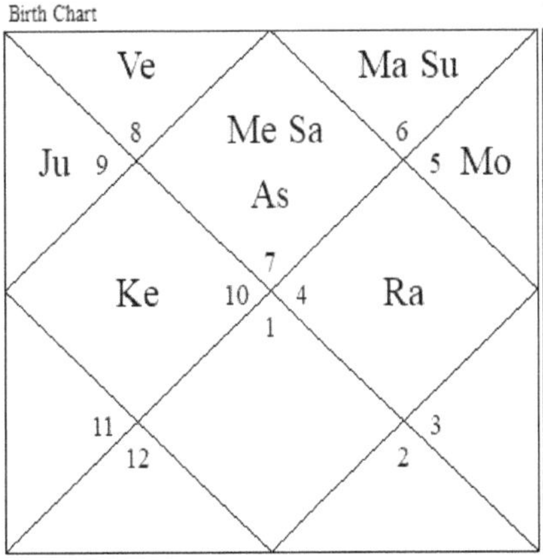

Birth Chart

			Ra
Ke			Mo
Ju	Ve	Me Sa As	Ma Su

Birth Nakshatra Magha

Progress chart for Bhramari/ Anuradha and Scorpio lagan.

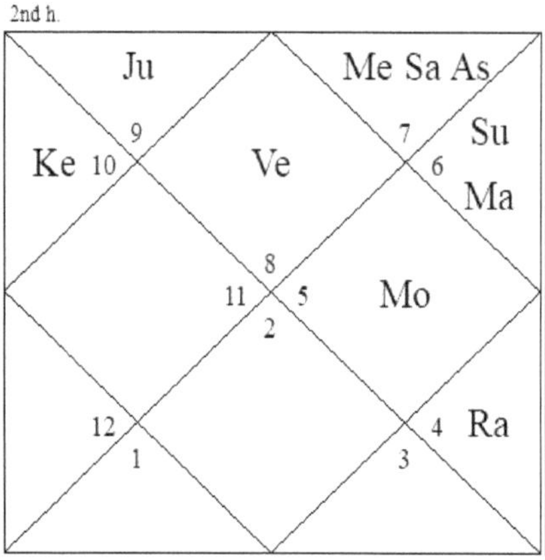

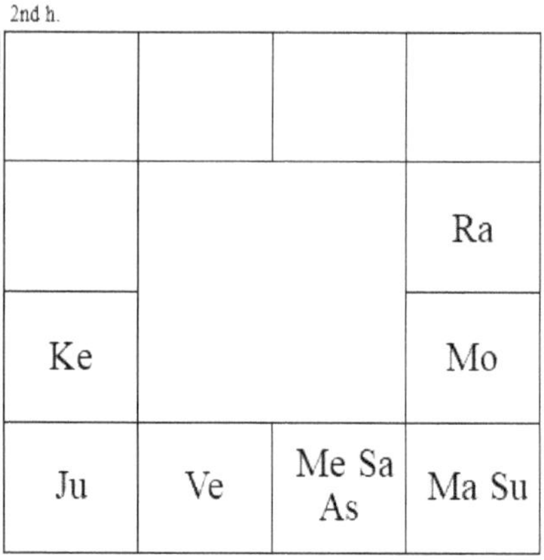

Dasa sequence

Yogini	Nakshatra	From	To
Bhadrika	Magha	13.10.1925	8.8.1928
Ulka	P. Phalguni	8.8.1928	8.8.1934
Siddha	U. Phalguni	8.8.1934	8.8.1941
Sankata	Hasta	8.8.1941	8.8.1949
Mangla	Chitra	8.8.1949	8.8.1950
Pingla	Swati	8.8.1950	8.8.1952
Dhanya	Visakha	8.8.1952	8.8.1955
Bharamari	Anuradha	8.8.1955	8.8.1959

She was elected MP for the first time in the general electionsheld on 8 Oct. 1959 after a big struggle.

Saturn is the yoga karaka of birth chart. It aspects the tenth house and is with ninth lord Mercury. Thus, Saturn is involved in Raj Yoga in birth chart.

In progress chart, ninth lord is in tenth an aspected by Jupiter. Seventh house is aspected by Venus.

She was elected in Bhadrika Sub. Mercury is involved in Yoga in birth chart and is eighth and eleventh lord of progress chart.

Example Birth of son DOB 27 November 1907 TOB 5.24.54 POB Allahabad

Birth Chart

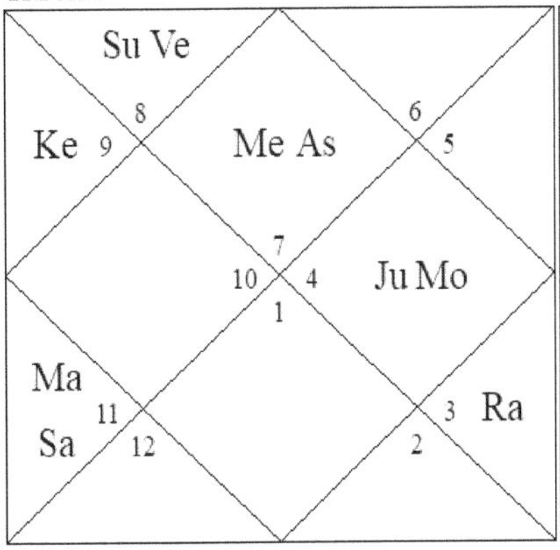

Birth Chart

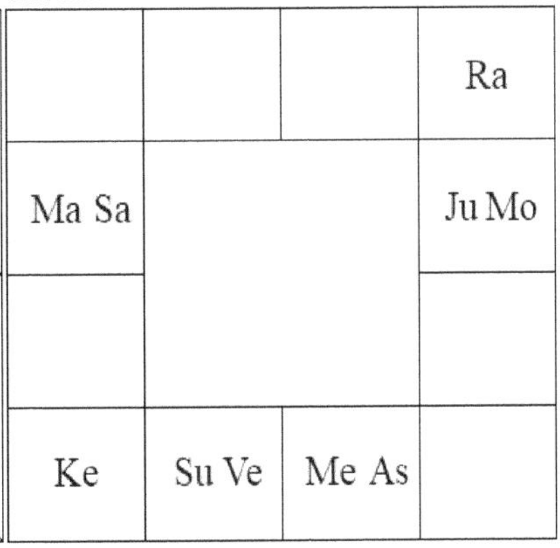

Birth Nakshatra Ashlesha

Dasa sequence

Yogini	Nakshatra	From	To
Bharamari	Ashlesha	27.11.1907	30.6.1908
Bhadrika	Magha	30.6.1908	30.6.1913
Ulka	P. Phalguni	30.6.1913	30.6.1919
Siddha	U. Phalguni	30.6.1919	30.6.1926
Sankata	Hasta	30.6.1926	30.6.1934
Mangla	Chitra	30.6.1934	30.6.1935
Pingla	Swati	30.6.1935	30.6.1937
Dhanya	Visakha	30.6.1937	30.6.1940
Bharamari	Anuradha	30.6.1940	30.6.1944

Progress chart for Bhramari/ Anuradha and Scorpio lagan.

2nd h.

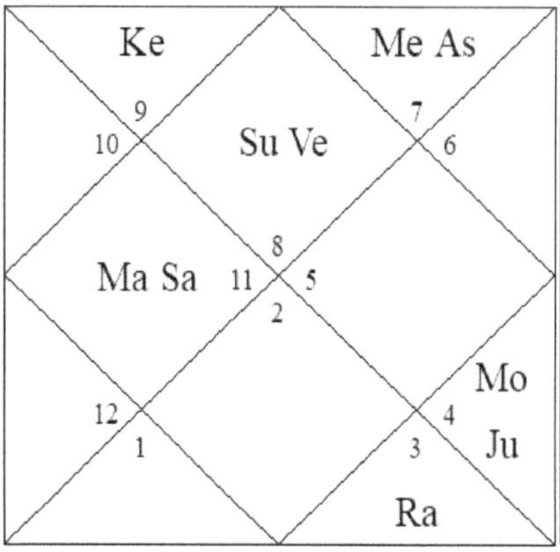

2nd h.

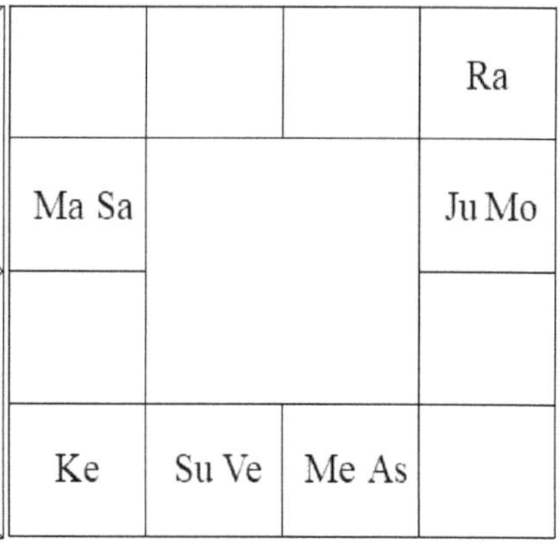

Saturn is the Yog Karak of birth Chart and is placed in fifthhouse.

The star lord is Saturn in the progress chart. It is aspectingVenus and Sun. Fifth Lord Jupiter is in Ninth house with ninthlord. The promise of fifth and fourth house are highlighted.

Amitabh was born in Bhramari / Siddha on 11 October 1942. Venus is aspectedby Saturn.

Example Marriage DOB 30 June 1960 TOB 6.57 POB Rohtak HR

Birth Chart

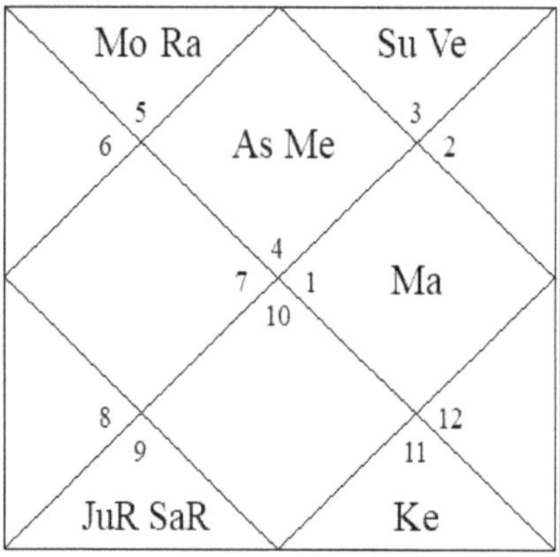

Birth Chart

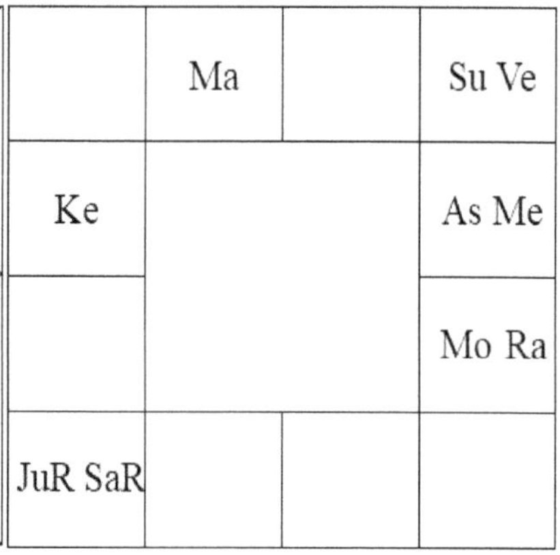

Birth Nakshatra P. Phalguni

Dasa sequence

Yogini	Nakshatra	From	To
Ulka	P. Phalguni	30.6.1960	16.5.1963
Siddha	U. Phalguni	16.5.1963	16.5.1970
Sankata	Hasta	16.5.1970	16.5.1978
Mangla	Chitra	16.5.1978	16.5.1979
Pingla	Swati	16.5.1979	16.5.1981
Dhanya	Visakha	16.5.1981	16.5.1984
Bharamari	Anuradha	16.5.1984	16.5.1988

Progress chart for Bhramari/ Anuradha and Scorpio lagan.

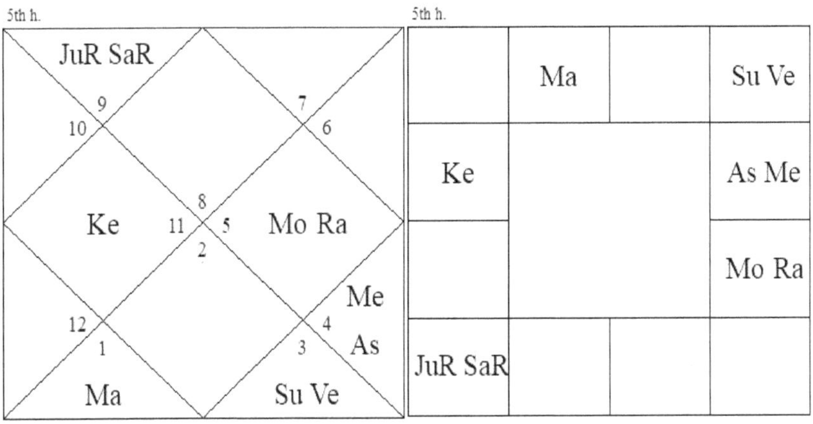

In the birth chart, Saturn is seventh lord and eighth lord. It is influencing Venus, Sun, Ketu and Mars. For Ketu we take Rahu or Sankata.

In the progress chart, seventh lord is Venus and is under the influence of Saturn. Now Saturn is placed in second housewhich is the secondary house for marriage.

The placement of Venus in eighth house is not good but itis with Sun. Rahu acts as Sun also. It was an inter caste marriage.

Example Business Expansion DOB 19 April 1964 TOB 10.25 POB Hoshiarpur

Birth Chart

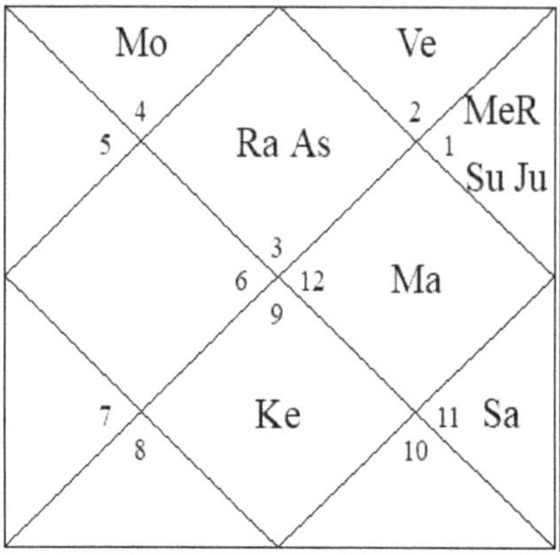

Birth Chart

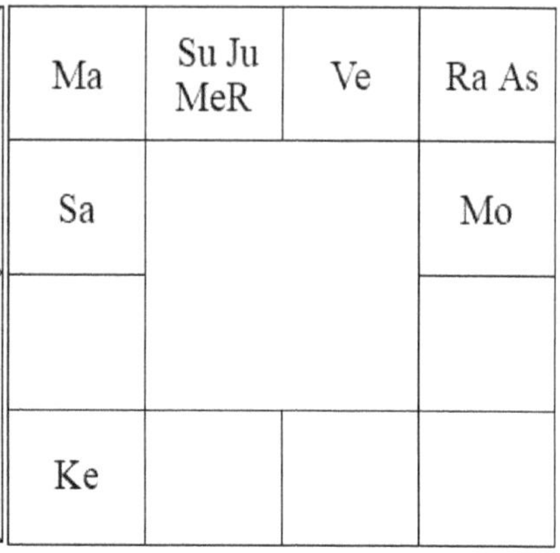

Birth Nakshatra Pushya

Dasa sequence

Yogini	Nakshatra	From	To
Dhanya	Pushya	19.4.1964	25.8.1966
Bharamari	Ashlesha	25.8.1966	25.8.1970
Bhadrika	Magha	25.8.1970	25.8.1975
Ulka	P. Phalguni	25.8.1975	25.8.1981
Siddha	U. Phalguni	25.8.1981	25.8.1988
Sankata	Hasta	25.8.1988	25.8.1996
Mangla	Chitra	25.8.1996	25.8.1997
Pingla	Swati	25.8.1997	25.8.1999
Dhanya	Visakha	25.8.1999	25.8.2002
Bharamari	Anuradha	25.8.2002	25.8.2006

Progress chart for Bhramari/ Anuradha and Scorpio lagan.

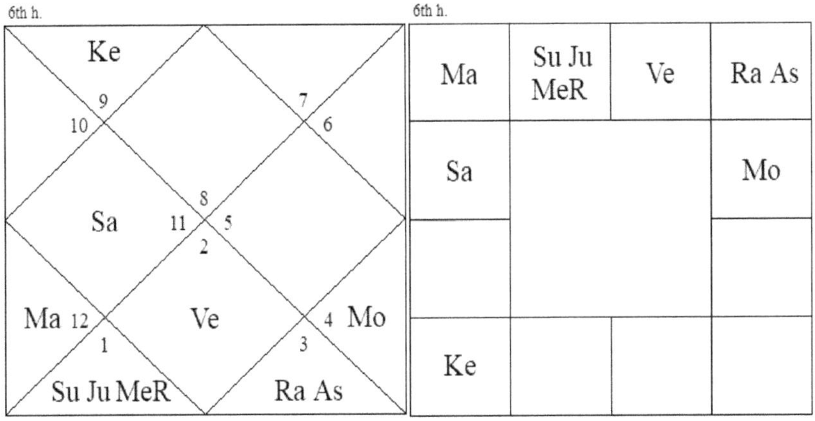

In birth chart Saturn is lord of eighth and ninth and placedin ninth house of Bhagya. It influences Mercury, Jupiter and Sun. Mars is in tenth house.

In the progress chart, Saturn is in fourth house and activatetenth house. Sun is the tenth lord and is under influence of Saturn.

He expanded his business in Jan. 2003 and started anotherfactory. Dasha was Bhramari / Bhramari.

Bhramari / P. Bhadrapad

The Nakshtra lord is Jupiter. The progress lagna is Aquarius and Pisces. For first three years the progress chart lagna will be Aquarius and for last one year it will be Pisces.

For Aquarius progress Lagna, Jupiter is the lord of eleventh and second house. A relation of Jupiter with trine lords of birth or progress chart will constitute a wealth giving yoga. With this progress lagna, Venus is yoga karaka. Relation of Venus with Jupiter give status and wealth. Saturn can add to the quantityand quality of this yoga. Sun and Moon are not good.

For Pisces lagna, Jupiter is the lagna and tenth lord. The personal and professional matters are highlighted. Venus is notfavorable and the signification of Venus suffers.

Example Death DOB 14 November 1889 TOB 23.05 POB Allahabad

Birth Chart

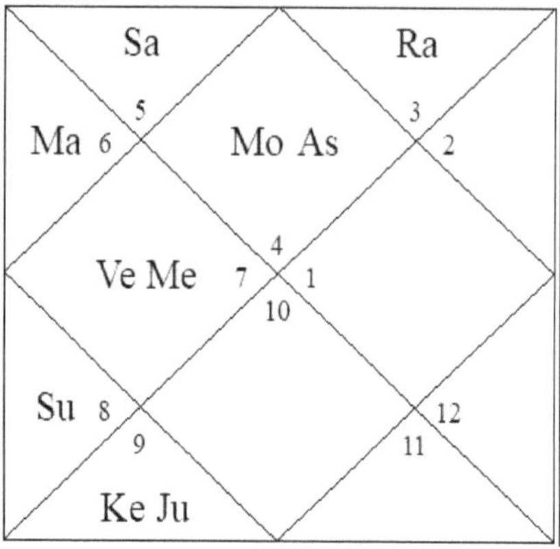

Birth Chart

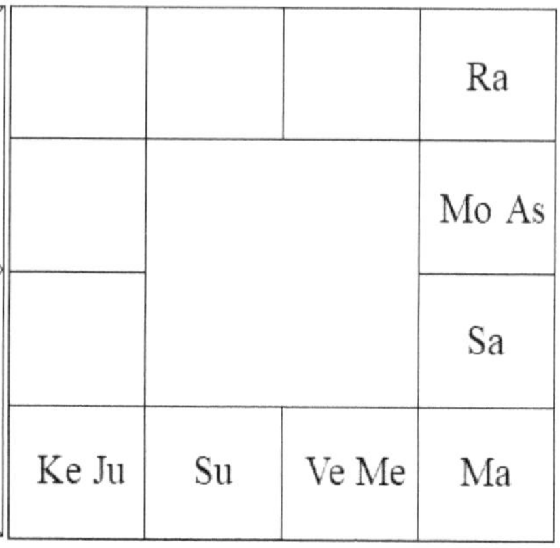

Birth Nakshatra Ashlesha

Dasa sequence

Yogini	Nakshatra	From	To
Bharamari	Ashlesha	14.11.1889	27.6.1893
Bhadrika	Magha	27.6.1893	27.6.1898
Ulka	P. Phalguni	27.6.1898	27.6.1904
Siddha	U. Phalguni	27.6.1904	27.6.1911
Sankata	Hasta	27.6.1911	27.6.1919
Mangla	Chitra	27.6.1919	27.6.1920
Pingla	Swati	27.6.1920	27.6.1922
Dhanya	Visakha	27.6.1922	27.6.1925
Bharamari	Anuradha	27.6.1925	27.6.1929
Bhadrika	Jyeshtha	27.6.1929	27.6.1934
Ulka	Moola	27.6.1934	27.6.1940
Siddha	P. Ashadha	27.6.1940	27.6.1947

Yogini	Nakshatra	From	To
Sankata	U. Ashadha	27.6.1947	27.6.1955
Mangla	Shravan	27.6.1955	27.6.1956
Pingla	Dhanishta	27.6.1956	27.6.1958
Dhanya	Shatbhisaj	27.6.1958	27.6.1961
Bharamari	P. Bhadrapad	27.6.1961	27.6.1965

Progress chart for Bhramari/ P. Bhadrapad and Aquarius lagan.

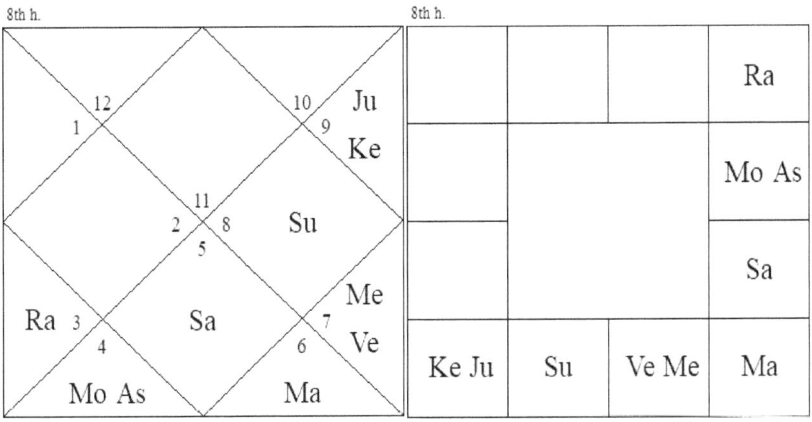

Jupiter is sixth lord in the birth chart and is placed in sixthhouse with Ketu.

This Jupiter in the progress chart is the second lord and isa maraca. Mars is aspecting Jupiter from eighth house.

Jupiter influences Rahu / Ketu and Saturn. The end camein sub period of Sankata.

Example Marriage DOB 1 February 1935 TOB 17.23 POB Birbhum

Birth Chart

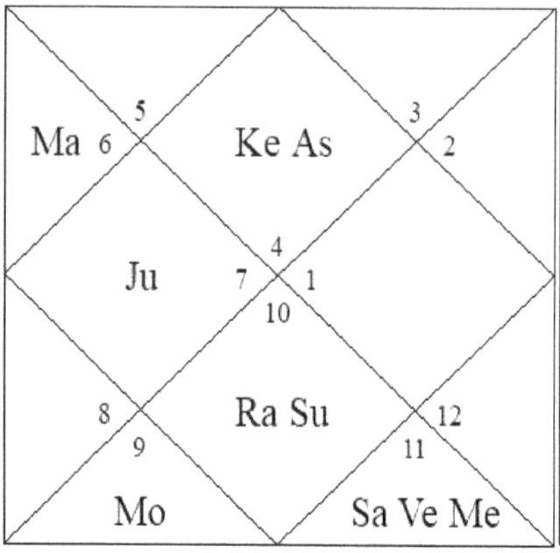

Birth Chart

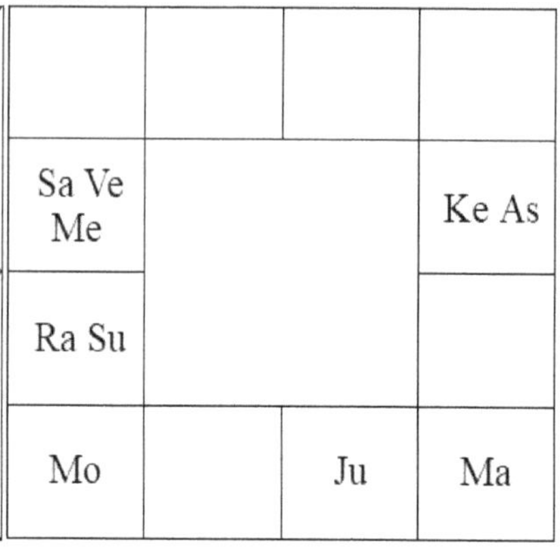

Birth Nakshatra P. Ashadha

Dasa sequence

Yogini	Nakshatra	From	To
Siddha	P. Ashadha	1.2.1935	13.8.1939
Sankata	U. Ashadha	13.8.1939	13.8.1947
Mangla	Shravan	13.8.1947	13.8.1948
Pingla	Dhanishta	13.8.1948	13.8.1950
Dhanya	Shatbhisaj	13.8.1950	13.8.1953
Bharamari	P. Bhadrapad	13.8.1953	13.8.1957

9th h.

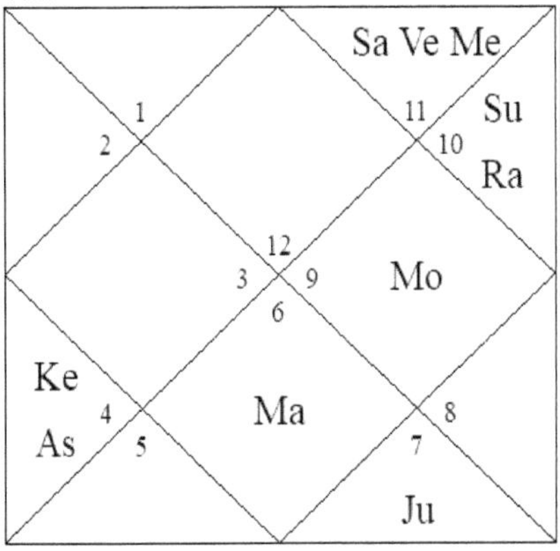

9th h.

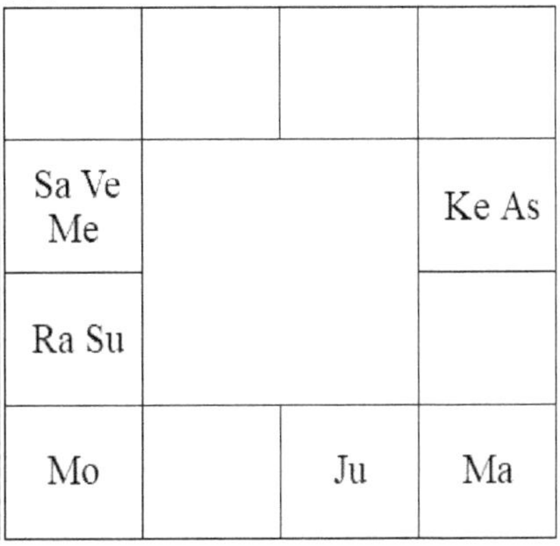

In the birth chart Jupiter is lord of ninth and sixth house and is placed in Kendra causing Yoga.

In the progress chart, Jupiter is in eighth house. It is influencing Mercury and Saturn. Mercury is the seventh lord ofprogress chart and Saturn is the seventh lord of birth chart.

He was married on 13 July, 1957 in the sub-Period of Dhanya.

Example Death of Husband DOB 17 April 1916 TOB 15.35.30 POB Colombo

Birth Chart

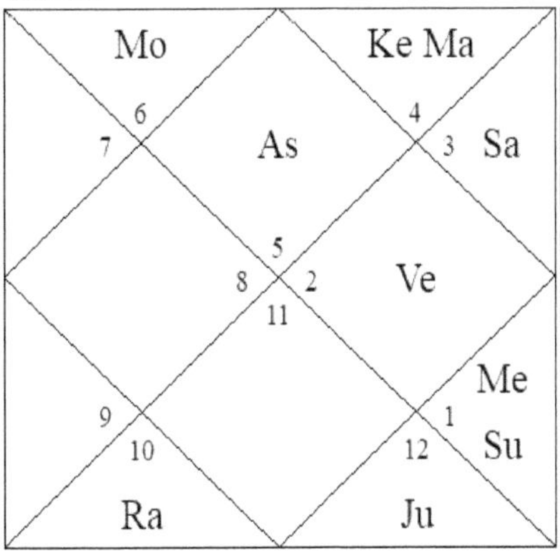

Birth Chart

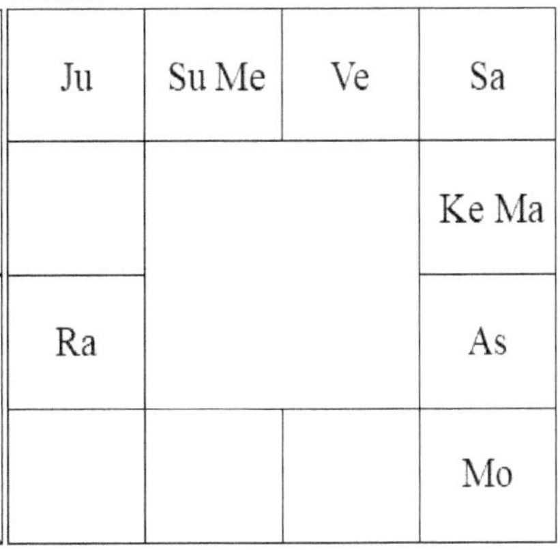

Birth Nakshatra Chitra

Dasa sequence

Yogini	Nakshatra	From	To
Mangla	Chitra	17.4.1916	29.3.1917
Pingla	Swati	29.3.1917	29.3.1919
Dhanya	Visakha	29.3.1919	29.3.1922
Bharamari	Anuradha	29.3.1922	29.3.1926
Bhadrika	Jyeshtha	29.3.1926	29.3.1931
Ulka	Moola	29.3.1931	29.3.1937
Siddha	P. Ashadha	29.3.1937	29.3.1944
Sankata	U. Ashadha	29.3.1944	29.3.1952
Mangla	Shravan	29.3.1952	29.3.1953
Pingla	Dhanishta	29.3.1953	29.3.1955
Dhanya	Shatbhisaj	29.3.1955	29.3.1958
Bharamari	P. Bhadrapad	29.3.1958	29.3.1962

Progress chart for Bhramari/ P. Bhadrapad and Aquarius lagan.

7th h.

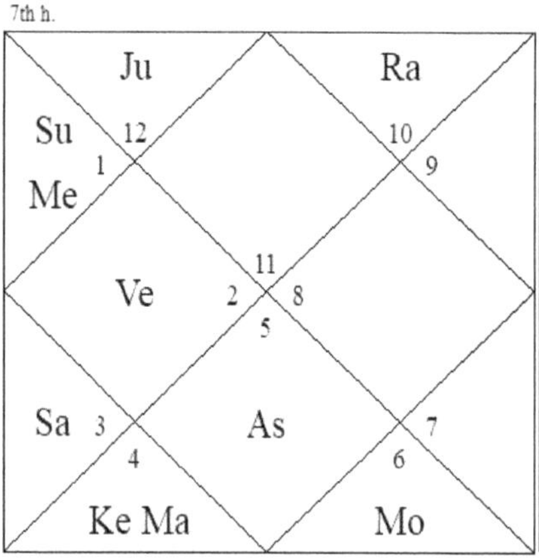

7th h.

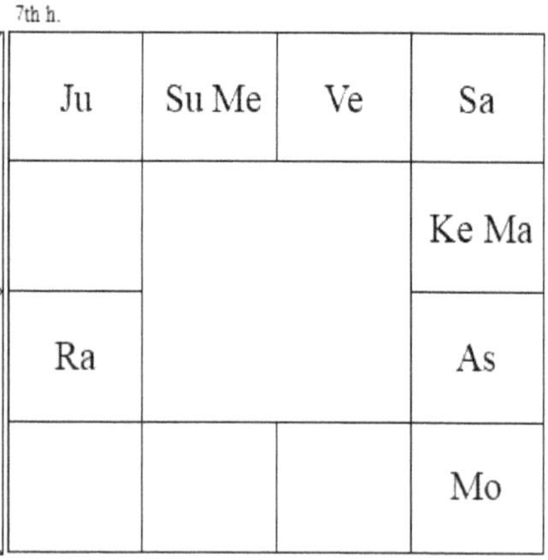

Her husband Solomon was assassinated by a Buddhist monk, on 26 Sept. 1959.

For husband we take seventh house as lagna. Jupiter andSun are maracas of progress chart. Jupiter is a strong maraca as it is in eighth house in own sign.

The progress Nakshtra lord is Jupiter. In the progress chart,it is in second house. The maracas of husband are Mercury andSaturn in the progress chart.

Saturn is aspecting Jupiter. The assassination was in subof Ulka.

She was appointed PM of Ceylon on 21 July 1960 in the sub of Venus. Venus is in tenth house of birth chart and aspects tenth house in progress chart. The Nakshtra lord Jupiter has aspect on tenth house and tenth lord.

Example resigned DOB 30 April 1945 TOB 9.27 POB Delhi

Birth Chart

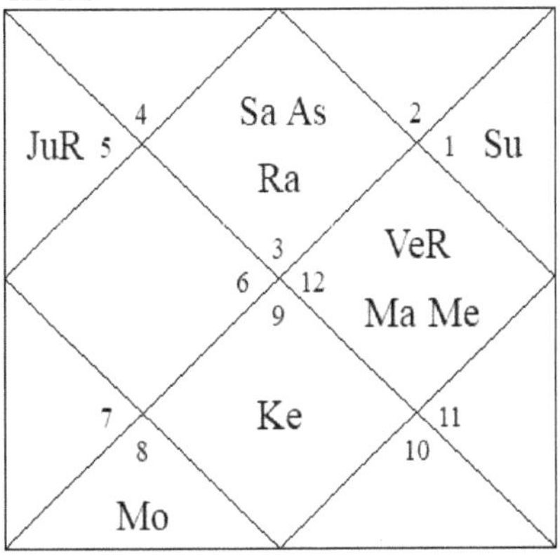

Birth Chart

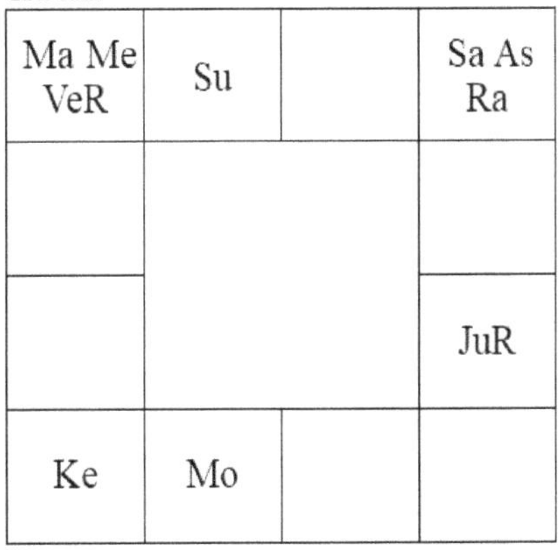

Birth Nakshtra Anuradha

Dasa sequence

Yogini	Nakshtra	From	To
Bharamari	Anuradha	30.4.1945	15.5.1945
Bhadrika	Jyeshtha	15.5.1945	15.5.1950

Ulka	Moola	15.5.1950	15.5.1956
Siddha	P. Ashadha	15.5.1956	15.5.1963
Sankata	U. Ashadha	15.5.1963	15.5.1971
Mangla	Shravan	15.5.1971	15.5.1972
Pingla	Dhanishta	15.5.1972	15.5.1974
Dhanya	Shatbhisaj	15.5.1974	15.5.1977
Bharamari	P. Bhadrapad	15.5.1977	15.5.1981

Progress chart for Bhramari/ P. Bhadrapad and Aquarius lagan.

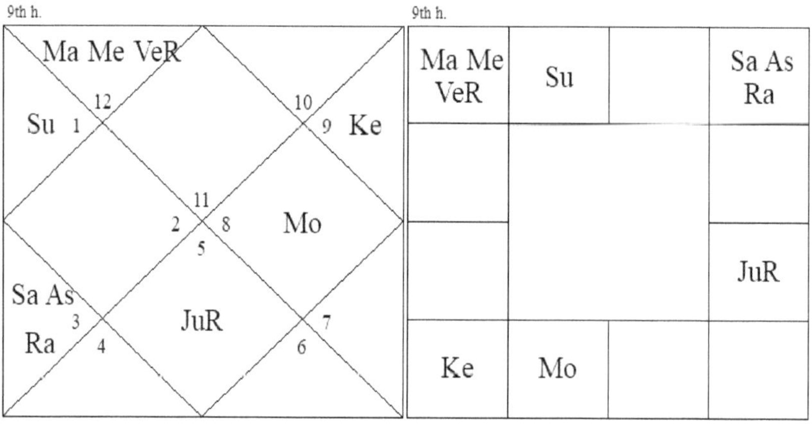

He was a Class I officer with Government of India.He resigned from Job on 19 November 1979 to work with a privatecompany.

The Nakshtra lord Jupiter is tenth lord of birth chart. It is retrograde and is a fallen planet. During this Jupiter the reversalof job is expected. In progress chart Jupiter is eleventh and second lord.

Planets in fifth house can cause loss of job being eighth from tenth. He resigned in Bhramari / Sankata.

Chapter 7

Bhadrika

Bhadrika maha dasha is generated by four Nakshtra. These are Bharani, Magha, Jyeshtha and U. Bhadrapad.

Nakshtra	Nakshtra Lord	Sign	Remarks
Bharani	Venus	Aries	Progress Lagna is Aries
Magha	Ketu	Leo	Progress lagna is Leo
Jyeshtha	Mercury	Scorpio	Progress lagna is Scorpio
U. Bhadrapad	Saturn	Pisces	Progress lagna is Pisces.

Bhadrika / Bharani

This dasha can operate up to the maximum age of 9 yearsin the scheme of progress yogini dasha. The childhood eventsrelating to family, parents, home etc. are seen in this dasha.

The progress lagna is Aries and the Nakshtra lord Venusis the second and seventh lord of progress chart. The placementof Venus in a house highlights the events of the house. Maleficrelation with Venus does not go well.

Example Birth of Younger Brother DOB 28November 1963 TOB 18.10 POB Bareilly

Birth Chart

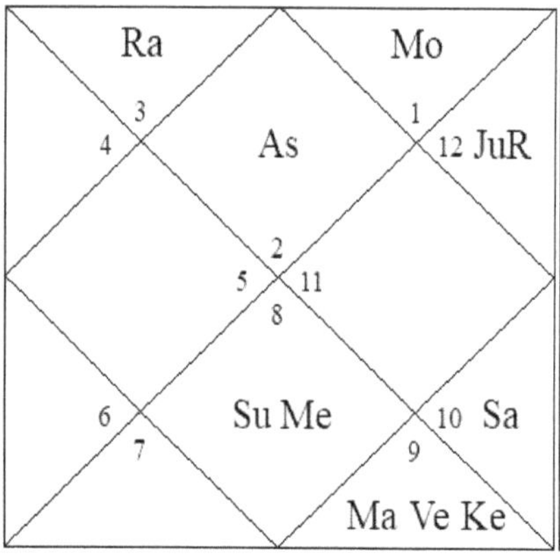

Birth Chart

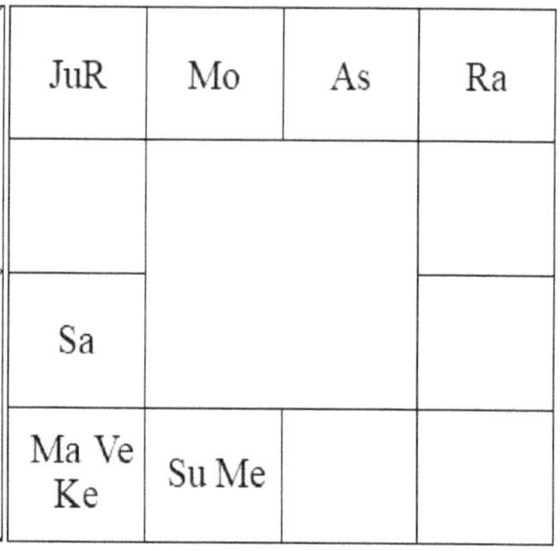

Birth Nakshatra Ashwini

Dasa sequence

Yogini	Nakshtra	From	To
Bharamari	Ashwini	28.11.1963	2.10.1965
Bhadrika	Bharani	2.10.1965	2.10.1970

Younger brother was born on 20 September 1969 in the dashaof Bhadrika / Pingla.

Progress chart for Bhadrika/ Bharani and Aries lagan.

12th h.

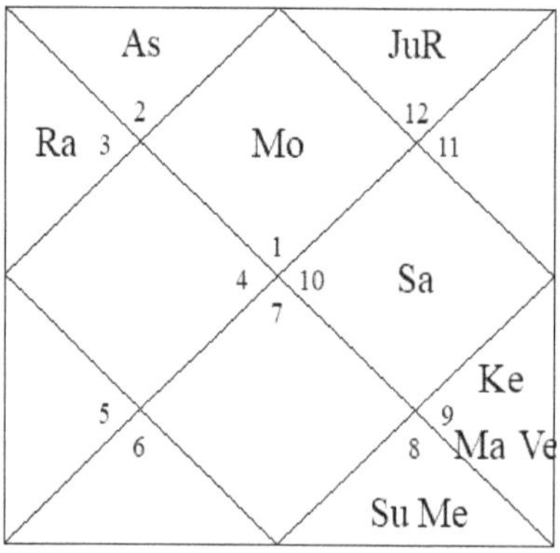

12th h.

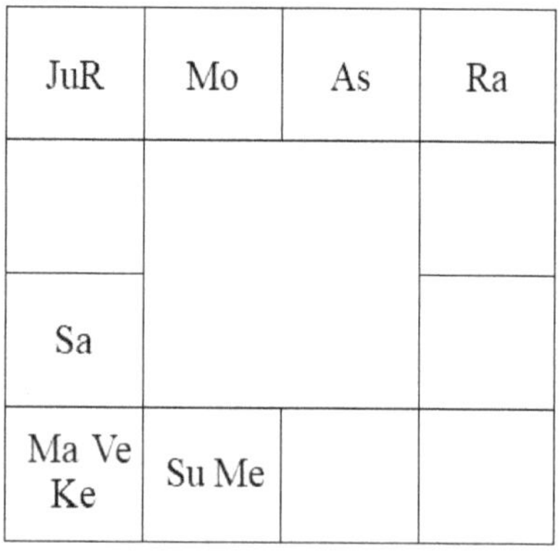

Venus is the Nakshtra Lord and is placed in ninth house.He is influencing the third house and can give results of third house. It is conjoined with Mars and Ketu and indicates problemsto co born also. In Bhadrika / Sankata there should be loss of coborn.

The sub period was Pingla when younger brother was born.
Sun is with the progress third lord.

Example Adoption and death of father DOB 15 December 1994 TOB 5.55 POB Mumbai

6th h.

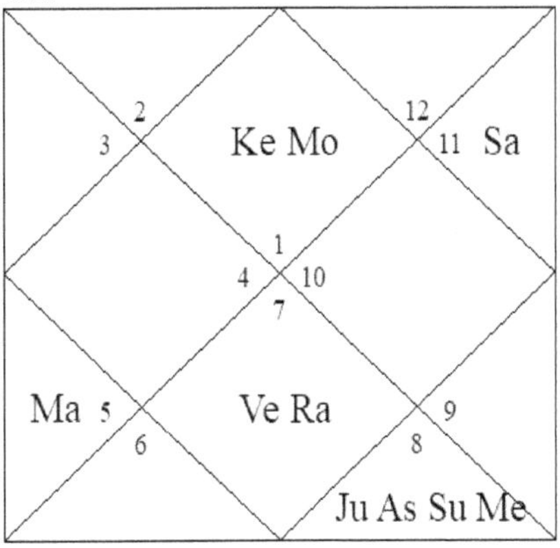

Birth Chart

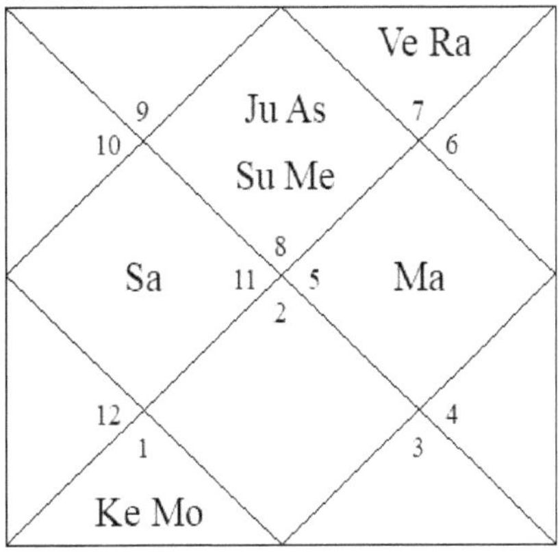

This boy was adopted soon after his birth. His father wasnot known and was feared dead. He was adopted by an Indiandoctor based in Dubai. The doctor was issueless.

In the birth chart, the ninth lord is in sixth house. It is withKetu and aspected by Saturn. The ninth house is also aspected by Jupiter.

Progress chart for Bhadrika/ Bharani and Aries lagan.

6th h. 6th h.

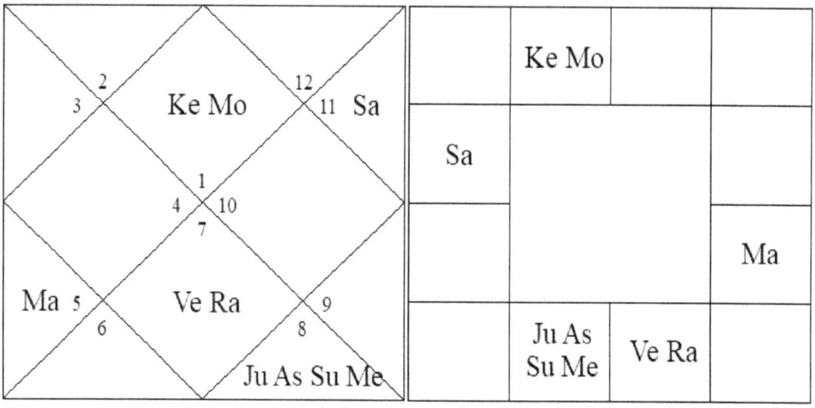

This is confirmed in the progress chart. The Nakshtra lordVenus is with Rahu. The ninth lord Jupiter is in eighth and aspected by Saturn and Mars. The ninth lord is seriously related to eighth house and lords.

The progress chart with Nakshtra lord gives a clear picture.

Example Death of Father DOB 19 August 1946 TOB 8.53 POB Hope

Birth Chart Birth Chart

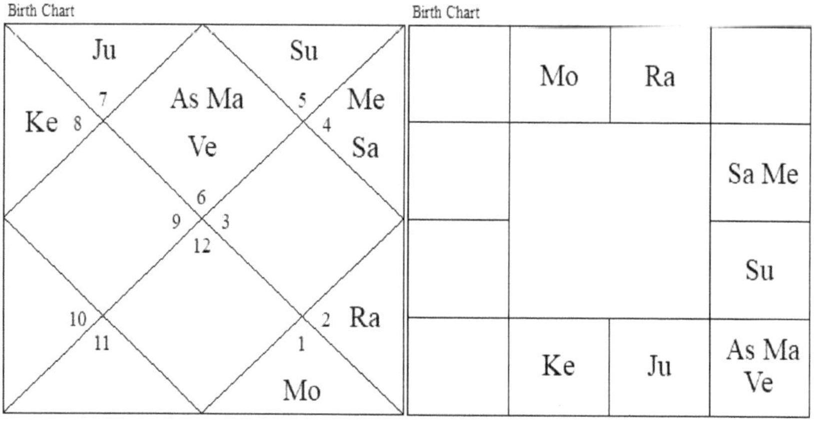

Birth Nakshatra Bharani

Dasa sequence

Bhadrika of Bharani Nakshatra lasted till 24 August 1946.

Progress chart for Bhadrika/ Bharani with Aries lagan.

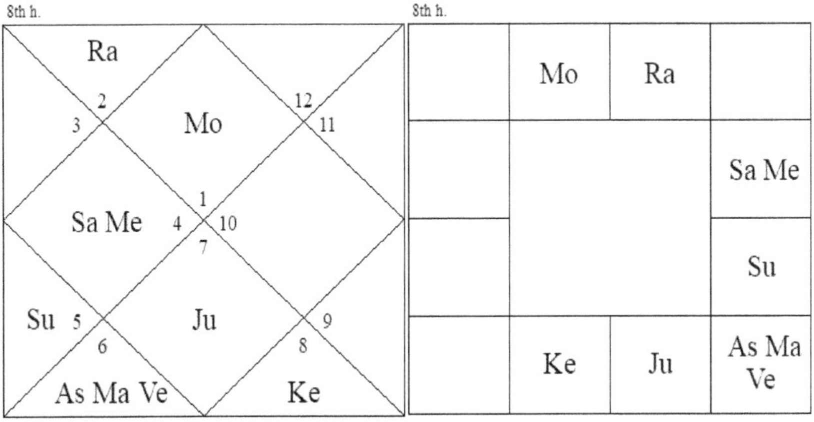

His father expired three months before his birth. The dashawas Bhadrika / Bhramari.

In the birth chart Rahu is placed in ninth house. The ninthlord is Venus and is with eighth lord Mars and aspected by Saturn.

Venus is the lord of ninth house of birth chart and is afflicted.

In the progress chart, this afflicted Venus is now in sixth house. It is again with the eighth lord of progress chart. For father we take the ninth house as lagna. Saturn and Mercury are maracas for father and both are together in the eighth housefrom ninth. The eighth lord from ninth, i.e. Moon is aspecting Jupiter. Mars is with Venus.

Example Separation from Family DOB 20 November 1942 TOB 8.30 POB Scranton

Birth Chart

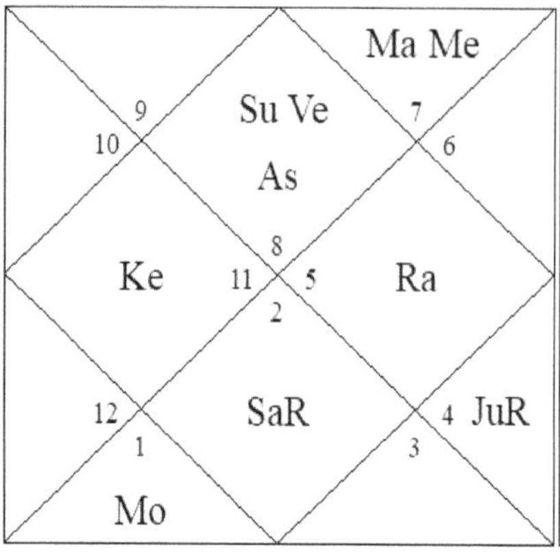

Birth Chart

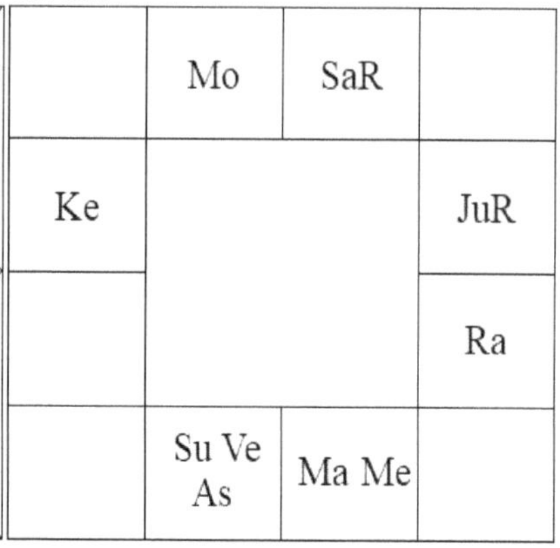

Birth Nakshatra Ashwini

Dasa sequence

Yogini	Nakshtra	From	To
Bharamari	Ashwini	20.11.1942	4.7.1944
Bhadrika	Bharani	4.7.1944	4.7.1949

He is President of USA. He lived with his maternal grandparents as his father was not doing well. This continued till 1956.

Venus is the lord of twelfth and seventh house in the birthchart. It is with Sun and aspected by Saturn and Jupiter.

Progress chart for Bhadrika/ Bharani with Aries lagan.

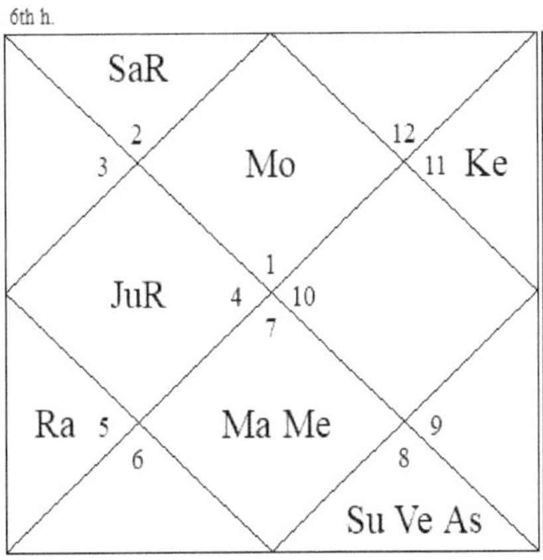

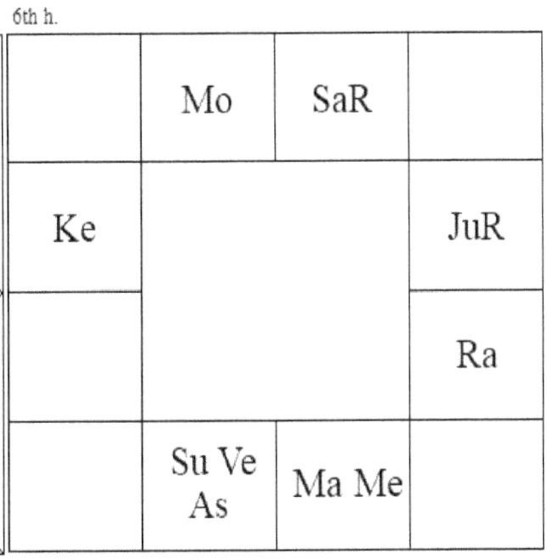

In the progress chart, this Venus is in eighth house with Sun. Eighth house is the twelfth house of father. Sun is the karaka of father. Placement of Venus and Sun in eighth house indicate losses to father.

Bhadrika / Magha

Lord of Nakshtra is Ketu and Ketu is not assigned any sign. Some scholars assign Scorpio as the sign of Ketu. Ketu itself is not in the eight Yoginis but its effects are felt. NormallyKetu acts as his sign dispositor and also as the planet it is conjoinedwith.

Example Big rise DOB 18 March 1914 TOB 12.22.35 POB Dungarpur

Birth Chart

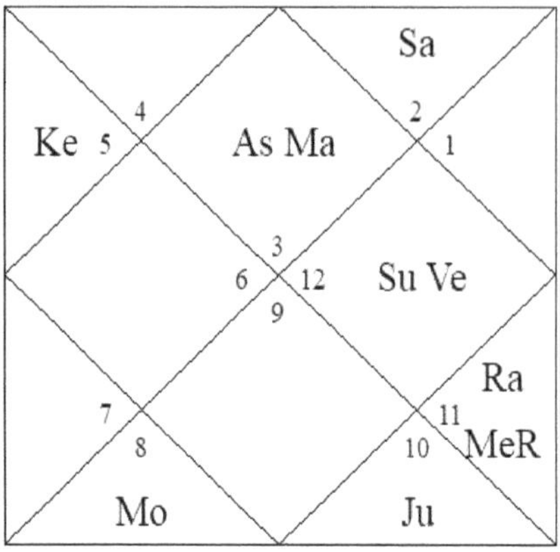

Birth Chart

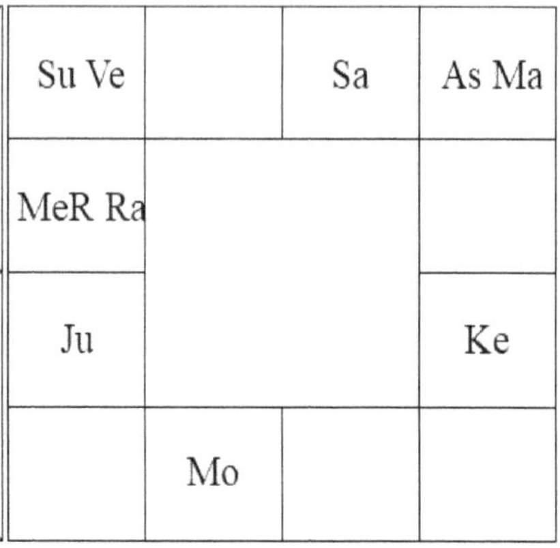

Birth Nakshatra Jyestha

Dasa sequence

Yogini	Nakshatra	From	To
Bhadrika	Jyeshtha	18.3.1914	19.2.1915
Ulka	Moola	19.2.1915	19.2.1921
Siddha	P. Ashadha	19.2.1921	19.2.1928
Sankata	U. Ashadha	19.2.1928	19.2.1936
Mangla	Shravan	19.2.1936	19.2.1937
Pingla	Dhanishta	19.2.1937	19.2.1939
Dhanya	Shatbhisaj	19.2.1939	19.2.1942
Bharamari	P. Bhadrapad	19.2.1942	19.2.1946
Bhadrika	U. Bhadrapad	19.2.1946	19.2.1951
Ulka	Revati	19.2.1951	19.2.1957

Yogini	Nakshatra	From	To
Siddha	Rohini	19.2.1957	19.2.1964
Sankata	Mrigshira	19.2.1964	19.2.1972
Mangla	Ardra	19.2.1972	19.2.1973
Pingla	Punarvasu	19.2.1973	19.2.1975
Dhanya	Pushya	19.2.1975	19.2.1978
Bharamari	Ashlesha	19.2.1978	19.2.1982
Bhadrika	Magha	19.2.1982	19.2.1987

He was elected as the President of International Court ofJustice in November 1985.

In the birth chart Ketu is in third house and acts as thirdlord. It is aspected by Mercury, the lagna lord.

Progress chart for Bhadrika/ Magha with Leo lagan.

3rd h.

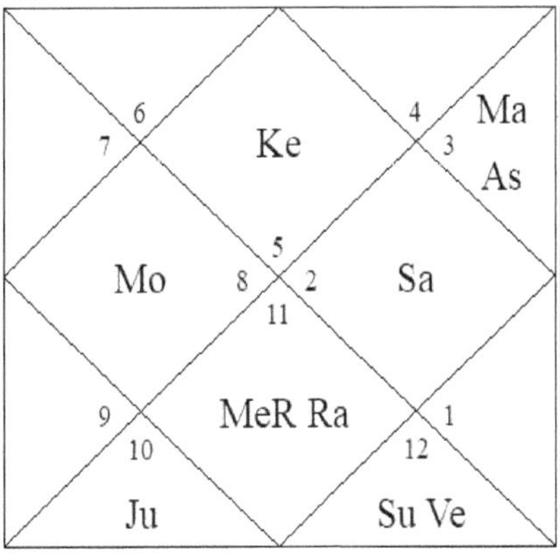

3rd h.

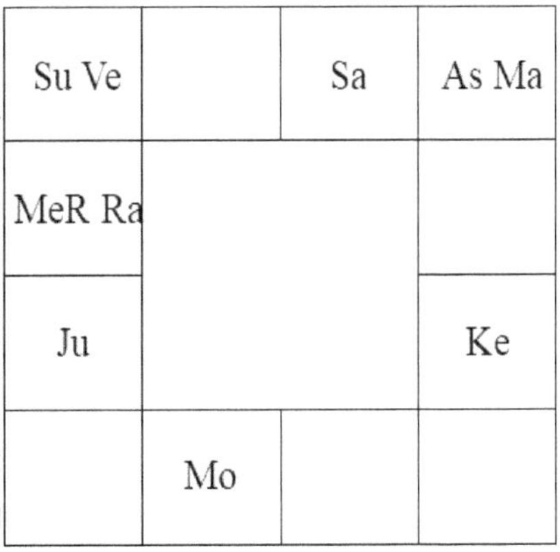

Ketu is in the lagna of progress chart and the self-efforts are highlighted. Ketu acts as Sun who is in eighth house and is with tenth lord Venus. Venus is also the third lord. The effortsare again seen.

The election for this post was to be held in September, 1985 when the sub was Mangla which is twelfth lord. The elections were postponed and were held when the Pingla sub period had commenced and he won the election.

Example Death DOB 23 December 1902 TOB 7.23 POB Baghpat

Birth Chart

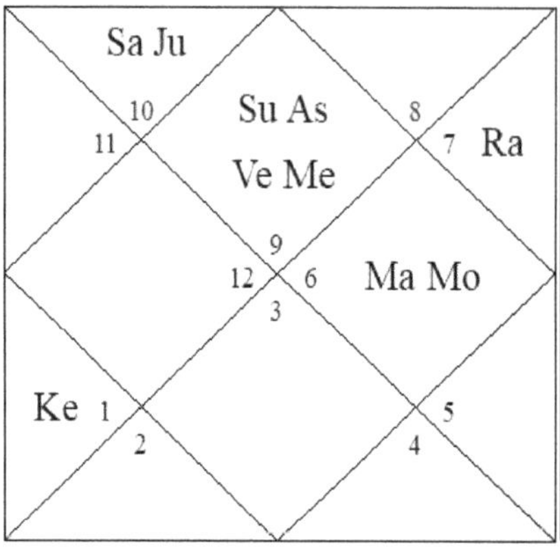

Birth Chart

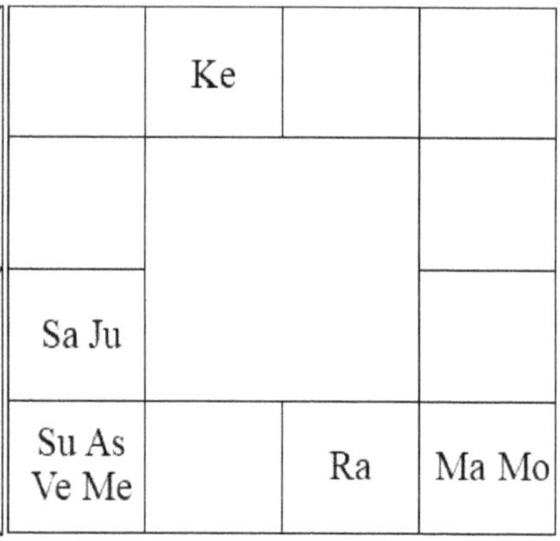

Birth Nakshatra Hasta

Dasa sequence

Yogini	**Nakshatra**	**From**	**To**
Sankata	Hasta	23.12.1902	26.5.1903
Mangla	Chitra	26.5.1903	26.5.1904
Pingla	Swati	26.5.1904	26.5.1906
Dhanya	Visakha	26.5.1906	26.5.1909
Bharamari	Anuradha	26.5.1909	26.5.1913
Bhadrika	Jyeshtha	26.5.1913	26.5.1918
Ulka	Moola	26.5.1918	26.5.1924
Siddha	P. Ashadha	26.5.1924	26.5.1931
Sankata	U. Ashadha	26.5.1931	26.5.1939
Mangla	Shravan	26.5.1939	26.5.1940
Pingla	Dhanishta	26.5.1940	26.5.1942

Yogini	Nakshatra	From	To
Dhanya	Shatbhisaj	26.5.1942	26.5.1945
Bharamari	P. Bhadrapad	26.5.1945	26.5.1949
Bhadrika	U. Bhadrapad	26.5.1949	26.5.1954
Ulka	Revati	26.5.1954	26.5.1960
Siddha	Rohini	26.5.1960	26.5.1967
Sankata	Mrigshira	26.5.1967	26.5.1975
Mangla	Ardra	26.5.1975	26.5.1976
Pingla	Punarvasu	26.5.1976	26.5.1978
Dhanya	Pushya	26.5.1978	26.5.1981
Bharamari	Ashlesha	26.5.1981	26.5.1985
Bhadrika	Magha	26.5.1985	26.5.1990

He expired on 23 May, 1987 in the Sub period of Siddha.

The maracas of birth chart are Mercury and Saturn. Moonis the lord of eighth house.

Progress chart for Bhadrika/ Magha with Leo lagan.

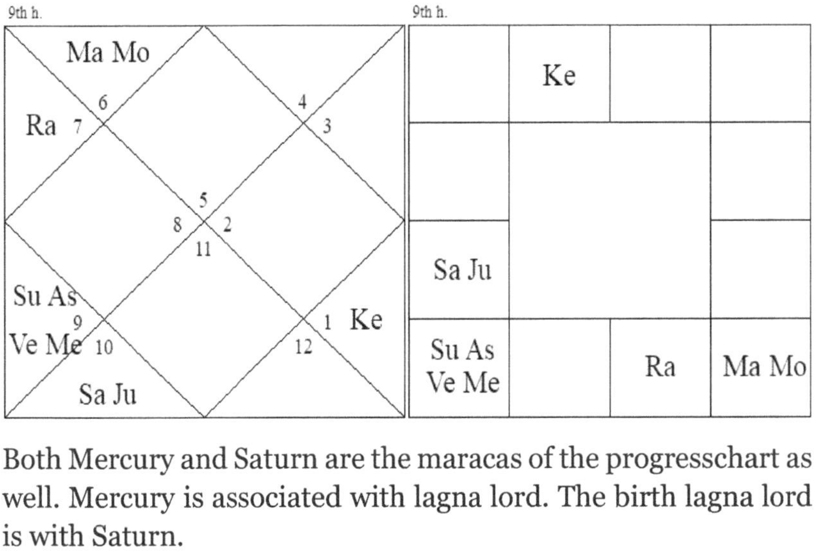

Both Mercury and Saturn are the maracas of the progresschart as well. Mercury is associated with lagna lord. The birth lagna lord is with Saturn.

Venus is associated with Lagna lord and Mercury. Therefore, the relation with Nakshtra lord and maracas is established.

Example Expansion of Business DOB 10 August 1955 TOB 22.0 POB Delhi

Birth Chart

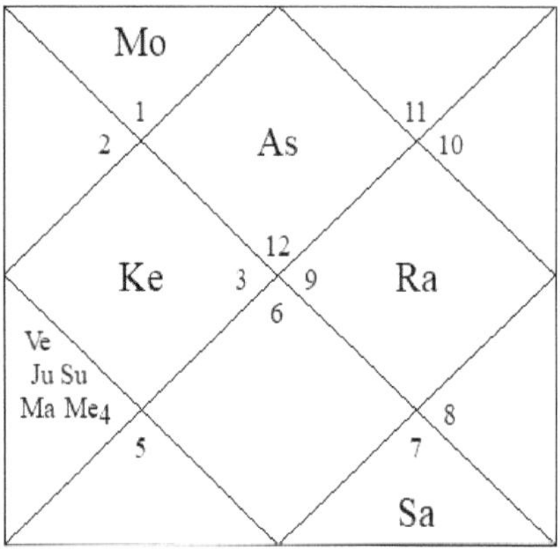

Birth Chart

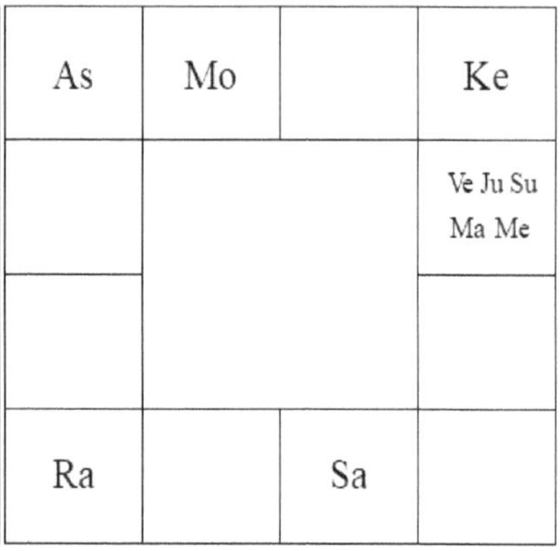

Birth Nakshatra Bharani

Dasa sequence

Yogini	Nakshatra	From	To
Bhadrika	Bharani	10.8.1955	23.8.1958
Ulka	Kritika	23.8.1958	23.8.1964
Siddha	Rohini	23.8.1964	23.8.1971
Sankata	Mrigshira	23.8.1971	23.8.1979
Mangla	Ardra	23.8.1979	23.8.1980
Pingla	Punarvasu	23.8.1980	23.8.1982
Dhanya	Pushya	23.8.1982	23.8.1985
Bharamari	Ashlesha	23.8.1985	23.8.1989
Bhadrika	Magha	23.8.1989	23.8.1994

Progress chart for Bhadrika/ Magha with Leo lagan.

6th h. | 6th h.

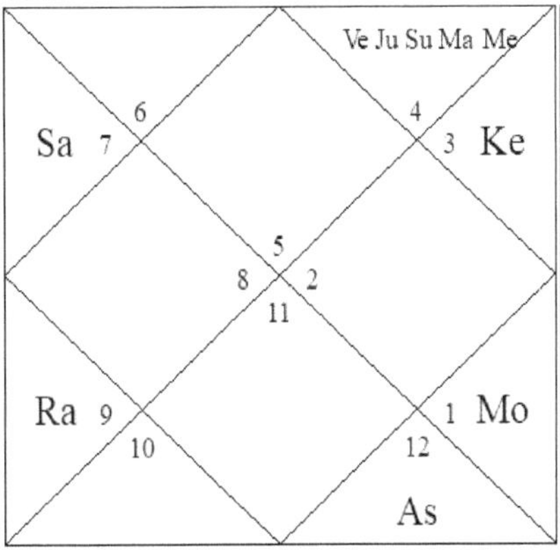

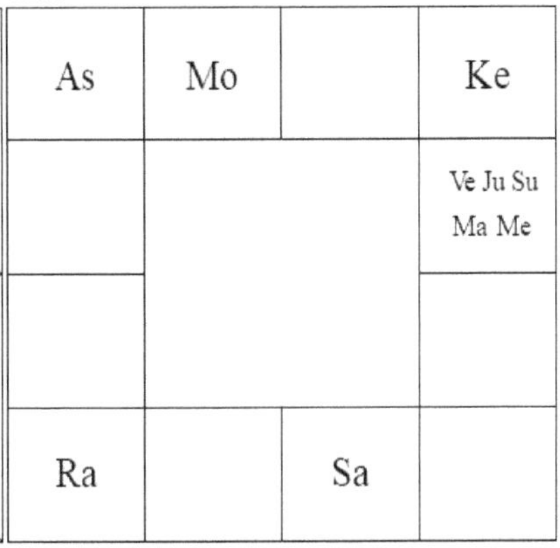

Ketu is the Nakshtra lord and is placed in eleventh house.Ketu acts as Mercury. Mercury is the lord of eleventh and is withboth the trine Lords Mars and Jupiter. An excellent Raj Yoga and Dhana Yoga is present.

During the Sub period of Siddha, Lord of tenth house, she founded Alps academy and the business flourished.

In the sub period of Sankata she opened many branchesin India and abroad.

Example Serious Accident DOB 13 September 1979 TOB 17.15 POB Allahabad

Birth Chart | Birth Chart

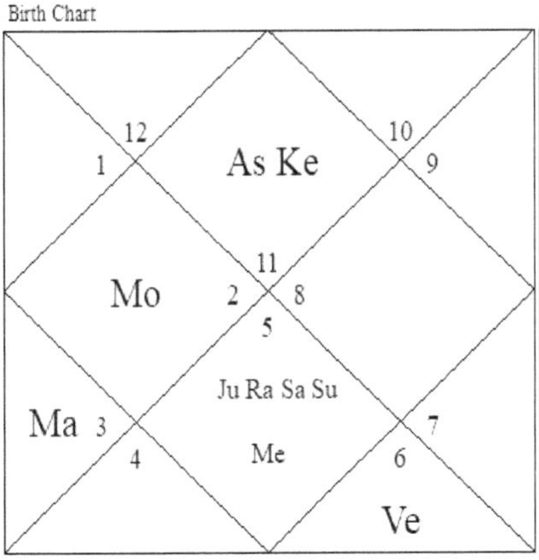

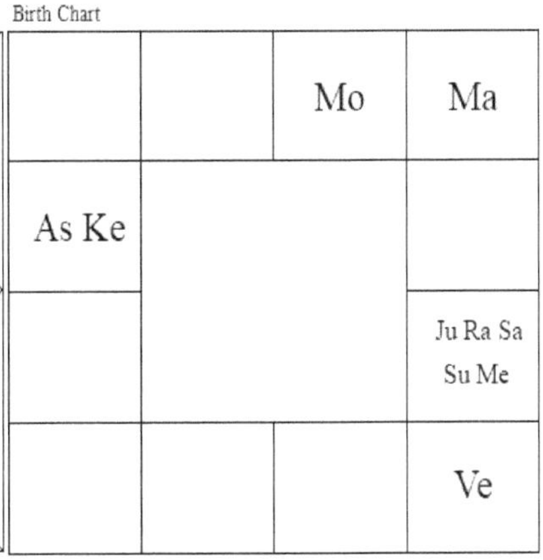

Birth Nakshatra Mrigshira

Dasa sequence

Yogini	Nakshatra	From	To
Sankata	Mrigshira	13.9.1979	2.3.1984
Mangla	Ardra	2.3.1984	2.3.1985
Pingla	Punarvasu	2.3.1985	2.3.1987
Dhanya	Pushya	2.3.1987	2.3.1990
Bharamari	Ashlesha	2.3.1990	2.3.1994
Bhadrika	Magha	2.3.1994	2.3.1999

Progress chart for Bhadrika/ Magha with Leo lagan.

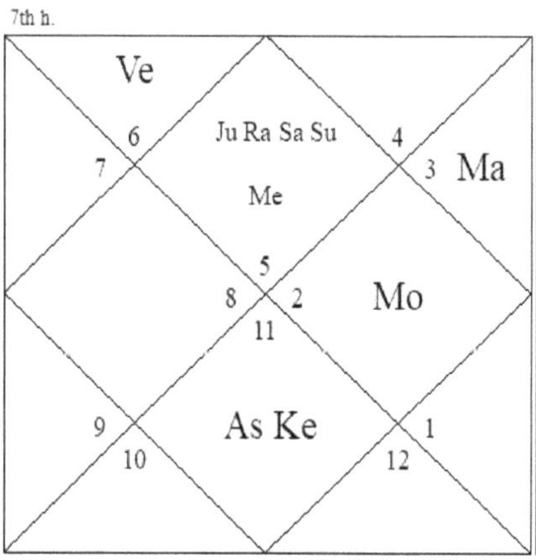

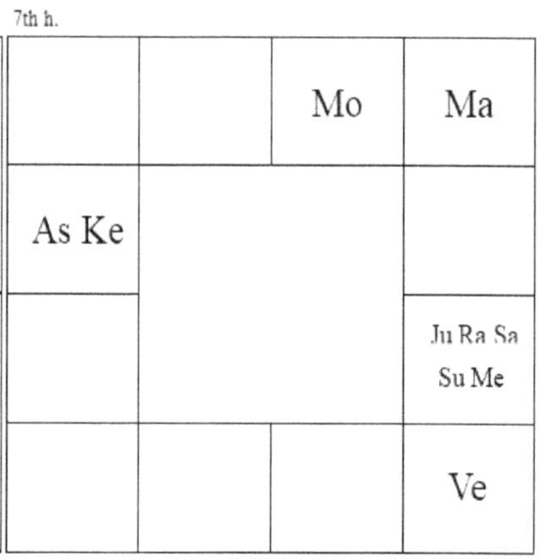

She had a serious accident while traveling with her family.Father died and she along with sister injured. Mother was seriously injured.

In the birth chart Mars is the maraca for father. In the progress chart, Venus is the killer of father. Venus is aspected by Mars. The accident happened on 26 Oct. 1995. The sub period was of Venus.

For mother, Mars is in the eighth house from fourth. Marsis in second from Moon. Mars or Moon is not aspected by Jupiterand she was saved with serious injuries.

For her the maraca connections are present. Ketu is like Saturn. The progress lagna lord and birth lagna lord are with birth and progress maracas. Her safety in the accident is a miracle.

Example Death DOB 17 April 1916 TOB 15.35.30 POB Colombo

Birth Chart

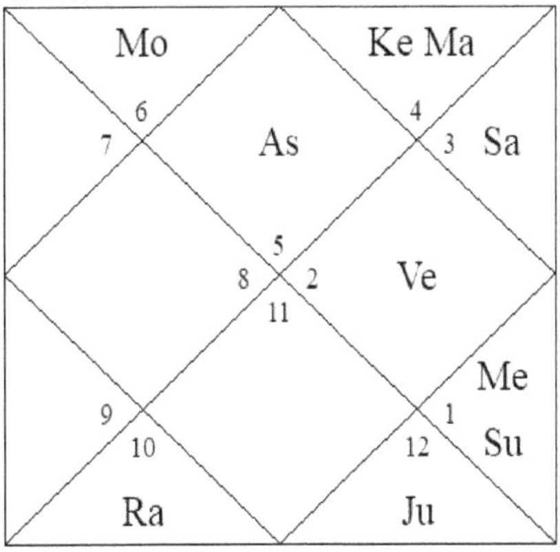

Birth Chart

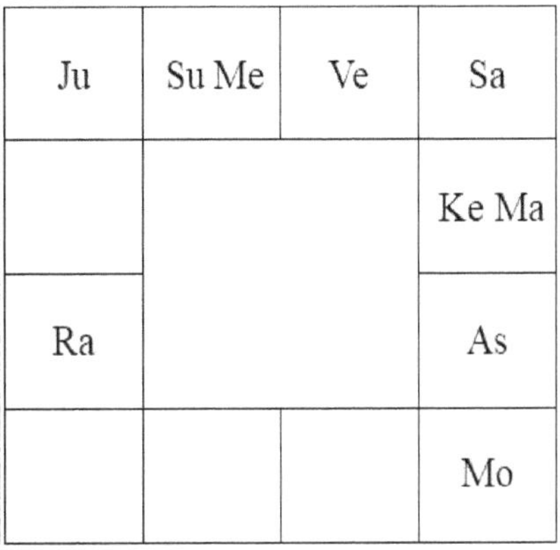

Birth Nakshatra Chitra

Dasa sequence

Yogini	Nakshatra	From	To
Mangla	Chitra	17.4.1916	29.3.1917
Pingla	Swati	29.3.1917	29.3.1919
Dhanya	Visakha	29.3.1919	29.3.1922
Bharamari	Anuradha	29.3.1922	29.3.1926
Bhadrika	Jyeshtha	29.3.1926	29.3.1931
Ulka	Moola	29.3.1931	29.3.1937
Siddha	P. Ashadha	29.3.1937	29.3.1944
Sankata	U. Ashadha	29.3.1944	29.3.1952
Mangla	Shravan	29.3.1952	29.3.1953
Pingla	Dhanishta	29.3.1953	29.3.1955

Yogini	Nakshatra	From	To
Dhanya	Shatbhisaj	29.3.1955	29.3.1958
Bharamari	P. Bhadrapad	29.3.1958	29.3.1962
Bhadrika	U. Bhadrapad	29.3.1962	29.3.1967
Ulka	Revati	29.3.1967	29.3.1973
Siddha	Rohini	29.3.1973	29.3.1980
Sankata	Mrigshira	29.3.1980	29.3.1988
Mangla	Ardra	29.3.1988	29.3.1989
Pingla	Punarvasu	29.3.1989	29.3.1991
Dhanya	Pushya	29.3.1991	29.3.1994
Bharamari	Ashlesha	29.3.1994	29.3.1998
Bhadrika	Magha	29.3.1998	29.3.2003

She died on 12 Oct. 2000 in the dasha of Bhadrika / Sankata.

The birth and the progress charts are same and the maracas are Mercury and Saturn.

Ketu is in twelfth house with debilitated Mars. The lord oflagna is with Mercury who stronger maraca being lord of Second house. Moon is in second house and thus Nakshtra is connectedto Maraca. Jupiter is the eighth lord an aspects Moon and Ketu. Jupiter is afflicted by maraca Saturn.

Bhadrika / Jyeshtha

The lord of Nakshtra and the dasha lord are same. Mercury is important planet for this dasha.

Scorpio is the progress lagna. Mercury is not a benefic planet for this lagna. Affliction to Mercury can give problems inthis dasha. Association with benefics can bring good news especially when Mercury is well placed. Mercury is eighth lord of progress chart and its association with eighth lord of birth chart can give serious accidents.

Example Plane Crash DOB 14 December 1946 TOB 9.24.44 POB Delhi

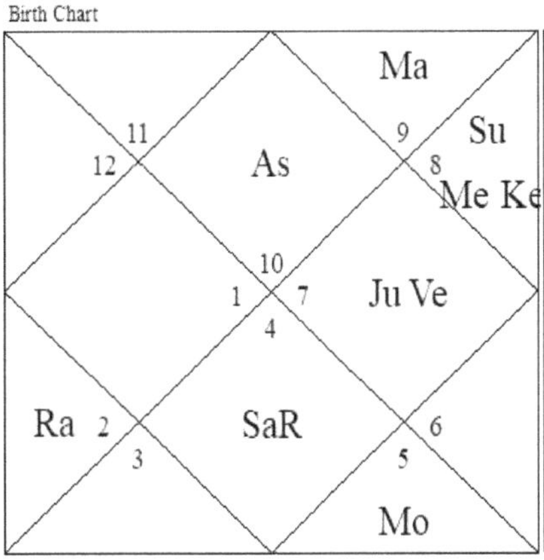

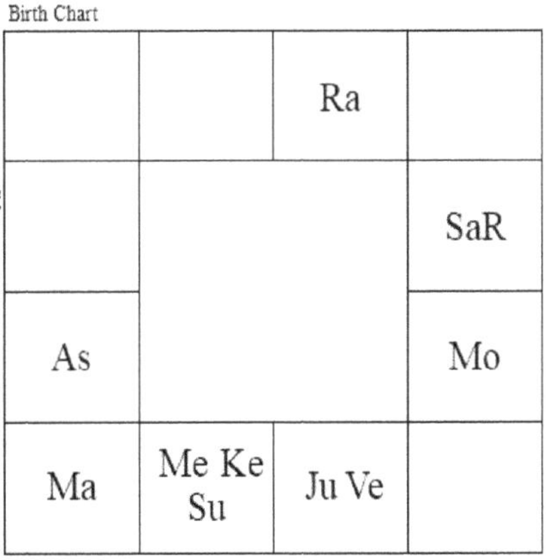

Birth Nakshatra Magha

Dasa sequence

Yogini	Nakshatra	From	To
Bhadrika	Magha	14.12.1946	10.4.1947
Ulka	P. Phalguni	10.4.1947	10.4.1953
Siddha	U. Phalguni	10.4.1953	10.4.1960
Sankata	Hasta	10.4.1960	10.4.1968
Mangla	Chitra	10.4.1968	10.4.1969
Pingla	Swati	10.4.1969	10.4.1971
Dhanya	Visakha	10.4.1971	10.4.1974
Bharamari	Anuradha	10.4.1974	10.4.1978
Bhadrika	Jyeshtha	10.4.1978	10.4.1983

Progress chart for Bhadrika/ Jyestha with Scorpio lagan.

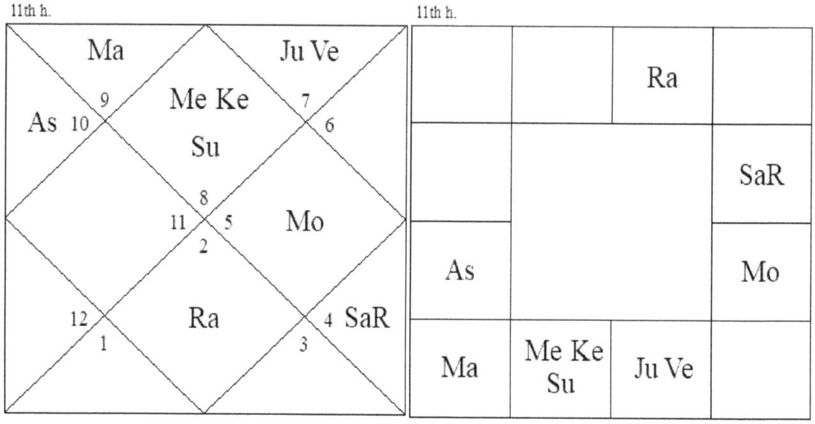

In the birth chart, Saturn is a maraca and lagna lord also.

He is retrograde.

Mercury is the Nakshtra lord. In the progress chart It is placed in lagna and afflicted by Ketu and the birth eighth lordSun.

Venus and Jupiter are maraca in progress chart. Both aretogether and placed in twelfth house.

He died in a plane crash on 23 June, 1980. The sub periodwas of Siddha. Venus is maraca and is with another maraca.

Example Noble Prize DOB 26 August 1910 TOB 14.24 POB Skopje

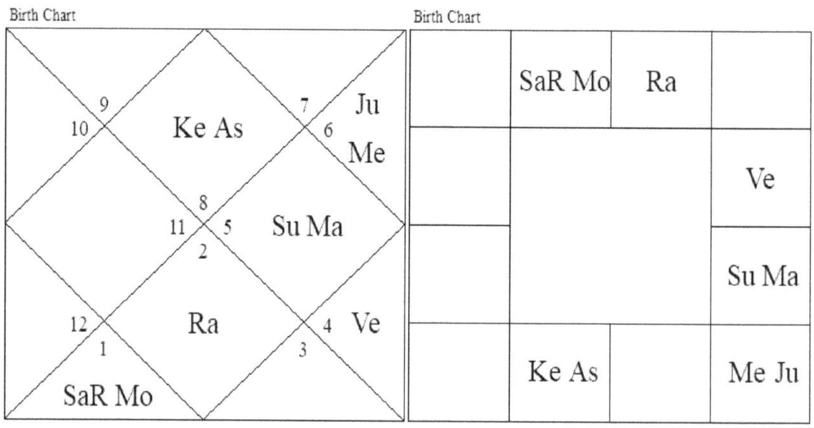

Birth Nakshatra Bharani

Dasa sequence

Yogini	Nakshatra	From	To
Bhadrika	Bharani	26.8.1910	25.11.1910
Ulka	Kritika	25.11.1910	25.11.1916
Siddha	Rohini	25.11.1916	25.11.1923
Sankata	Mrigshira	25.11.1923	25.11.1931
Mangla	Ardra	25.11.1931	25.11.1932
Pingla	Punarvasu	25.11.1932	25.11.1934
Dhanya	Pushya	25.11.1934	25.11.1937
Bharamari	Ashlesha	25.11.1937	25.11.1941
Bhadrika	Magha	25.11.1941	25.11.1946
Ulka	P. Phalguni	25.11.1946	25.11.1952
Siddha	U. Phalguni	25.11.1952	25.11.1959
Sankata	Hasta	25.11.1959	25.11.1967
Mangla	Chitra	25.11.1967	25.11.1968
Pingla	Swati	25.11.1968	25.11.1970
Dhanya	Visakha	25.11.1970	25.11.1973
Bharamari	Anuradha	25.11.1973	25.11.1977
Bhadrika	Jyeshtha	25.11.1977	25.11.1982

Progress chart is same as birth chart.

She was awarded the Noble prize in 1980. The dasha wasBhadrika / Siddha of Jyeshtha Nakshtra.

Mercury is not afflicted and is in eleventh house of gain and is exalted. Jupiter is trine lord and joins this Mercury - A gainful period.

Venus is in ninth house and is in eleventh from Mercury. The honor is seen from tenth house. The lagna lord and tenth lord are together in tenth house.

Example Death of father DOB 14 November 1889 TOB 23.05 POB Allahabad

Birth Chart

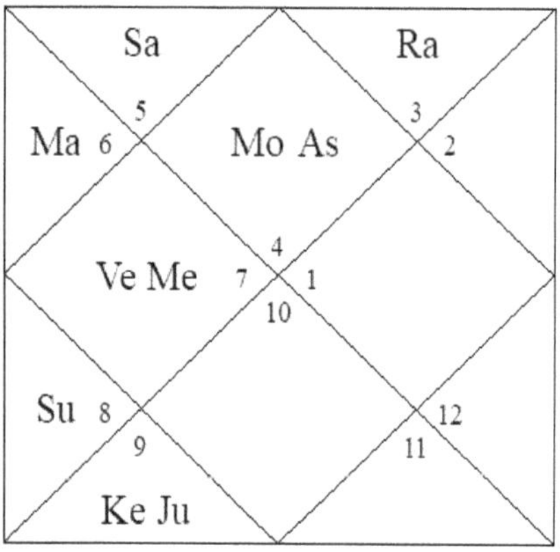

Birth Chart

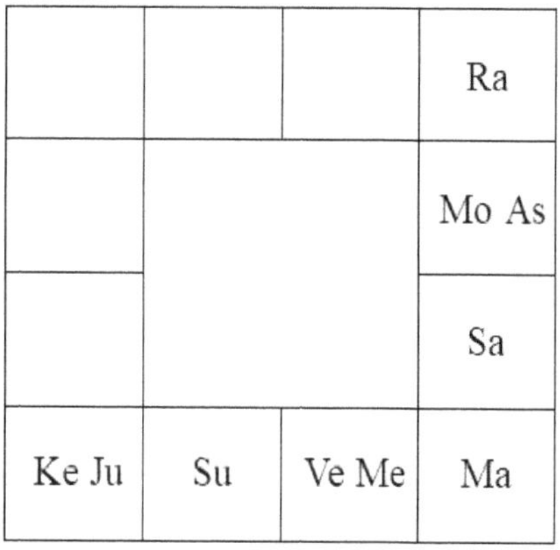

Birth Nakshatra Ashlesha

Dasa sequence

Yogini	Nakshatra	From	To
Bharamari	Ashlesha	14.11.1889	27.6.1893
Bhadrika	Magha	27.6.1893	27.6.1898
Ulka	P. Phalguni	27.6.1898	27.6.1904
Siddha	U. Phalguni	27.6.1904	27.6.1911
Sankata	Hasta	27.6.1911	27.6.1919
Mangla	Chitra	27.6.1919	27.6.1920
Pingla	Swati	27.6.1920	27.6.1922
Dhanya	Visakha	27.6.1922	27.6.1925
Bharamari	Anuradha	27.6.1925	27.6.1929
Bhadrika	Jyeshtha	27.6.1929	27.6.1934

Progress chart for Bhadrika/ Jyestha and Scorpio lagan.

5th h.

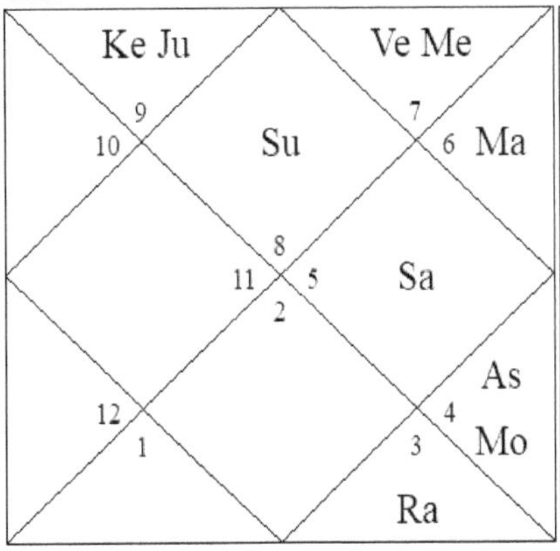

5th h.

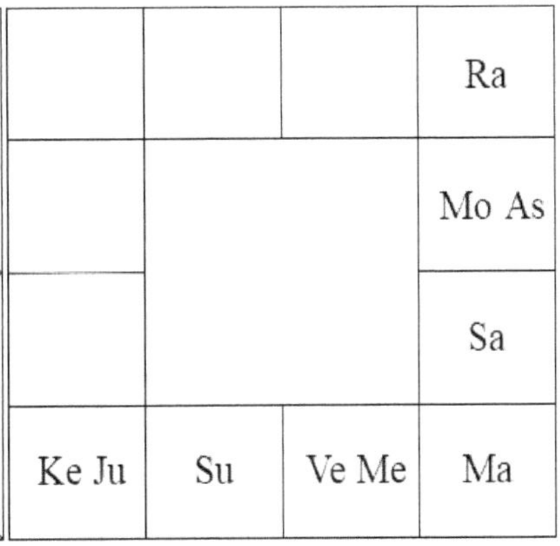

In the birth chart, Mercury is maraca of father. Mercury is in fourth house which is eighth for father and is with Venus. Thus, Mercury is a strong maraca for father.

In the progress chart, this combination has moved to twelfthhouse. His father expired on 6 Feb. 1931 in the Sub period of Siddha. Venus and Mercury are aspected by Saturn who is the lord of Seventh and eighth lord for father.

Example Job and Marriage DOB 24 December 1937 TOB 4.27 POB Darbhanga

Birth Chart

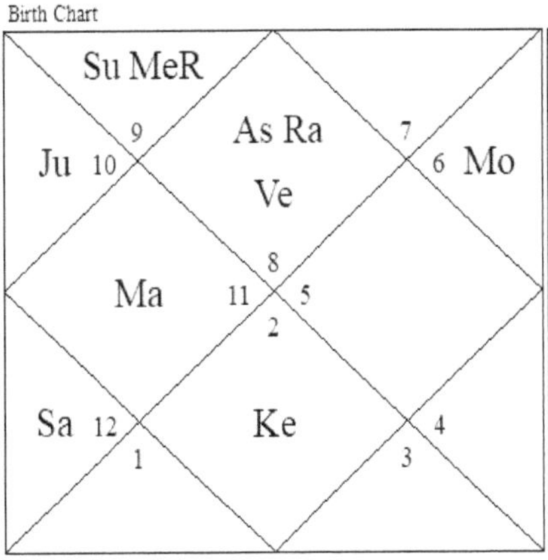

Birth Chart

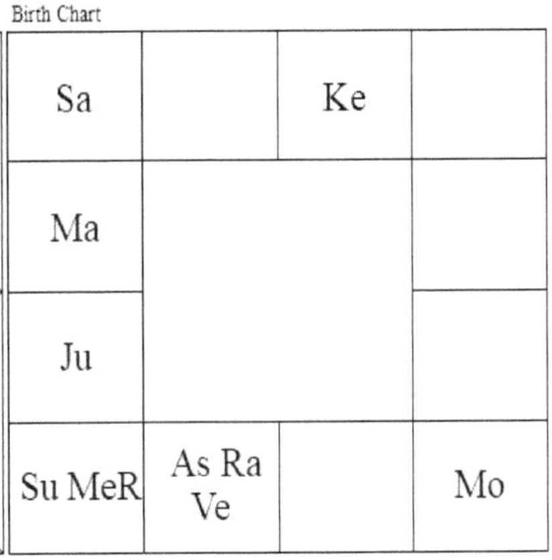

Birth Nakshatra U. Phalguni

Dasa sequence

Yogini	Nakshatra	From	To
Siddha	U. Phalguni	14.12.1937	18.9.1942
Sankata	Hasta	18.9.1942	18.9.1950
Mangla	Chitra	18.9.1950	18.9.1951
Pingla	Swati	18.9.1951	18.9.1953
Dhanya	Visakha	18.9.1953	18.9.1956
Bharamari	Anuradha	18.9.1956	18.9.1960
Bhadrika	Jyeshtha	18.9.1960	18.9.1965

The birth and progress chart are same. Mercury is retrograde and aspects his own eighth house. Sun is the lord oftenth house and is with Mercury. Saturn is aspecting this Mercury. He started his career in Ulka sub on 5 February 1962.

In the progress chart Venus aspects, his own sign in seventhhouse. Venus is with Rahu. He was married on 10 December 1963 inthe sub of Sankata.

We will see the same chart for Bhadrika of U. Bhadrapad and how the results differ for same dasha but of different Nakshtra.

Example Marriage and Child DOB 12 June 1951 TOB 11.20 POB Delhi

Birth Chart

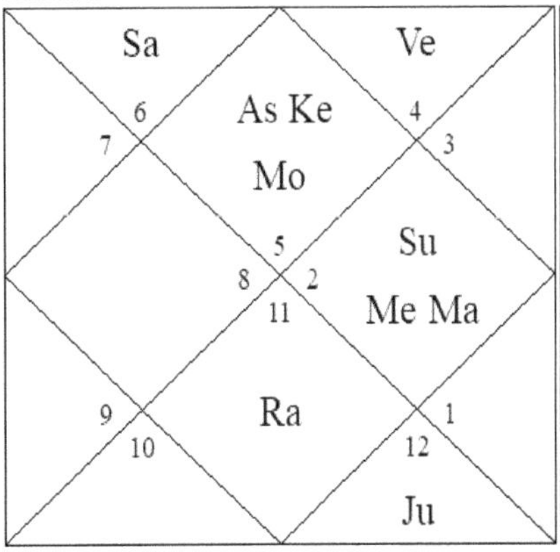

Birth Chart

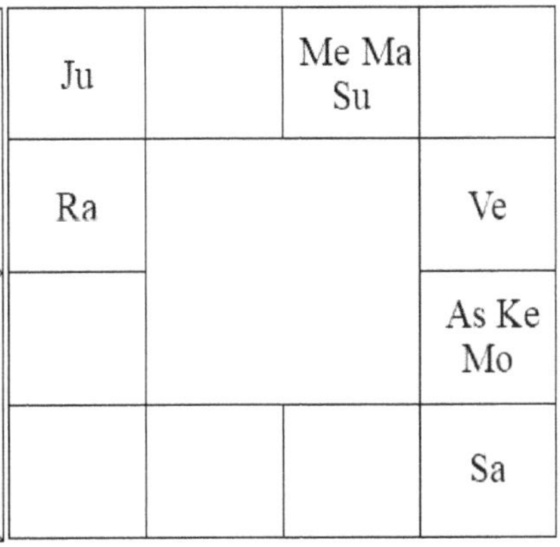

Birth Nakshatra P. Phalguni

Dasa sequence

Yogini	Nakshatra	From	To
Ulka	P. Phalguni	12.6.1951	17.1.1954
Siddha	U. Phalguni	17.1.1954	17.1.1961
Sankata	Hasta	17.1.1961	17.1.1969
Mangla	Chitra	17.1.1969	17.1.1970
Pingla	Swati	17.1.1970	17.1.1972
Dhanya	Visakha	17.1.1972	17.1.1975
Bharamari	Anuradha	17.1.1975	17.1.1979
Bhadrika	Jyeshtha	17.1.1979	17.1.1984

Mercury is eleventh and second lord of the birth chart and is conjoined with lagna lord and the Yoga karaka Mars in the tenth house.

We can expect good results during dasha of Mercury Nakshtra.

Progress chart for Bhadrika/ Jyestha and Scorpio lagan.

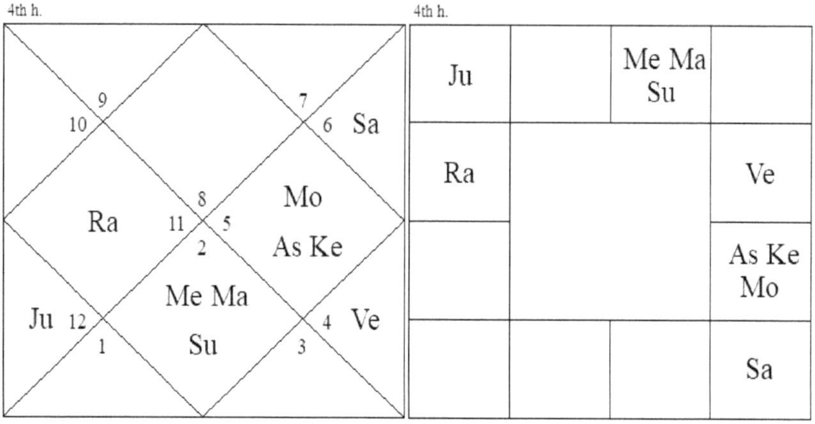

In the progress chart, Mercury is now in seventh house and gives results of this house. He was married in May 1979 in the sub period of Bhadrika itself.

A son was born in March 1980 in the sub of Ulka. Saturn is aspected by fifth lord Jupiter. Jupiter is strongly placed in ownsign in fifth house.

Bhadrika / U. Bhadrapad

Saturn is the Nakshtra lord. A strong un-afflicted Saturnof birth chart promise good results in this dasha period. Normally a retrograde Saturn is not good. An afflicted Saturn can give adverse results of the house, if he is placed badly in progress chart.

Jupiter is the lord of tenth house of progress lagna as wellas the lagna lord. Association of Jupiter with Moon or Mars assures a smooth job when tenth house is not under malefic influence.

Example Coronation DOB 14 December 1895 TOB 03.05 POB York

Birth Chart

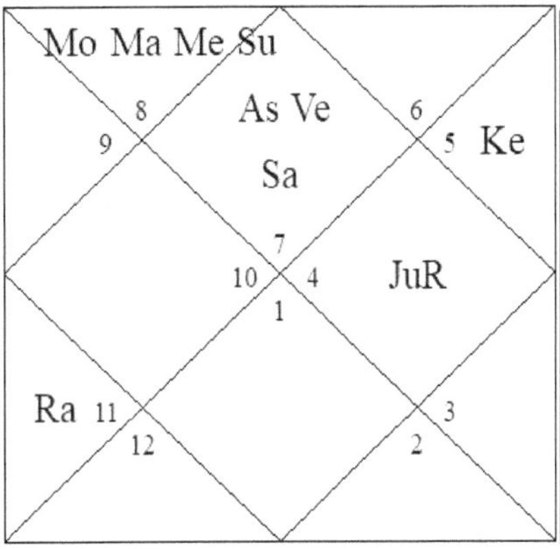

Birth Chart

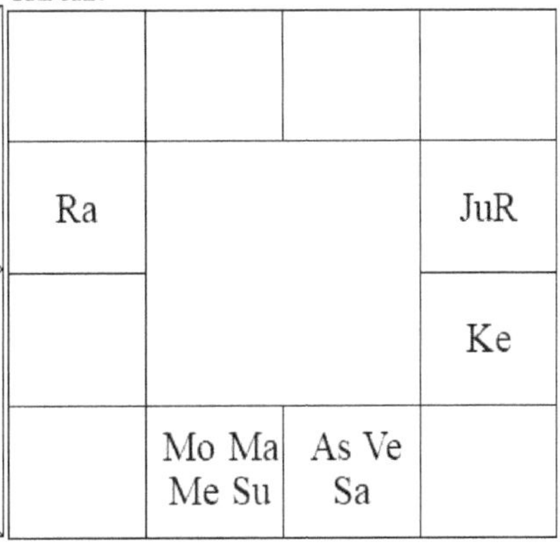

Birth Nakshatra Vishakha

Dasa sequence

Yogini	Nakshatra	From	To
Dhanya	Visakha	14.12.1895	24.2.1896
Bharamari	Anuradha	24.2.1896	24.2.1900
Bhadrika	Jyeshtha	24.2.1900	24.2.1905
Ulka	Moola	24.2.1905	24.2.1911
Siddha	P. Ashadha	24.2.1911	24.2.1918
Sankata	U. Ashadha	24.2.1918	24.2.1926
Mangla	Shravan	24.2.1926	24.2.1927
Pingla	Dhanishta	24.2.1927	24.2.1929
Dhanya	Shatbhisaj	24.2.1929	24.2.1932
Bharamari	P. Bhadrapad	24.2.1932	24.2.1936
Bhadrika	U. Bhadrapad	24.2.1936	24.2.1941

Progress chart for Bhadrika/ U. Bhadrapad and Pisces lagan.

6th h.

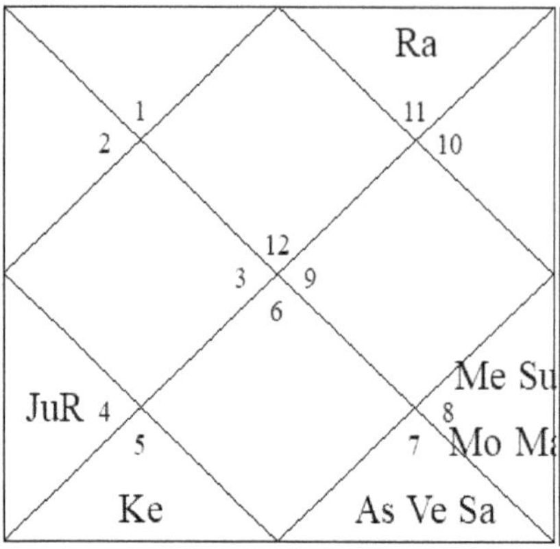

6th h.

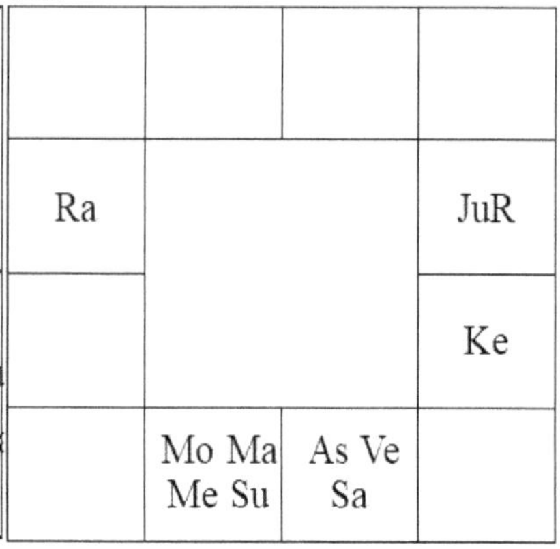

Saturn is powerfully placed and is yoga karaka of birth chart. He is exalted and is with lagna lord. He is expected to give good results.

King George VI was not expected to be the king. His elderbrother Edward ascended the throne as Edward VII. He desiredto marry Walls Simpson, a divorcee. This was not permitted and he abdicated the throne to marry her.

King George was coroneted on 11 December 1936 in the sub period of Ulka, the Nakshtra lord. The Ulka period started on5 November, 1936.

We have seen in birth chart that Saturn is strong to give good result. The progress chart is again strong. The lagna lordis exalted and aspects lagna. Ninth lord is with fourth and seventhlord in ninth house. The placement of eleventh lord in eighth house did harms the elder brother.

Example Job in Foreign DOB 30 April 1945 TOB 9.27 POB Delhi

Birth Chart

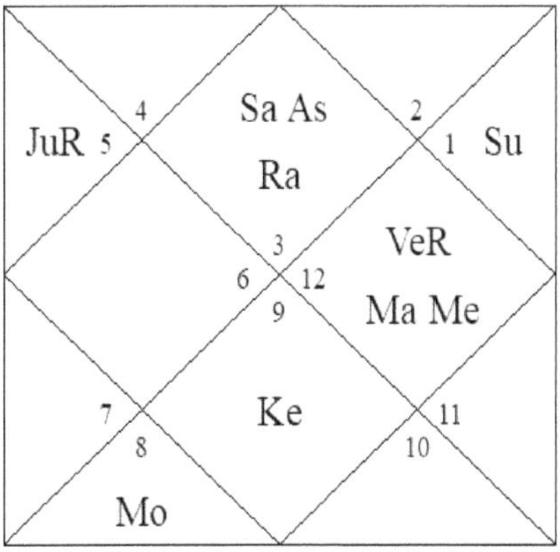

Birth Chart

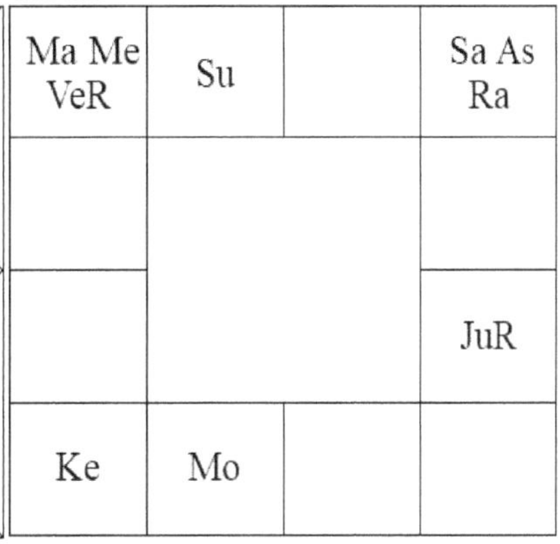

Birth Nakshtra Anuradha

Dasa sequence

Yogini	Nakshtra	From	To
Bharamari	Anuradha	30.4.1945	15.5.1945
Bhadrika	Jyeshtha	15.5.1945	15.5.1950
Ulka	Moola	15.5.1950	15.5.1956
Siddha	P. Ashadha	15.5.1956	15.5.1963
Sankata	U. Ashadha	15.5.1963	15.5.1971
Mangla	Shravan	15.5.1971	15.5.1972
Pingla	Dhanishta	15.5.1972	15.5.1974
Dhanya	Shatbhisaj	15.5.1974	15.5.1977
Bharamari	P. Bhadrapad	15.5.1977	15.5.1981
Bhadrika	U. Bhadrapad	15.5.1981	15.5.1986

Progress chart for Bhadrika/ U. Bhadrapad and Pisces lagan.

10th h.

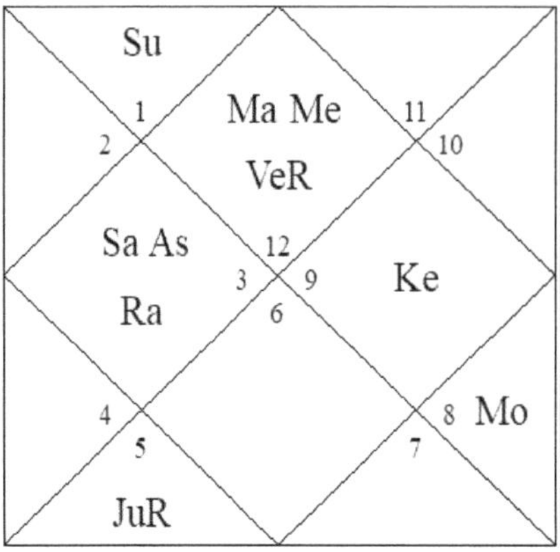

10th h.

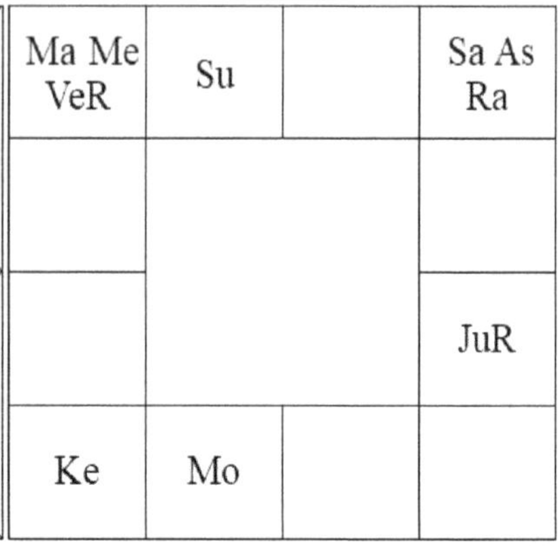

Saturn is the lord of eighth and ninth in the birth Chart. He is with Rahu and is aspected by Mars. Saturn is expectedto give average results.

In the progress chart, Saturn is in fourth house. It is aspecting tenth house and tenth lord. He left the country in August, 1982 to take up a job in Nigeria. The stay abroad wasnot happy. He moved out of country in Ulka sub period and came back in Mangla sub period.

Example Death DOB 24 December 1937 TOB 4.27 POB Darbhanga

Birth Chart

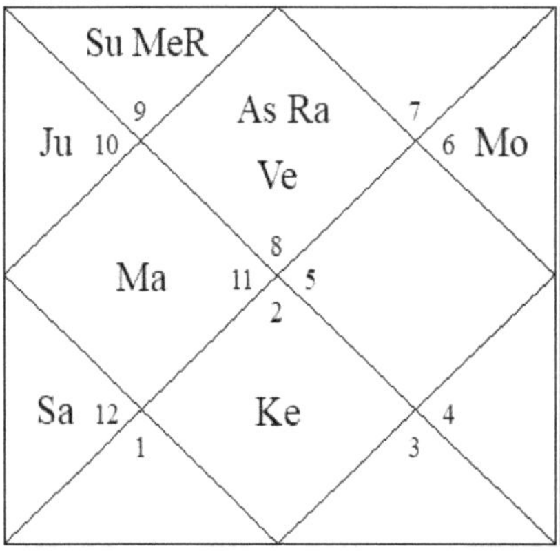

Birth Chart

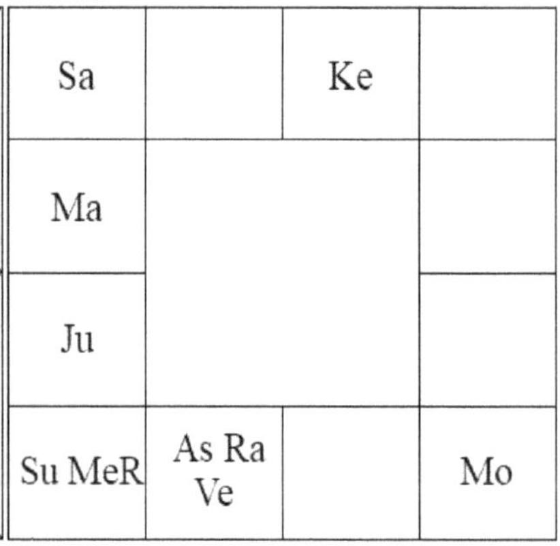

Birth Nakshatra U. Phalguni

Dasa sequence

Yogini	Nakshatra	From	To
Siddha	U. Phalguni	14.12.1937	18.9.1942
Sankata	Hasta	18.9.1942	18.9.1950
Mangla	Chitra	18.9.1950	18.9.1951
Pingla	Swati	18.9.1951	18.9.1953
Dhanya	Visakha	18.9.1953	18.9.1956
Bharamari	Anuradha	18.9.1956	18.9.1960
Bhadrika	Jyeshtha	18.9.1960	18.9.1965
Ulka	Moola	18.9.1965	18.9.1971
Siddha	P. Ashadha	18.9.1971	18.9.1978
Sankata	U. Ashadha	18.9.1978	18.9.1986
Mangla	Shravan	18.9.1986	18.9.1987
Pingla	Dhanishta	18.9.1987	18.9.1989
Dhanya	Shatbhisaj	18.9.1989	18.9.1992
Bharamari	P. Bhadrapad	18.9.1992	18.9.1996
Bhadrika	U. Bhadrapad	18.9.1996	18.9.2001

Progress chart for Bhadrika/ U. Bhadrapad and Pisces lagan.

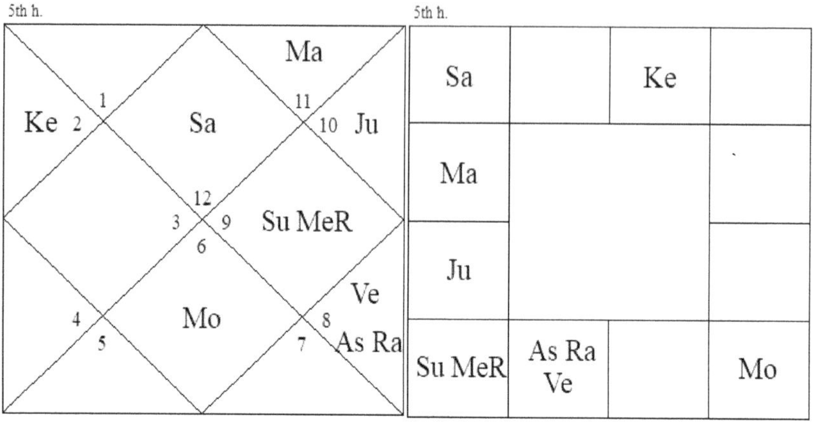

We repeat the chart example of job and marriage discussed in Bhadrika ofJyeshtha. He started his job and got married in this dasha.

Next Bhadrika of U. Bhadrapad commenced on 18 September 1996 and lasted till 18 September 2001. He died in July 2001.

The classical period was Bhadrika but for progress Yogini,the

Progress lagna and the Nakshtra lords have changed. The progress chart for Bhadrika / U. Bhadrapad is given.

In the birth chart Saturn is in fifth house. Jupiter is maracaof birth chart. Jupiter and Saturn have exchanged places and thus Saturn is capable of giving maraca effects.

In the progress chart, Saturn is lord of twelfth and placedin lagna. Saturn influences Moon, Sun and Mercury. Sun is sixthlord and Karaka of heart.

He suffered a heart attack and died. The sub period was of Bhramari.

Chapter 8
Ulka

Ulka period is of six years and in classics this period is not considered good since it is ruled by Saturn. Four Nakshtra can generate this Ulka dasha. These are Kritika, P. Phalguni, Moola and Revati. The results are dependent on the strength ofNakshtra lords.

Nakshtra	Nakshtra Lord	Sign	Remarks
Kritika	Sun	Aries / Taurus	For first one yearsix months, the progress lagna isAries and for lastfour year six months it is Taurus.
P. Phalguni	Venus	Leo	Progress Lagna isLeo
Moola	Ketu	Sagittarius	Progress lagna is Sagittarius
Revati	Mercury	Pisces	Progress lagna isPisces

Ulka / Kritika

Sun is the Nakshtra lord and the progress lagna are Ariesor Taurus.

This dasha period can operate up to a maximum age of 15years in this scheme of progress yogini dasha.

When Aries is the progress lagna, Sun is the lord of fifth house. Depending upon status of Sun in birth chart, it will influence the education.

With Taurus progress lagna, Sun is fourth lord and thus is capable of giving fourth house effects like home, mother, accidents etc.

Example Death of Mother DOB 8 November 1927 TOB 8.09.48 POB Karachi

Birth Chart

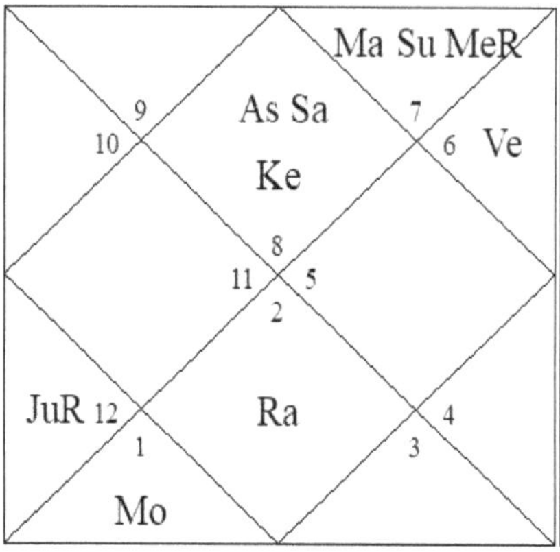

Birth Chart

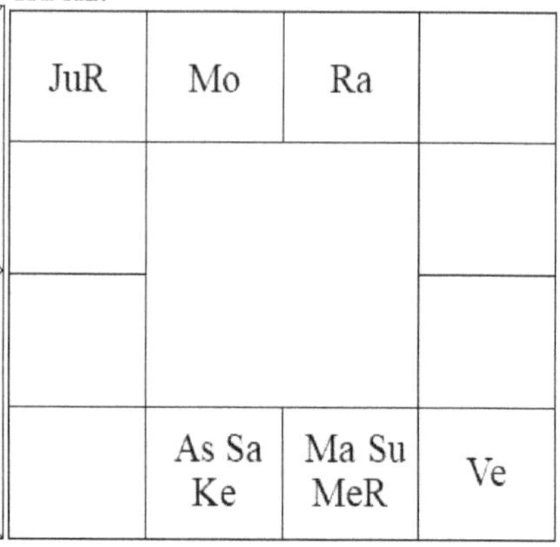

Birth Nakshatra Ashwini

Dasa sequence

Yogini	Nakshatra	From	To
Bharamari	Ashwini	8.11.1927	8.4.1930
Bhadrika	Bharani	8.4.1930	8.4.1935
Ulka	Kritika	8.4.1935	8.4.1941

In the birth chart Sun is in twelfth house and is debilitated.

It is afflicted by Mars.

Progress chart for Ulka/ Kritika and Taurus lagan.

7th h.

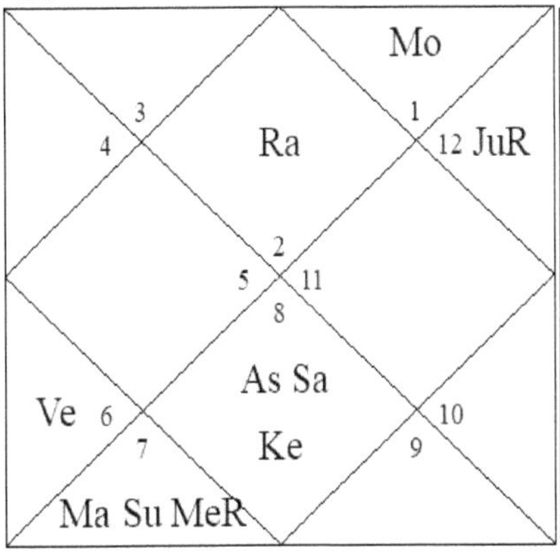

7th h.

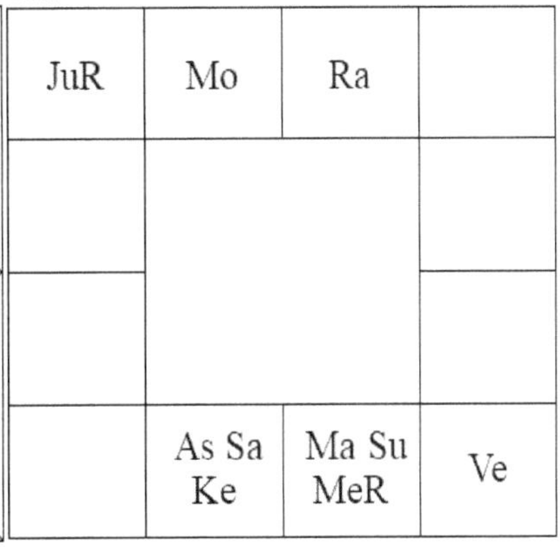

Now see the progress chart. Sun is the fourth lord and placed in sixth house. The fourth house is aspected by Saturn. The fourth lord is with Mercury and Mars.

For fourth house, maracas are Saturn and Mercury. Both are making relation with fourth house and fourth lord.

His mother died when he was thirteen years of age and the sub period was of Bhadrika.

Example Re Marriage of mother DOB 19 August 1946 TOB 8.53 POB Hope

Birth Chart

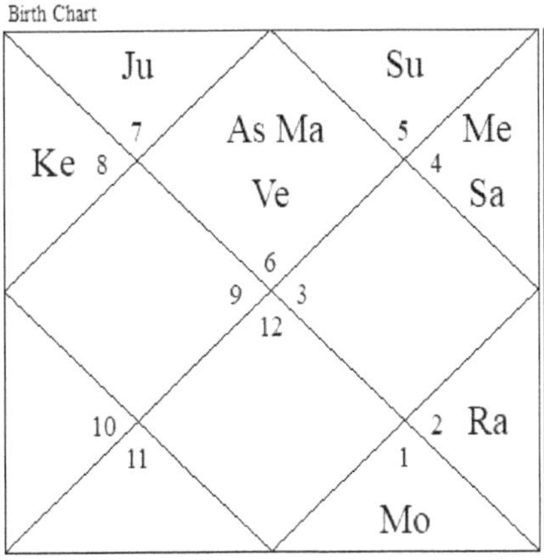

Birth Chart

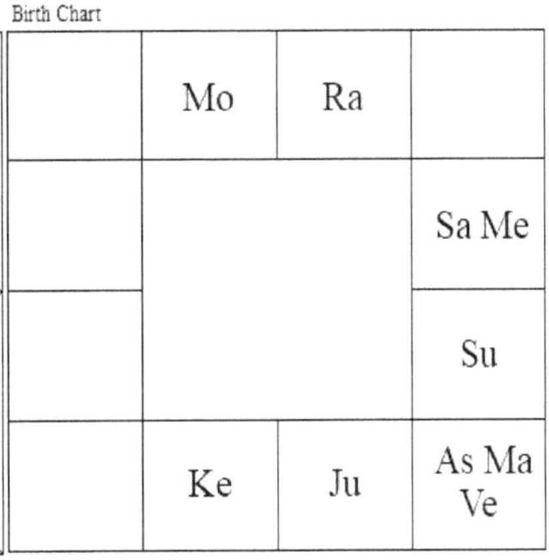

Birth Nakshatra Bharani

Dasa sequence

Yogini	Nakshatra	From	To
Bhadrika	Bharani	19.8.1946	24.8.1946
Ulka	Kritika	24.8.1946	24.8.1952

Progress chart for Ulka/ Kritika and Taurus lagan.

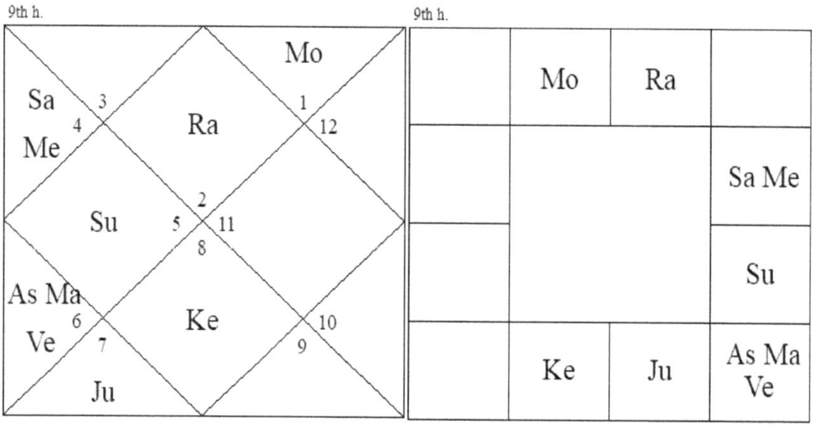

Sun is twelfth lord and is placed in twelfth house of changein birth chart. It is in Kartari indicating dependence and externalsupport.

Sun is placed in fourth house of progress chart and the events of home and mother are seen. He moved to hot springs when his mother married Roger Clinton who owned an automobile dealership.

Re marriage of mother is confirmed from fourth house. The seventh lord from fourth is Saturn in the progress chart and it is Mercury in birth chart. Both are together. The tenth house, i.e. seventh from fourth is aspected by seventh lord ofbirth chart.

Example Change of Residence DOB 20 November 1942 TOB 8.30 POB Scranton

Birth Chart

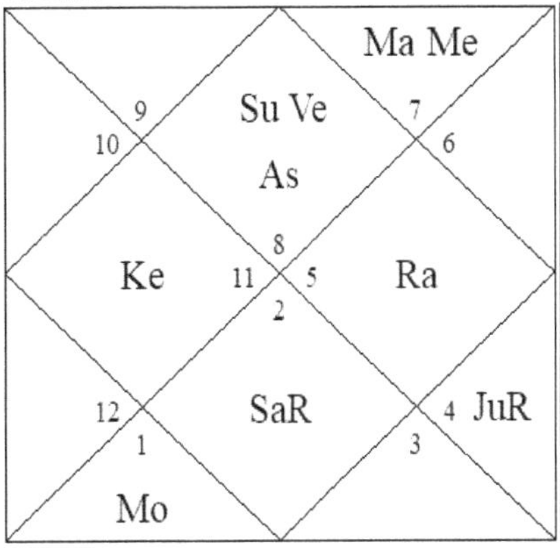

Birth Chart

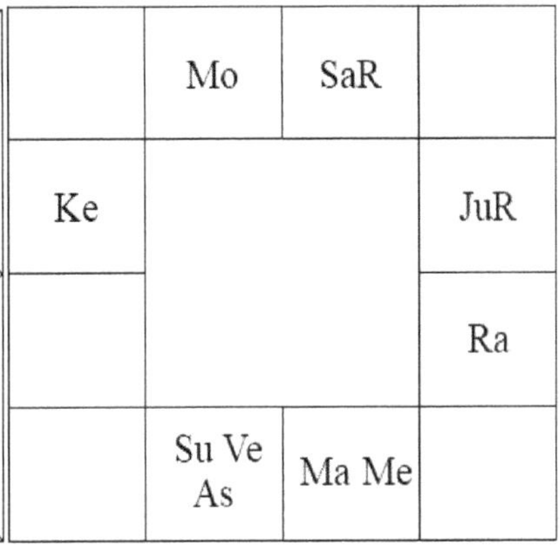

Birth Nakshatra Ashwini

Dasa sequence

Yogini	Nakshatra	From	To
Bharamari	Ashwini	20.11.1942	4.7.1944
Bhadrika	Bharani	4.7.1944	4.7.1949
Ulka	Kritika	4.7.1949	4.7.1955

Progress chart for Ulka/ Kritika and Taurus lagan.

7th h.

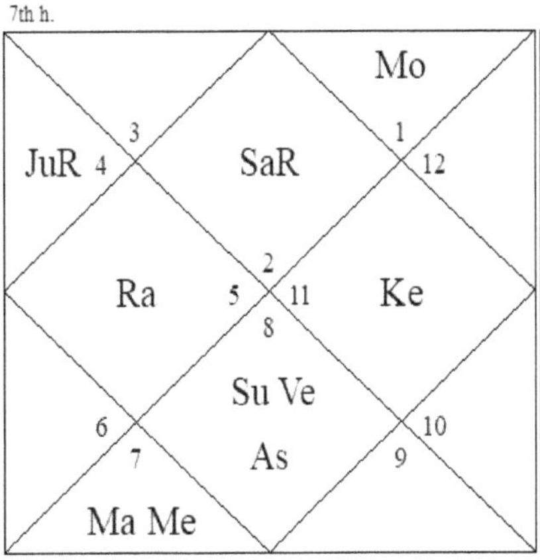

7th h.

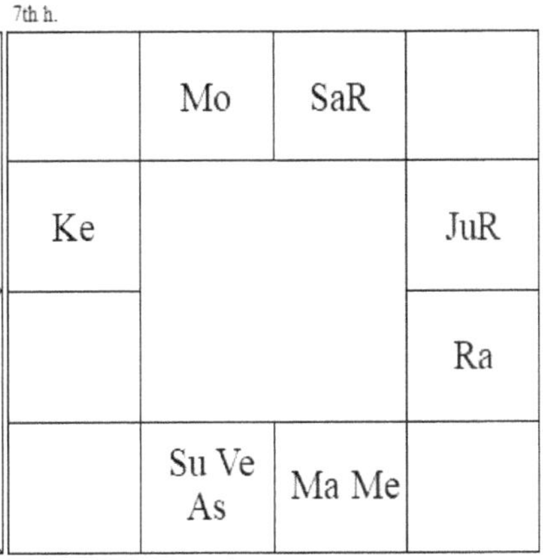

In the birth chart Sun is in lagna. It is with twelfth lord Venus.

Retrograde Saturn and Jupiter aspects it. This aspect isof Kendra and trikona lords but retrograde. Sun given mixed results being tenth lord and related with yoga karakas.

In the progress chart fourth house has Rahu. Now Sun asfourth lord is in seventh house and aspected by eighth lord Jupiter.

Due to lack of work, his father moved to an apartment inClaymont in 1953. The sub period was Pingla

Ulka / P. Phalguni

Venus is the Nakshtra lord and Leo is the progress lagna. When Venus is a favorable planet in birth chart it gives rise incareer since it is now the tenth lord of progress chart. When Venus is afflicted in birth chart it is not a good period for careeror reputation. Venus is a maraca for father. If Venus is also maraca of father in birth chart, then problems to father is seen.

Mars is the yoga karaka for Leo lagna. A good Mars in birthchart will give good results in this dasha period. Any planet inrelation with this Mars will have a say in its dasha period.

In the birth chart Venus is with Rahu in sixth house. It isnot aspected by any planet. Venus is thus afflicted in birth chart.

Example Honor and Defeat DOB 19 November 1917 TOB 23.11 POB Allahabad

Birth Chart

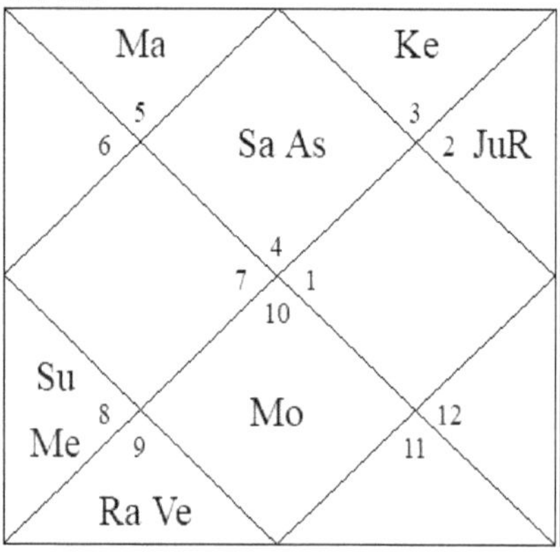

Birth Chart

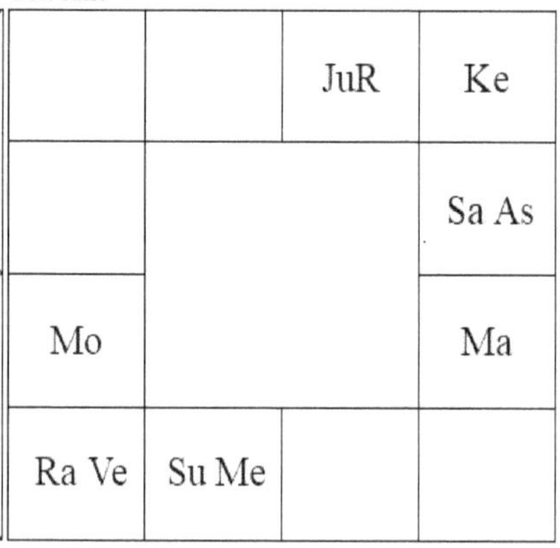

Birth Nakshatra U. Ashadha

Dasa sequence

Yogini	Nakshatra	From	To
Sankata	U. Ashadha	19.11.1917	13.7.1920
Mangla	Shravan	13.7.1920	13.7.1921
Pingla	Dhanishta	13.7.1921	13.7.1923
Dhanya	Shatbhisaj	13.7.1923	13.7.1926
Bharamari	P. Bhadrapad	13.7.1926	13.7.1930
Bhadrika	U. Bhadrapad	13.7.1930	13.7.1935
Ulka	Revati	13.7.1935	13.7.1941
Siddha	Rohini	13.7.1941	13.7.1948
Sankata	Mrigshira	13.7.1948	13.7.1956
Mangla	Ardra	13.7.1956	13.7.1957
Pingla	Punarvasu	13.7.1957	13.7.1959
Dhanya	Pushya	13.7.1959	13.7.1962
Bharamari	Ashlesha	13.7.1962	13.7.1966
Bhadrika	Magha	13.7.1966	13.7.1971
Ulka	P. Phalguni	13.7.1971	13.7.1977

Progress chart for Ulka/ P. Phalguni and Leo lagan.

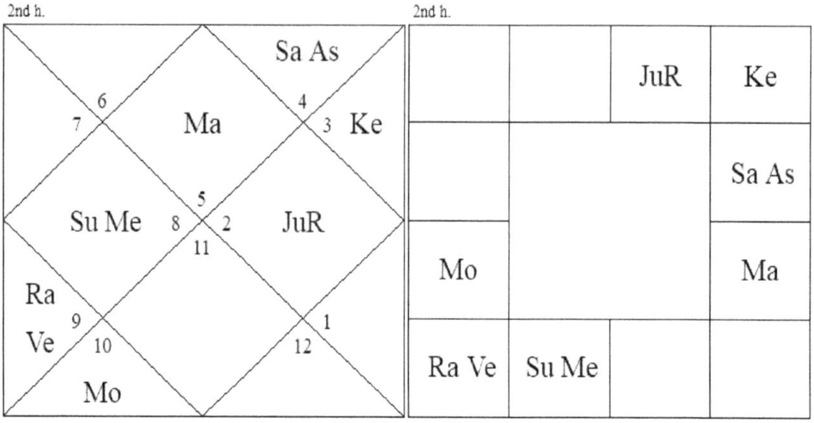

In the progress chart, Venus is in fifth house which is eighth from tenth. The exchange of Jupiter and Venus is now the exchange of tenth and fifth lords and is Yoga karaka.

The Ulka dasha started on 13 July, 1971 and the situation in Bangladesh came up at the mind of nation.

She was hailed as Durga when Bangladesh was created and Pakistan was divided.

Then came the sub period of Pingla in this dasha. On12 June 1975, Allahabad High Court ruled against her. Emergencywas declared. Sun is lagna lord of progress chart and is involvedin exchange with Mars. The iron rule was imposed. Retrogradeeighth lord Jupiter is aspecting it. We should not forget the effects of this Jupiter. Venus has to give its adverse effects also.

The last sub period was of Bhadrika. Mercury is third andtwelfth lord of birth chart. In the progress chart Mercury is aspecting tenth house. Emergency was lifted in 1977 and general elections were held. Indira Gandhi lost the elections and congresssuffered heavy losses. It was reduced to 153 seats from 350 seats.

Example Elevation of husband DOB 26 October 1947 TOB 20.0 POB Chicago

Birth Chart

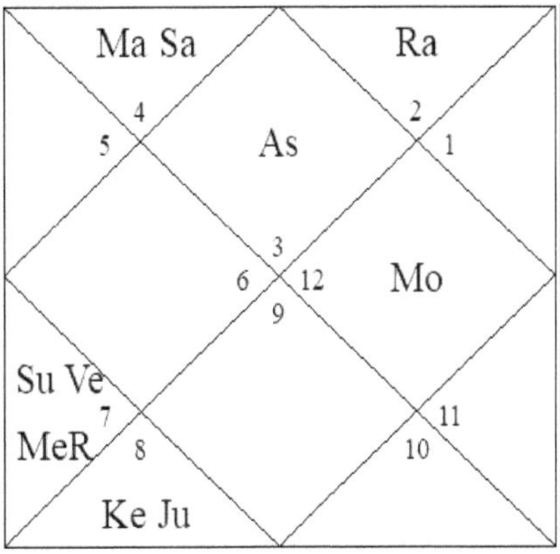

Birth Chart

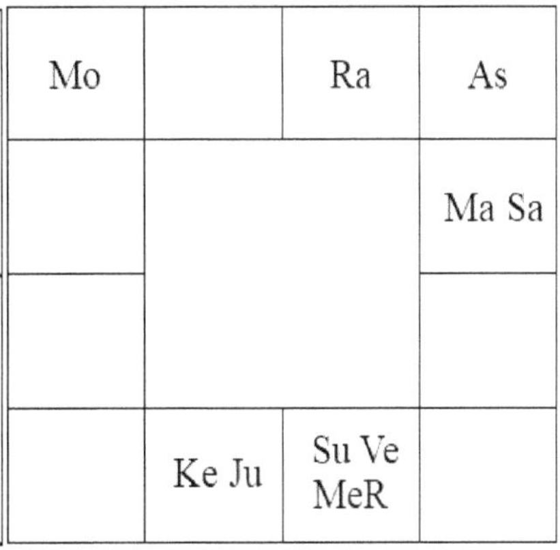

Birth Nakshatra U. Bhadrapad

Dasa sequence

Yogini	Nakshatra	From	To
Bhadrika	U. Bhadrapad	26.10.1947	17.10.1951
Ulka	Revati	17.10.1951	17.10.1957
Siddha	Rohini	17.10.1957	17.10.1964
Sankata	Mrigshira	17.10.1964	17.10.1972
Mangla	Ardra	17.10.1972	17.10.1973
Pingla	Punarvasu	17.10.1973	17.10.1975
Dhanya	Pushya	17.10.1975	17.10.1978
Bharamari	Ashlesha	17.10.1978	17.10.1982
Bhadrika	Magha	17.10.1982	17.10.1987
Ulka	P. Phalguni	17.10.1987	17.10.1993

Progress chart for Ulka/ P. Phalguni and Leo lagan.

3rd h.

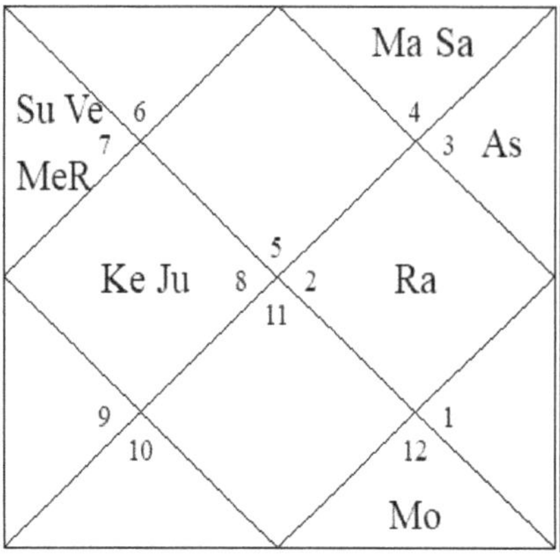

3rd h.

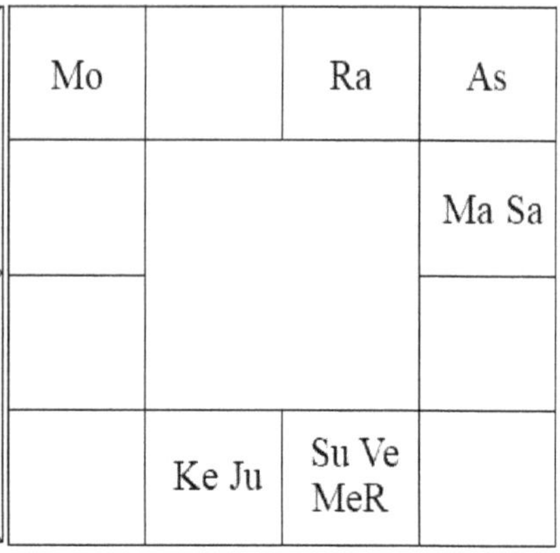

Venus is yoga karaka of birth chart. It is in own sign in fifthhouse and its placement with fourth lord Mercury is a great Rajyoga.

In the progress chart he is well placed. Mars is the Yoga karaka of progress chart. It is with Saturn who is seventh lord.Mars aspects Mercury. Mercury is with Venus. Her husband became President of USA on 20 Jan 1993 and she became thefirst lady.

Example Death DOB 18 March 1914 TOB 12.22.35 POB Dungarpur

Birth Chart

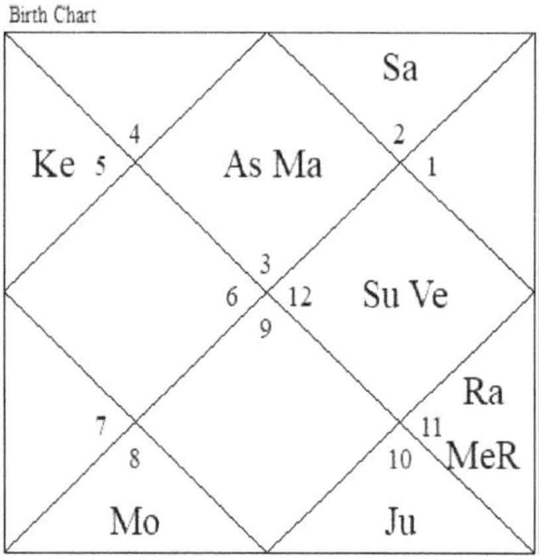

Birth Chart

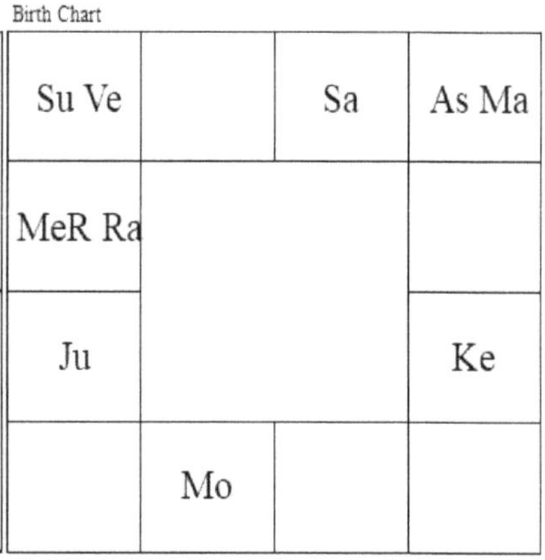

Birth Nakshatra Jyestha

Dasa sequence

Yogini	Nakshatra	From	To
Bhadrika	Jyeshtha	18.3.1914	19.2.1915
Ulka	Moola	19.2.1915	19.2.1921
Siddha	P. Ashadha	19.2.1921	19.2.1928
Sankata	U. Ashadha	19.2.1928	19.2.1936
Mangla	Shravan	19.2.1936	19.2.1937
Pingla	Dhanishta	19.2.1937	19.2.1939
Dhanya	Shatbhisaj	19.2.1939	19.2.1942
Bharamari	P. Bhadrapad	19.2.1942	19.2.1946
Bhadrika	U. Bhadrapad	19.2.1946	19.2.1951
Ulka	Revati	19.2.1951	19.2.1957
Siddha	Rohini	19.2.1957	19.2.1964
Sankata	Mrigshira	19.2.1964	19.2.1972
Mangla	Ardra	19.2.1972	19.2.1973
Pingla	Punarvasu	19.2.1973	19.2.1975
Dhanya	Pushya	19.2.1975	19.2.1978
Bharamari	Ashlesha	19.2.1978	19.2.1982
Bhadrika	Magha	19.2.1982	19.2.1987

Progress chart for Ulka/ P. Phalguni and Leo lagan.

3rd h.

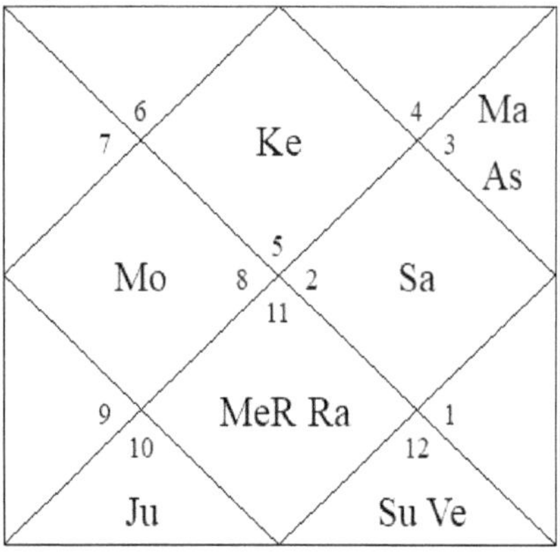

3rd h.

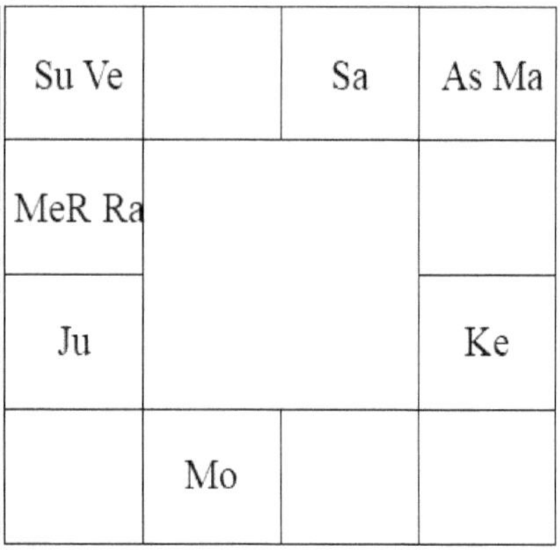

In the progress chart, Venus is placed in eighth house with lagna Lord Sun. No planet is aspecting this combination. Lagnais afflicted by Ketu and aspected by maraca Mercury. Mercury isaspected by Saturn.

He left this world on 11 December 1988 in the sub period of Siddha, the Nakshtra lord. The Pratyantar was of Bhadrika which commenced on 11 December, 1988.

Example Successful dasa DOB 14 June 1969 TOB 04.40 POB Manheim

Birth Chart

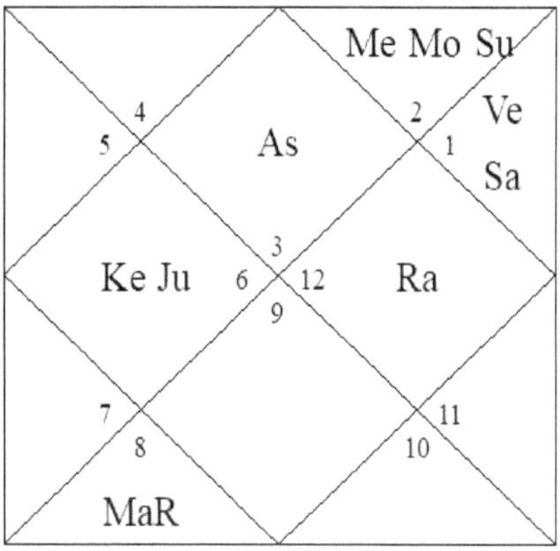

Birth Chart

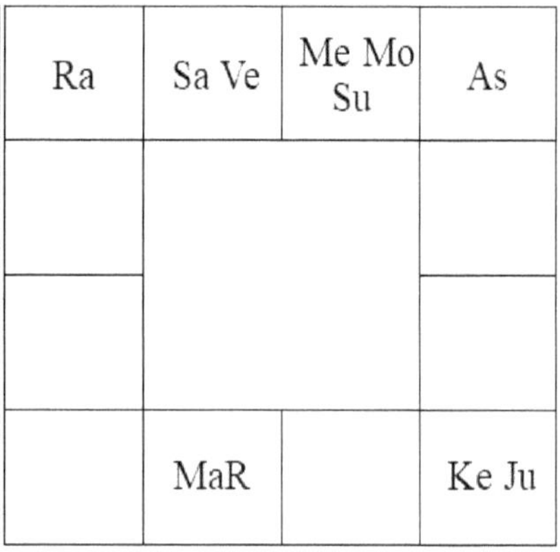

Birth Nakshatra Rohini

Dasa sequence

Yogini	Nakshatra	From	To
Siddha	Rohini	14.6.1969	30.11.1970
Sankata	Mrigshira	30.11.1970	30.11.1978
Mangla	Ardra	30.11.1978	30.11.1979
Pingla	Punarvasu	30.11.1979	30.11.1981
Dhanya	Pushya	30.11.1981	30.11.1984
Bharamari	Ashlesha	30.11.1984	30.11.1988
Bhadrika	Magha	30.11.1988	30.11.1993
Ulka	P. Phalguni	30.11.1993	30.11.1999

Progress chart for Ulka/ P. Phalguni and Leo lagan.

3rd h.

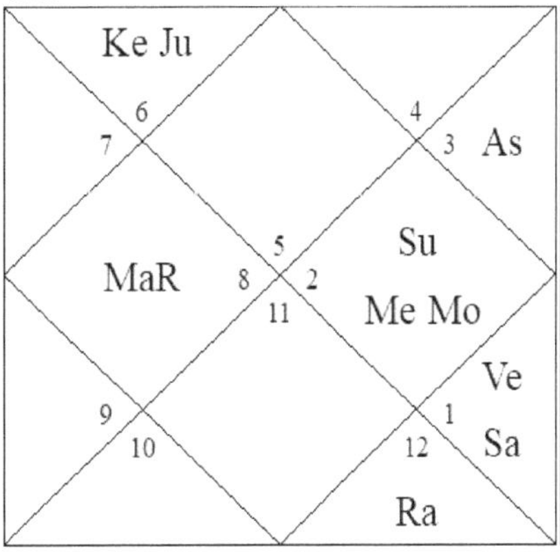

3rd h.

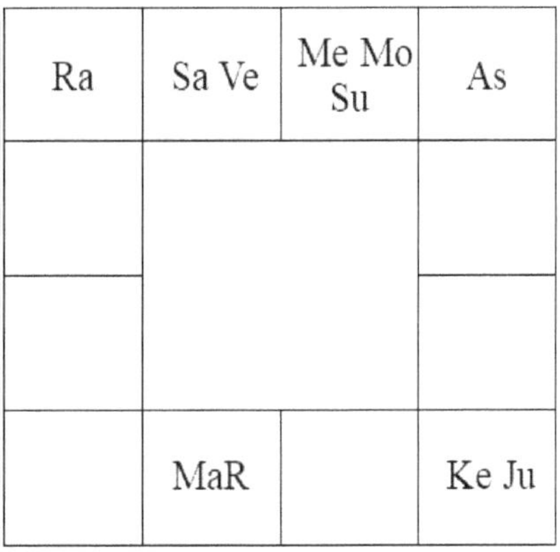

In the birth chart Venus is fifth lord and is placed with ninth lord in eleventh house. The luck factor is present.

In the progress chart Venus is in ninth house. There are four planets in four – ten axes. Now the ninth lord is aspectingtenth house and tenth lord is in ninth house. Mars is yoga karakaand gives great strength to professional matters.

She remained on top during this Ulka period which lastedtill 1999.

Soon when Siddha of U Phalguni commenced, she retired from active game. Sun is third lord of birth, placed in twelfth and aspected by Mars.

Example Promotion DOB 6 June 1948 TOB 10.25 POB Palampur

Birth Chart

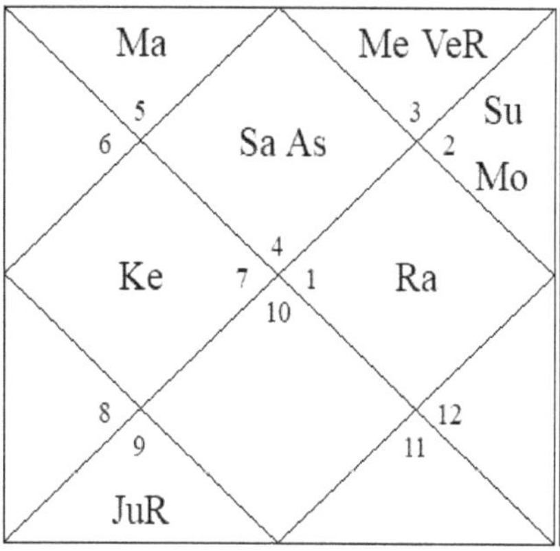

Birth Chart

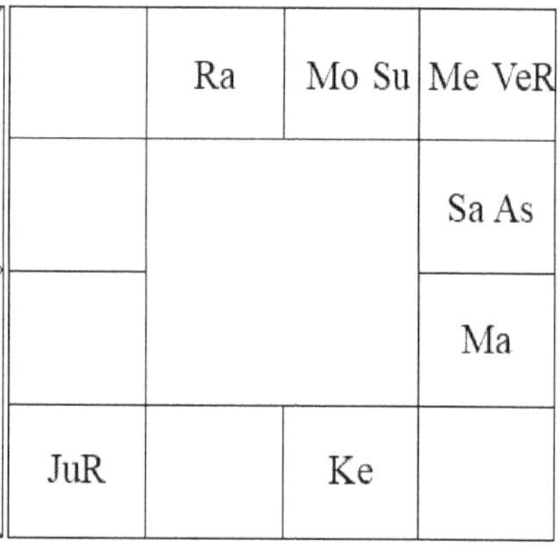

Birth Nakshatra Kritika

Dasa sequence

Yogini	Nakshatra	From	To
Ulka	Kritika	6.6.1948	27.8.1950
Siddha	Rohini	27.8.1950	27.8.1957
Sankata	Mrigshira	27.8.1957	27.8.1965
Mangla	Ardra	27.8.1965	27.8.1966
Pingla	Punarvasu	27.8.1966	27.8.1968
Dhanya	Pushya	27.8.1968	27.8.1971
Bharamari	Ashlesha	27.8.1971	27.8.1975
Bhadrika	Magha	27.8.1975	27.8.1980
Ulka	P. Phalguni	27.8.1980	27.8.1986

Progress chart for Ulka/ P. Phalguni and Leo lagan.

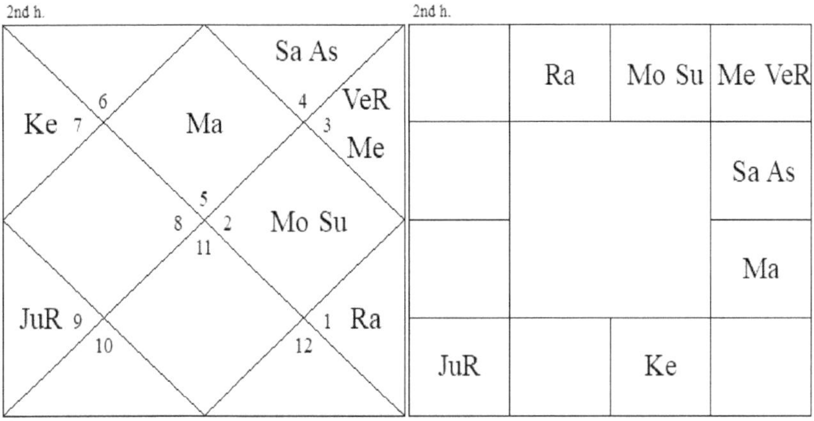

Venus is fourth and eleventh lord of birth chart. Venus cannot be termed as a good planet itself. The mutual aspect offourth and ninth lord makes it participate in yoga.

The progress chart is having strength. The tenth house contains lagna lord Sun which is with exalted Moon. The Yogakaraka Mars is in lagna. Mars is yoga karaka of birth and progresschart.

He got an excellent promotion on 28 June, 1984 in the subperiod of Pingla.

Ulka / Moola

Ketu is the Nakshtra lord. The progress lagna is Sagittarius.Ketu gives results of its dispositor in the birth chart. Ketu can beunpredictable and indicate unexpected events.

A good placement of Ketu in birth chart can auger well inthis dasha. Sagittarius is the ninth house of Kaal Purush and Ketu is the planet to grant salvation. It gives detachment if connected with Jupiter and trine lords.

Example Death of wife and son DOB 15 November 1918 TOB 21.49.26 POB Srinagar

Birth Chart

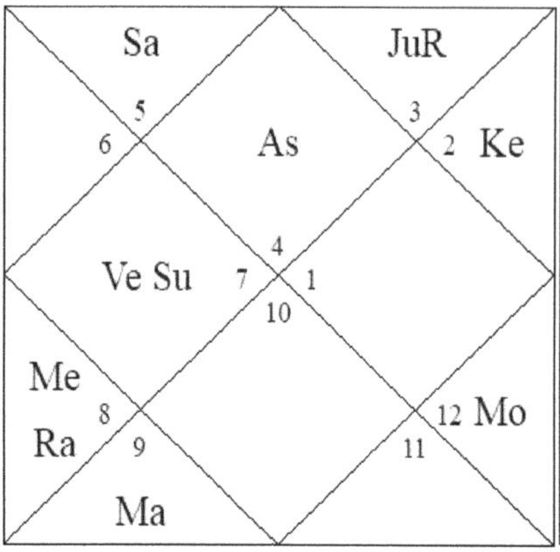

Birth Chart

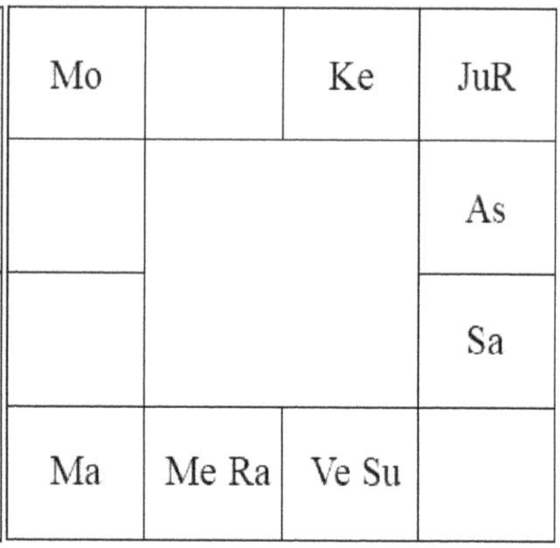

Birth Nakshatra Revati

Dasa sequence

Yogini	Nakshatra	From	To
Ulka	Revati	15.11.1918	11.2.1922
Siddha	Rohini	11.2.1922	11.2.1929
Sankata	Mrigshira	11.2.1929	11.2.1937
Mangla	Ardra	11.2.1937	11.2.1938
Pingla	Punarvasu	11.2.1938	11.2.1940
Dhanya	Pushya	11.2.1940	11.2.1943
Bharamari	Ashlesha	11.2.1943	11.2.1947
Bhadrika	Magha	11.2.1947	11.2.1952
Ulka	P. Phalguni	11.2.1952	11.2.1958
Siddha	U. Phalguni	11.2.1958	11.2.1965
Sankata	Hasta	11.2.1965	11.2.1973
Mangla	Chitra	11.2.1973	11.2.1974

Yogini	Nakshatra	From	To
Pingla	Swati	11.2.1974	11.2.1976
Dhanya	Visakha	11.2.1976	11.2.1979
Bharamari	Anuradha	11.2.1979	11.2.1983
Bhadrika	Jyeshtha	11.2.1983	11.2.1988
Ulka	Moola	11.2.1988	11.2.1994

Progress chart for Ulka/ Moola and Sagittarius lagan.

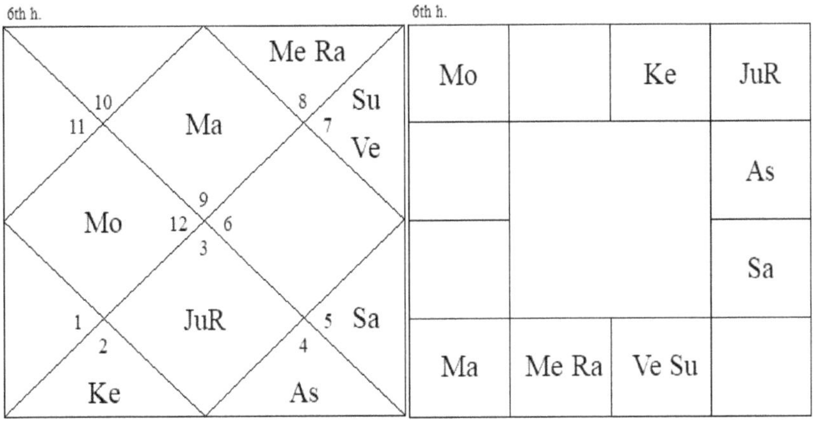

In the birth chart, Ketu is in eleventh house and is aspectedby Saturn. Saturn is lord of eighth and is a maraca for wife. The axis of Rahu/Ketu is five / eleven.

Ketu is in sixth house of progress chart and Saturn is againeighth lord from seventh house. His wife died in Ulka / Ulka.

From birth chart, Ketu is capable of giving results of fifthhouse also. He is with Mercury who is eighth lord from fifth.

In the progress chart Sun and Venus are aspecting the fifth house. This combination is aspected by Saturn. Venus is maraca for child and Ketu is acting as Venus. His elder son diedin Ulka / Pingla.

Example Death of wife DOB 14 November 1889 TOB 23.05 POB Allahabad

Birth Chart

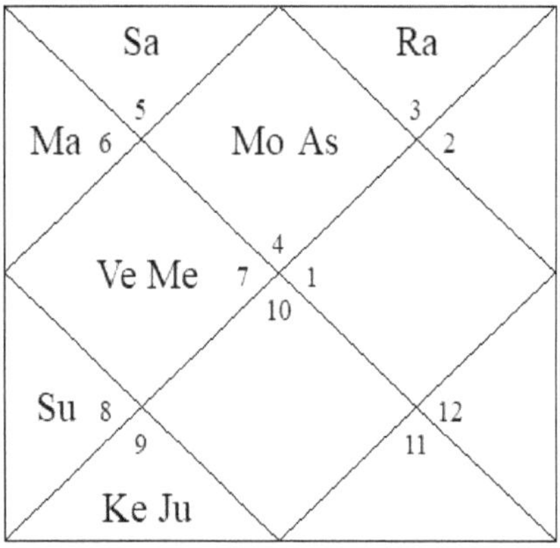

Birth Chart

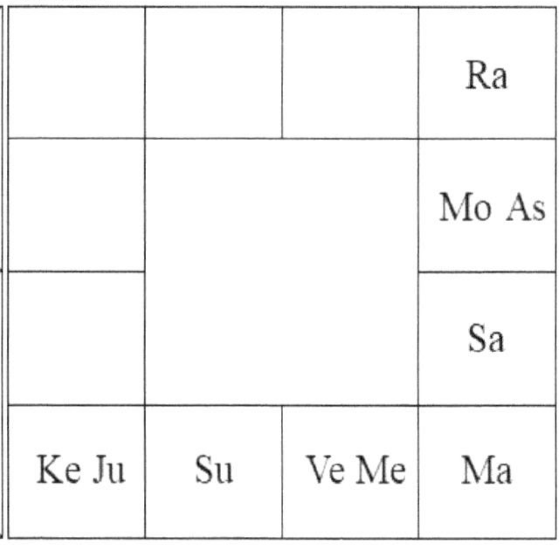

Birth Nakshatra Ashlesha

Dasa sequence

Yogini	Nakshatra	From	To
Bharamari	Ashlesha	14.11.1889	27.6.1893
Bhadrika	Magha	27.6.1893	27.6.1898
Ulka	P. Phalguni	27.6.1898	27.6.1904
Siddha	U. Phalguni	27.6.1904	27.6.1911
Sankata	Hasta	27.6.1911	27.6.1919
Mangla	Chitra	27.6.1919	27.6.1920
Pingla	Swati	27.6.1920	27.6.1922
Dhanya	Visakha	27.6.1922	27.6.1925
Bharamari	Anuradha	27.6.1925	27.6.1929
Bhadrika	Jyeshtha	27.6.1929	27.6.1934
Ulka	Moola	27.6.1934	27.6.1940

Progress chart for Ulka/ Moola and Sagittarius lagan.

6th h.

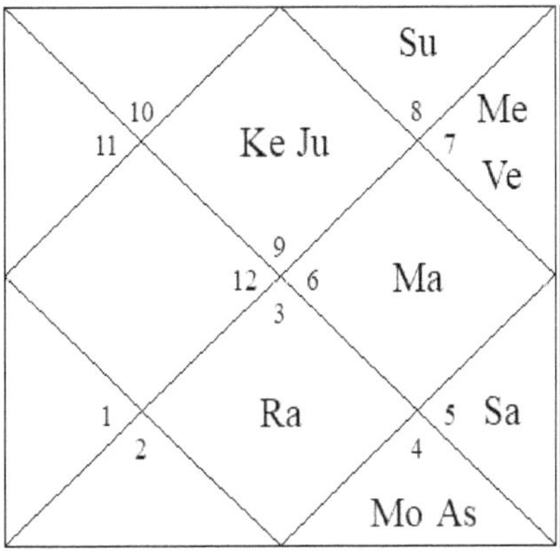

6th h.

			Ra
			Mo As
			Sa
Ke Ju	Su	Ve Me	Ma

Ketu is in sixth house of birth chart. The sixth lord Jupiterjoins him. Thus, Ketu is capable of giving illness.

In the progress chart Ketu is in lagna and afflicts one seven axis. Jupiter and Ketu are maraca for wife. The eighth lord of wife is Saturn. Saturn aspects Venus and Mercury.

Kamala Nehru expired on 28 Feb. 1936 in a T.B. Sanitorium in Switzerland. The dasha was Ulka / Siddha/ Dhanya.

Example Marriage and child DOB 29 December 1942 TOB 18.05 POB Burewala

Birth Chart

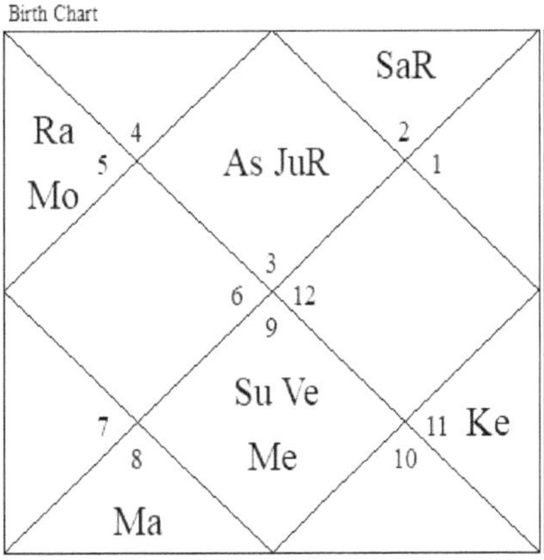

Birth Chart

		SaR	As JuR
Ke			
			Ra Mo
Su Ve Me	Ma		

Birth Nakshatra U. Phalguni

Dasa sequence

Yogini	Nakshatra	From	To
Siddha	U. Phalguni	29.12.1942	3.10.1948
Sankata	Hasta	3.10.1948	3.10.1956
Mangla	Chitra	3.10.1956	3.10.1957
Pingla	Swati	3.10.1957	3.10.1959
Dhanya	Visakha	3.10.1959	3.10.1962
Bharamari	Anuradha	3.10.1962	3.10.1966
Bhadrika	Jyeshtha	3.10.1966	3.10.1971
Ulka	Moola	3.10.1971	3.10.1977

Progress chart for Ulka/ Moola and Sagittarius lagan.

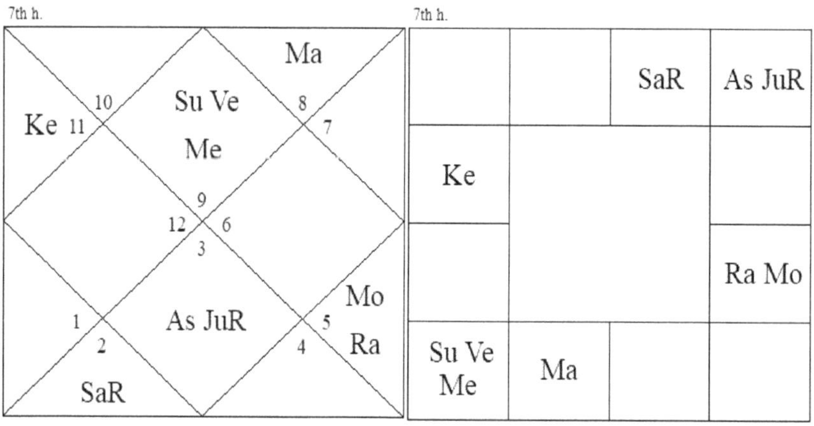

The Rahu / Ketu axis is in three / nine axis in both the charts.

With Sagittarius progress lagna, the seventh and lagna lords are in mutual aspect. He married Dimple Kapadia in March 1973 in the dasha of Ulka / Siddha.

The three nine axis indicate the arrival of child also. His daughter was born in Ulka / Sankata.

Example Marriage DOB 10 March 1955 TOB 20.55 POB Dehradun

Birth Chart

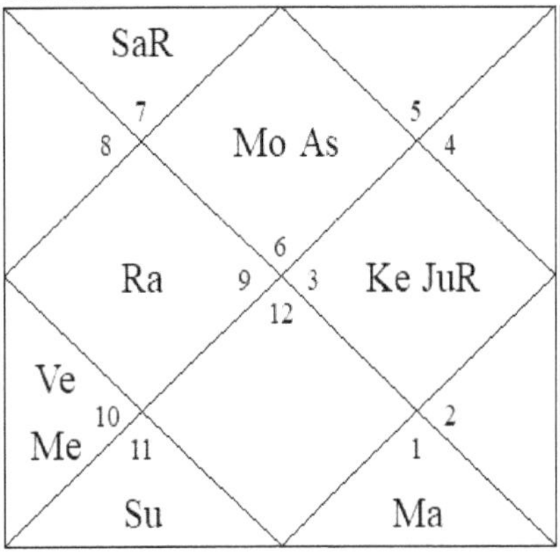

Birth Chart

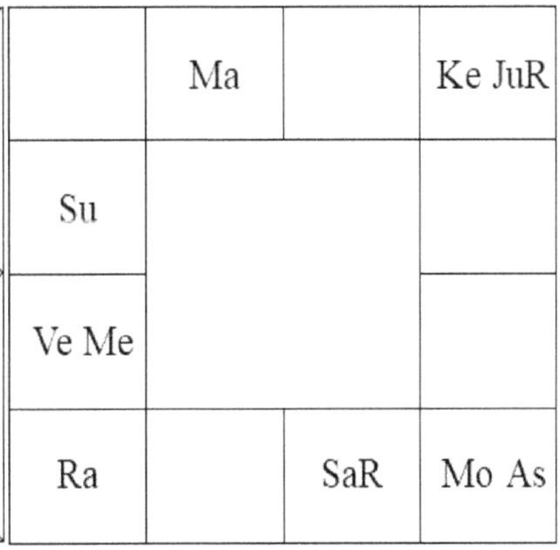

Birth Nakshatra Hasta

Dasa sequence

Yogini	Nakshatra	From	To
Sankata	Hasta	10.3.1955	8.7.1957
Mangla	Chitra	8.7.1957	8.7.1958
Pingla	Swati	8.7.1958	8.7.1960
Dhanya	Visakha	8.7.1960	8.7.1963
Bharamari	Anuradha	8.7.1963	8.7.1967
Bhadrika	Jyeshtha	8.7.1967	8.7.1972
Ulka	Moola	8.7.1972	8.7.1978

Progress chart for Ulka/ Moola and Sagittarius lagan.

4th h.

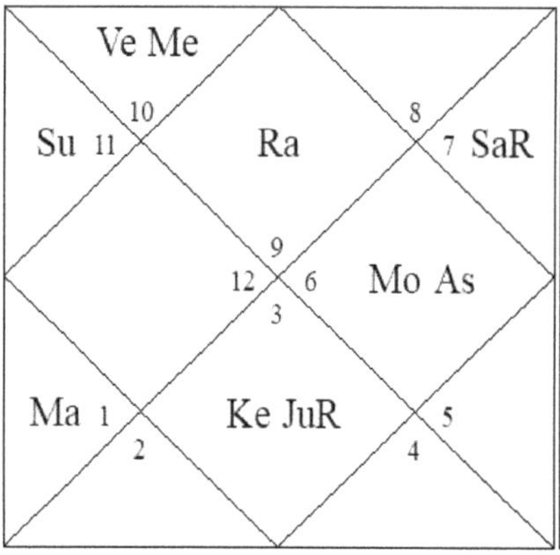

4th h.

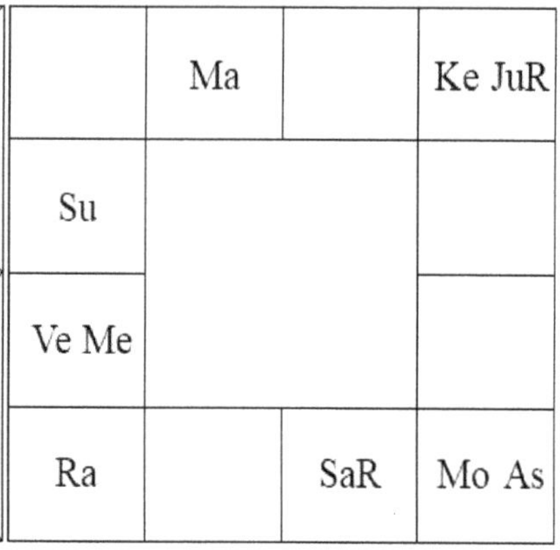

Ketu is with Jupiter in birth chart. Jupiter is lord of fourth and seventh house.

Now Ketu is moved to seventh house and is with lagna andfourth lord. The promise of seventh and fourth house is highlighted. He married on 30 Jan. 1975 in the dasha of Ulka /Sankata.

Is the dasha of Ulka / Sankata is bad?

Example Scorpion bite DOB 7 November 1953 TOB 22.30 POB Gaya

Birth Chart

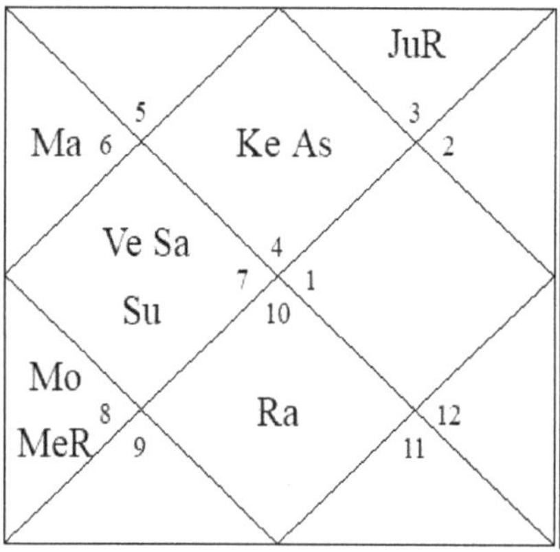

Birth Chart

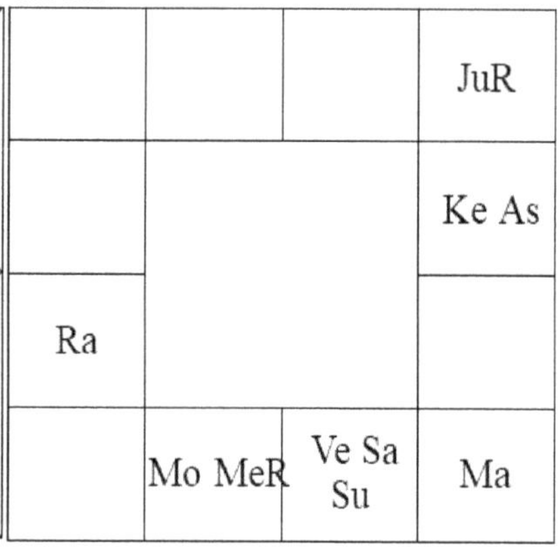

Birth Nakshatra Visakha

Dasa sequence

Yogini	Nakshatra	From	To
Dhanya	Visakha	7.11.1953	6.1.1954
Bharamari	Anuradha	6.1.1954	6.1.1958
Bhadrika	Jyeshtha	6.1.1958	6.1.1963
Ulka	Moola	6.1.1963	6.1.1969

Progress chart for Ulka/ Moola and Sagittarius lagan.

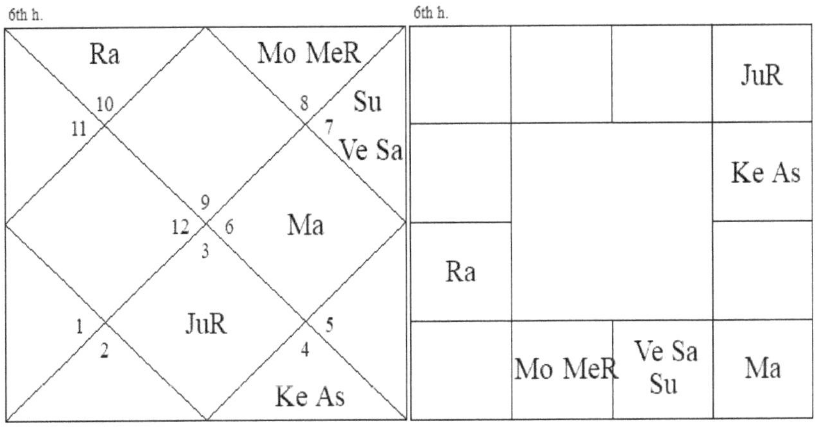

In the birth chart Ketu is in Lagna and is aspected by Saturn.Saturn is lord of eighth and seventh house of birth. The Positionof Ketu is not good for the body.

This Ketu has moved to eighth house of progress chart. Aserious condition and to make matters worse, it is now aspectedby second and third lord Saturn.

A Scorpion bit him in December 1964 in the sub period ofSiddha. Siddha is with Saturn and is a malefic planet for Sagittarius lagna. He survived. Lagna lord Jupiter is aspectinglagna.

Ulka / Revati

Mercury is the Nakshtra lord and Pisces is the progress lagna. Mercury is the lord of fourth and seventh house. The events at home like mother, house and are related to spouse, deathpartners are seen in this dasha.

When Mercury is afflicted in the birth chart or is not a benefic, there are problems related to fourth or seventh house.

A well associated and having good lordship in the birth chart, Mercury will do well in his affairs.

Jupiter is the tenth and lagna lord of progress Chart. Jupiterhaving malefic lordship in birth chart can give problems of health or in profession.

Example PM DOB 17 April 1916 TOB 15.35.30 POB Colombo

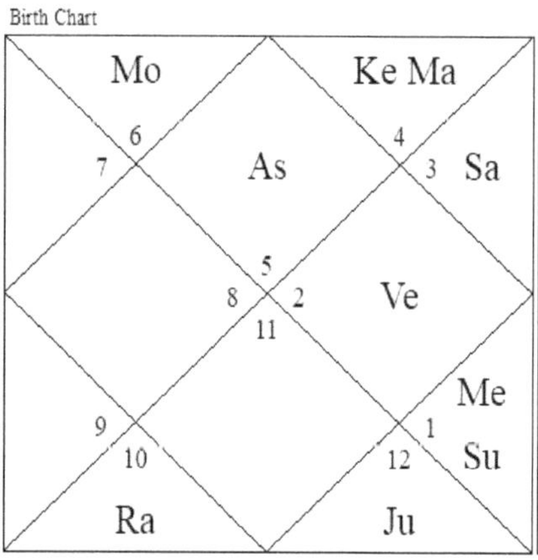

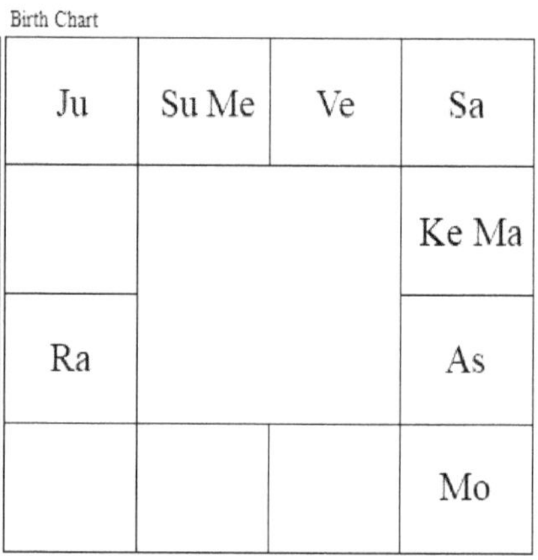

Birth Nakshatra Chitra

Dasa sequence

Yogini	Nakshatra	From	To
Mangla	Chitra	17.4.1916	29.3.1917
Pingla	Swati	29.3.1917	29.3.1919
Dhanya	Visakha	29.3.1919	29.3.1922
Bharamari	Anuradha	29.3.1922	29.3.1926
Bhadrika	Jyeshtha	29.3.1926	29.3.1931

Yogini	Nakshatra	From	To
Ulka	Moola	29.3.1931	29.3.1937
Siddha	P. Ashadha	29.3.1937	29.3.1944
Sankata	U. Ashadha	29.3.1944	29.3.1952
Mangla	Shravan	29.3.1952	29.3.1953
Pingla	Dhanishta	29.3.1953	29.3.1955
Dhanya	Shatbhisaj	29.3.1955	29.3.1958
Bharamari	P. Bhadrapad	29.3.1958	29.3.1962
Bhadrika	U. Bhadrapad	29.3.1962	29.3.1967
Ulka	Revati	29.3.1967	29.3.1973

Progress chart for Ulka/ Revati and Pisces lagan.

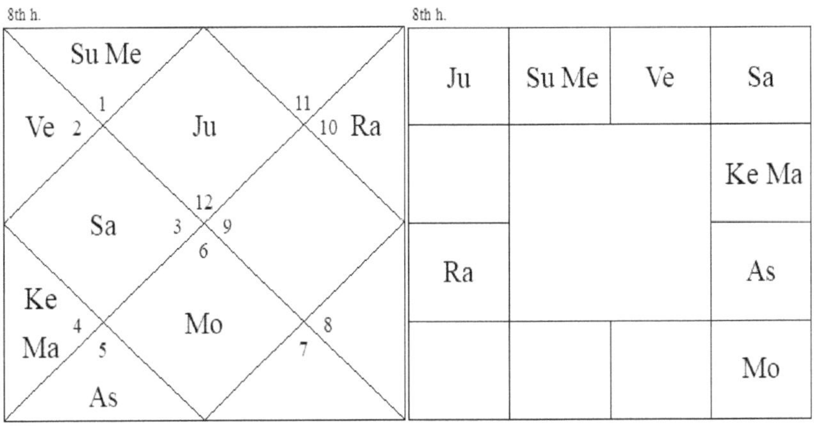

Mercury is the lord of second and eleventh lord in birth chart. It is with exalted lagna lord causing Dhana yoga and alsoa maraca.

In the progress chart, lagna lord is in lagna. Jupiter is alsotenth lord. Mercury is in second house with exalted fifth lord.Sun is birth lagna lord. She was elected Prime Minister in Ulka /Sankata. Rahu is in eleventh from Progress lagna and in tenthfrom Mercury.Sri Lanka became a republic on 22 May, 1972. The sub period was Bhadrika and she was again elected P.M. for secondterm.

Example Death DOB 30 August 1927 TOB 7.16 POB Bulandshahar

Birth Chart

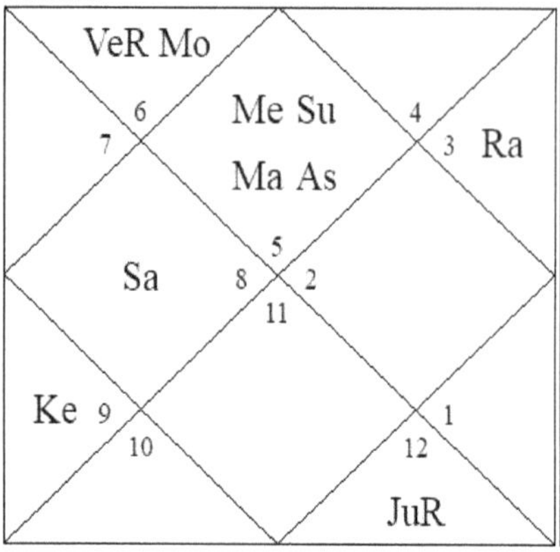

Birth Chart

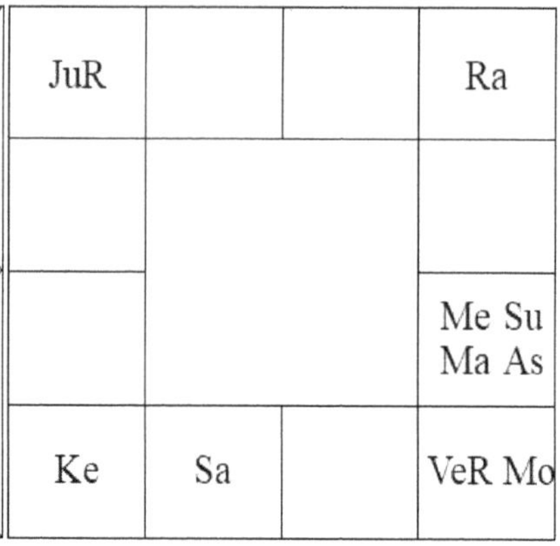

Birth Nakshatra Hasta

Yogini	Nakshatra	From	To
Sankata	Hasta	30.8.1927	4.4.1933
Mangla	Chitra	4.4.1933	4.4.1934
Pingla	Swati	4.4.1934	4.4.1936
Dhanya	Visakha	4.4.1936	4.4.1939
Bharamari	Anuradha	4.4.1939	4.4.1943
Bhadrika	Jyeshtha	4.4.1943	4.4.1948
Ulka	Moola	4.4.1948	4.4.1954
Siddha	P. Ashadha	4.4.1954	4.4.1961
Sankata	U. Ashadha	4.4.1961	4.4.1969
Mangla	Shravan	4.4.1969	4.4.1970
Pingla	Dhanishta	4.4.1970	4.4.1972
Dhanya	Shatbhisaj	4.4.1972	4.4.1975

Yogini	Nakshatra	From	To
Bharamari	P. Bhadrapad	4.4.1975	4.4.1979
Bhadrika	U. Bhadrapad	4.4.1979	4.4.1984
Ulka	Revati	4.4.1984	4.4.1990

Progress chart for Ulka/ Revati and Pisces lagan.

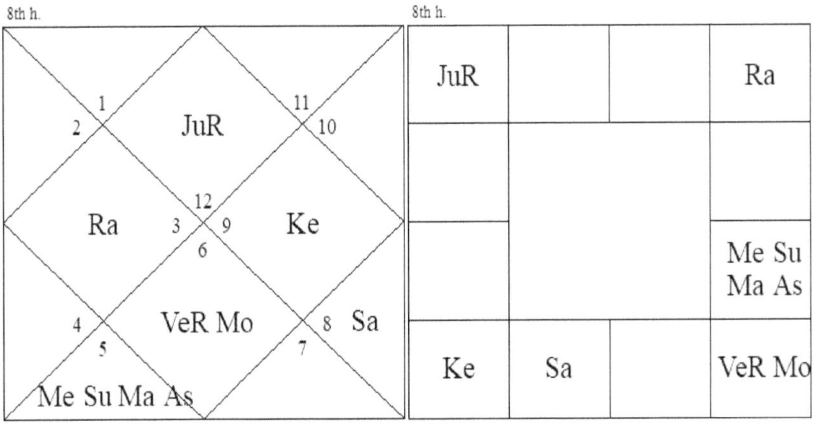

Compare this with previous example. Both charts have Leoas birth lagna. The association of Jupiter and placement of Mercury in progress chart have made the difference.

In the progress chart, Mercury is in sixth house with sixthlord. The maracas of progress chart are Mercury and Mars. Mercury is maraca of birth chart as well.

The eighth lord Venus and the second lord Mars are nowaspecting lagna and lagna lord Jupiter. Rahu acts as Mercury.

He died on 26 Aug. 1986 in the sub period of Sankata.

Example Death of Mother DOB 19 November 1917 TOB 23.11 POB Allahabad

Birth Chart

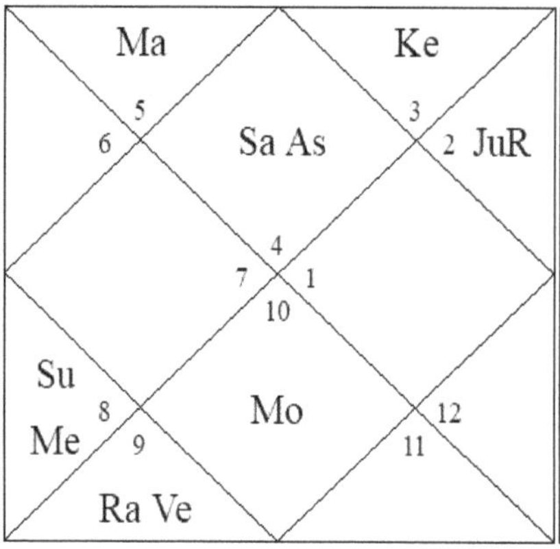

Birth Chart

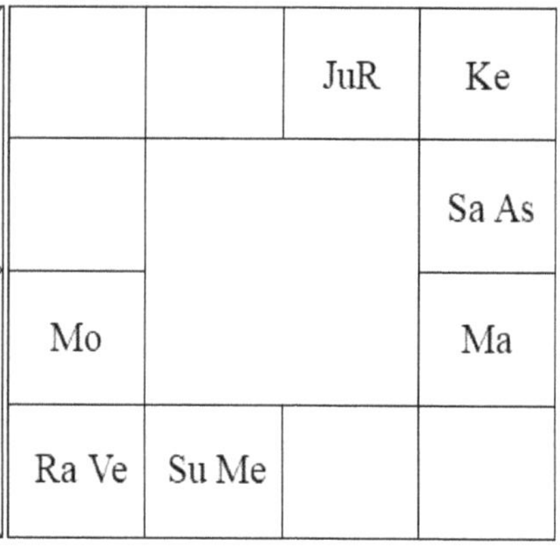

Birth Nakshatra U. Ashadha

Dasa sequence

Yogini	Nakshatra	From	To
Sankata	U. Ashadha	19.11.1917	13.7.1920
Mangla	Shravan	13.7.1920	13.7.1921
Pingla	Dhanishta	13.7.1921	13.7.1923
Dhanya	Shatbhisaj	13.7.1923	13.7.1926
Bharamari	P. Bhadrapad	13.7.1926	13.7.1930
Bhadrika	U. Bhadrapad	13.7.1930	13.7.1935
Ulka	Revati	13.7.1935	13.7.1941

Progress chart for Ulka/ Revati and Pisces lagan.

9th h.

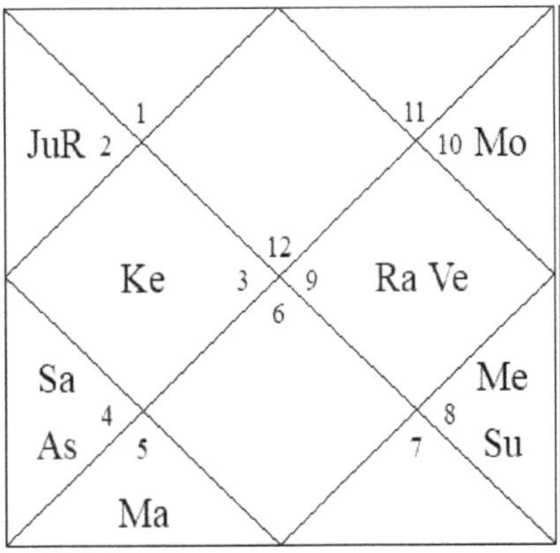

9th h.

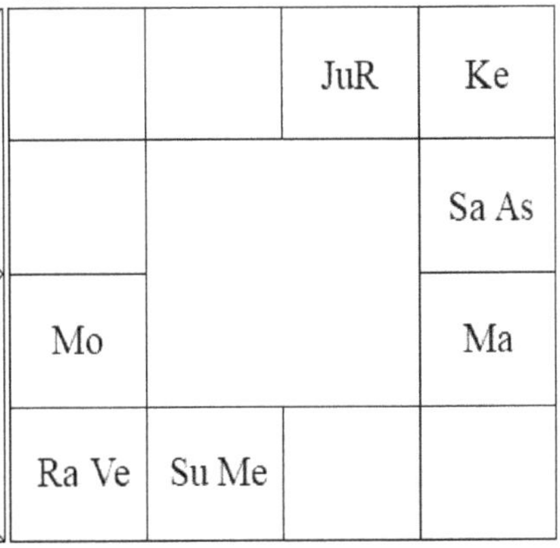

In birth chart, Mercury is with Sun and aspected by ninth lord Jupiter. Mercury is lord of third and twelfth house. It promises mixed results in the birth chart.

In the progress chart, Mercury is in ninth house of father and aspected by maraca of mother and father Jupiter. Saturn isplaced in fifth house. For mother it is maraca house and is aspected by maraca lord Moon. Her mother expired on 22 June,1936 in the sub period of Ulka.

Example President of USA DOB 6 July 1946 TOB 7.46 POB New Heaven

Birth Chart

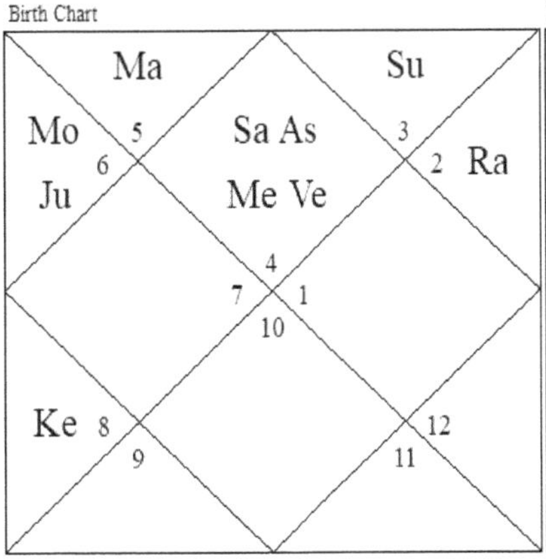

Birth Chart

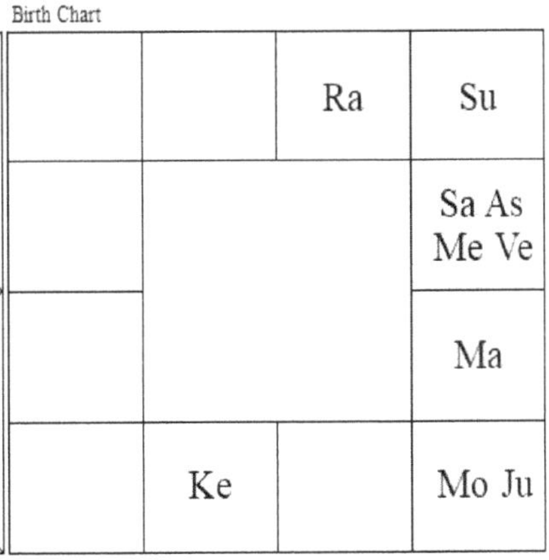

Birth Nakshatra Chitra

Dasa sequence

Yogini	Nakshatra	From	To
Mangla	Chitra	6.7.1946	28.6.1947
Pingla	Swati	28.6.1947	28.6.1949
Dhanya	Visakha	28.6.1949	28.6.1952
Bharamari	Anuradha	28.6.1952	28.6.1956
Bhadrika	Jyeshtha	28.6.1956	28.6.1961
Ulka	Moola	28.6.1961	28.6.1967
Siddha	P. Ashadha	28.6.1967	28.6.1974
Sankata	U. Ashadha	28.6.1974	28.6.1982
Mangla	Shravan	28.6.1982	28.6.1983
Pingla	Dhanishta	28.6.1983	28.6.1985
Dhanya	Shatbhisaj	28.6.1985	28.6.1988
Bharamari	P. Bhadrapad	28.6.1988	28.6.1992
Bhadrika	U. Bhadrapad	28.6.1992	28.6.1997
Ulka	Revati	28.6.1997	28.6.2003

Progress chart for Ulka/ Revati and Pisces lagan.

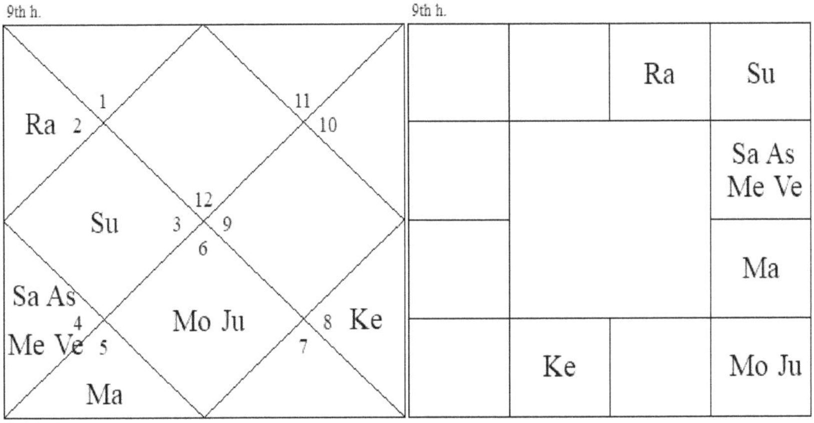

Mercury is in the lagna in birth chart. It is involved in exchange with lagna lord. The ninth house is aspected by lagnalord, ninth lord and the tenth lord.

The position in progress chart improves. Now Mercury is in exchange with fifth lord, Kendra trikona yoga. The tenth and lagna lord aspects lagna.

He assumed office of president of USA on 20 Jan. 2001. The sub period was of Mangla. Moon is with tenth lord and involved in exchange with dasha Nakshtra lord.

Example Death DOB 29 February 1904 TOB 11.54 POB Madurai

Birth Chart

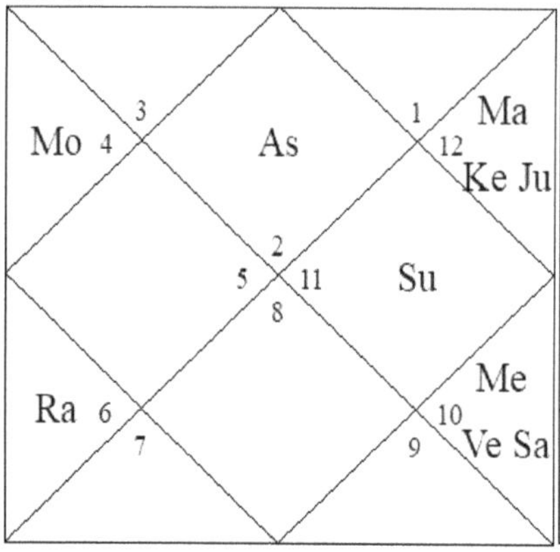

Birth Chart

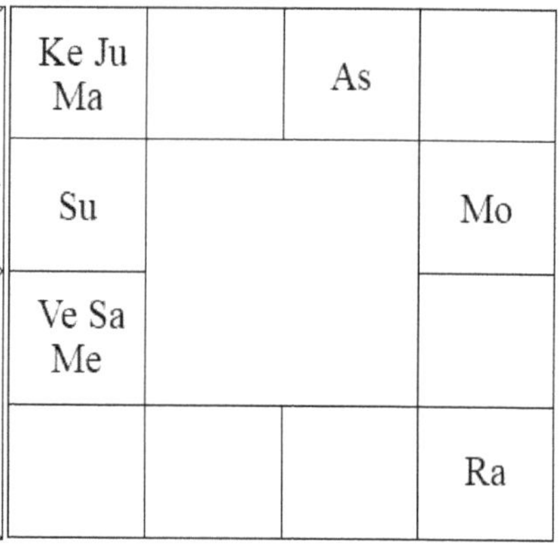

Birth Nakshatra Ashlesha

Dasa sequence

Yogini	Nakshatra	From	To
Bharamari	Ashlesha	29.2.1904	27.12.1906
Bhadrika	Magha	27.12.1906	27.12.1911
Ulka	P. Phalguni	27.12.1911	27.12.1917
Siddha	U. Phalguni	27.12.1917	27.12.1924
Sankata	Hasta	27.12.1924	27.12.1932
Mangla	Chitra	27.12.1932	27.12.1933
Pingla	Swati	27.12.1933	27.12.1935
Dhanya	Visakha	27.12.1935	27.12.1938
Bharamari	Anuradha	27.12.1938	27.12.1942
Bhadrika	Jyeshtha	27.12.1942	27.12.1947
Ulka	Moola	27.12.1947	27.12.1953
Siddha	P. Ashadha	27.12.1953	27.12.1960

Yogini	Nakshatra	From	To
Sankata	U. Ashadha	27.12.1960	27.12.1968
Mangla	Shravan	27.12.1968	27.12.1969
Pingla	Dhanishta	27.12.1969	27.12.1971
Dhanya	Shatbhisaj	27.12.1971	27.12.1974
Bharamari	P. Bhadrapad	27.12.1974	27.12.1978
Bhadrika	U. Bhadrapad	27.12.1978	27.12.1983
Ulka	Revati	27.12.1983	27.12.1989

Progress chart for Ulka/ Revati and Pisces lagan.

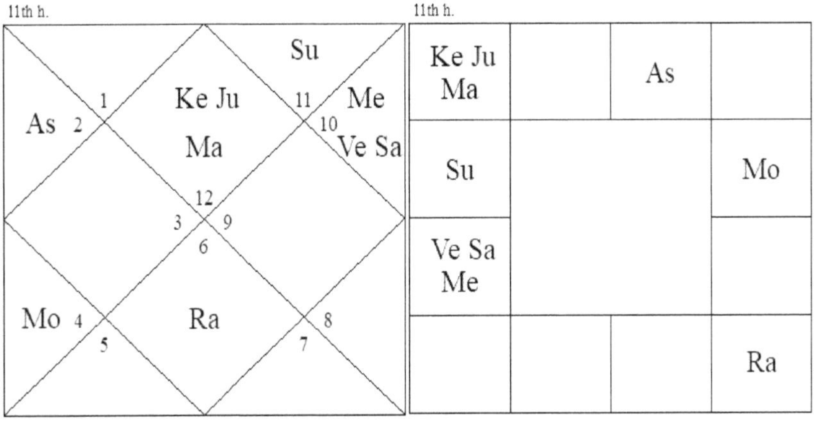

Mercury is lord of second house of birth chart. It is also fifth lord but Rahu is in fifth house. Jupiter is the eighth lord.

In the progress chart also, Mercury and Mars are the maracas as they were in the birth chart. Mars is now in lagna with Ketu and eighth lord of birth chart. Jupiter is now the lagna lord.

The lagna and lagna lord are badly afflicted. It is aspectedby Saturn. Venus is with dasha and Nakshtra lord.

She died on 24 Feb. 1986. The Sankata sub started on the same day.

Chapter 9
Siddha

Siddha dasha is considered as giver of all desired results as per classics.We cannot generalize the results of a dasha in this way. It depends on the total horoscope and dasha is the dynamic unfolding of events.

Siddha is generated by three Nakshtra

Nakshtra	Nakshtra Lord	Sign	Remarks
Rohini	Moon	Taurus	Taurus is the progress lagna
U. Phalguni	Sun	Leo/ Virgo	First one year nine months Leo is progress lagna. For last five years and three months progress lagna isVirgo.
P. Ashadha	Venus	Sagittarius	Sagittarius is the progress lagna

Siddha / Rohini

We must note that after Revati we jump to Rohini in thisscheme of progress yogini dasha.

Moon is the Nakshtra lord and Taurus is the progress lagna.Moon is lord of third house and gets exalted in lagna. Moon is easily influenced by other planets and the results will depend on his placement and strength.

For this progress lagna, Mercury and Mars are Maraca. Saturn is

Yoga karaka. Jupiter is a malefic planet being lord ofeighth and eleventh house.

Example Death DOB 14 December 1895 TOB 03.05 POB York

Birth Chart

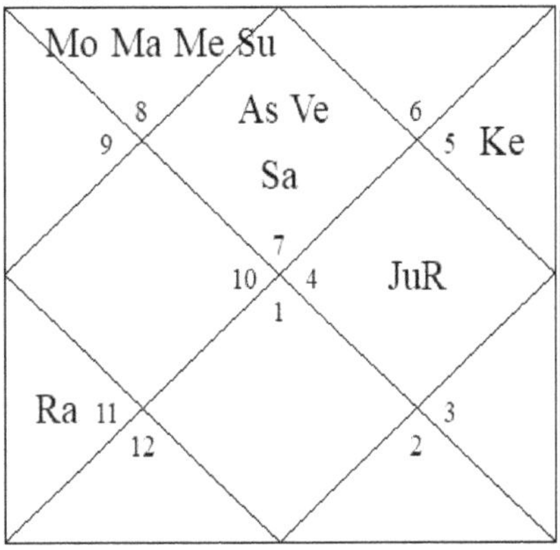

Birth Chart

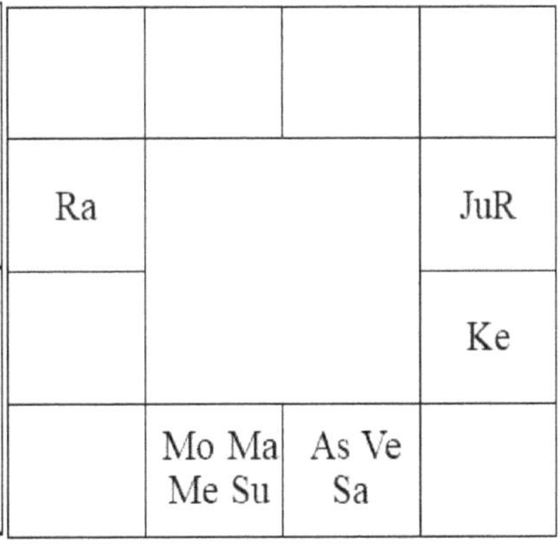

Birth Nakshatra Vishakha

Dasa sequence

Yogini	Nakshatra	From	To
Dhanya	Visakha	14.12.1895	24.2.1896
Bharamari	Anuradha	24.2.1896	24.2.1900
Bhadrika	Jyeshtha	24.2.1900	24.2.1905
Ulka	Moola	24.2.1905	24.2.1911
Siddha	P. Ashadha	24.2.1911	24.2.1918
Sankata	U. Ashadha	24.2.1918	24.2.1926
Mangla	Shravan	24.2.1926	24.2.1927
Pingla	Dhanishta	24.2.1927	24.2.1929
Dhanya	Shatbhisaj	24.2.1929	24.2.1932
Bharamari	P. Bhadrapad	24.2.1932	24.2.1936
Bhadrika	U. Bhadrapad	24.2.1936	24.2.1941

Yogini	Nakshatra	From	To
Ulka	Revati	24.2.1941	24.2.1947
Siddha	Rohini	24.2.1947	24.2.1954

Progress chart for Siddha/ Rohini and Taurus lagan.

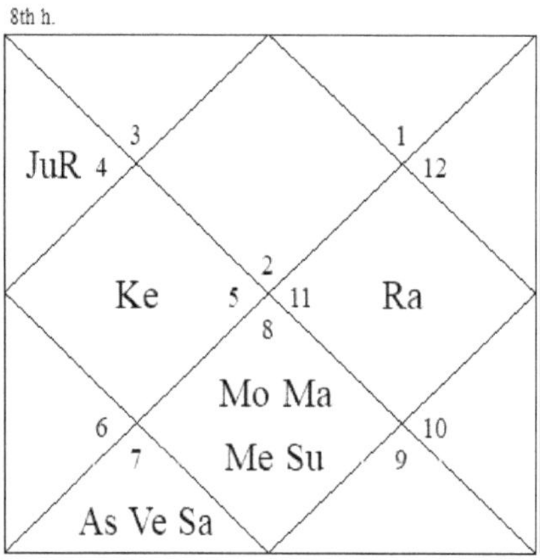

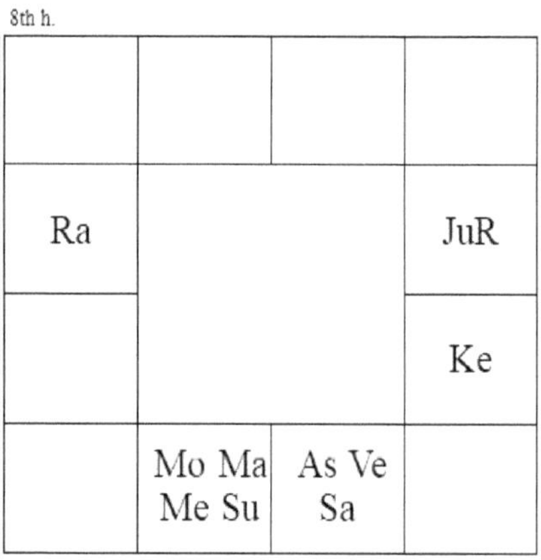

Moon is the tenth lord of Birth Chart and is placed in secondhouse with three planets and aspected by Jupiter. Lagna is having Yoga Karaka Saturn with lagna lord.

The progress lagna is Taurus. Moon is now in seventh house with seventh, fourth and fifth lord. Mars also join it. Mars is the strong maraca of birth Chart. Mars and Mercury are maraca of progress chart. Both of them join Moon. It was a period of glory but the maraca effects are also present.

He died in sleep in May 1952 in the sub period of Bhadrika.

Example PM and Death DOB 9 October 1904 TOB 11.17 POB Varanasi

Birth Chart

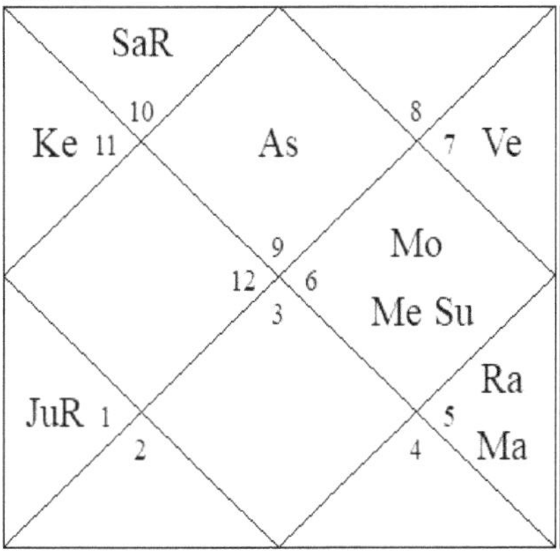

Birth Chart

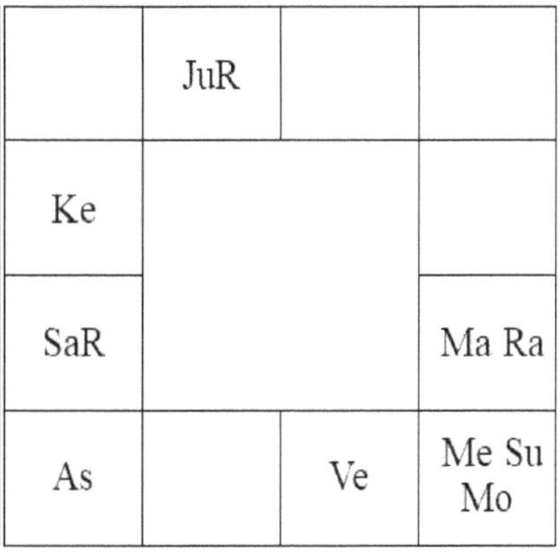

Birth Nakshatra Hasta

Dasa sequence

Yogini	Nakshatra	From	To
Sankata	Hasta	9.10.1904	19.10.1904
Mangla	Chitra	19.10.1904	19.10.1905
Pingla	Swati	19.10.1905	19.10.1907
Dhanya	Visakha	19.10.1907	19.10.1910
Bharamari	Anuradha	19.10.1910	19.10.1914
Bhadrika	Jyeshtha	19.10.1914	19.10.1919
Ulka	Moola	19.10.1919	19.10.1925
Siddha	P. Ashadha	19.10.1925	19.10.1932
Sankata	U. Ashadha	19.10.1932	19.10.1940
Mangla	Shravan	19.10.1940	19.10.1941
Pingla	Dhanishta	19.10.1941	19.10.1943
Dhanya	Shatbhisaj	19.10.1943	19.10.1946

Yogini	Nakshatra	From	To
Bharamari	P. Bhadrapad	19.10.1946	19.10.1950
Bhadrika	U. Bhadrapad	19.10.1950	19.10.1955
Ulka	Revati	19.10.1955	19.10.1961
Siddha	Rohini	19.10.1961	19.10.1968

Progress chart for Siddha/ Rohini and Taurus lagan.

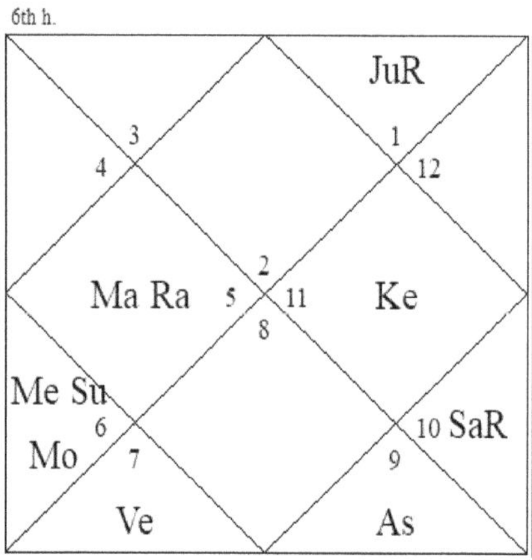

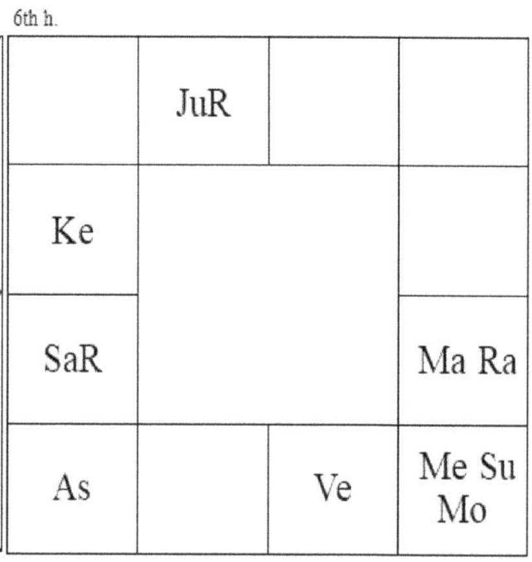

Moon is in the tenth house of Birth chart. He is joined by Sun and Mercury which are tenth and ninth lords. Moon is in Yoga. Remember Moon is eighth lord. The dasha of Moon Nakshtra will give Yoga effects beside effect of eighth house.

Moon is in fifth house of progress chart and in again withKendra trikona lords. Rahu / Ketu are in four ten axis.

He became Prime Minister after death of Jawaharlal Lal Nehru. He took office in 9 June 1964 in sub Of Sankata.

The sinister role of Moon was to unfold in dasha of maracaMars. He died in mysterious circumstances on 10 Jan. 1966 inthe sub of Mars.

Example Marriage and child DOB 19 November 1917 TOB 23.11 POB Allahabad

Birth Chart

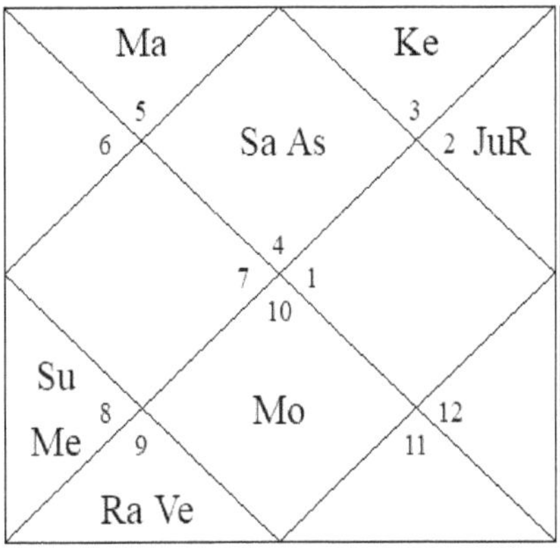

Birth Chart

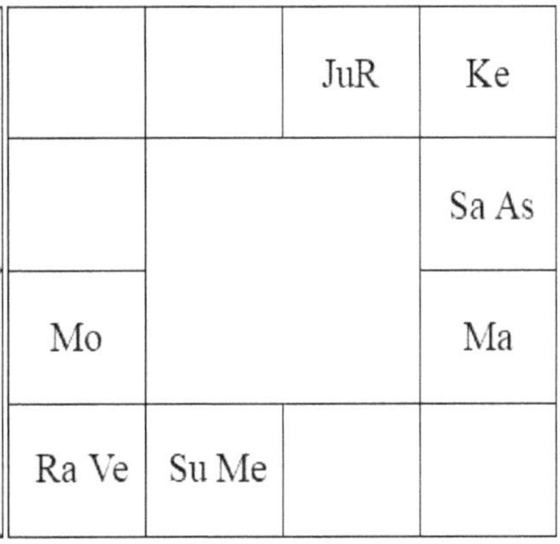

Birth Nakshatra U. Ashadha

Dasa sequence

Yogini	Nakshatra	From	To
Sankata	U. Ashadha	19.11.1917	13.7.1920
Mangla	Shravan	13.7.1920	13.7.1921
Pingla	Dhanishta	13.7.1921	13.7.1923
Dhanya	Shatbhisaj	13.7.1923	13.7.1926
Bharamari	P. Bhadrapad	13.7.1926	13.7.1930
Bhadrika	U. Bhadrapad	13.7.1930	13.7.1935
Ulka	Revati	13.7.1935	13.7.1941
Siddha	Rohini	13.7.1941	13.7.1948

Progress chart for Siddha/ Rohini and Taurus lagan.

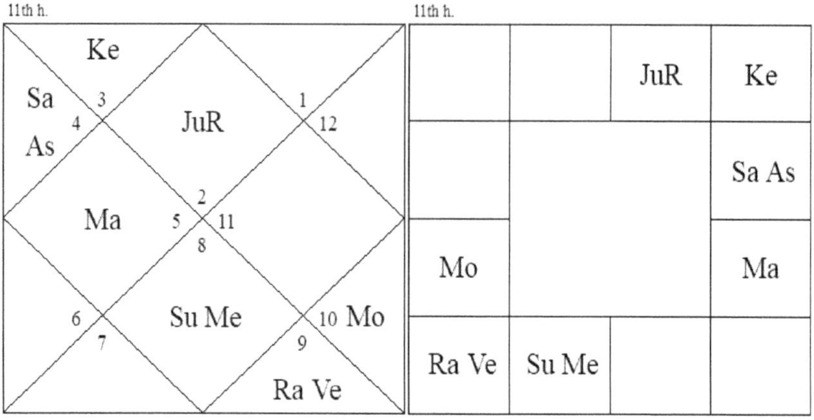

Many personal events took place in this Siddha dasha. Inthe birth chart Moon is the lagna lord and placed in seventh. Being lagna lord it announces the personnel matters. It is aspected by Saturn, lord of seventh and eighth house.

In the progress chart, seventh house is aspected by seventhlord Mars and eighth lord Jupiter. Venus is lagna lord. She married Feroze Gandhi on 26 March 1942 in the sub Of Siddha.

Moon is in the ninth house and aspected by Jupiter. Rajivwas born on 14 Dec. 1946 in the sub of Bhadrika. Mercury is fifth lord.

The promise of Moon relation with seventh, ninth and lagnahas fully materialized.

Example Marriage DOB 26 August 1956 TOB 4.36 POB Delhi

Birth Chart

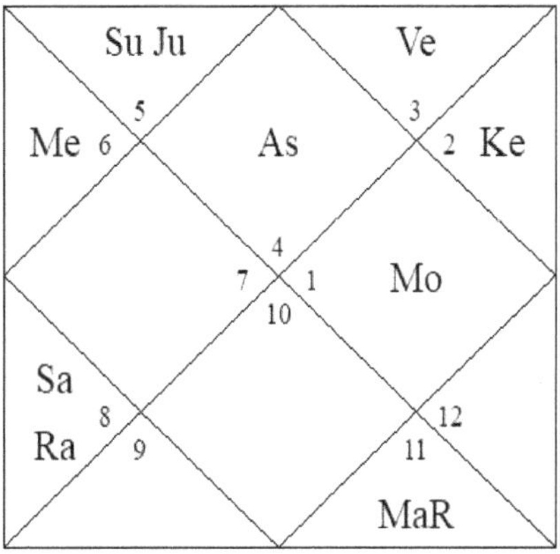

Birth Chart

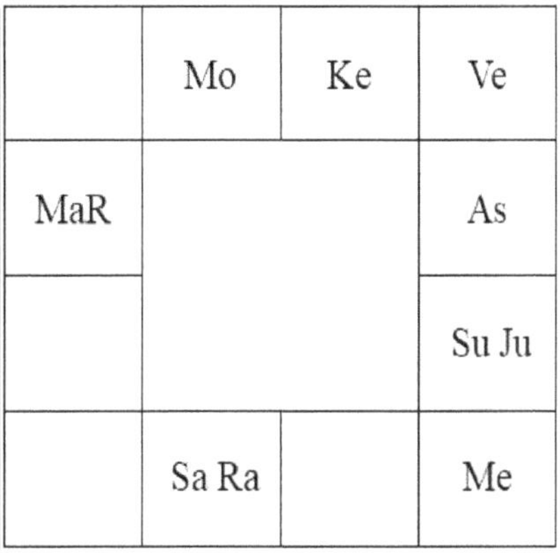

Birth Nakshatra Ashwini

Dasa sequence

Yogini	Nakshatra	From	To
Bharamari	Ashwini	26.8.1956	7.8.1960
Bhadrika	Bharani	7.8.1960	7.8.1965
Ulka	Kritika	7.8.1965	7.8.1971
Siddha	Rohini	7.8.1971	7.8.1978

Progress chart for Siddha/ Rohini and Taurus lagan.

11th h.

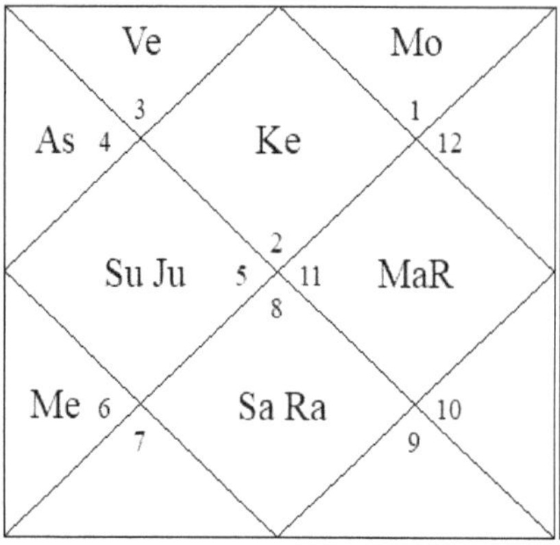

11th h.

	Mo	Ke	Ve
MaR			As
			Su Ju
	Sa Ra		Me

In the birth chart Moon is the lagna lord. The personal matters are important. He is aspected by Jupiter.

Moon moves to twelfth housc of progress chart.

Seventh lord of birth chart aspects lagna. The seventh lord of progress chart also aspects lagna. Mars is influencing Sun and Jupiter and Mercury.

She was married to Sanjay Gandhi on 23 Dec. 1974 in thesub of Pingla. The aspect of eighth lord Jupiter on the seventhlord Mars is not welcomed.

Example Death of husband DOB 6 February 1967 TOB 3.58 POB Chamba

Birth Chart

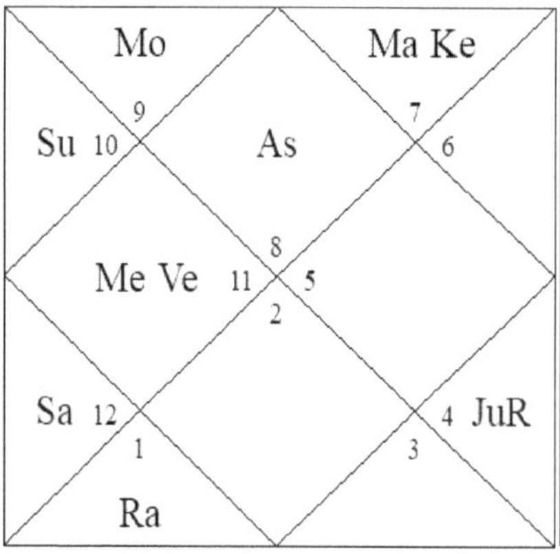

Birth Chart

Sa	Ra		
Me Ve			JuR
Su			
Mo	As	Ma Ke	

Birth Nakshatra Moola

Dasa sequence

Yogini	Nakshatra	From	To
Ulka	Moola	6.2.1967	13.8.1967
Siddha	P. Ashadha	13.8.1967	13.8.1974
Sankata	U. Ashadha	13.8.1974	13.8.1982
Mangla	Shravan	13.8.1982	13.8.1983
Pingla	Dhanishta	13.8.1983	13.8.1985
Dhanya	Shatbhisaj	13.8.1985	13.8.1988
Bharamari	P. Bhadrapad	13.8.1988	13.8.1992
Bhadrika	U. Bhadrapad	13.8.1992	13.8.1997
Ulka	Revati	13.8.1997	13.8.2003
Siddha	Rohini	13.8.2003	13.8.2010

Progress chart for Siddha/ Rohini and Taurus lagan.

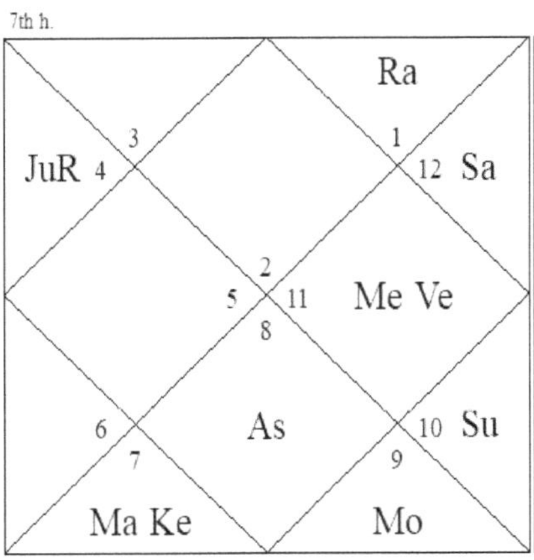

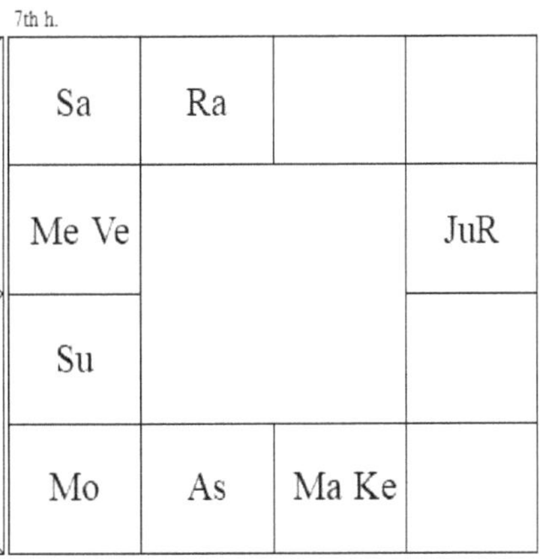

In the birth chart Moon is placed in the second house whichis eighth for husband. Moon is aspected by Saturn. Moon is lord of ninth house. The Siddha of Rohini gives results of ninth, second and that of Saturn.

Moon has moved to eighth house in the progress chart. Lagna is aspected by Mars and Saturn. The seventh house is aspected by eighth lord. Grief is seen during this period.

The husband died on 19 December, 2008 in the sub period of Bhadrika. Mercury is eighth lord of birth chart.

Siddha / U. Phalguni

Sun is the Nakshtra Lord. For the first one fourth of Siddha, the progress lagna is Leo. Sun is the lagna lord. Afflicted Sun gives problems to self. A good Sun keeps the things in good shape.

Mars is the lord of Kendra / Trikona of progress chart. Relation of Mars with Venus, tenth lord, can give good positionin this progress lagna.

When the progress lagna moves to Virgo after one year nine months of Siddha. The change comes in Sankata sub period. The events can take big change towards good or bad. Sun is now twelfth lord.

Example Many events DOB 19 November 1917 TOB 23.11 POB Allahabad

Birth Chart

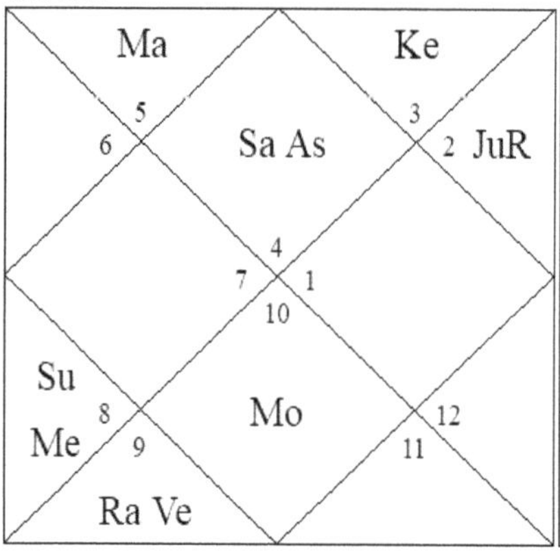

Birth Chart

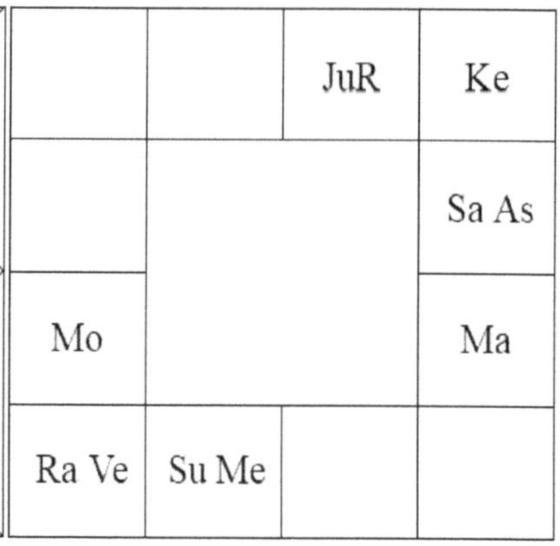

Birth Nakshatra U. Ashadha

Dasa sequence

Yogini	Nakshatra	From	To
Sankata	U. Ashadha	19.11.1917	13.7.1920
Mangla	Shravan	13.7.1920	13.7.1921
Pingla	Dhanishta	13.7.1921	13.7.1923
Dhanya	Shatbhisaj	13.7.1923	13.7.1926
Bharamari	P. Bhadrapad	13.7.1926	13.7.1930
Bhadrika	U. Bhadrapad	13.7.1930	13.7.1935
Ulka	Revati	13.7.1935	13.7.1941
Siddha	Rohini	13.7.1941	13.7.1948
Sankata	Mrigshira	13.7.1948	13.7.1956
Mangla	Ardra	13.7.1956	13.7.1957
Pingla	Punarvasu	13.7.1957	13.7.1959
Dhanya	Pushya	13.7.1959	13.7.1962
Bharamari	Ashlesha	13.7.1962	13.7.1966
Bhadrika	Magha	13.7.1966	13.7.1971
Ulka	P. Phalguni	13.7.1971	13.7.1977
Siddha	U. Phalguni	13.7.1977	13.7.1984

Sun is the lord of second house and placed in fifth house with Mercury in the birth chart. Jupiter is aspecting this Sun.

Progress chart for Siddha/ U. Phalguni and Leo lagan.

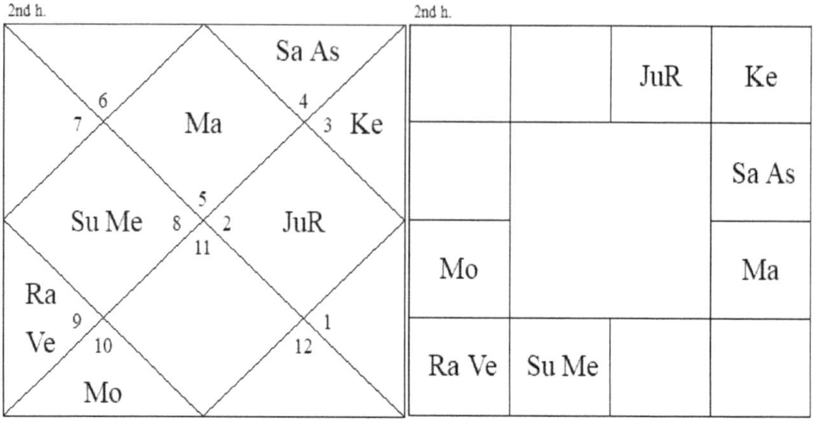

For Leo Progress Lagna, Sun is in fourth house and aspects tenth house. The tenth house is not making any relation with tenth lord. Tenth lord is afflicted by Rahu. Sun is in twelfthfrom Venus. She was rather humiliated and was out of power.

Progress chart for Siddha/ U. Phalguni and Virgo lagan.

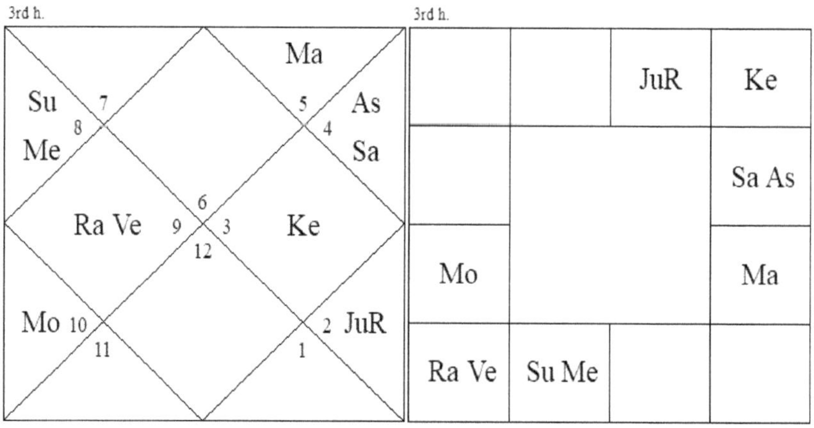

The progress lagna changes to Virgo on 12 April 1979. The things looked up. Now Sun is with tenth lord Mercury. Ninth lord is aspecting tenth lord and tenth lord is aspecting ninth house. This is RAJ yoga situation.

She fought back and came back to power on 14 Jan. 1980and was

Prime Minister till the end of Siddha period. She came back in Sankata sub period. Ketu is in tenth house.

For her son, Sun is the eighth lord from fifth. Mars is in eighth house and aspected by Saturn. Moon is in fifth house aspects Sun. Moon is in fifth house aspected by Saturn. Sanjaydied on 23 June 1980 in the sub of Mangla.

Example Problem to husband DOB 26 October 1947 TOB 20.0 POB Chicago

Birth Chart

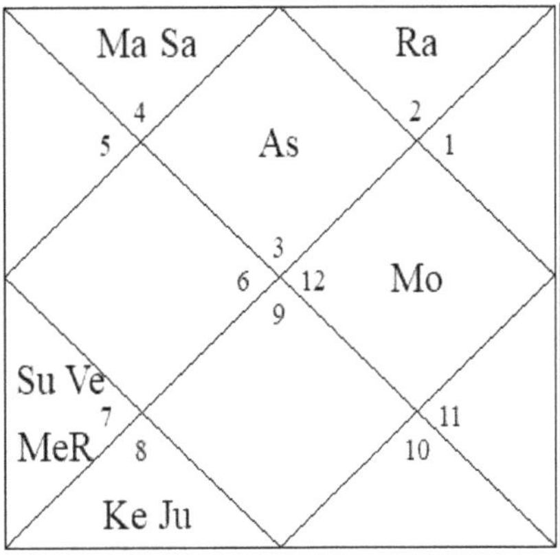

Birth Chart

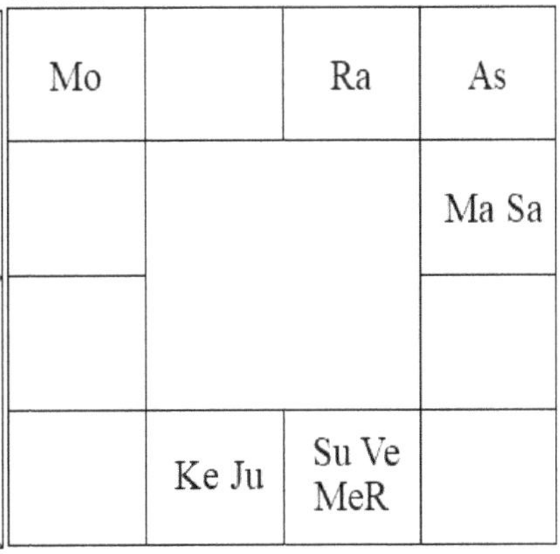

Birth Nakshatra U. Bhadrapad

Dasa sequence

Yogini	Nakshatra	From	To
Bhadrika	U. Bhadrapad	26.10.1947	17.10.1951
Ulka	Revati	17.10.1951	17.10.1957
Siddha	Rohini	17.10.1957	17.10.1964
Sankata	Mrigshira	17.10.1964	17.10.1972
Mangla	Ardra	17.10.1972	17.10.1973
Pingla	Punarvasu	17.10.1973	17.10.1975
Dhanya	Pushya	17.10.1975	17.10.1978
Bharamari	Ashlesha	17.10.1978	17.10.1982

Yogini	Nakshatra	From	To
Bhadrika	Magha	17.10.1982	17.10.1987
Ulka	P. Phalguni	17.10.1987	17.10.1993
Siddha	U. Phalguni	17.10.1993	17.10.2000

Progress chart for Siddha/ U. Phalguni and Virgo lagan.

4th h.

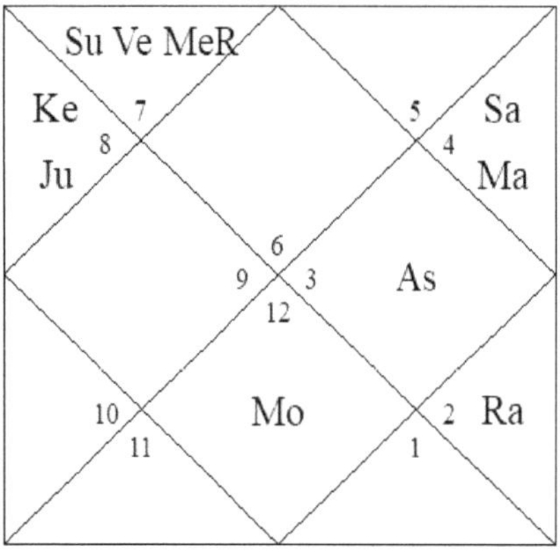

4th h.

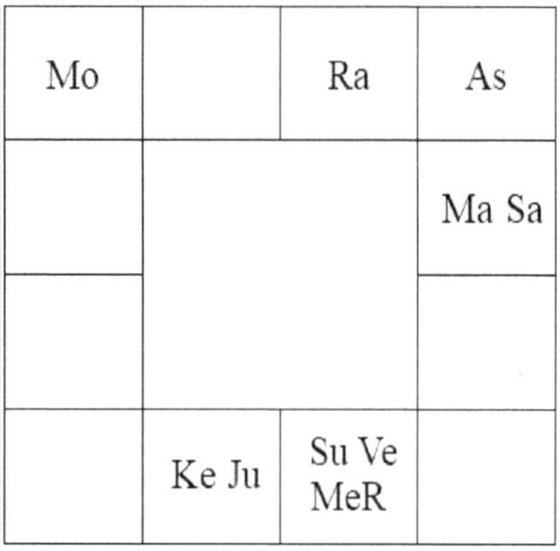

In the birth chart Sun is debilitated with cancellation of debilitation. It is participating in Raj yoga with Venus and Mercury.

Aspect of sixth lord Mars is not welcome even though Mars debilitated is Yoga Karaka.

In the progress chart, we examine the husband. The lordof seventh house is with Ketu giving secret affairs. Sun is placedin eighth house from the seventh and with seventh and eighthlord. Worst is the aspect of debilitated Mars on this combination.

Her husband was involved in an affair with a girl and it became public. He was holding the post of President of USA. For husband we see the seventh house of progress chart. Placement of Moon, fifth lord and aspect of lagna lord and tenthlord saved him.

Example Marriage DOB 22 February 1964 TOB 13.10.20 POB Delhi

Birth Chart

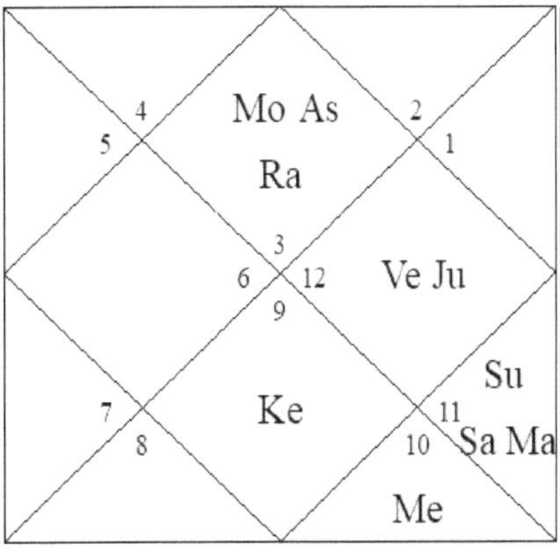

Birth Chart

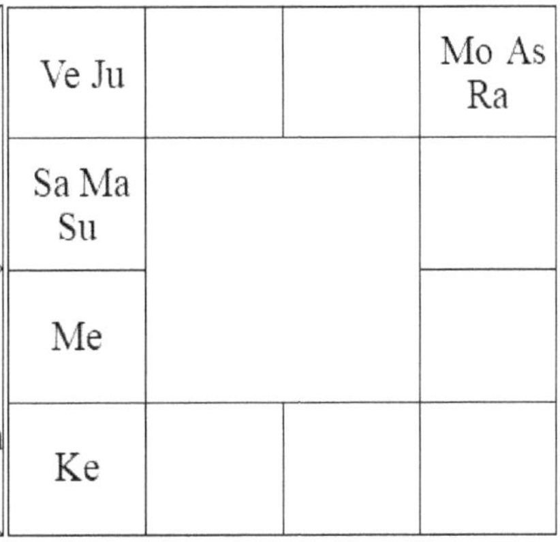

Birth Nakshatra Mrigshira

Dasa sequence

Yogini	Nakshatra	From	To
Sankata	Mrigshira	22.2.1964	3.9.1966
Mangla	Ardra	3.9.1966	3.9.1967
Pingla	Punarvasu	3.9.1967	3.9.1969
Dhanya	Pushya	3.9.1969	3.9.1972
Bharamari	Ashlesha	3.9.1972	3.9.1976
Bhadrika	Magha	3.9.1976	3.9.1981
Ulka	P. Phalguni	3.9.1981	3.9.1987
Siddha	U. Phalguni	3.9.1987	3.9.1994

Progress chart for Siddha/ U. Phalguni and Leo lagan.

3rd h. 3rd h.

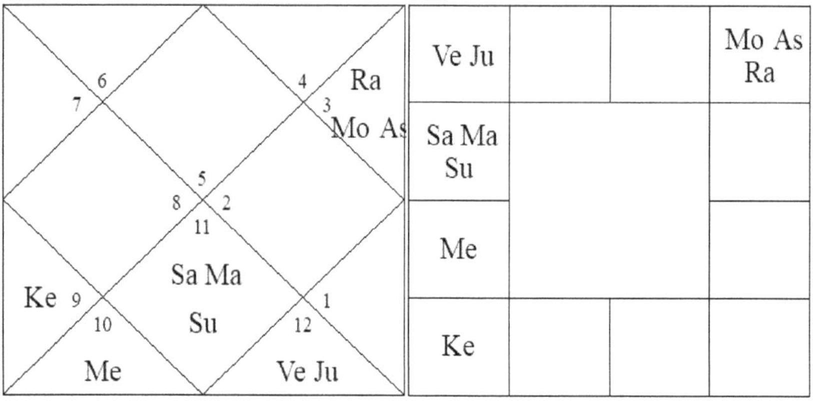

Sun is the third lord of birth chart. It is placed in ninth house with ninth lord.

With progress lagna as Leo, Sun moves to seventh houseas lagna lord. He is conjoined with Saturn, the seventh lord. Mars is now the fourth and ninth lord.

She got married in the sub period of Sankata before the progress lagna changes to Virgo.

Example Higher education DOB 24 December 1942 TOB 0.21.40 POB Gazipur

Birth Chart Birth Chart

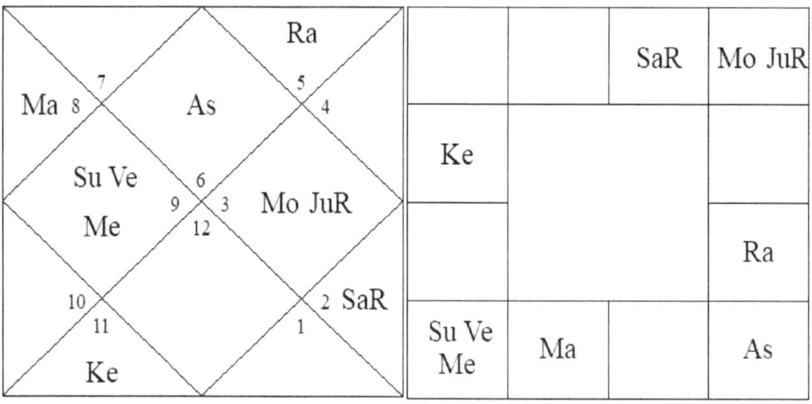

Birth Nakshatra Punarvasu

Dasa sequence

Yogini	Nakshatra	From	To
Pingla	Punarvasu	24.12.1942	5.12.1944
Dhanya	Pushya	5.12.1944	5.12.1947
Bharamari	Ashlesha	5.12.1947	5.12.1951
Bhadrika	Magha	5.12.1951	5.12.1956
Ulka	P. Phalguni	5.12.1956	5.12.1962
Siddha	U. Phalguni	5.12.1962	5.12.1969

Progress chart for Siddha/ U. Phalguni and Virgo lagan is same as birth chart.

Sun is twelfth lord of birth chart and progress chart. It is placed in fourth house. Lord of twelfth in fourth can give shift from home. It iswith ninth and tenth lord. Sun is thus participating in Yoga.

He got admission in engineering college and moved to hostel in Siddha sub period.

Example Wealth DOB 22 August 1954 TOB 20.33 POB Calcutta

Birth Chart

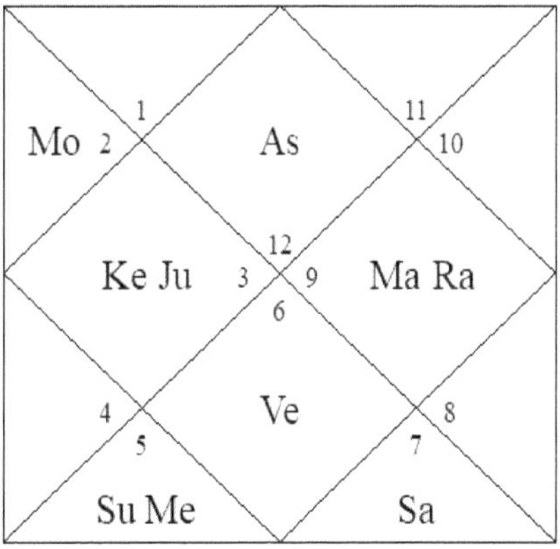

Birth Chart

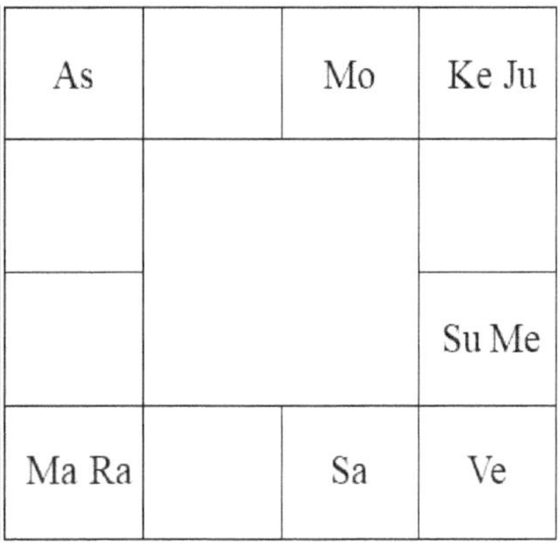

Birth Nakshatra Mrigshira

Dasa sequence

Yogini	Nakshatra	From	To
Sankata	Mrigshira	22.8.1954	24.1.1962
Mangla	Ardra	24.1.1962	24.1.1963
Pingla	Punarvasu	24.1.1963	24.1.1965
Dhanya	Pushya	24.1.1965	24.1.1968
Bharamari	Ashlesha	24.1.1968	24.1.1972
Bhadrika	Magha	24.1.1972	24.1.1977
Ulka	P. Phalguni	24.1.1977	24.1.1983
Siddha	U. Phalguni	24.1.1983	24.1.1990

Progress chart for Siddha/ U. Phalguni and Leo lagan.

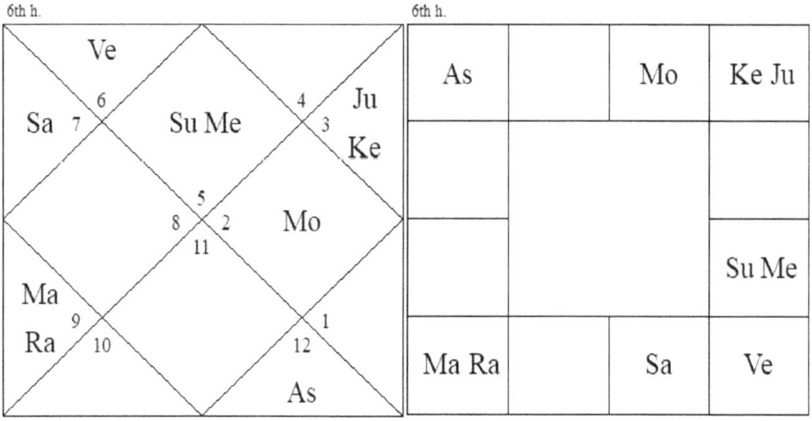

This chart was given as test case in the research class of Bhartiya Vidya Bhavan for approval of progress Yogini dasa method. We were to assess the event in January 1983 of thischart.

The progress yogini dasha was used and the reading wascorrect.

In the birth chart Sun is the sixth lord and is in own sign with Kendra lord Mercury.

In the progress chart the picture is clear. Now Sun is lagnalord in Lagna and with eleventh and second lord. Great Dhanayoga is forming. Moon as twelfth lord is exalted in tenth house.

He started a steel rolling mill in Houston USA and earned alot in this period. This chart is again discussed in Sankata/ Hasta.

Siddha/P Ashadha

Venus is the progress Nakshtra and Sagittarius in the progress lagna. Venus is not favorable planet for this lagna. Any malefic relation with this Venus do not promise good results.It will be a troublesome period. Venus is both dasha and Nakshtra lord and assumes importance.

For good results Venus should not be connected to any planet.

This dasha period needs careful examination as troubles are expected.

Example Death DOB 20 August 1944 TOB 8.10.59 POB Mumbai

Birth Chart

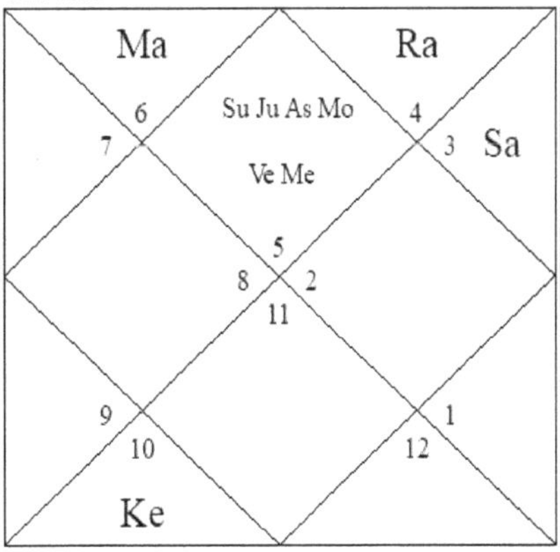

Birth Chart

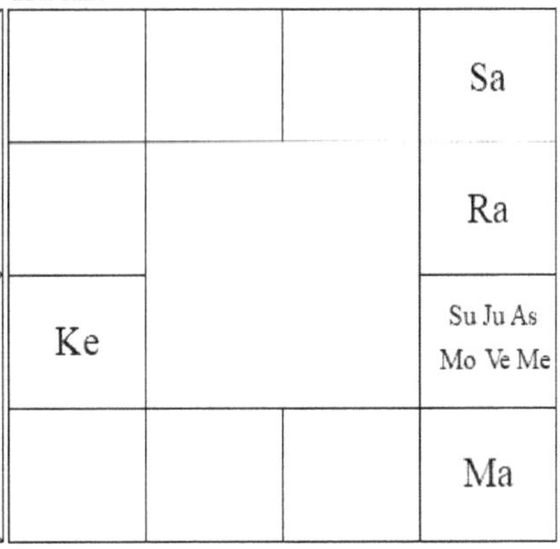

Birth Nakshatra P. Phalguni

Dasa sequence

Yogini	Nakshatra	From	To
Ulka	P. Phalguni	20.8.1944	30.11.1948
Siddha	U. Phalguni	30.11.1948	30.11.1955
Sankata	Hasta	30.11.1955	30.11.1963
Mangla	Chitra	30.11.1963	30.11.1964
Pingla	Swati	30.11.1964	30.11.1966
Dhanya	Visakha	30.11.1966	30.11.1969
Bharamari	Anuradha	30.11.1969	30.11.1973
Bhadrika	Jyeshtha	30.11.1973	30.11.1978
Ulka	Moola	30.11.1978	30.11.1984
Siddha	P. Ashadha	30.11.1984	30.11.1991

Progress chart for Siddha/ U. Ashadha and Sagittarius lagan.

5th h.

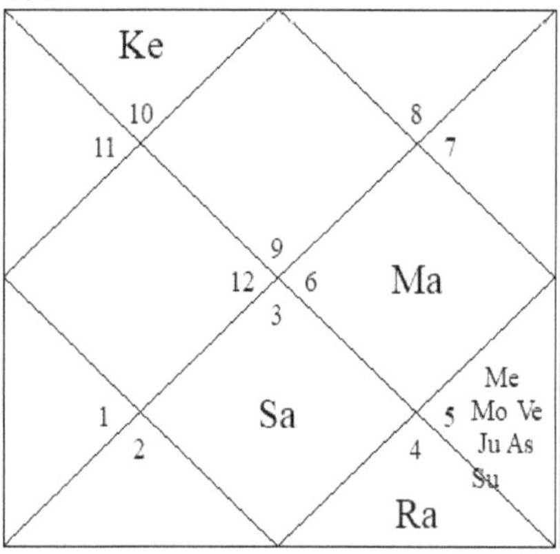

5th h.

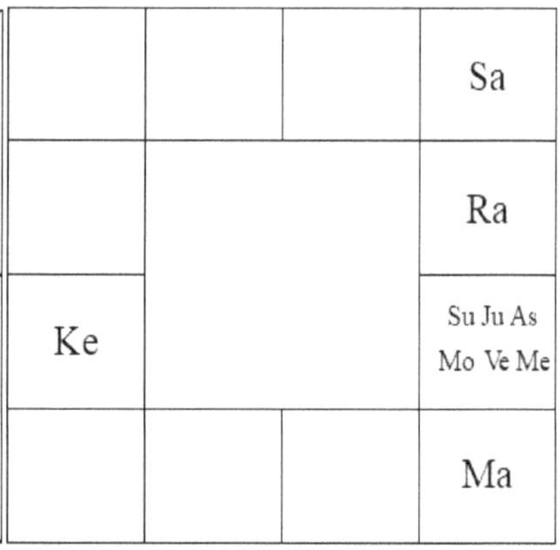

The birth lagna is Leo. Venus is not friendly to the lagna lord. He is with second and eighth lord and aspected by seventhlord Saturn. These planets have other lordship also and have given their due results.

The condition is not improved in progress chart. All the maraca combinations are repeated. Saturn and Mercury are maraca again. In addition to birth eighth lord, Sun is nowjoinedby progress eighth lord.

He was killed by a human bomb on 21 May 1991 in the subperiod of Ulka. The sub- sub was Sankata. Rahu is in eighth house.

Example Birth and death of daughter DOB 23 December 1902 TOB 7.23 POB Bagpat

Birth Chart

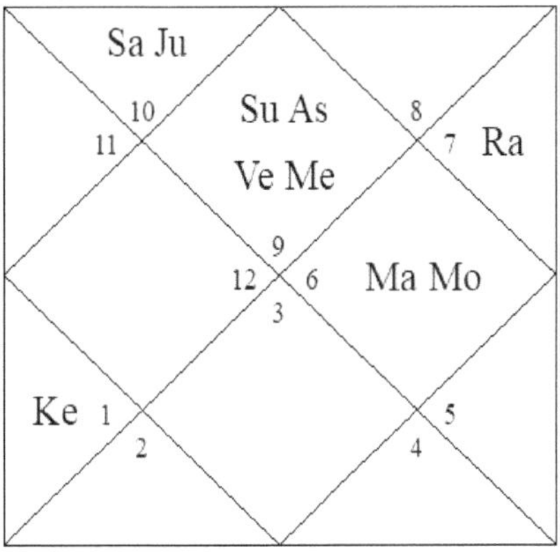

Birth Chart

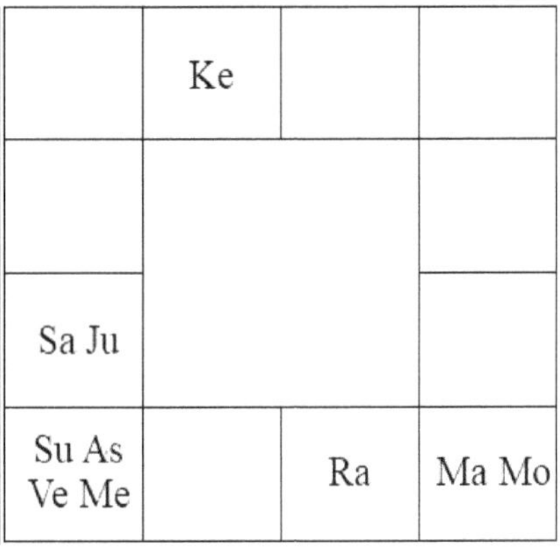

Birth Nakshatra Hasta

Dasa sequence

Yogini	Nakshatra	From	To
Sankata	Hasta	23.12.1902	26.5.1903
Mangla	Chitra	26.5.1903	26.5.1904
Pingla	Swati	26.5.1904	26.5.1906
Dhanya	Visakha	26.5.1906	26.5.1909
Bharamari	Anuradha	26.5.1909	26.5.1913
Bhadrika	Jyeshtha	26.5.1913	26.5.1918
Ulka	Moola	26.5.1918	26.5.1924
Siddha	P. Ashadha	26.5.1924	26.5.1931

The birth and progress chart are same. Venus is in lagna. It iswith ninth lord and aspected by fifth lord Mars. Mars is also thetwelfth lord. Venus is in exact degree conjunction with seventh lord Mercury. He got married in Siddha sub period.

Mars is with eighth lord Moon and not favorable. A daughter was born in Pingla sub period but could not survive.

Example President of India DOB 3 December 1884 TOB 8.18.30 POB Chapra

Birth Chart

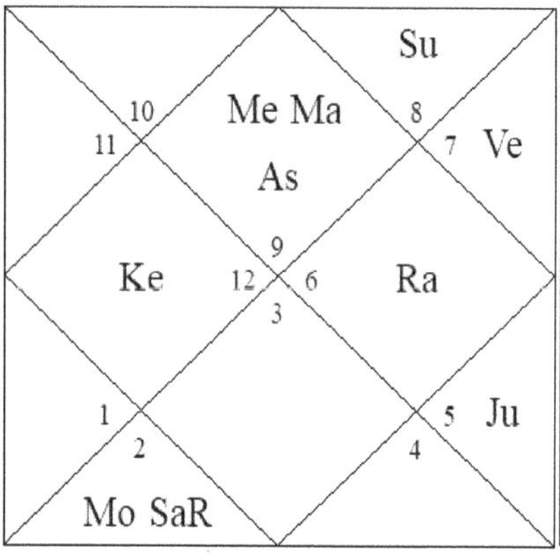

Birth Chart

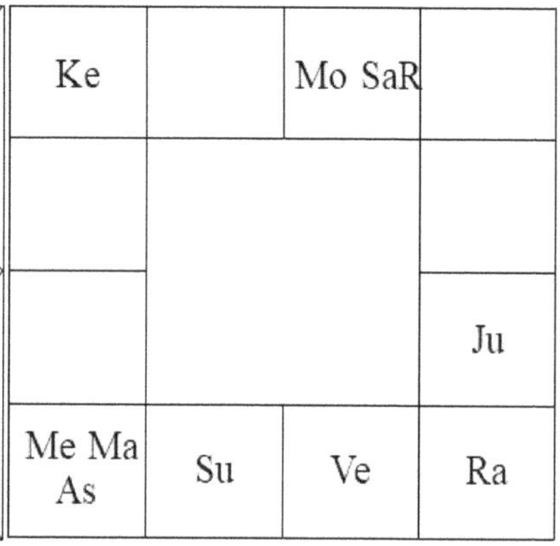

Birth Nakshatra Mrigshira

Dasa sequence

Yogini	Nakshatra	From	To
Sankata	Mrigshira	3.12.1884	28.2.1892
Mangla	Ardra	28.2.1892	28.2.1893
Pingla	Punarvasu	28.2.1893	28.2.1895
Dhanya	Pushya	28.2.1895	28.2.1898
Bharamari	Ashlesha	28.2.1898	28.2.1902
Bhadrika	Magha	28.2.1902	28.2.1907
Ulka	P. Phalguni	28.2.1907	28.2.1913

Siddha	U. Phalguni	28.2.1913	28.2.1920
Sankata	Hasta	28.2.1920	28.2.1928
Mangla	Chitra	28.2.1928	28.2.1929
Pingla	Swati	28.2.1929	28.2.1931
Dhanya	Visakha	28.2.1931	28.2.1934
Bharamari	Anuradha	28.2.1934	28.2.1938
Bhadrika	Jyeshtha	28.2.1938	28.2.1943
Ulka	Moola	28.2.1943	28.2.1949
Siddha	P. Ashadha	28.2.1949	28.2.1956

The birth lagna and the progress lagna are same.

Venus is eleventh lord and placed in eleventh house. Venusis not having any aspect or association.

The lord of tenth house is in lagna and aspected by lagnalord from ninth house. A very good tenth house and tenth lord.

He was elected first president of republic of India in theSankata sub period. Rahu is in tenth house and Venus isin eleventh house.

Example Closure of business DOB 30 June 1960 TOB 12.20 POB Mumbai

Birth Chart

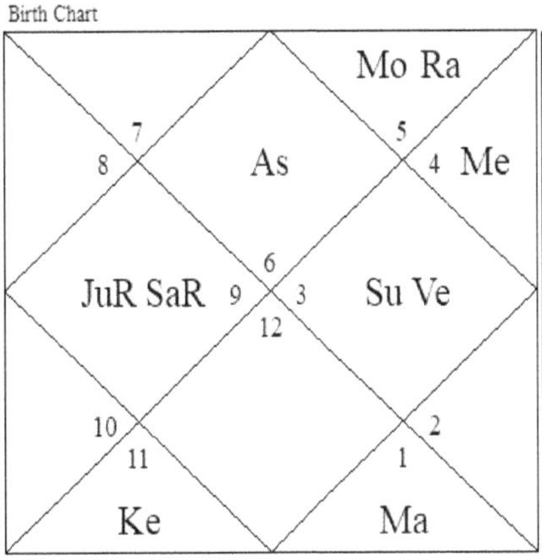

Birth Chart

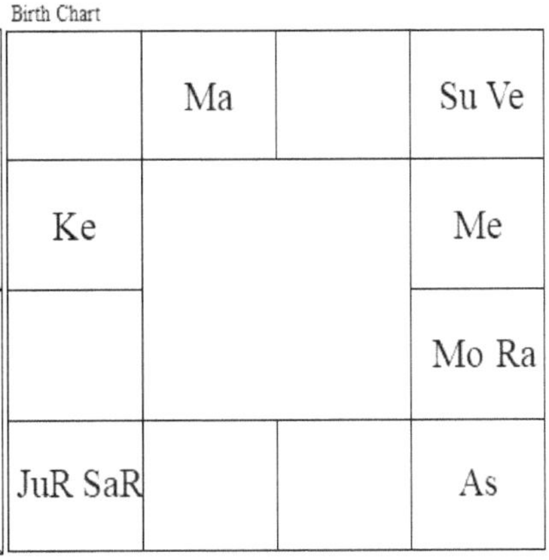

Birth Nakshatra P. Phalguni

Dasa sequence

Yogini	Nakshatra	From	To
Ulka	P. Phalguni	30.6.1960	12.2.1962
Siddha	U. Phalguni	12.2.1962	12.2.1969
Sankata	Hasta	12.2.1969	12.2.1977
Mangla	Chitra	12.2.1977	12.2.1978
Pingla	Swati	12.2.1978	12.2.1980
Dhanya	Visakha	12.2.1980	12.2.1983
Bharamari	Anuradha	12.2.1983	12.2.1987
Bhadrika	Jyeshtha	12.2.1987	12.2.1992
Ulka	Moola	12.2.1992	12.2.1998
Siddha	P. Ashadha	12.2.1998	12.2.2005

Progress chart for Siddha/ P. Ashadha and Sagittarius lagan.

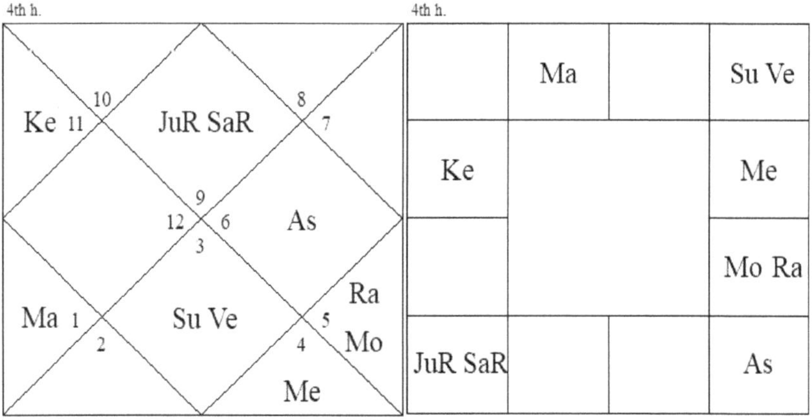

Venus is the ninth lord of birth chart. He is with twelfth lordSun and is aspected by retrograde lords of fourth and fifth house.This gives yoga. The other lordship of Jupiter and Saturn is notgood and they are retrograde.

Now see the progress chart. Venus is with ninth lord Sunand is in seventh house. Jupiter and Saturn are not so powerfulnow.

The lord of tenth house has moved to eighth house with an aspect of twelfth lord Mars. The ninth house is spoiled withthe placement of Rahu and eighth lord.

The luck has run out. He had to close down his business inJuly 2002 in the sub period of Bhramari.

Example Up and down in profession DOB 28 May 1969 TOB 9.55 POB Coimbatore

Birth Chart

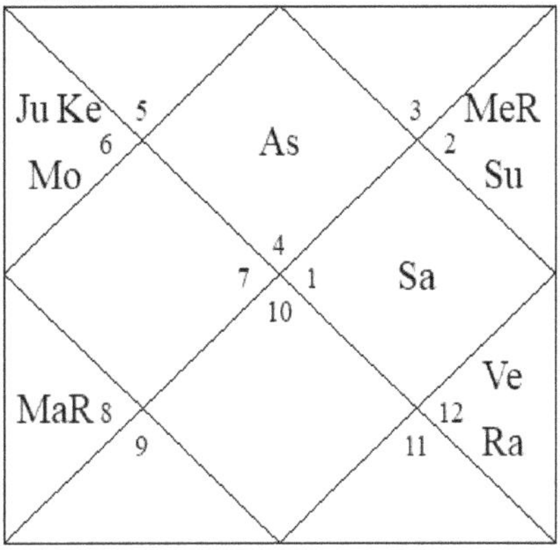

Birth Chart

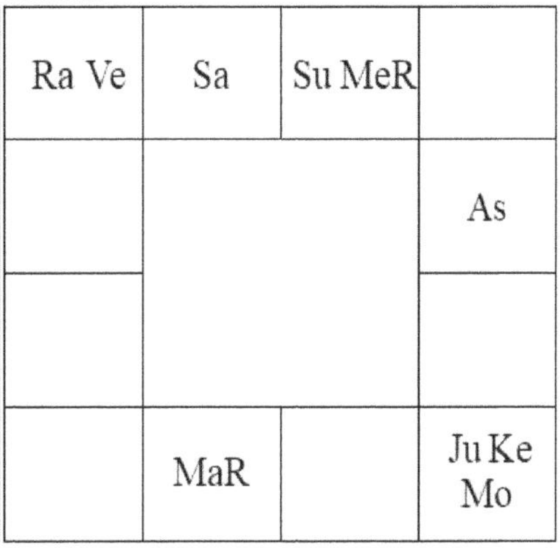

Birth Nakshatra Chitra

Dasa sequence

Yogini	Nakshatra	From	To
Mangla	Chitra	28.5.1969	4.2.1970
Pingla	Swati	4.2.1970	4.2.1972
Dhanya	Visakha	4.2.1972	4.2.1973
Bharamari	Anuradha	4.2.1973	4.2.1977
Bhadrika	Jyeshtha	4.2.1977	4.2.1982
Ulka	Moola	4.2.1982	4.2.1988
Siddha	P. Ashadha	4.2.1988	4.2.1995

Progress chart for Siddha/ P. Ashadha and Sagittarius lagan.

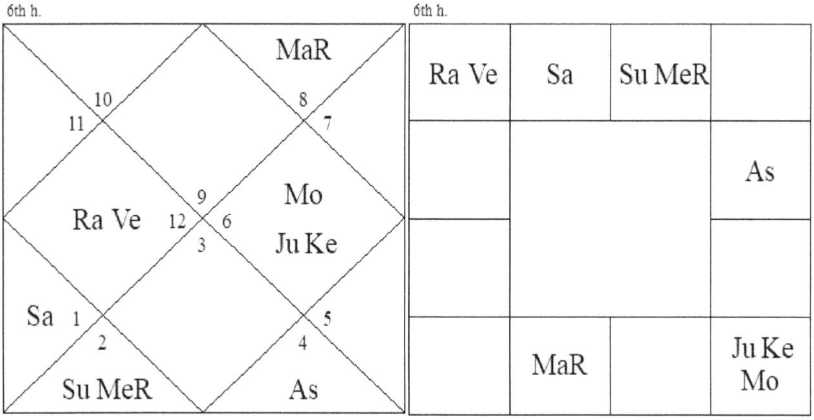

Venus is exalted in birth chart. It is with Rahu and aspectedby ninth lord and the lagna lord. Not a bad position.

In the progress chart Venus moves to fourth house along with Rahu. The eighth lord Moon is in tenth house. Moon was lagna lord of birth chart and now it is eighth lord in tenth. It gives problems and dissatisfaction in profession.

He started work in October 1992 in the sub of Sankata. Ketu is in tenth house. By the time Mangla sub period commenced the trouble started and he begin to look for otherwork.

In the Bhadrika sub period, he landed a good governmentjob on 16 December 1994. Mercury is tenth Lord and is with ninth Lord Sun. The government job is indicated.

Example Death of child DOB 20 June 1956 TOB 13.53 POB Chennai

Birth Chart

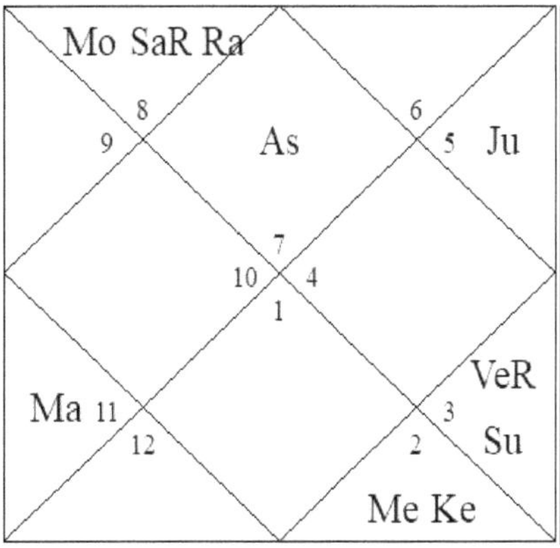

Birth Chart

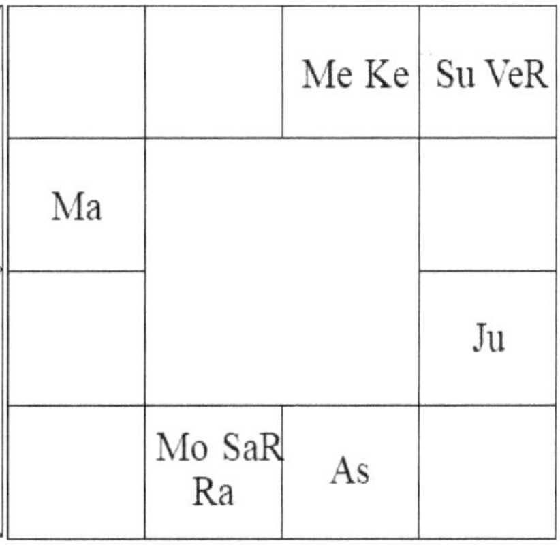

Birth Nakshatra Anuradha

Dasa sequence

Yogini	Nakshatra	From	To
Bharamari	Anuradha	20.6.1956	11.6.1960
Bhadrika	Jyeshtha	11.6.1960	11.6.1965
Ulka	Moola	11.6.1965	11.6.1971
Siddha	P. Ashadha	11.6.1971	11.6.1978

Progress chart for Siddha/ P. Ashadha and Sagittarius lagan.

3rd h.

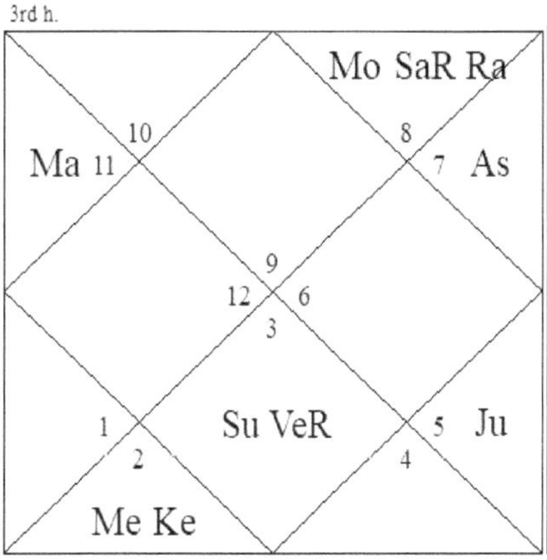

3rd h.

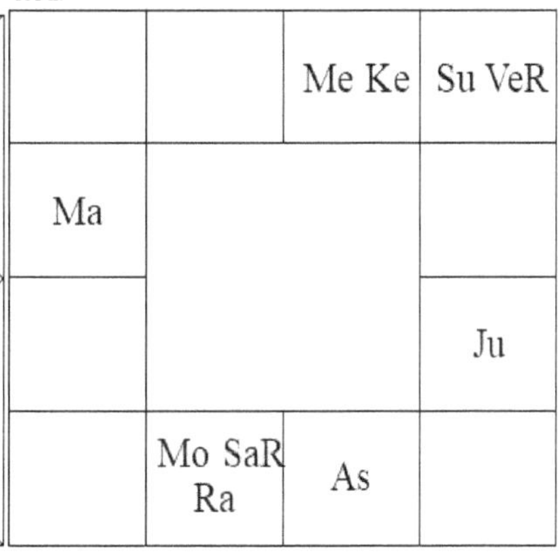

This case was also a test case for verification of yogini dasha. The case was also put up in the research class of BhartiVidya Bhavan.

Venus is Lagna Lord of birth chart and is with Sun. It is placed in ninth house. There is an exchange of ninth and eighth Lord. Venus is retrograde.

This chart is examined for events related to her 1-year-oldchild. The event took place in December 1974. In the progresschart, Venus is the Lord of second and seventh house from fifth house. It is a maraca for child. The fifth lord of birth chart is now in twelfth house. It is with eighth Lord and Rahu.

Her one-year-old child fell down from chair and could notsurvive. The sub period was Dhanya.

After applying the method of progress Yogini in BVB on many such cases, this was accepted as an excellent method of timing and nature of events.

Chapter 10
Sankata

Sankata is the longest dasha period in yogini. Rahu is themother yogini of Sankata. Ketu is not assigned any dasha period.Rahu and Ketu are always forming an axis. We can thus take Ketu also in this axis.

In our scheme of progressive Yogini, it is the Nakshtra lord which is given importance along with the progress lagna.Therefore, Rahu / Ketu axis is not very important consideration.

Sankata is generated by three Nakshtra. These are Mrigshira, Hasta and U. Ashadha. These three Nakshtra lords are Mars, Moon and Sun. Sun and Moon are enemies of Rahu.It may be a reason that this dasha of Sankata is not welcomed in classics. However, we have witnessed many important eventsin every one's life in Sankata period.

Nakshtra	Nakshtra Lord	Sign of Progress Lagna	Remarks
Mrigshira	Mars	Taurus/ Gemini	For first four years, progress lagna is Taurus. For last four yearsit is Gemini.
Hasta	Moon	Virgo	Virgo is progresslagna
U. Ashadha	Sun	Sagittarius / Capricorn	For first two years, progress lagna is Sagittarius. For last six years it isCapricorn.

Sankata / Mrigshira

For Taurus lagna, Mars is the lord of seventh and twelfth.It can give marriage, death, long travels, expenditure illness etc. when Mars is related to these houses in the birth chart. ForTaurus lagna, Saturn is a good planet as it is lord of ninth andtenth house. Venus is the lagna lord and sixth lord.

When Gemini is the progress lagna, Mars is the sixth andeleventh lord. It is capable of giving illness and gain also. Whenafflicted it gives expenditure etc.

This dasha period gives sudden events.

Example PM DOB 17 April 1927 TOB 6.47.30 POB Balia

Birth Chart

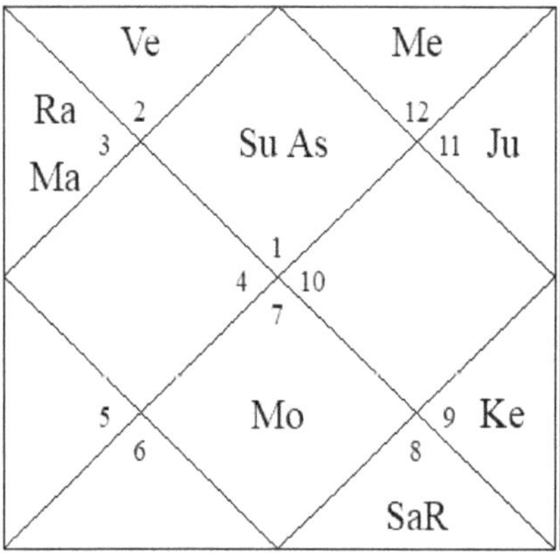

Birth Chart

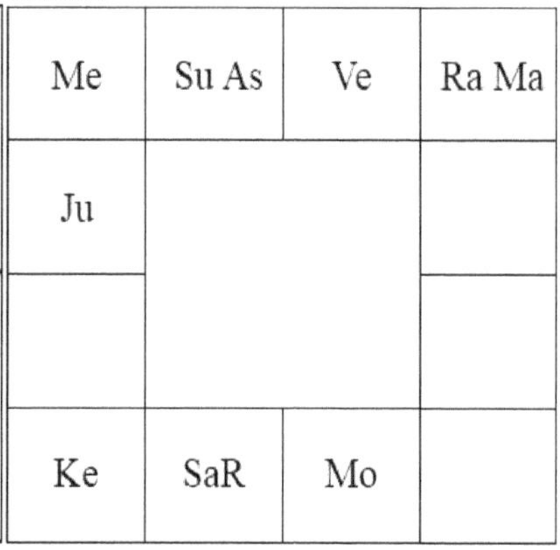

Birth Nakshatra Chitra

Dasa sequence

Yogini	Nakshatra	From	To
Mangla	Chitra	17.4.1927	18.8.1927
Pingla	Swati	18.8.1927	18.8.1929
Dhanya	Visakha	18.8.1929	18.8.1932
Bharamari	Anuradha	18.8.1932	18.8.1936
Bhadrika	Jyeshtha	18.8.1936	18.8.1941

Yogini	Nakshatra	From	To
Ulka	Moola	18.8.1941	18.8.1947
Siddha	P. Ashadha	18.8.1947	18.8.1954
Sankata	U. Ashadha	18.8.1954	18.8.1962
Mangla	Shravan	18.8.1962	18.8.1963
Pingla	Dhanishta	18.8.1963	18.8.1965
Dhanya	Shatbhisaj	18.8.1965	18.8.1968
Bharamari	P. Bhadrapad	18.8.1968	18.8.1972
Bhadrika	U. Bhadrapad	18.8.1972	18.8.1977
Ulka	Revati	18.8.1977	18.8.1983
Siddha	Rohini	18.8.1983	18.8.1990
Sankata	Mrigshira	18.8.1990	18.8.1998

Progress chart for Sankat/ Mrigshira and Taurus lagan.

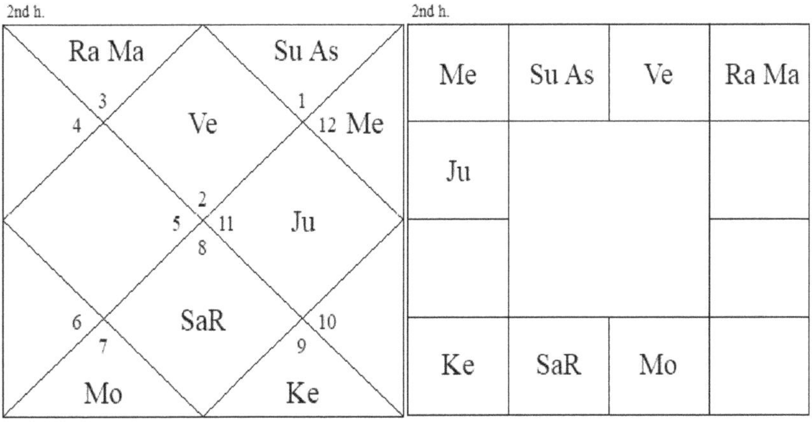

Mars is the lagna lord and eighth lord of birth chart. Marsis aspected by ninth lord Jupiter. Mars influences tenth house of birth chart. He is with Rahu.

Now the progress chart with Taurus lagna. Lagna lord andtenth lords are in mutual aspect in one seven axes. Jupiter is intenth house as eighth and eleventh lord. Eighth lord is good intenth for politicians.

Association of Rahu with Nakshtra lord Mars gives the promise of the chart.He became Prime Minister of India on 27 November 1990to 21 June 1991 in the sub period of Sankata itself.

Can it be explained by classic interpretation?

Example Forced resignation DOB 22 August 1931 TOB 23.08 POB Bulandshahr

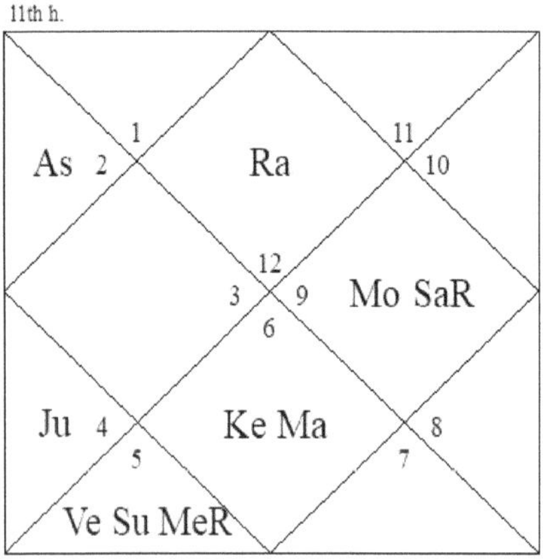

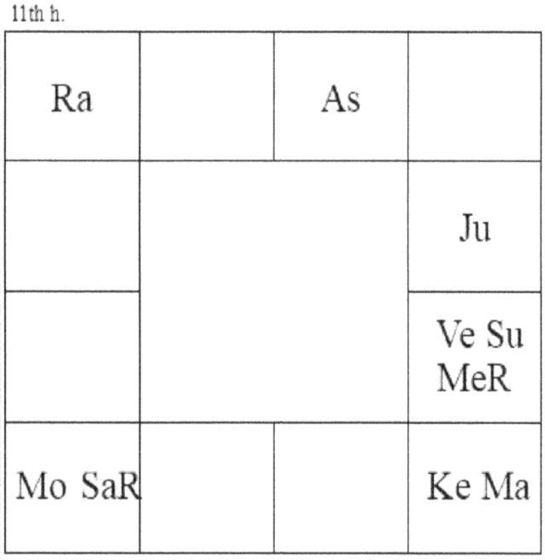

Birth Nakshatra Moola

Dasa sequence

Yogini	Nakshatra	From	To
Ulka	Moola	22.8.1931	29.12.1935
Siddha	P. Ashadha	29.12.1935	29.12.1942
Sankata	U. Ashadha	29.12.1942	29.12.1950
Mangla	Shravan	29.12.1950	29.12.1951
Pingla	Dhanishta	29.12.1951	29.12.1953
Dhanya	Shatbhisaj	29.12.1953	29.12.1956
Bharamari	P. Bhadrapad	29.12.1956	29.12.1960
Bhadrika	U. Bhadrapad	29.12.1960	29.12.1965
Ulka	Revati	29.12.1965	29.12.1971
Siddha	Rohini	29.12.1971	29.12.1978
Sankata	Mrigshira	29.12.1978	29.12.1986

The birth chart and the progress chart are same.

Mars is in fifth house which is eighth from tenth. It is withKetu and aspected by retrograde Saturn from eighth house. Saturn is tenth lord and its retrogression indicate reversal.

In 1980 he was forced to resign his job as a very senior doctor in a well-known Government hospital. He is also honored byPadam Vibhushan for his good work.

He resigned in the sub period of Mangla. Moon is in eighthhouse with tenth lord and aspected by Nakshtra lord Mars.

Example Birth of son and death of husband DOB 26 August 1956 TOB 4.36 POB Delhi

Birth Chart

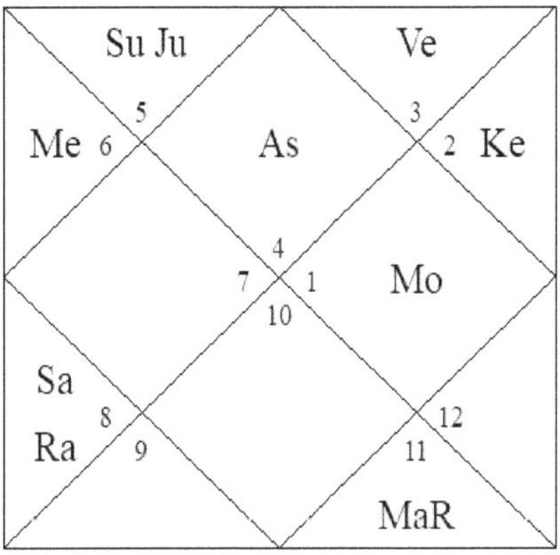

Birth Chart

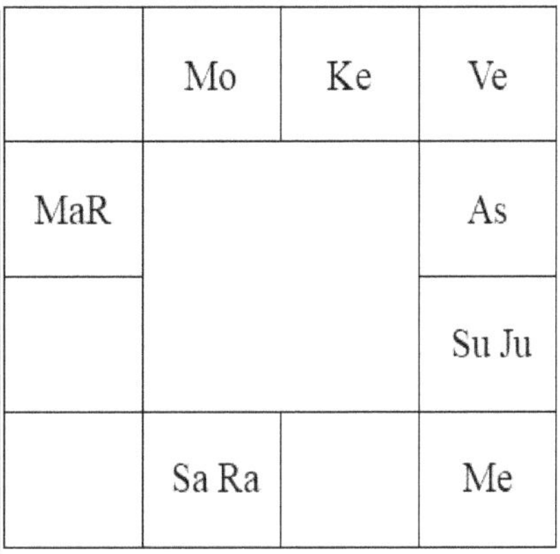

Birth Nakshatra Ashwini

Dasa sequence

Yogini	Nakshatra	From	To
Bharamari	Ashwini	26.8.1956	7.8.1960
Bhadrika	Bharani	7.8.1960	7.8.1965
Ulka	Kritika	7.8.1965	7.8.1971
Siddha	Rohini	7.8.1971	7.8.1978
Sankata	Mrigshira	7.8.1978	7.8.1986

Progress chart for Sankata/ Mrigshira and Taurus lagan.

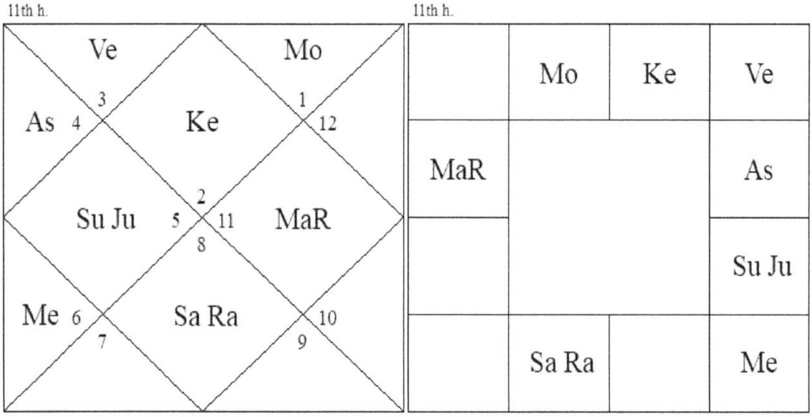

In the birth chart, Mars is the lord of fifth and tenth. It isplaced in eighth house which is the maraca house for husband.

The progress lagna is Taurus and Mars moves to tenth house. It is aspecting fifth house and fifth lord Mercury. Her son Varun was born on 13 March, 1980 in the sub of Sankata.

From tenth house it is aspecting lagna which is maraca house for husband. The lagna is also aspected by Saturn. Saturn is birth seventh and eighth lord. The aspect of Jupiter is no good as it is eighth lord. Eighth house is Mangalya house.

Sanjay died in an air crash on 23 June 1980 in the sub period of Moon. Moon is lagna lord of birth chart (seventh fromseventh).

Example Purchase of house and Heart Problem DOB 30 April 1945 TOB 9.27 POB Delhi

Birth Chart

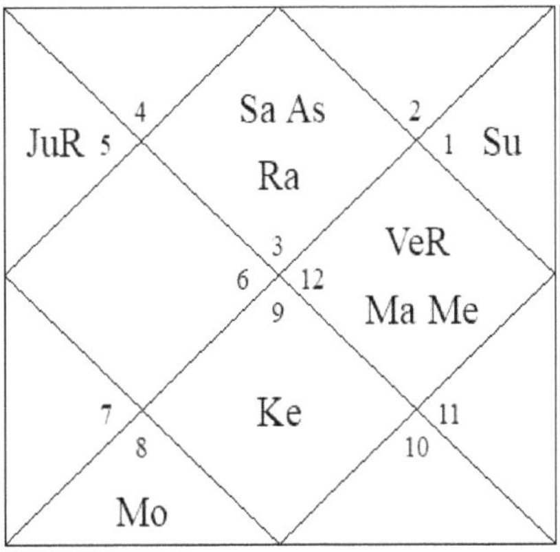

Birth Chart

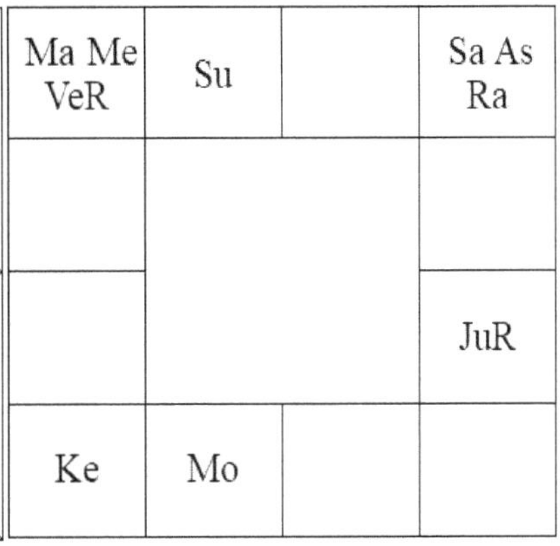

Birth Nakshatra Anuradha

Dasa sequence

Yogini	Nakshatra	From	To
Bharamari	Anuradha	30.4.1945	15.5.1945
Bhadrika	Jyeshtha	15.5.1945	15.5.1950
Ulka	Moola	15.5.1950	15.5.1956
Siddha	P. Ashadha	15.5.1956	15.5.1963
Sankata	U. Ashadha	15.5.1963	15.5.1971
Mangla	Shravan	15.5.1971	15.5.1972
Pingla	Dhanishta	15.5.1972	15.5.1974
Dhanya	Shatbhisaj	15.5.1974	15.5.1977
Bharamari	P. Bhadrapad	15.5.1977	15.5.1981
Bhadrika	U. Bhadrapad	15.5.1981	15.5.1986
Ulka	Revati	15.5.1986	15.5.1992
Siddha	Rohini	15.5.1992	15.5.1999
Sankata	Mrigshira	15.5.1999	15.5.2007

In the birth chart, Mars is in tenth house with Mercury andVenus and aspected by Saturn. It gives rise to multiple activities.Mars is also lord of sixth giving health problems.

Progress chart for Sankata/ Mrigshira and Taurus lagan.

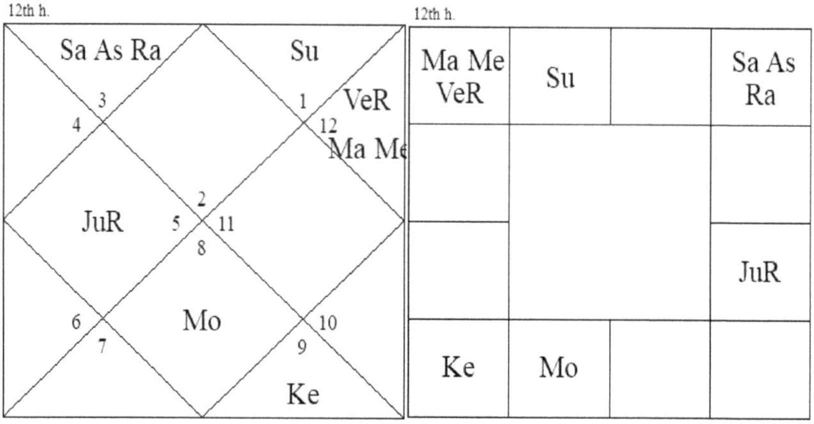

Mars is in eleventh house. It is now twelfth lord. Lord of fourth house is in twelfth house and is exalted. It is aspected byJupiter from fourth house. He purchased a house on 27November, 2001. The Dhanya Sub started on 4 November, 2001.Fourth lord is in twelfth house giving a change of residence.

Mars is aspecting fifth house along with fifth lord. The fifthlord of birth chart is also with it. In July 2003 he was asked tojoin the teaching facility of institute of astrology.

The progress chart with Gemini lagan is same as birth chart. Now Mars is sixth lord. It is with fifth and twelfth lord Venus. Both Venus andMars are aspected by eighth lord Saturn. The Siddha period started on 4 November, 2005. On 27 November, 2005 he suffereda stroke and was rushed to hospital. He was advised immediate surgery. He had open heart surgery in 2013.

Sankata / Hasta

Moon is the Nakshtra lord and Virgo is the progress lagna.The relation of Moon in birth chart and its placement in progresschart is important.

The paksha Bala of Moon in the birth chart is important. Awaxing

Moon tends to give favorable results. A waning Moon will tend to give adverse result.

Mercury and Jupiter are the lords of Kendra's or the SukhSthana. Their relation with Moon in a good house and having benefic association will provide happiness. Adverse relation can give disappointment in these affairs.

When Moon is maraca or lagna lord in birth chart and is related to malefic, it can give physical or mental problems. Even death can occur.

Example Marriage and birth of daughter DOB 14 November 1889 TOB 23.05 POB Allahabad

Birth Chart

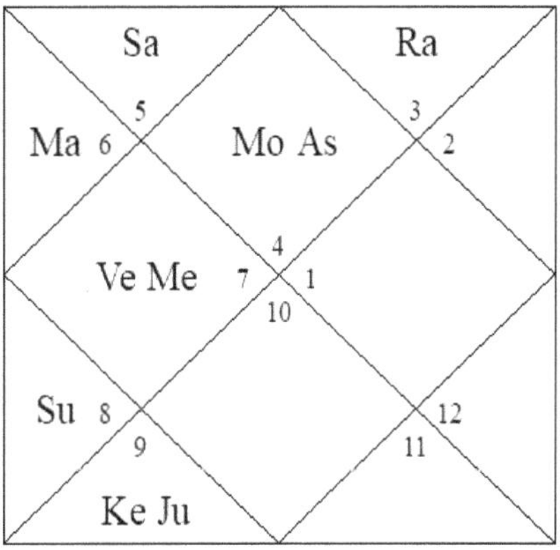

Birth Chart

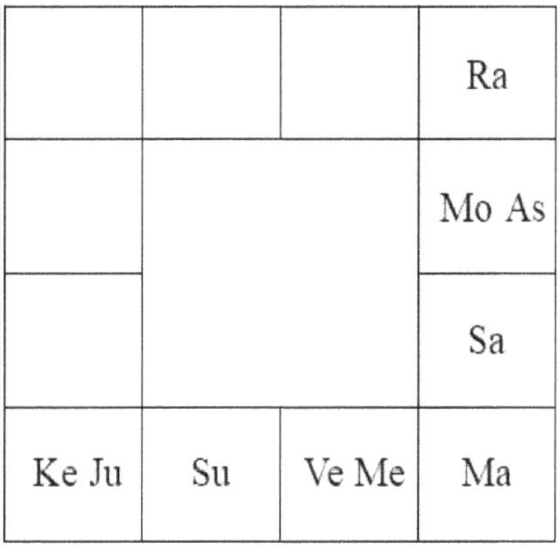

Birth Nakshatra Ashlesha

Dasa sequence

Yogini	Nakshatra	From	To
Bharamari	Ashlesha	14.11.1889	27.6.1893
Bhadrika	Magha	27.6.1893	27.6.1898
Ulka	P. Phalguni	27.6.1898	27.6.1904
Siddha	U. Phalguni	27.6.1904	27.6.1911
Sankata	Hasta	27.6.1911	27.6.1919

Progress chart for Sankata/ Hasta and Virgo lagan.

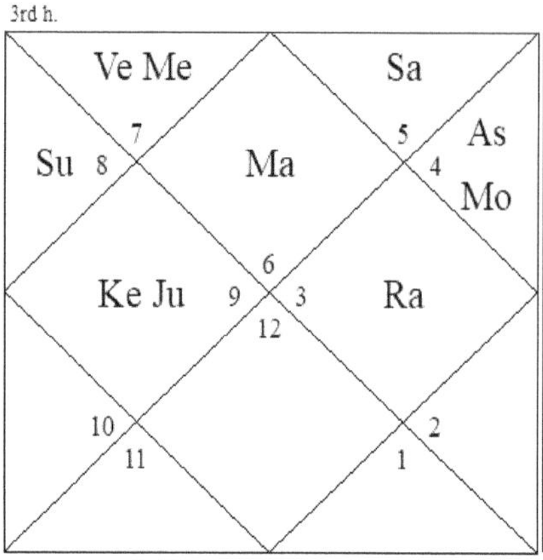

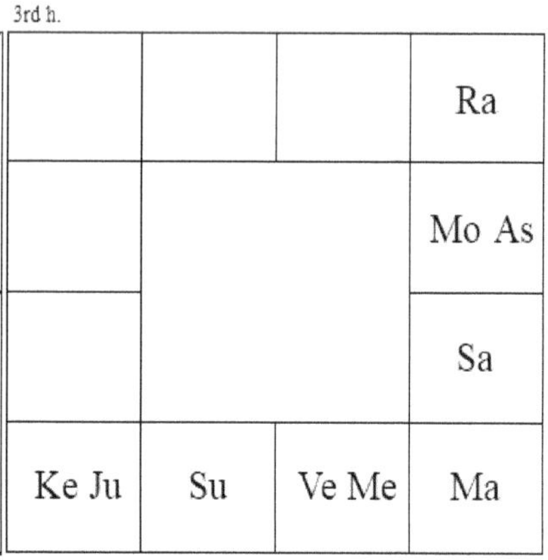

Moon is the lagna lord of birth chart and is in lagna. He is not aspected by any planet.

In the progress chart Moon is in eleventh house. The birthseventh lord has moved to twelfth house and aspects progresslagna lord.

Jupiter is progress seventh lord an aspects birth seventh lord.

He married on 7 Feb 1916 in the sub of Bhadrika.

Saturn is also aspecting Venus. Venus is the ninth lord of progress chart. For even Lagna, ninth is the housc of first child.

Daughter Indira Gandhi was born on 19 November 1917 in thesub period of Siddha.

Example Death DOB 19 November 1917 TOB 23.11 POB Allahabad

Birth Chart

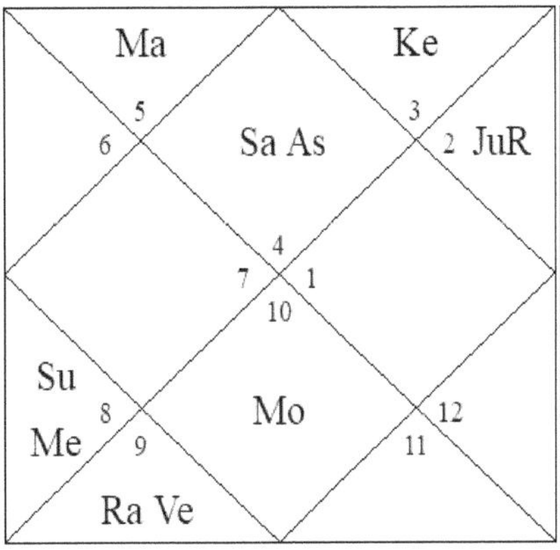

Birth Chart

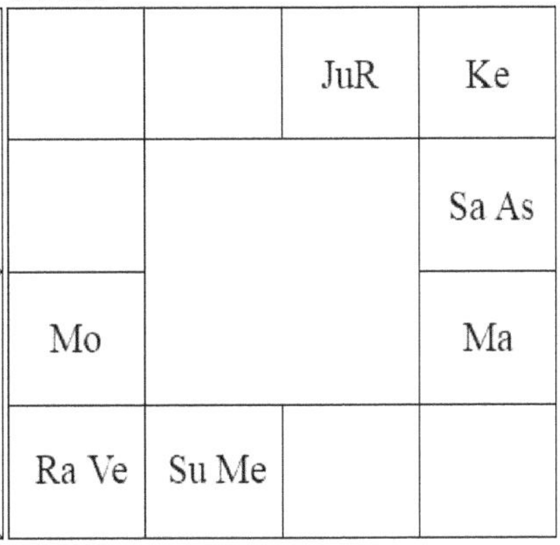

Birth Nakshatra U. Ashadha

Dasa sequence

Yogini	Nakshatra	From	To
Sankata	U. Ashadha	19.11.1917	13.7.1920
Mangla	Shravan	13.7.1920	13.7.1921
Pingla	Dhanishta	13.7.1921	13.7.1923
Dhanya	Shatbhisaj	13.7.1923	13.7.1926
Bharamari	P. Bhadrapad	13.7.1926	13.7.1930
Bhadrika	U. Bhadrapad	13.7.1930	13.7.1935
Ulka	Revati	13.7.1935	13.7.1941
Siddha	Rohini	13.7.1941	13.7.1948
Sankata	Mrigshira	13.7.1948	13.7.1956
Mangla	Ardra	13.7.1956	13.7.1957
Pingla	Punarvasu	13.7.1957	13.7.1959
Dhanya	Pushya	13.7.1959	13.7.1962
Bharamari	Ashlesha	13.7.1962	13.7.1966
Bhadrika	Magha	13.7.1966	13.7.1971

Yogini	Nakshatra	From	To
Ulka	P. Phalguni	13.7.1971	13.7.1977
Siddha	U. Phalguni	13.7.1977	13.7.1984
Sankata	Hasta	13.7.1984	13.7.1992

Progress chart for Siddha/ Hasta and Virgo lagan.

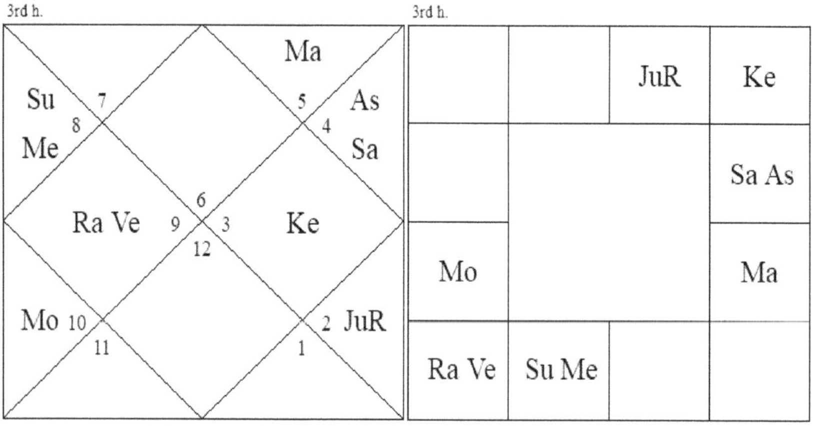

Moon is the lagna lord of birth chart and aspects lagna. Itis fully connected with lagna. It is aspected by Saturn, who is maraca and lord of eighth house.

With the progress lagna moving to Virgo and Moon as Nakshtra lord and Jupiter becomes maraca along with Venus.

Now Moon is influenced by birth maraca and progress maraca. Rahu is with Venus.

She was shot by her security guard on 31 Oct 1984 andwas killed.

Example Suicide by wife DOB 22 August 1954 TOB 20.33 POB Calcutta

Birth Chart

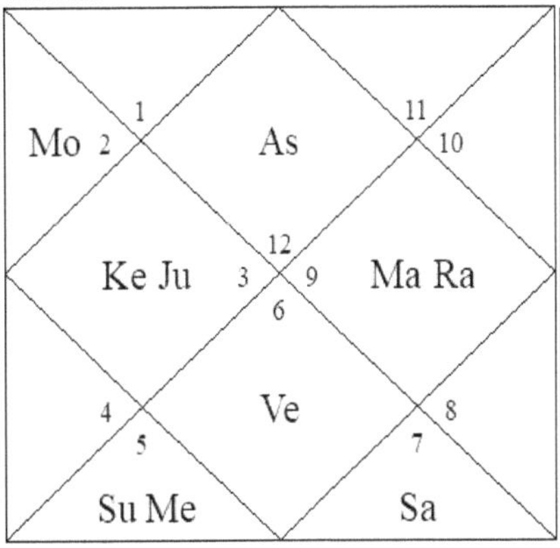

Birth Chart

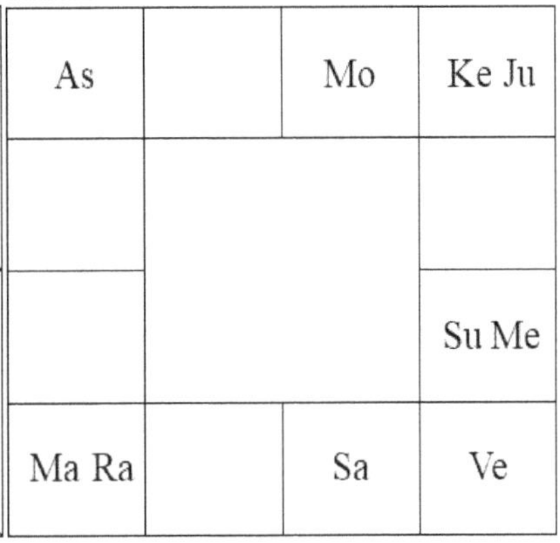

Birth Nakshatra Mrigshira

Dasa sequence

Yogini	Nakshatra	From	To
Sankata	Mrigshira	22.8.1954	24.1.1962
Mangla	Ardra	24.1.1962	24.1.1963
Pingla	Punarvasu	24.1.1963	24.1.1965
Dhanya	Pushya	24.1.1965	24.1.1968
Bharamari	Ashlesha	24.1.1968	24.1.1972
Bhadrika	Magha	24.1.1972	24.1.1977
Ulka	P. Phalguni	24.1.1977	24.1.1983
Siddha	U. Phalguni	24.1.1983	24.1.1990
Sankata	Hasta	24.1.1990	24.1.1998

Progress chart for Siddha/ Hasta and Virgo lagan.

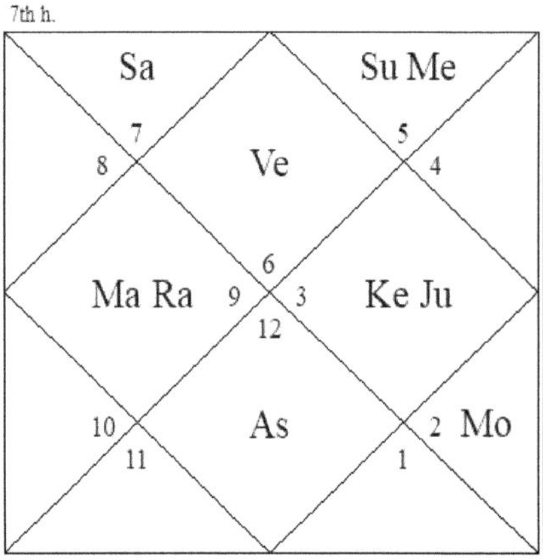

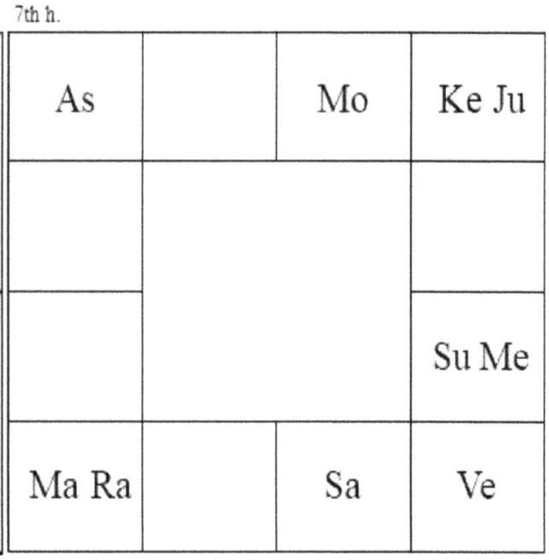

This chart has been discussed in Siddha / U. Phalguni. In the dasha of Siddha in 1983, he was earning very well in USA.

We now discuss his Sankata / Hasta. With this progresschart, the fourth house is badly afflicted. The eighth lord Mars is placed in fourth with Rahu. He aspects seventh house and seventh lord. He is aspected by Saturn.

It gives a clear indication that there is trouble in the domestic front.

His wife committed suicide due to outside influence on her husband and problems in in her married life. His business was ruined and he faced lots of problems.

Example President of India DOB 1 February 1935 TOB 17.23 POB Birbhum

Birth Chart

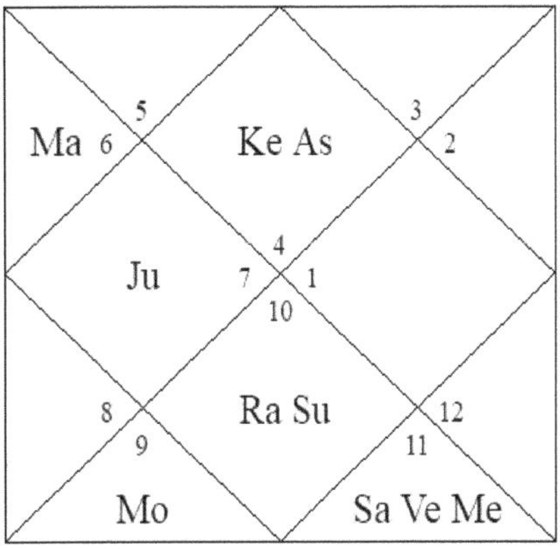

Birth Chart

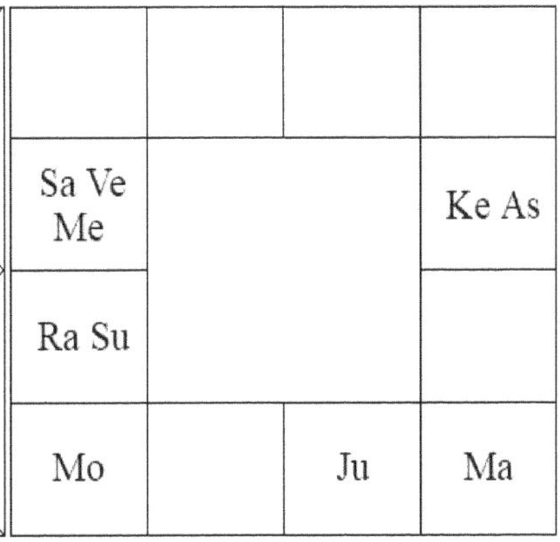

Birth Nakshatra P. Ashadha

Dasa sequence

Yogini	Nakshatra	From	To
Siddha	P. Ashadha	1.2.1935	13.8.1939
Sankata	U. Ashadha	13.8.1939	13.8.1947
Mangla	Shravan	13.8.1947	13.8.1948
Pingla	Dhanishta	13.8.1948	13.8.1950
Dhanya	Shatbhisaj	13.8.1950	13.8.1953
Bharamari	P. Bhadrapad	13.8.1953	13.8.1957
Bhadrika	U. Bhadrapad	13.8.1957	13.8.1962
Ulka	Revati	13.8.1962	13.8.1968
Siddha	Rohini	13.8.1968	13.8.1975
Sankata	Mrigshira	13.8.1975	13.8.1983
Mangla	Ardra	13.8.1983	13.8.1984
Pingla	Punarvasu	13.8.1984	13.8.1986
Dhanya	Pushya	13.8.1986	13.8.1989
Bharamari	Ashlesha	13.8.1989	13.8.1993

Yogini	Nakshatra	From	To
Bhadrika	Magha	13.8.1993	13.8.1998
Ulka	P. Phalguni	13.8.1998	13.8.2004
Siddha	U. Phalguni	13.8.2004	13.8.2011
Sankata	Hasta	13.8.2011	13.8.2019

Progress chart for Siddha/ Hasta and Virgo lagan.

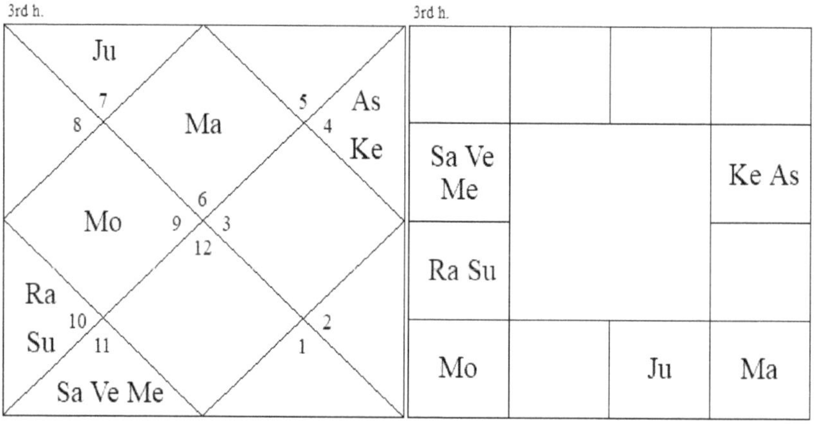

Moon is lagna lord of birth chart. He is aspected by Yoga karaka Mars. Moon can give yoga karaka effect as well eventsrelating to body and self.

In the progress chart, this Moon is eleventh lord and aspects tenth house. The tenth lord, ninth lord and lagna lord are joinedtogether forming a Raj Yoga in sixth house of competition.

He was elected President of India and took oath of office on 25 July, 2013 in the sub period of Mangla.

Mars is not a benefic planet for Virgo lagna.

Example Selection in IFS DOB 21 January 1932 TOB 23.01 POB Rawalpindi

Birth Chart

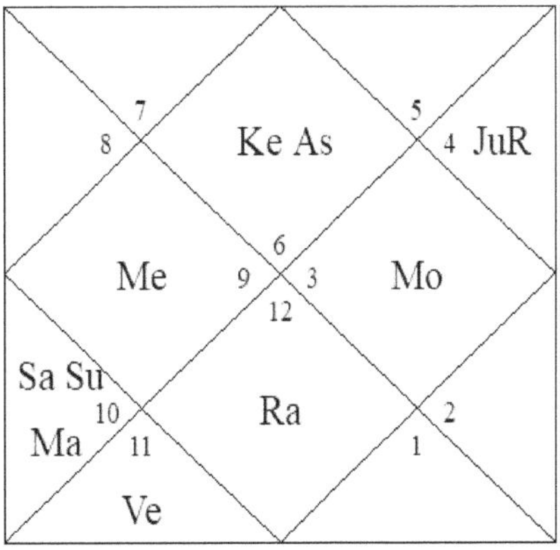

Birth Chart

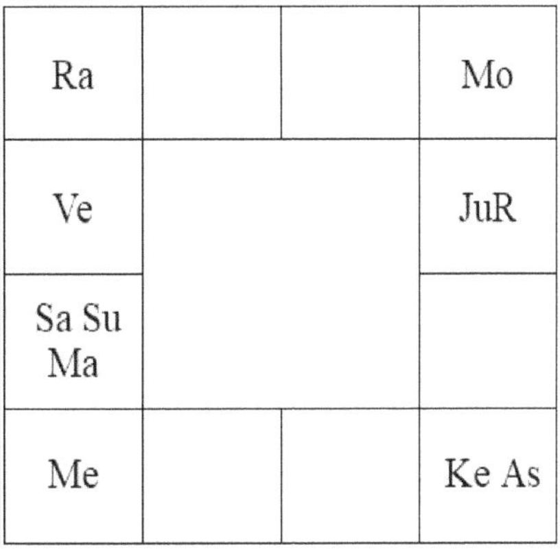

Birth Nakshatra Ardra

Dasa sequence

Yogini	Nakshatra	From	To
Mangla	Ardra	21.1.1932	25.6.1932
Pingla	Punarvasu	25.6.1932	25.6.1934
Dhanya	Pushya	25.6.1934	25.6.1937
Bharamari	Ashlesha	25.6.1937	25.6.1941
Bhadrika	Magha	25.6.1941	25.6.1946
Ulka	P. Phalguni	25.6.1946	25.6.1951
Siddha	U. Phalguni	25.6.1951	25.6.1958
Sankata	Hasta	25.6.1958	25.6.1966

The birth and progress chart are same.

Moon is eleventh lord and placed in tenth house. It isaspected by tenth and lagna lord Mercury.

Moon is the giver of position. He joined IFS in May 1961 in the sub-period of Mangla.

A clear picture emerges with progress Nakshtra interpretation.

Example Marriage Death of Father and Coronation DOB 21 April 1926 TOB 2.48 POB London

Birth Chart

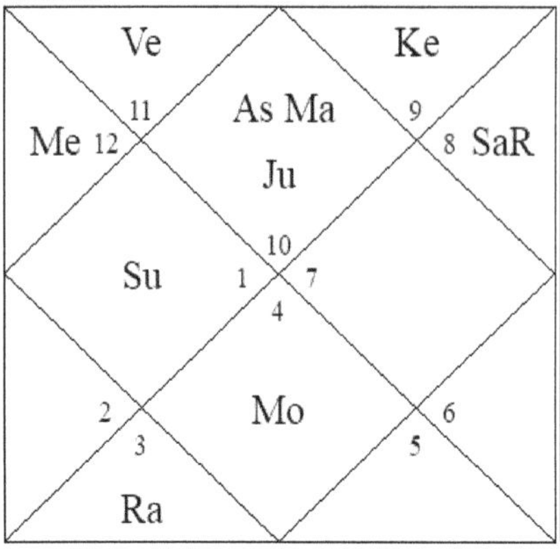

Birth Chart

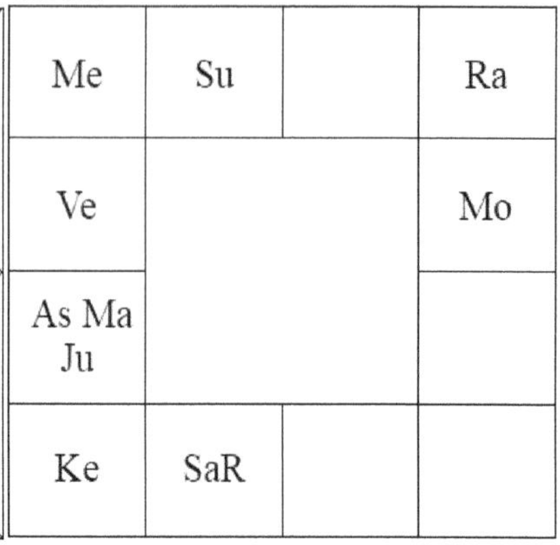

Birth Nakshatra Ashlesha

Dasa sequence

Yogini	Nakshatra	From	To
Bharamari	Ashlesha	21.4.1926	29.6.1929
Bhadrika	Magha	29.6.1929	29.6.1934
Ulka	P. Phalguni	29.6.1934	29.6.1940
Siddha	U. Phalguni	29.6.1940	29.6.1947
Sankata	Hasta	29.6.1947	29.6.1955

Progress chart for Siddha/ Hasta and Virgo lagan.

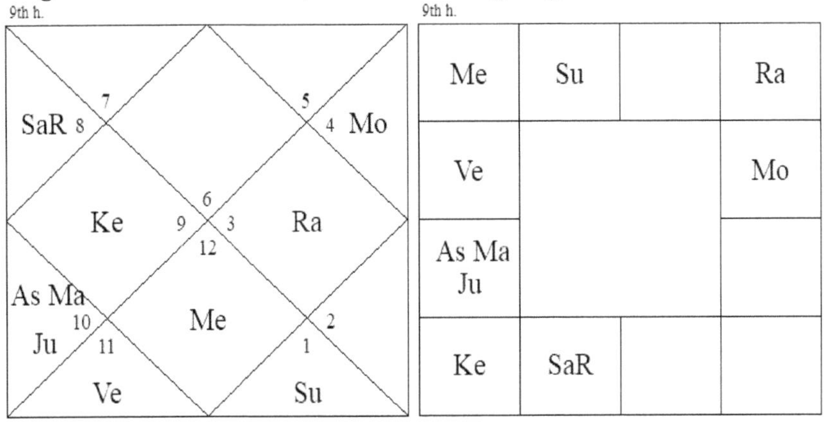

Moon is the seventh lord of birth chart and is placed in seventh house. He is aspected by Mars and Jupiter. Jupiter is debilitated third lord and giver of yoga.

In the progress chart, Moon is in eleventh house. He is now aspected by progress seventh lord. Rahu acts as Mercury of tenth lord. Mercury is placed in seventh house. She married on 20 Nov., 1947. Theaspect of Mars on this Moon gave controversies in this marriage.

For father we take ninth house. The maracas are Mercuryand Mars. The eighth lord from ninth house is Jupiter. Moon is aspected by both Mars and Jupiter. Her father died on 6 Feb., 1952 in sub of Bhadrika. Mercury is birth ninth lord. After the death of father, she was virtually the queen. Mercury is tenth lord of progress chart.

Can we see these events with Sankata dasha? Rahu is nothaving any relation with seventh house or lord.

Example Eternal Samadhi DOB 1 May 1896 TOB 3.01.30 POB Kheora

Birth Chart

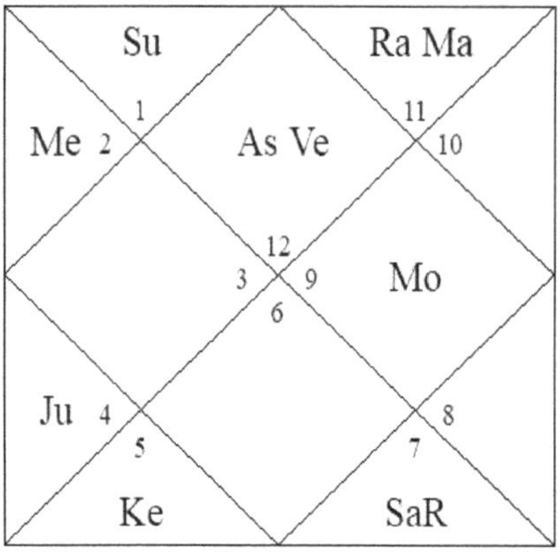

Birth Chart

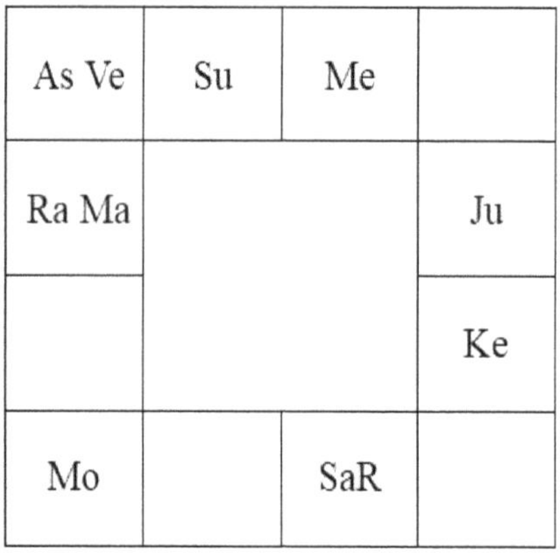

Birth Nakshatra Moola

Dasa sequence

Yogini	Nakshatra	From	To
Ulka	Moola	1.5.1896	22.10.1900
Siddha	P. Ashadha	22.10.1900	22.10.1907
Sankata	U. Ashadha	22.10.1907	22.10.1915
Mangla	Shravan	22.10.1915	22.10.1916
Pingla	Dhanishta	22.10.1916	22.10.1918
Dhanya	Shatbhisaj	22.10.1918	22.10.1921
Bharamari	P. Bhadrapad	22.10.1921	22.10.1925
Bhadrika	U. Bhadrapad	22.10.1925	22.10.1930
Ulka	Revati	22.10.1930	22.10.1936
Siddha	Rohini	22.10.1936	22.10.1943
Sankata	Mrigshira	22.10.1943	22.10.1951
Mangla	Ardra	22.10.1951	22.10.1952
Pingla	Punarvasu	22.10.1952	22.10.1954

Yogini	Nakshatra	From	To
Dhanya	Pushya	22.10.1954	22.10.1957
Bharamari	Ashlesha	22.10.1957	22.10.1961
Bhadrika	Magha	22.10.1961	22.10.1966
Ulka	P. Phalguni	22.10.1966	22.10.1972
Siddha	U. Phalguni	22.10.1972	22.10.1979
Sankata	Hasta	22.10.1979	22.10.1987

Progress chart for Sankata/ Hasta and Virgo lagan.

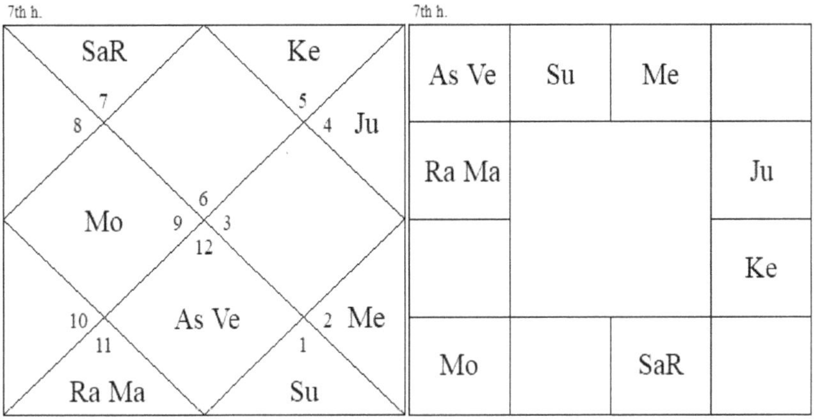

Moon is in tenth house of birth chart. Moon has Mercury and Jupiter is sixth and eighth from it. Moon is aspected by exalted Saturn from eighth house. This Moon gives eternal Samadhi.

In the progress chart Moon is in fourth house. It is aspected by Saturn from second house. Saturn also aspects Jupiter who is seventh lord of progress chart.

She took eternal Samadhi on 27 August 1982 in the sub period of Jupiter.

Sankata / U. Ashadha

Sun is the Nakshtra lord. In the progress chart with Sagittarius progress lagna, Sun is the lord of ninth house. WhenSun is related to tenth house in birth chart or in progress chart,it can give yoga karaka results of tenth house.

For Sagittarius lagna, Venus is not a good planet. When ill-disposed in birth chart, it is not good for its significations.

The position is not good generally for the Capricorn progresslagna. Sun is now the eighth lord. Even now if Sun is exalted or debilitated it can give favorable results. Venus now becomes a yoga karaka and can give very good result if it is favorable in birth chart.

The progress lagna changes to Capricorn with the start ofPingla Sub period.

Example Selection in Class I service DOB 30 April 1945 TOB 9.27 POB Delhi

Birth Chart

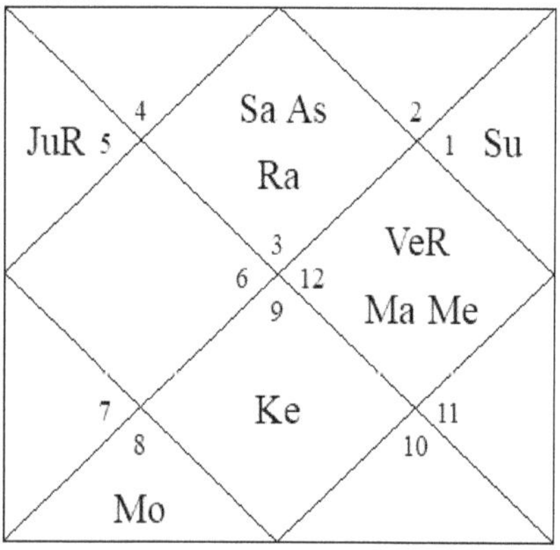

Birth Chart

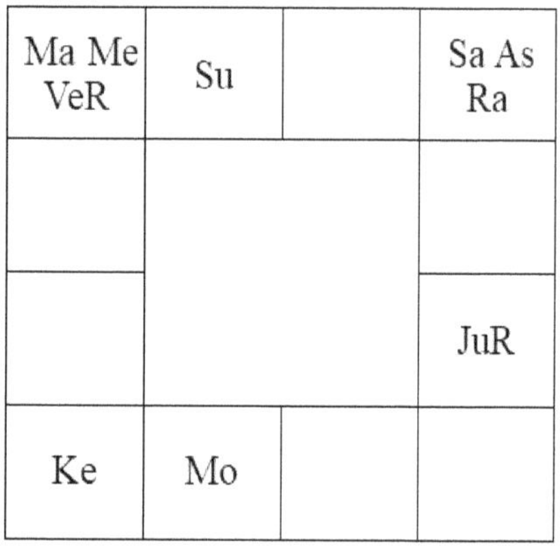

Birth Nakshatra Anuradha

Dasa sequence

Yogini	Nakshatra	From	To
Bharamari	Anuradha	30.4.1945	15.5.1945
Bhadrika	Jyeshtha	15.5.1945	15.5.1950
Ulka	Moola	15.5.1950	15.5.1956
Siddha	P. Ashadha	15.5.1956	15.5.1963
Sankata	U. Ashadha	15.5.1963	15.5.1971

He joined class I service on 1 November 1969.

In the birth chart, Sun is exalted in eleventh house. He is aspected by Jupiter who is tenth lord. Sun promises good eventsregarding profession.

Progress chart for Sankata/ U. Ashadha and Capricorn lagan.

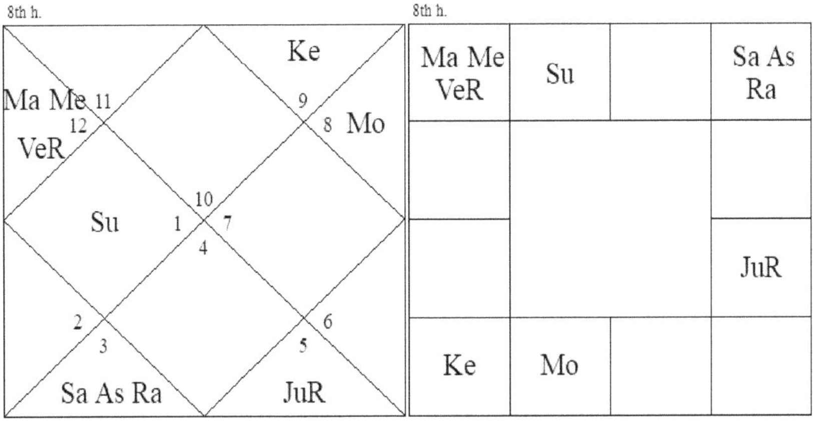

In the progress chart, Sun is now in fourth house an aspectstenth house. The lord of tenth house is exalted in third house. The relation of Sun is again established with tenth house in progress chart.

He joined when the Siddha sub period started.

Example Big start in professional life DOB 24 April 1973 TOB 13.00 POB Mumbai

Birth Chart

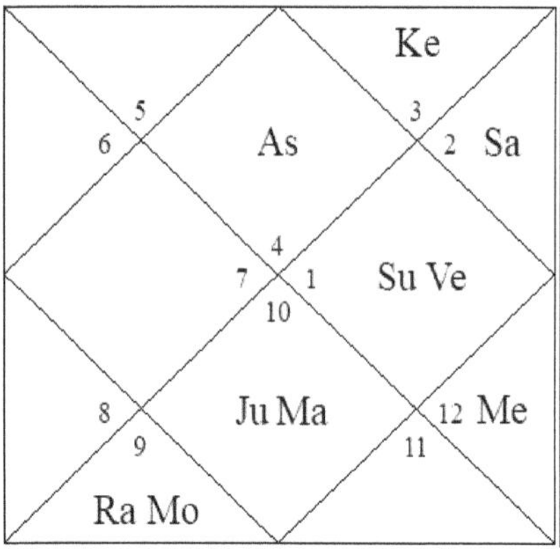

Birth Chart

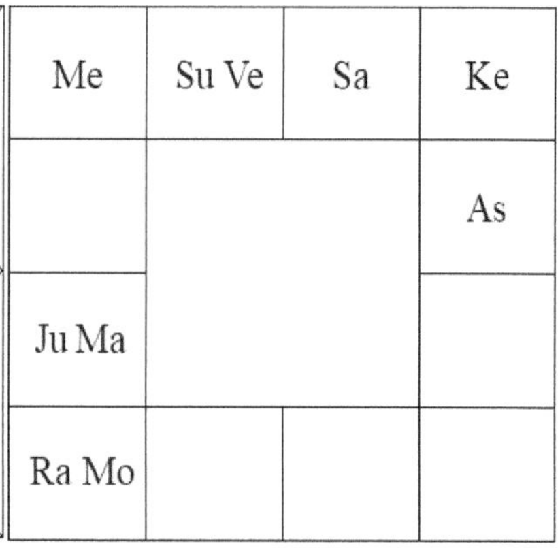

Birth Nakshatra P. Ashadha

Dasa sequence

Yogini	Nakshatra	From	To
Siddha	P. Ashadha	24.4.1973	26.5.1974
Sankata	U. Ashadha	26.5.1974	26.5.1982

Progress chart for Sankata/ U. Ashadha and Capricorn lagan.

7th h.

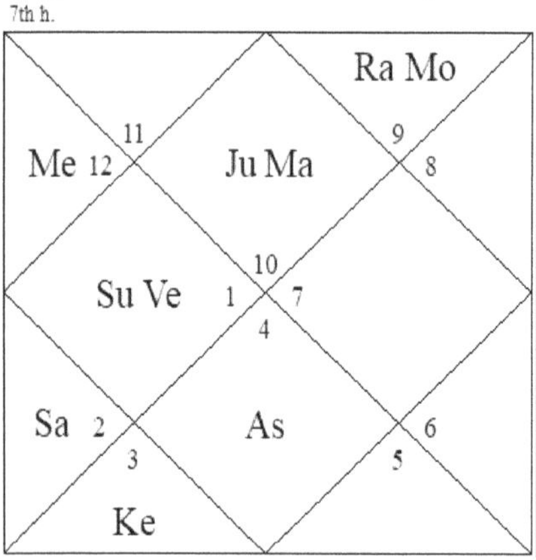

7th h.

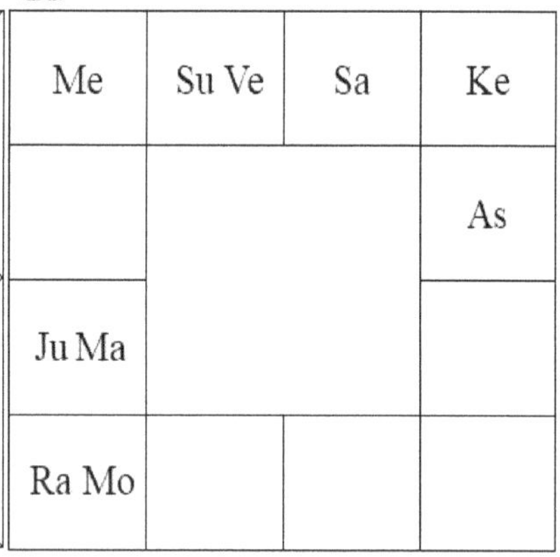

In the birth chart Sun is exalted in tenth house. He is placedwith

Venus. Venus is the fourth and eleventh lord. He can give much wealth. Sun is aspected by Mars and is very good for Cancer Lagna.

In the progress chart, Sun is in fourth house with Yoga Karaka Venus.

In the Sankata dasa he was introduced to his coach, Achrekar. He changed his school and started his coaching. This was a big step for his professional career.

Example Death DOB 15 November 1918 TOB 21.49.26 POB Srinagar

Birth Chart

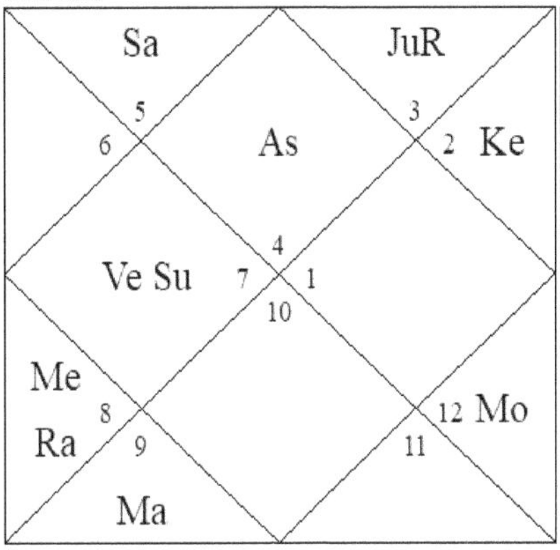

Birth Chart

Birth Nakshtra Revati

Dasa sequence

Yogini	Nakshatra	From	To
Ulka	Revati	15.11.1918	11.2.1922
Siddha	Rohini	11.2.1922	11.2.1929
Sankata	Mrigshira	11.2.1929	11.2.1937
Mangla	Ardra	11.2.1937	11.2.1938
Pingla	Punarvasu	11.2.1938	11.2.1940
Dhanya	Pushya	11.2.1940	11.2.1943
Bharamari	Ashlesha	11.2.1943	11.2.1947
Bhadrika	Magha	11.2.1947	11.2.1952

Yogini	Nakshatra	From	To
Ulka	P. Phalguni	11.2.1952	11.2.1958
Siddha	U. Phalguni	11.2.1958	11.2.1965
Sankata	Hasta	11.2.1965	11.2.1973
Mangla	Chitra	11.2.1973	11.2.1974
Pingla	Swati	11.2.1974	11.2.1976
Dhanya	Visakha	11.2.1976	11.2.1979
Bharamari	Anuradha	11.2.1979	11.2.1983
Bhadrika	Jyeshtha	11.2.1983	11.2.1988
Ulka	Moola	11.2.1988	11.2.1994
Siddha	P. Ashadha	11.2.1994	11.2.2001
Sankata	U. Ashadha	11.2.2001	11.2.2009

Progress chart for Sankata/ U. Ashadha and Sagittarius lagan.

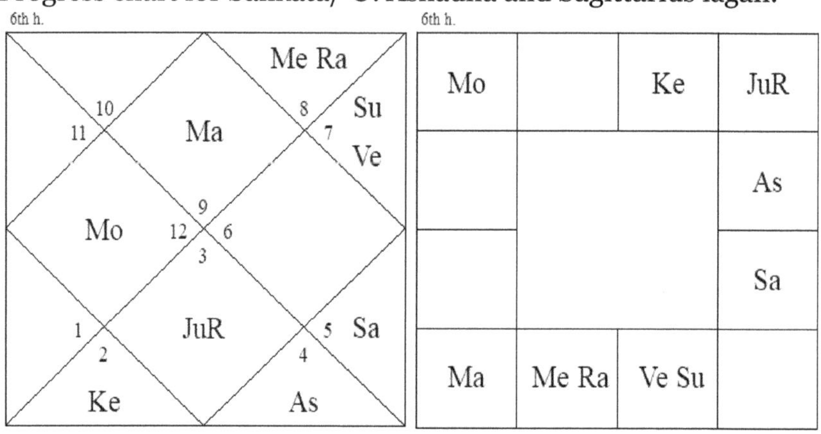

In the birth chart, Sun is the maraca lord of second house.He is aspected by the other maraca Saturn from second house.Saturn is the lord of eighth also. Saturn influences Ketu also.

In the progress chart, Saturn is again a maraca along with Mercury. Mercury is in Rahu Ketu axis. Sun is now badly afflicted. He is with Venus and aspected by Saturn.

He died on 18 May, 2002 in the sub of Sankata and sub sub of Ulka.

Example PM DOB 14 November 1889 TOB 23.05 POB Allahabad

Birth Chart

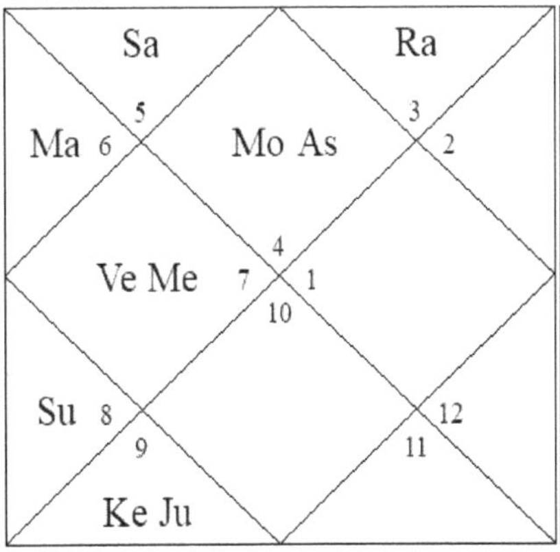

Birth Chart

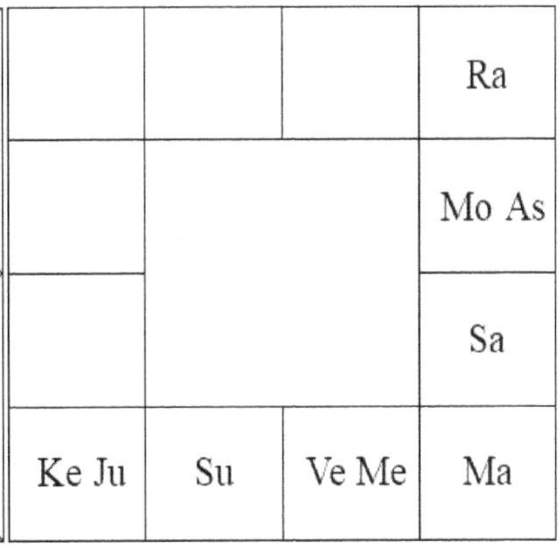

Birth Nakshatra Ashlesha

Dasa sequence

Yogini	Nakshatra	From	To
Bharamari	Ashlesha	14.11.1889	27.6.1893
Bhadrika	Magha	27.6.1893	27.6.1898
Ulka	P. Phalguni	27.6.1898	27.6.1904
Siddha	U. Phalguni	27.6.1904	27.6.1911
Sankata	Hasta	27.6.1911	27.6.1919
Mangla	Chitra	27.6.1919	27.6.1920
Pingla	Swati	27.6.1920	27.6.1922
Dhanya	Visakha	27.6.1922	27.6.1925
Bharamari	Anuradha	27.6.1925	27.6.1929
Bhadrika	Jyeshtha	27.6.1929	27.6.1934
Ulka	Moola	27.6.1934	27.6.1940
Siddha	P. Ashadha	27.6.1940	27.6.1947
Sankata	U. Ashadha	27.6.1947	27.6.1955

Sun is the second lord of birth chart. He is placed in fifth house and is not aspected by any planet. Sun is in Subh Kartari.It can give good results.

Progress chart for Sankata/ U. Ashadha and Sagittarius lagan.

6th h. 6th h.

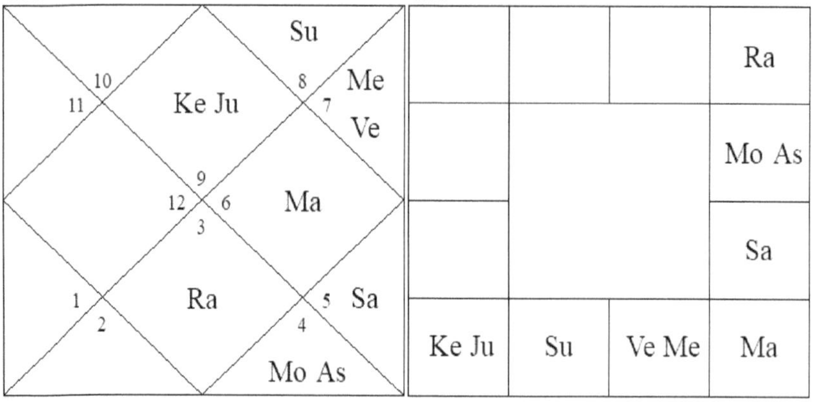

In the progress chart, Sun has moved to twelfth house. The tenth lord of birth chart is now in tenth house. The birth lagna lord is in eighth and the self and mind are involved in creating a scam. Rahuacts as Mercury. Mercury is in eleventh house. The strength is placement of Progress lagan lord in lagan.

He became PM in Sankata sub itself.

Example Death DOB 24 May 1819 TOB 2.26.54 POB London

Birth Chart Birth Chart

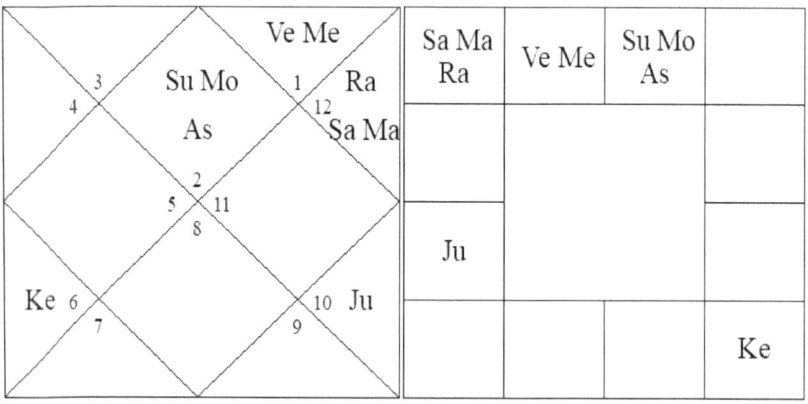

Birth Nakshatra Rohini

Dasa sequence

Yogini	Nakshatra	From	To
Siddha	Rohini	24.5.1819	27.2.1825
Sankata	Mrigshira	27.2.1825	27.2.1833
Mangla	Ardra	27.2.1833	27.2.1834
Pingla	Punarvasu	27.2.1834	27.2.1836
Dhanya	Pushya	27.2.1836	27.2.1839
Bharamari	Ashlesha	27.2.1839	27.2.1843
Bhadrika	Magha	27.2.1843	27.2.1848
Ulka	P. Phalguni	27.2.1848	27.2.1854
Siddha	U. Phalguni	27.2.1854	27.2.1861
Sankata	Hasta	27.2.1861	27.2.1869
Mangla	Chitra	27.2.1869	27.2.1870
Pingla	Swati	27.2.1870	27.2.1872
Dhanya	Visakha	27.2.1872	27.2.1875
Bharamari	Anuradha	27.2.1875	27.2.1879
Bhadrika	Jyeshtha	27.2.1879	27.2.1884
Ulka	Moola	27.2.1884	27.2.1890
Siddha	P. Ashadha	27.2.1890	27.2.1897
Sankata	U. Ashadha	27.2.1897	27.2.1905

Progress chart for Sankata/ U. Ashadha and Capricorn lagan.

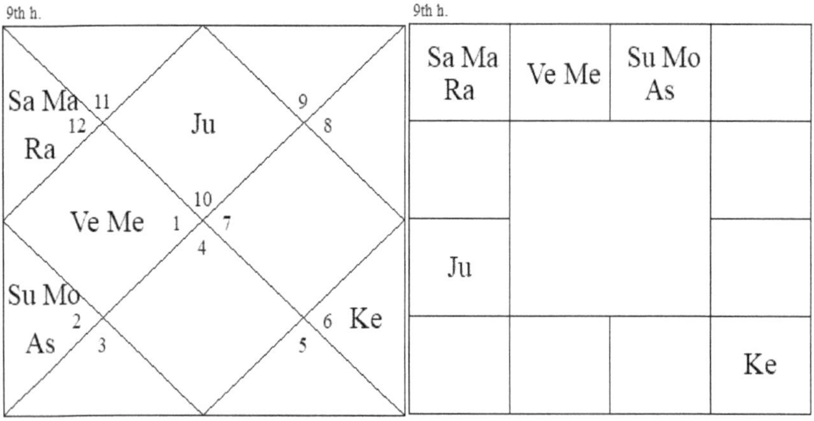

Sun is the fourth lord of birth chart and is in lagna with exalted third lord Moon. He is aspected by eighth lord Jupiter. Sun can give longevity related events. He is also aspected by Saturn.

In progress chart, Saturn and Moon are the maracas. Moonis with Sun and is aspected by Saturn. For this progress lagna,Sun is the eighth lord, connected with birth eighth lord.

She died on 22 Jan. 1901 in the sub of Mars. Mars is the birth maraca.

www.ingramcontent.com/pod-product-compliance
Ingram Content Group UK Ltd.
Pitfield, Milton Keynes, MK11 3LW, UK
UKHW021405190726
13845UKWH00028B/883

9 788198 213457